The Successful Sunday School and Teachers Guidebook

Elmer Towns

Creation House 🌼 Carol Stream, Illinois

Biblical quotations are from the King James Version or the New American Standard Bible unless otherwise noted. Quotations from the New American Standard Bible, © 1971, are used with permission of the Lockman Foundation. Quotations from the Revised Standard Version Bible are used with the permission of the National Council of Churches of Christ, 1946, 1952, © 1971, 1973.

Printed in the United States of America
Second Printing—September, 1976
Third Printing—June, 1977
ISBN 0-88419-118-4
Library of Congress Catalog Card Number 75-23009

Contents

SECTION II: GETTING THE SUNDAY SCHOOL ORGANIZED

SECTION III: FACILITIES FOR LEARNING

SECTION IV: BUSES—ONE KEY TO GROWTH

SECTION V: PERSONNEL DEVELOPMENT

SECTION VI: PROMOTION AND OUTREACH

SECTION VII: CLASS IN SESSION

SECTION VIII: ORIGIN OF THE SUNDAY SCHOOL

SECTION IX: YOUR SUNDAY SCHOOL TOMORROW

Introduction

I love Sunday School and have dedicated my life to its ministry. I still believe Sunday School is the most powerful tool that God has in His hand. I faithfully attend a class, and teach every opportunity I get. The Sunday School is the church at work . . . reaching . . . teaching . . . winning the lost . . . then training them for Christian service.

This book is written for every Sunday School teacher who believes the Bible and loves children. There is no denominational slant. The pages are committed to an authoritative teaching of the Bible and the winning of people to Jesus Christ. It is committed to helping the local church carry out the Great Commission through the Sunday School.

You are the aim of this book. These pages contain *almost* everything you need to be a better Sunday School worker. This was a gigantic undertaking. It has been several years since a comprehensive volume on Sunday School has been published. Of course, everything about Sunday School couldn't be packed into one volume. I have included both old workable ideas and the newest innovations.

For example, it will help you implement such "tried and proven" methods as:

Workable Sunday School contests
How to get good discipline
How to prepare a lesson
Twenty suggestions to double a class
Memory work
Puppets

. . . But this guidebook has more than the proven techniques. We live in a modern age with new problems. Different needs emerge daily. These burgeoning problems have tested Sunday School to the ultimate. Some teachers have thrown in the towel, and some Sunday Schools have lost their effectiveness because they cannot incorporate new ideas and methods.

Here are some of the new techniques which are explained in this guidebook:

Team teaching

Dyads and multi-media

Open session teaching

Dioramas

The laws of Sunday School growth for the 80s

New trends in Sunday School busing

The astonishing list of 100 Largest Sunday Schools is in this book, along with information about the fastest growing Sunday School in each state. Charts on curriculum, statistics on trends and profiles of successful churches also are here. The best from the pages of *Christian Life* is available in this volume, along with material never before published. I wrote a 50-page questionnaire to evaluate today's Sunday Schools. This questionnaire was used in preparing the best-selling book *The 10 Largest Sunday Schools* (Baker Book House, 1970). Many have asked for a copy of this questionnaire. It is printed here for the first time. Fill out this questionnaire and find out where your church is weak. Then apply the principles in this *Sunday School Guidebook* so your church can become even stronger and more effective.

Also, I have included new laws of Sunday School growth. These laws were gathered from churches that are growing. They are different from the former laws compiled by the Southern Baptists. Read them. You can be used of God to help your Sunday School grow.

Poor teaching is the screaming weakness of Sunday School. There was a time when boring teachers simply irritated students. Not any more. Students don't attend classes which have poor teachers. Teaching techniques are thoroughly analyzed in this guidebook. You need to try more than one or two methods of teaching. This guidebook is designed to add diversification to your teaching. An interesting teacher is an effective teacher.

The *Successful Sunday School and Teachers Guidebook* is dedicated to you, the greatest person in the world: the Sunday School teacher. May God use you to defeat insurmountable foes, even if you have little time, marginal facilities, and limited education. May God use you in the life of every one of your pupils.

Elmer L. Towns

section I

The Sunday School Scene Today

1

The revival of the workable is sprouting up in many denominations. It is a trend that cannot be ignored.

The Newest Innovation Is a Return to the Old Workable Methods

Sunday School apparently has gone full cycle in its search for success, and its return to normalcy is applauded by many. During the sixties when attendance in Sunday Schools plunged, experiments in techniques attempted to attract the multitude on Sunday morning. Classes in sex education, and discussion groups on socially practical topics were tried. Panels, colloquies and debates were introduced to keep people in Sunday School. But after exploring the hinterlands of sensitivity training, experiencing the fruitlessness of activity-play classes, and coping with the frustration of mass bus-in crowds, Sunday Schools have returned to the old workable formulas. Leaders are finding Bible teaching, memory work, singing to the Lord and obedience to Biblical principles can build a Sunday School.

However, the return does not mean that every modern Robert Raikes should lead children by the hand to Sunday School down a sooty alley. Nor does the return to old workable forms mean that wires and sheets should be strung across church basements to make classrooms. The "tried and tested" methods that are finding their way into modern buildings and that are being used by dedicated teachers include instruction in Bible content, memory work, enthusiastic singing, workbooks, rally days, and captivating teaching aids such as puppets, flash cards and flannelgraph.

But the total Sunday School picture does not show a clear repudiation of the latest fads from John Dewey experimental schools. Many branches of Christendom continue to search for progressive educational techniques. They employ psycho-drama, simulation games, writing creative poetry, and neighbor nudge. But like the first trickle of water wearing down the sand hill, there is an obvious trend among Sunday Schools to return to old workable techniques.

Back of the search for effective workable techniques is a philosophic question for the experts, "Do we use only those techniques found in Scripture or can the methods from educational research work in the Sunday School?" No one questions that content must come from the Word of God, but many believe that modern techniques lead to modernism in doctrine. This presents many problems.

Opening exercises are making a comeback. They were kicked out. One Sunday School expert maintained, "They don't open anything or exercise anything." However, teachers are finding that a link must be made with pupils before teaching can begin. Just because pupils walk into class doesn't mean they are mentally and emotionally ready to learn. The opening exercise (some call it opening worship) draws the class together through testimonies, special music, singing and announcements. When a proper contact is established between pupil and teacher, better teaching takes place.

Not one Sunday School used closing exercises, according to a 1964 survey. However, teachers found they were just ending class rather than bringing the lesson to a natural conclusion. Poor teachers who did their best still found attention at a low ebb at the end of class. Many students were leaving Sunday School with a bad taste in their mouths. Today, closing exercises are being re-introduced to rally enthusiasm after the lesson is over. They permit the master teacher to apply the lesson, make announcements regarding the next week's events and send pupils away on a high note.

The use of Sunday School quarterlies was discontinued by many churches for varying reasons. Some claimed quarterlies were too expensive; a few said quarterlies introduced liberalism; many claimed students only lost quarterlies; others maintained quarterlies were too sophisticated or too simple. Those who threw out the quarterlies forgot that Sunday School is the one agency in the church that gives a systematic, comprehensive, complete coverage of Scripture and doctrine. When the local church doesn't have a systematic curriculum, it usually goes off on tangents, omits important doctrines or over-emphasizes the preacher's pet hobby-horse. Today, most leaders call the quarterly a manual or lesson book. But some who are returning to quarterlies

aren't providing them for pupils. Instead, Sunday Schools are purchasing the manuals for teachers (to give them assistance and resources). Even so, many publishers are now providing an in-class workbook rather than a manual to take home for lesson preparation together with a quarterly to be used in the class as a teaching aid. Few churches ask a student to prepare a Sunday School lesson before coming on Sunday. However, the First Baptist Church, Elkhart, Indiana, still reports approximately 75 percent of its students do homework.

Puppets are popping their heads up all over. A few years ago, some Christian educators were claiming that puppets were a superficial way to teach Bible. However, today's Sunday School teachers are snapping them up in Christian bookstores, and publishers recently have put out several new lines of puppets. Why? Because Sesame Street, the Electric Company and other children's television programs have proved that children are fascinated by characters like Cookie Monster and Mr. Moose.

Educators who claimed that stimulus-response psychology was on its way out and that a new day of human relationships in education would grow have had to eat their words. One educator insisted that "It's not what the teacher does on the platform that determines

Once again a hot item in religious supply stores, flannelgraph can be used to teach Bible lessons, doctrine, missions and practical lessons. (First Baptist Church, West Hollywood, FL)

learning, but how the pupils interact that measures the success of Sunday School." So liberal educators introduced finger paint, play centers, expression activities and did away with teaching techniques that appeared to force-feed the Bible to kids. But to the consternation of progressive educators, Sesame Street demonstrated that more children learn more things earlier through repetitive stimulus-response situations. Children learned by watching the teacher on the screen. This is one reason that Sunday School is experiencing a return to "things that teachers do," such as flannelgraph, flash cards, picture stories, illustrated song books, and other teaching aids that assist in communicating the Bible.

Memory verse flash cards are being waved by Sunday School teachers and children repeat them en masse or individually. This means Bible memorization is being revived. (A junior boy in Immanuel Baptist Church, Moore, Oklahoma, repeated over 100 verses from Proverbs to win a contest.)

Flannelgraph is once again a big seller, according to Child Evangelism Fellowship, one of the largest suppliers. Not only are Bible stories taught by pictures; doctrine, missions, and practical lessons are visualized for young minds.

Indoctrination was ridiculed by secular educators. If anyone claimed to believe in indoctrination, he was laughed down in our universities. Secular educators falsely claimed that indoctrination meant: (1) insensitivity to pupils, (2) facts communicated without understanding, (3) lessons taught with no relevancy to life, and (4) teaching methods that have no meaning to pupils.

If anyone taught the Bible without applying it to life, he was considered a Neanderthal Christian. However, today's kids want more than groovy "relaters." They want answers from the Bible. One of the shocking phenomena in the publishing world is the run-away success of *The Late Great Planet Earth.* This book doesn't have an exciting plot, captivating characterizations or even practical knowledge. Hal Lindsey's book became a best seller because it gave simple answers on the second coming of Jesus Christ.

The same phenomenon is happening in Sunday Schools. Those with a strong Bible teaching program are prospering. Dr. Jack Hudson, pastor of Northside Baptist Church, Charlotte, North Carolina, indicates he uses contests to attract children to Sunday School, but Bible content to keep them. He says the contests are the worm, but the Bible content is the hook. "We keep pupils in Sunday School the way we catch them," he explains.

Today's kids want more than groovy "relaters." They want answers from the Bible.

Rally Day was almost gone—at least in name. Traditionally, Rally Day was held on the first Sunday in October when children were "rallied" for the new Sunday School year. At that time, public schools began during the last week in September, so the Sunday School year was kicked off on the first Sunday of October. Today Rally Day is back. Some call it High Attendance Day, others call it Friend Day, Anniversary Sunday or Homecoming. The First Baptist Church of Bossier City, Louisiana, called it Hallelujah Day. Attendance jumped from 1,200 to over 2,000 and they all shouted for joy.

Modern-day Rally Days are held when the Sunday School can be most effectively rallied. Some have it in the middle of summer; others two weeks before Christmas (First Baptist Church in Hammond, Indiana, had 23,024 on December 16, 1973).

The new Rally Days can: (1) get new prospects to attend church, (2) attract former attenders, (3) create excitement and generate optimism, usually the greatest need in an old church. Whereas the goal of a big attendance motivates some to hard work, the threat of not making the goal (along with its embarrassment) motivates others. The opportunity to meet former friends attracts some to attend on Rally Day. But whatever the reason, all hear the Gospel which if presented properly, will result in some being converted to Jesus Christ.

Teacher training seemed to have lost its place in the Sunday School. In the panic to stop the attendance erosion of the 1960s, new methods were introduced to involve students in the educational process. But educators forgot that the teacher is the measure of the learning experience. Better-trained teachers would have kept pupils in class, but equipping teachers for better teaching was a long involved process. Quickie techniques were tried. Now, however, teacher training classes are being revived. The Evangelical Teacher Training Association reports an all-time high in enrollment. And over 8,000 laymen paid to attend the ICL (International Center for Learning) seminars conducted across our nation. When leaders stress teachers meetings and give quality training, attendance goes up.

Finally, evangelism is returning to center stage. The Sunday School was originally built on soulwinning. Two hundred years ago, faithful Sunday School workers walked the streets to gather children to learn the Word of God. But during the '60s, the concept of nurture seemed to control the Sunday School. The desire for quality blinded workers to the need for reaching the multitude. But a Sunday School also should emphasize numbers, attracting the lost to hear the Bible. Now leaders realize a program of evangelism and education must complement each other.

A REAR VIEW MIRROR LOOK:

During the '60s, many thought television would make a great impact on the Sunday Schools of the '70s. We are five years into that decade and we can count on one hand the Sunday Schools that have employed television.

Predictions claimed that computers would revolutionize Sunday School through programmed instruction, record keeping and educational assistance. But Sunday Schools that effectively use computers can be counted on the other hand. Two companies that offered computerized record assistance to Sunday Schools went bankrupt. True, a few Sunday Schools have toyed with computerized mailing to students. But in spite of our electronic miracles, a computerized program instruction package is not available, even though some hand-scored texts have been printed.

If proof for the most effective methods were growing Sunday Schools, those returning to basic fundamentals would be reinforced in their assurance. But many critics of "the numbers game" in Sunday School claim quality is measured by self-individualized attainment. They repudiate numbers and almost everything that is employed by those who have numbers.

Those who are fed up with experimentation and tangents want basic Christianity. They could be experiencing the same motivation that attracts people to the simplicity of home Bible groups, or they could be pulled back to the traditional Sunday School by a desire for realism, or they could be merely reflecting America's nostalgia kick. Whatever the reason, if they help carry out the Great Commission, the idea that prompted them may have come from the Holy Spirit.

The revival of the workable is sprouting up in many denominations. It is a trend that can't be ignored.

2

The house of God should be a refuge, open only to God and intimate fellowship with other believers, say proponents of the small Sunday School.

The Small Personal Sunday School

Most every institution in America is big and getting bigger: schools, government, and shopping centers. The family that owned the corner grocery store has long since been replaced by the impersonal supermarket administrators. There are many arguments for largeness. For example, combined purchasing, administration and advertising result in low overhead, lower prices and perhaps better quality. But why should the church get large? Can we judge the success of Christ's ministry by American business standards?

The answer to a Biblically relevant and person-centered ministry is found in congregations small enough to allow for meaningful relationships between Christians so they can nurture one another, yet churches large enough (socially) to allow for individual differences.

Many of America's youth are rebelling against depersonalization and anonymity. Zip codes, draft numbers and universities of gigantic dimensions threaten young people because they reduce them to a digit instead of accepting them as individuals. A church, therefore, should not be allowed to become a large impersonal factory, producing assembly-line Christians. The house of God should be a refuge where a man can have private thoughts, open only to God and intimate fellowship with other believers.

The Sunday School movement found in the major denominations of America is definitely placing more emphasis on the small group. They are attempting to appeal to those who reject the church as a large organized business complex on the corner. Those who are alienated believe that the church should be a place where a man becomes truly human, where God is fully known; where the Word is honestly studied, and where Christians realistically face the problems of being like Jesus. The following reasons are given for the small church.

1. *The New Testament emphasis on "person."* Ralph Harris, editor-in-chief, Assembly of God publications, is one who goes on record against the large church. "The Lord likened people in large churches to those who are lost in the crowd," he says. He states that a church should never have more than 300 members; that the whole emphasis in the New Testament is on the individual man. "On nineteen occasions, Jesus talked to one person," he says.

2. *The New Testament purpose of "church."* The small church in Philippi, Ephesus and Athens is further proof that churches should be small. But there's a deeper argument for the small church than its size during New Testament times. That argument is philosophy. The church should be a "service station" where the Christian, like the car owner, comes in to "fill up." Church should be a place of edifying and equipping the believer in light of

26

Ephesians 4:11-13, so that the Christian can go out from the church into the world and witness.

3. *Greater impact on the local neighborhood.* Large churches tend to be built upon a city-wide ministry, whereas smaller local churches can more easily deal with the issues of the community. Such a pastor is more apt to speak to a local bond issue, and the local church usually is quicker to exercise influence on pornography, X-rated movies, segregation or busing school children. And the Sunday School teacher as well as the church member who is identified with a local church will find it easier to witness for God to his neighbors.

Downtown stores have learned to bring their business to the shopping centers near where people live. Churches must follow the same pattern of identifying with a neighborhood if they are to make an impact.

4. *Pastoral care is personal.* The Rev. Dan Bauman, Central Baptist Church, St. Louis, Mo., asks, "How can a pastor give personal care to more than 300 people?" He indicates that a minister cannot fulfill the responsibilities of a large church requiring hospital visitation, counseling, preparation of sermons, program planning, attendance at meetings, besides the daily responsibility of spiritual oversight of thousands of people.

Pastoral care is more than preaching, according to Dr. Carroll Wise, professor of pastoral counseling, Garrett Theological Seminary. "It's the communication of the Gospel to individuals at the point of their need," he says. Time and energy limit a pastor from knowing the needs of more than 300 people, much less allowing space in his schedule to talk

Pastoral care is more than preaching. It is the communication of the Gospel to individuals at the point of their need. (Photo by Raymond L. Cox)

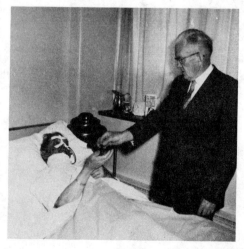

Sunday Schools in the major denominations are placing more emphasis on the small group.

to them. And Dr. Lee Roberson, minister of the several-thousand-member Highland Park Baptist Church in Chattanooga, Tenn., once confessed in a public meeting he could not give more than 15 minutes to counseling individual church members.

5. *Education is built on interaction.* The very nature of the teaching-learning relationship needed for personal growth in Christians is found in small churches. Teaching is more than passing out ideas via lecture, as a huckster sells programs at a football game. A hundred years ago, John Milton Gregory, president of the University of Illinois, stated, "Knowledge cannot be passed from mind to mind as apples are passed from one basket to another, but must in every case be recognized and rethought by the receiving mind." Today, Gregory's statement is being reflected in effective educational centers, both Christian and secular. Students are demanding the opportunity to interact with ideas, with experiments, with teachers and other pupils. The growth of home Bible study groups shows that people want to get involved with the Word of God.

The success of Circle Church, pastored by the Rev. Dave Mains in Chicago, is built upon small group discussions following the morning message. The small groups discuss the pastor's sermon, which is designed to be relevant to contemporary needs.

6. *Responsibility leads to individual growth.* One of the major contributions of the small church is the obligation and opportunity of the layman to become involved in ministry. David Moberg, in his book *The Church As a Social Institution,* states, "As a church grows larger ... the spontaneity, informality and intimacy of the primary group member tends to disappear; laymen are used proportionately less. The member accepts less and less personal responsibility for the work of his church, shifting it to paid workers. He tends to give proportionately less money to the church." Moberg suggests a continuing decline in life as the church gets larger: "The usefulness of the individual church member has decreased in direct proportion to the increase in the size of the congregation." Members may have as many as three responsibilities in a small church. The small church may not be well organized or financially efficient, but it does belong to the laymen.

The traditional strength of the Sunday School movement has been laymen-inspired, laymen-directed, and laymen-supported. When the professional (minister, director of Christian education, or full-time Sunday School superintendent) takes over, the church usually suffers a decline in congregational autonomy. Laymen show lack of concern when there is a centralization of the decision-making process. The attendance may continue to grow because of the charisma of the minister, but the church has already begun to die from lack of laymen interest.

Many Christian educators do not agree that a church should remain small, however. Dr. Virgil Foster, in his book *How a Small Church Can Have Good Christian Education,* pinpointed many of the problems of small churches and suggested ways of growth. Although all agree that a church must start small, not all agree that it should remain small—nor on how large a church should become. This is a subject that must be "prayed through" carefully by every church.

3

To understand the phenomenon of the world's largest Sunday School, it is necessary to understand Jack Hyles' unique abilities.

The World's Largest Sunday School

The world's largest Sunday School is not secluded in a southern city where the Bible-belt mentality perpetuates the past. Rather, the world's largest Sunday School (average weekly attendance 13,561) thrives in Hammond, Ind., an unexpected setting for an old-fashioned Bible-teaching Sunday School. Freight trains delay traffic to the church, soot from the steel mills of Gary coat everything in view, stagnant water in surrounding lowlands refuses to drain into Lake Michigan, and the city's predominant blue-collar inhabitants should be racially prejudiced.

Yet none of these things has stopped Dr. Jack Hyles, minister of the First Baptist Church, nor his staff of dedicated workers who have masterfully injected the old-fashioned Gospel into an expressway society. More than 50 of the church's 139 buses go 40 miles into Chicago's inner-city to bring children to a Bible-teaching Sunday School for which Hyles writes the Sunday School lesson. Whereas many large Sunday Schools have accommodated their teaching to large classes under the master teacher plan, the world's largest Sunday School is still organized on the traditional 10-students-per-class basis, with a small room for each teaching unit.

Hyles startled the Sunday School world with his announcement of an average of more than 13,561 pupils during the 10-week campaign in 1974. This all-time record was achieved when the Sunday School was divided into three sec-

tions: the traditional Sunday School at 9:30 a.m.; second Sunday School at 11:00 a.m., with its own teachers, bus workers, staff and administrators; third Sunday School for children at 1:30 with children's church stretching till 4:00 in the afternoon.

To understand the phenomenon of the world's largest Sunday School, it is necessary to understand Jack Hyles' unique ability to motivate others to extraordinary service. Hyles was born and reared in poverty, he says, in Dallas, Texas. His father was an alcoholic. Today his mother is a member of the Hammond church where he receives an annual salary of $8,450 plus housing allowance. Even though the deacons have tried, he will not accept a raise in pay.

When Hyles was 19, he worked at the J. C. Penney Company, Bogata, Texas. A fellow employee mentioned a church was without a pastor. Young Hyles preached, then got the assignment the following week when the vote for a minister was taken. The first candidate got 19; the second, 8; Hyles, 28 (all write-ins).

The deacons were furious; three of them phoned Hyles and demanded he come to the church immediately. It was 12:00 midnight.

"Young man, you're not old enough to pastor this church," said one deacon, towering over Hyles who sat in the front pew.

"I won't write a check for your salary," the treasurer threatened.

29

"You will not walk into this pulpit next Sunday morning," another deacon concluded.

Hyles confesses he was young and insecure. He drove around that night and finally stopped to pray in an east Texas pine thicket, kneeling on a sand hill. He determined five things that would ultimately help him build the largest church in America: (1) No man would ever tell him what to preach. (2) Money would never be the object of his ministry. (3) He would always be loyal to his friends. (4) He would be faithful to Biblical principles, not to institutions. (5) He would never go against his conscience, but make decisions based on what he knew was right.

Hyles preached that Sunday and the following seven, although he did not get a single pay check. But he soon won the confidence of both the congregation and the recalcitrant deacons.

Today one deacon at the Hammond church testifies, "I *know* my pastor will do the will of God; therefore, I would never oppose him on anything."

Once Hyles chewed out an usher publicly before 3,000 people for setting up chairs at the wrong time of the service. When asked how he felt, the chagrined bricklayer confessed, "Before Hyles came to this church we never had anyone saved; now the aisles are filled every service. I'm glad we have a preacher that makes us do right, even if he embarrasses me."

When preaching on how to rear children Hyles warns, "You spoil them, you let them wear long hair and short dresses, you let them listen to ungodly rock music and you never discipline them . . . you don't love them and when you get old they won't love you. They'll put you in an old folks home and let you rot!"

But Hyles is more than a hard-nosed fundamentalist preacher. One Sunday as he hurried down the back alley to speak to his 3,000 waiting parishioners, Hyles heard someone say, "Hi, Preacher." It was an admiring preschooler. The busy pastor took time to tie the boy's shoestring before delivering a scorching sermon.

Hyles also takes time to counsel people. On Friday and Saturday before Father's Day, for example, he counseled 44 different persons, remaining at his study past 11:00 each night. Then after each service that weekend, a line of more than 20 people stretched down the hall into the educational building waiting to see their pastor. (In fact, Hyles will counsel patiently more than two hours after *every* service. This pays off in great pastor/parishioner relationships: Hyles received more than 400 Father's Day cards from those who view him as a father!)

The Hammond church's Sunday School workers reflect the influence of the hard-working Hyles. More than 100 bus workers for the second Sunday School arrive between 6:30 and 7:00 a.m. Sunday morning to start their routes to Chicago, the long distance requiring approximately two hours to gather children and return to Sunday School by 11:00. Most of the buses average 100 riders each. Other drivers arrive later. All are required to spend at least two hours on Saturday visiting along their route.

Dave Hyles, son of the pastor, is in charge of the youth program and directs the teenagers during the second and third service where 700 teens gather. A quick look around tells you these are not typical suburban teens. They wear flashy flares, cheap plastic coats and the screaming colors of the Latins. A number of blacks are sprinkled throughout the teen crowd. Many girls come dressed in dirty, dragging

Pastor of the church with America's largest Sunday School, Jack Hyles poses with a friend. (Graves Spotshot)

30

jeans (in the first Sunday School, girl bus riders are exhorted to wear dresses).

When I visited him, Dave Hyles opened an office desk drawer to show me the weapons of warfare brought by the teenagers to Sunday School . . . two sawed-off baseball bats . . . two brass knuckles . . . seven knives . . . two bicycle chains . . . some mangled joints of marijuana and a cheap portable radio.

"Since I preach against rock and roll," young Hyles explained, "a kid left the radio on the altar because he felt he couldn't give up filthy music any other way."

A not-unusual incident Sunday mornings comes when a rowdy who has goofed off is led to young Hyles' office. There staff members counsel him privately. The teen is then brought back to class when he agrees to behave.

Sunday School workers have short hair cuts, and each week Dave invites teenagers to "come forward to get a hair cut." Two barbers in the church bring their instruments and go to work as soon as the invitation is over. Fifteen haircuts were given one Sunday recently.

Children are disciplined, as are adults. Miss Gail McKinny, a high school German teacher who superintends the 900-member junior department, points her finger during opening exercises. "You . . . once more and you stand against the wall."

Gail began as superintendent in the second Sunday School with approximately 100 pupils in a refurbished furniture showroom. When 755 children showed up a few months later to sit on the 275'chairs, two shared each chair. Others sat in the aisles or stood around the walls. The next week, all chairs were removed and children sat on the red-carpeted floor. That Sunday, with a barnyard theme, Gail stood in her bonnet and Calico dress and asked the children, "Have you ever seen chairs in a barnyard?"

After opening exercises with Gail McKinney, the children march to small classrooms throughout the furniture store where Sunday School lasts approximately 50 minutes, long by traditional standards.

I talked with one 9-year-old boy who was crying after Jim Vineyard, bus director, had given him a paddling with a Ping Pong paddle.

"I've been coming for months but daddy and mommy are getting a divorce this week. That's why I skipped out of class. They are going to make me quit coming and put me in a detention home . . ."

Vineyard sat with his arm around the boy, reminding him that God loved him and he personally would do what he could.

"How many times have you been whipped in Sunday School?" I asked.

"Seven times."

"Why do you keep coming back?"

"Because they love me and this is the only place that will make me do right."

Several years ago, Hyles faced a major decision in his ministry. He had 22 invitations on his desk to preach city-wide revivals, in addition to an appeal to become president of a college and seminary. After a day of fasting and praying, Hyles determined he could not do everything, but he would concentrate on three objectives: (1) pastoring the First Baptist Church to make it one of the most effective, (2) writing books (he already has authored 18) to help ministers become more effective, and (3) speaking primarily to ministers (in pastors conferences) to help them build great churches. Hyles is away from his church only on Monday and Tuesday each week and will miss only about one service a year.

Back of Hyles' desire to motivate preachers is deep concern. "I've cried for the United States many times," he replied. "Our country is going to the devil and we've got to build strong fundamental churches to save our nation before it is too late."

When asked why other preachers imitate him, Hyles responded, "I'm not a big shot—I'm just common . . . an average preacher who follows the Bible."

Hyles has pictures of over 90 ministers on his office wall, those whom he influenced into full-time Christian service.

The First Baptist Church of Hammond also is the motivation behind Baptist City, a 39-acre, multi-million dollar project in Schererville, Indiana, some 20 miles from downtown Hammond. The Hyles-Anderson College, which enrolled almost 400 students its first year, is located there along with Hammond Baptist High School (500 students) and a grade school. In the future, Hyles dreams of opening an orphanage.

The church has 450 retarded persons on the roll, six classes for them, and an up-to-date fleet of vans to bring them to church. Nine classes accommodate the 250 deaf. One class is organized for the blind.

When riders pile off buses, they are greeted with a sign-carrying usher, "If you speak Spanish, follow me." There are five classes for those who speak only Spanish.

The Hammond Rescue Mission operated by the church has two services daily and serves three hot meals a day to those who attend its meetings. Also, there is a full-time church worker who ministers to the shut-ins and handicapped of the city.

The church has the largest Sunday School, the largest fleet of buses, leads more to Christ and baptizes more than any other church in the U.S. today. Yet Hyles sets no unreachable numerical goals. The church auditorium now accommodates 5,000. The Sunday School already has reached a one-day high of 30,527.

4

When *Christian Life* magazine began to compile statistics on the nation's largest Sunday Schools in 1968, only 12 averaged 2,000 or more a week. By 1975, there were 33. Will there be 100 in 1980, as predicted?

The 100 Largest Sunday Schools

The listing of the nation's largest Sunday Schools by *Christian Life* magazine first appeared in 1968, shocking the complacency of the church world. Whereas many thought Sunday Schools were dying, the opposite was apparent. Crowds were attending some Sunday Schools. Neighborhoods were reached by busing. Attendance contests didn't turn off sophisticated Americans, but rather got them excited. Large Sunday Schools were getting the job done, most of them using old-fashioned methods. Their workers canvassed neighborhoods and gathered for all-night prayer meetings. Their ministers preached to great crowds and gave invitations to come forward and receive Christ. These large churches had soul-winning Sunday Schools.

In 1968 only 12 Sunday Schools in America averaged 2,000 or more a week. *Christian Life* predicted there would be 100 that large by 1980. By 1975 there were 33.

Christian Life predicted an individual Sunday School would average 10,000 by 1980. Many thought it was an unrealistic guess. When Jerry Falwell of Thomas Road Baptist Church, Lynchburg, Va., skyrocketed to 10,187 for a one-time big day in November 1970, many still thought the 10,000 barrier couldn't be broken on a weekly basis. But First Baptist Church, Hammond, Ind., averaged 13,561 in 1975. Pastor Jack Hyles seems to have no limitations, attracting an unbelievable crowd

of 30,527 to Sunday School in December 1974.

"Hyles is unreal; he shouldn't be counted with other churches. He's a whole denomination in one building," one pastor said.

Hyles challenged Alvin Dark, manager of the Oakland A's, to an attendance contest. The world's largest Sunday School believes it can have more in Sunday School than the world champion A's can attract to a baseball game.

"That's one game I want to lose," replied Dark.

In 1968 most of the large Sunday Schools were independent Baptist. "We were shocked to discover we were not the leaders," declared a Southern Baptist magazine. The independent Baptists basked in the light of new-found glory. Then *Christian Life* discovered the growth of the Baptist Bible Fellowship and labeled them "The fastest growing denomination in the U.S." (they grew from 13 churches to over 2,700 in a short 25-year span).

Criticism

Christian Life continues to receive complaints about the listing. First, some charge that Sunday Schools are lying about their size. However, the magazine requires that two officers in each church verify the attendance figures and state that these figures have been published to the congregation. It is assumed that a whole congregation can't be deceived.

Beyond that, *Christian Life* cannot guarantee the published figures.

Second, protesting letters claim that *Christian Life* is frustrating average pastors by publicizing impossible goals. Some communities respond more rapidly than others. "When you publish a story of a church growing from 150 to 1,538 in five years (the Open Door Church, Chambersburg, Pa.), you frustrate average pastors with average abilities," a critic charged.

For example, one pastor of a small Free Will Baptist Church set a goal of 5,000 in Sunday School. When he couldn't reach 300, he wrote a suicide note and left his clothes on the bank of a lake. After a short time, his conscience smote him. He returned to town confessing to the "embarrassment of failure," and not realizing that he might have qualified for the fastest growing!

However, although some Sunday School workers may have been frustrated, thousands have written appreciation. "I read where Dallas Billington built the world's largest Sunday School with an eighth grade education, so I figured I could do it too," wrote Pastor Bill Monroe who began Florence Baptist Temple five years ago and averaged 1,034 this past year.

Third, critics have accused *Christian Life* of emphasizing quantity while neglecting quality. This is a reckless charge. A careful count of articles will reveal more pages attributed to small churches with good programs than to large churches.

Criticism also has been leveled against Sunday Schools that have gone to single services which combine Sunday School and worship services.

"They are not a Sunday School," claimed one West Coast pastor. "If I counted my 11 a.m. crowd, I'd be larger." But those who have visited single services notice that they are more like an adult Sunday School class than a worship service. And because they call themselves Sunday Schools, they are listed by *Christian Life.*

Finally, cries of foul-play have been heard through the years about large Sunday Schools which list their chapels. Highland Park Baptist Church, Chattanooga, averaged 6,819 last year. Half attended 73 chapels away from the main campus, yet they were listed in the total because (1) the church could have bused them to the main location but chose to keep a neighborhood witness, (2) the property (assets and liabilities) is controlled by the mother church, and (3) the chapels are pastored by students from Tennessee Temple College, located in the main church. Since the attendance thrust for all the Sunday School missions have come from the mother church, *Christian Life* has listed the total attendance.

Busing Boom Tops Out
Many large churches rode the busing crest to

Several years ago Dallas Billington, with only an eighth grade education, built America's largest Sunday School and inspired many other pastors to attempt the same. Here Billington, (center) received the award. (Carpenter's Studio, Inc.)

33

new attendance heights. A few years ago, everyone seemed to be buying buses. Today the picture has changed. The Sunday School bus movement seems to have "topped out." There are many who still reach communities with buses, and thousands are won to Christ through bus visitation. But we no longer find unbridled optimism. Some churches are selling off extra buses.

"What happened to all the bus conferences?" someone recently asked. Thomas Road Baptist Church once registered over 5,000 to study its busing program; this year a reported 300 were there. Many others closed down their busing seminars.

There are several reasons why super-enthusiasm over the buses has waned. First, the recession hit. Soaring gas prices and spiraling costs of used buses forced some out of the ministry.

"We once bought gas for 17 cents, now we pay 47 cents. It used to cost us 85 cents to bring one child to Sunday School, now we pay $2.25 per bus rider," says Dr. Greg Dixon, Indianapolis Baptist Temple. He observed those who bused just to hike attendance are scattering, and that "we who win souls through buses will pay the price."

Those who thought buses would work like magic found it wasn't so easy to get people to Sunday School. The bus ministry is *hard work*. When they discovered that it took 10 hours of visitation on Saturday to get 100 riders, superficial enthusiasts sold their buses. Those with a compassion for the lost stuck by the stuff. Their bus ministry continues to prosper.

Others found they brought busloads of kids to Sunday School but had no space or teachers to instruct the children properly. The teachers were hardly more than babysitters. The First Baptist Church, Riverdale, Md., is one church

Carl Godwin, one of the new breed of church "planters," tells the story of David and Goliath. Godwin started Bible Baptist Church in an office building, which members could enter only through a garage door. Using Sunday School campaigns, busing, visitation, and advertisements, Godwin and his workers built the church into a going concern. (Bible Baptist Church, Lincoln, NB)

which cut back so they could do a better job teaching those they reached.

Guarded Optimism

A few years ago, the super-churches ran with wide open throttle. Planning to double their

The 100 Largest Sunday Schools

Rank	Church City - State Minister	Weekly Attendance	Change in Attendance From Last Year	Denomination
1	First Baptist Church Hammond, Indiana Dr. Jack Hyles	13,561	+2,258	Independent Baptist
2	Highland Park Baptist Church Chattanooga, Tennessee Dr. Lee Roberson	7,453	+617	Independent Baptist

attendance, many went on television and radio, built larger buildings, hired more staff and incurred debts.

"The super aggressive churches ended up with super debts," one noted.

Today's sky has some clouds for the large churches. Rex Humbard and Jerry Falwell had an encounter with the Securities and Exchange Commission, but both appear to be pulling out of financial trouble. Others pulled in their financial belt when the recession hit. With less money to advertise and hire staff, expansion slowed. When others reached their debt-ceiling, they hit another plateau in their growth pattern.

The large churches continue to push upward at their own rate. Those whose mushroom growth was tied to the media and busing have topped out.

"Why does First Baptist Church of Hammond continue to grow?" many have asked.

"Because our growth has been tied to soul-winning," pastor Jack Hyles answers. The lost are won to Christ in the homes, streets and factories of the Calumet region of Indiana—busing happens to be the way they get these people to church. Their growth has not been tied to expensive techniques. Then again, the explanation of growth resides in Jack Hyles. He will not be quenched in his desire to win men and women to Jesus Christ. And as long as he has that aim, the church will not stop growing.

Today, although most pastors believe their churches will grow, few boast of a goal of 10,000. *Guarded optimism* is the by-word for those in the large churches; they have become realistic.

Public-grabbing excitement no longer is being generated by the Sunday School at the top of the list. Even when Hyles has a one-year increase of 2,258, he gets a ho-hum reaction from some who expected him to pull people from a hat. There is more happiness in the maternity ward than in the old folks home, so today's excitement is sparked by new churches.

The focus of Sunday School growth today is on a new breed of church "planters" who believe that the old denominations have had it and that the stagnant churches are filled with problems. This new breed rebels against bureaucracy and professional Christianity. They want to win souls and teach their converts. These young preachers coming out of colleges usually are not looking for a fat salary, parsonage, health insurance, vacation and country club membership. They go to a neighborhood, knock on the doors, raise money, build an auditorium, and organize people into a church. Sacrifice is their slogan; the power of God their franchise. These pioneers read how Jack Hyles, Dallas Billington and Jerry Falwell captured the attention of their towns. They plan to do the same. They want to build a church large enough to enter the "100 Largest" listing.

Within 10 years, a second generation of super-church builders will emerge in our nation.

There always will be large Sunday Schools. There always will be a "100 List" in the vision of spiritual revolutionaries, even if it doesn't appear on paper. Just as young men aspire to be president of a corporation before the elderly retire, there will be other Criswells, Spurgeons and Wesleys who see themselves preaching to the masses and teaching the multitude. God always will have His large church because He is a great Lord who is concerned about the millions. He will raise up His gifted servants to reach them. The 70s and the 80s will still be the decades of the large church.

Number of Missions	Professions of Faith	Number of Baptisms	Total Income	Number of Buses	Number of Riders	Literature
0	24,059	7,273	$3,740,000	220	7,101	Write own.
73	1,795	1,249	1,342,502	15	950	1) Write own. 2) Baptist Publications 3) Regular Bapt. Press

Rank	Church City - State Minister	Weekly Attendance	Change in Attendance From Last Year	Denomination
3	First Baptist Church Dallas, Texas Dr. W. A. Criswell	6,703	+764	Southern Baptist
4	Akron Baptist Temple Akron, Ohio Dr. Charles Billington	5,801*	--	Baptist Bible Fellowship
5	Thomas Road Baptist Church Lynchburg, Virginia Dr. Jerry Falwell	5,566*	--	Baptist Bible Fellowship
6	Canton Baptist Temple Canton, Ohio Dr. Harold Henniger	4,574	+34	Baptist Bible Fellowship
7	Landmark Baptist Temple Cincinnati, Ohio Dr. John Rawlings	4,315*	--	Baptist Bible Fellowship
8	Temple Baptist Church Detroit, Michigan Dr. G. B. Vick	4,043*	--	Baptist Bible Fellowship
9	First Baptist Church of Van Nuys Van Nuys, California Dr. Harold Fickett	3,829*	--	Independent Baptist
10	Trinity Baptist Church Jacksonville, Florida Dr. Robert Gray	3,776	+230	Independent Baptist
11	Indianapolis Baptist Temple Indianapolis, Indiana Dr. Greg Dixon	3,517	+255	Independent Baptist
12	Calvary Temple Denver, Colorado Dr. Charles Blair	3,418	+38	Interdenominational
13	The Chapel in University Park Akron, Ohio Dr. David Burnham	3,200	+226	Independent Baptist
14	Madison Church of Christ Madison, Tennessee Dr. Ira North	3,185	+212	Church of Christ
15	First Baptist Church Hollywood, Florida Dr. Verle S. Ackerman	2,934	+175	Baptist Bible Fellowship
16	First Baptist Church Jacksonville, Florida Dr. Homer Lindsay	2,846	-118	Southern Baptist

Number of Missions	Professions of Faith	Number of Baptisms	Total Income	Number of Buses	Number of Riders	Literature
6	107	537	5,297,062	18	500	Southern Baptist
0	--	--	--	19	640	1) Write own. 2) Baptist Publications
0	--	--	--	41	1,201	Baptist Publications
0	--	--	--	40	1,200	1) Regular Bapt. Press 2) Baptist Publications
1	--	--	--	--	--	Write own.
0	--	--	--	--	--	Write own.
--	--	--	--	10	350	1) Southern Baptist 2) Gospel Light Publications
0	2,594	1,223	600,000	60	2,700	Write own.
9	1,692	284	750,409	39	1,515	Write own.
0	--	--	2,028,495	4	150	1) Gospel Light 2) Scripture Press
0	596	152	784,000	5	150	1) Gospel Light 2) David C. Cook 3) Scripture Press 4) Baptist Publications
1	--	120	998,451	11	191	1) 20th Century 2) Christian Advocate
0	875	563	814,632	36	1,200	Write own.
0	769	668	1,751,525	16	540	1) Southern Baptist 2) Scripture Press 3) Baptist Publications

Rank	Church City - State Minister	Weekly Attendance	Change in Attendance From Last Year	Denomination
17	First Baptist Church Riverdale, Maryland Dr. Herbert Fitzpatrick	2,308	+238	Independent Baptist
18	Beth Haven Baptist Church Louisville, Kentucky Dr. Tom Wallace	2,534	-701	Baptist Bible Fellowship
19	New Testament Baptist Church Miami, Florida Dr. A. C. Janney	2,521	+95	Baptist Bible Fellowship
20	Emmanuel Baptist Church Pontiac, Michigan Dr. Tom Malone	2,517*	+28	Independent Baptist
21	Bethesda Missionary Temple Detroit, Michigan Dr. James Lee Beall	2,505	+155	Independent
22	High Street Baptist Church Springfield, Missouri Dr. D. A. Cavin	2,381	+100	Baptist Bible Fellowship
23	Bellevue Baptist Church Memphis, Tennessee Dr. Adrian Rogers	2,301	+465	Southern Baptist
24	Northside Baptist Church Charlotte, North Carolina Dr. W. Jack Hudson	2,248*	--	Independent Baptist
25	First Baptist Church Del City, Oklahoma Rev. Bailey Smith	2,235*	--	Southern Baptist
26	First Baptist Church Lubbock, Texas Dr. Jaroy Weber	2,204	-171	Southern Baptist
27	Forrest Hills Baptist Church Decatur, Georgia Dr. Curtis W. Hutson	2,195	+82	Independent Baptist
28	Dauphin Way Baptist Church Mobile, Alabama	2,185*	--	Southern Baptist
29	North Phoenix Baptist Church Phoenix, Arizona Rev. Richard A. Jackson	2,159	+363	Southern Baptist
30	Los Gatos Christian Church Los Gatos, California Rev. Marvin G. Rickard	2,089	+548	Non-Denominational
31	Gospel Light Baptist Church Walkertown, North Carolina Rev. Bobby Roberson	2,058	+300	Independent Baptist

Number of Missions	Professions of Faith	Number of Baptisms	Total Income	Number of Buses	Number of Riders	Literature
1	701	244	762,858	22	1,000	Write own.
1	3,251	940	--	23	1,250	Write own.
0	550	174	700,000	30	700	1) Write own. 2) Christian Publications
3	--	1,419	795,100	55	1,478	Write own.
0	--	592	1,000,000	--	--	1) Write own. 2) Scripture Press
0	290	109	822,850	18	525	Write own.
1	--	--	--	5	75	Southern Baptist
0	--	--	--	30	1,188	1) Write own. 2) Baptist Publications
0	--	--	--	3	110	Southern Baptist
0	175	243	1,200,000	1	35	Southern Baptist
0	2,627	541	611,572	30	1,045	1) Baptist Publications 2) Scripture Press
0	--	--	--	17	460	Southern Baptist
0	796	643	1,227,487	0	0	Southern Baptist
0	--	389	734,673	0	0	1) Gospel Light 2) Scripture Press
0	274	104	430,161	40	1,100	1) Write own. 2) Child Evangelism

Rank	Church City - State Minister	Weekly Attendance	Change in Attendance From Last Year	Denomination
32	Travis Avenue Baptist Church Fort Worth, Texas Dr. James Coggin	2,047*	--	Southern Baptist
33	Calvary Temple Springfield, Illinois Rev. M. C. Johnson	2,017	+687	Assemblies of God
34	Tallowood Baptist Church Houston, Texas Dr. Lester B. Collins, Jr.	1,989	+153	Southern Baptist
35	First Assembly of God Oklahoma City, Oklahoma Rev. Daniel T. Sheaffer	1,967	+441	Assemblies of God
36	Garden Grove Community Church Garden Grove, California Dr. Robert Schuller	1,947*	--	Reformed Church in America
37	Grace Community Church Tempe, Arizona Rev. Guy Davidson	1,912	+442	Non-Denominational
38	Allapattah Baptist Church Miami, Florida Dr. Donald G. Manuel	1,893*	--	Southern Baptist
39	First Baptist Church Pomona, California Dr. Edward Cole	1,882	+87	American Baptist Convention
40	Park Cities Baptist Church Dallas, Texas Dr. Herbert Howard	1,850*	--	Southern Baptist
41	Massillon Baptist Church Massillon, Ohio Dr. Bruce D. Cummons	1,842	+97	Independent Baptist
42	First Baptist Church Wichita Falls, Texas Dr. William Pinson	1,840	+150	Southern Baptist
43	The Peoples Church Willowdale, Ontario Dr. Paul B. Smith	1,839	+285	Independent
44	Westside Assembly of God Davenport, Iowa Rev. Tommy Barnett	1,825	+618	Assemblies of God
45	Dawson Memorial Baptist Church Birmingham, Alabama Dr. Edgar M. Arendall	1,814	-15	Southern Baptist
46	Scott Memorial Baptist Church San Diego, California Dr. Tim F. LaHaye	1,801	+142	Independent Baptist

Number of Missions	Professions of Faith	Number of Baptisms	Total Income	Number of Buses	Number of Riders	Literature
--	--	--	--	15	375	Southern Baptist
0	871	414	605,030	19	600	1) Gospel Light 2) Write own.
0	66	58	1,013,200	0	0	Southern Baptist
1	655	--	374,354	6	105	Gospel Publishing House
0	--	--	--	0	0	Gospel Light
1	--	--	712,374	--	--	Gospel Light
4	--	--	700,000	19	675	1) Write own. 2) Southern Baptist
0	204	204	669,888	2	25-40	1) David C. Cook 2) Gospel Light
0	--	--	--	0	0	Southern Baptist
0	--	202	513,423	17	500	Write own.
2	190	162	1,178,978	19	450	Southern Baptist
1	65	60	1,500,000	8	140	Scripture Press
0	3,210	542	211,000	21	771	Gospel Publishing House
0	140	140	1,046,000	6	85	Southern Baptist
1	--	127	863,000	4	80	Gospel Light

Rank	Church City - State Minister	Weekly Attendance	Change in Attendance From Last Year	Denomination
47	South Sheridan Baptist Church Denver, Colorado Dr. Ed Nelson	1,777	+119	Independent Baptist
48	Good Shepherd Baptist Church Tampa, Florida Rev. Scotty Drake	1,756	+308	Independent Baptist
49	Roswell Street Baptist Church Marietta, Georgia Dr. Nelson Rice	1,726	+251	Southern Baptist
50	Moline Gospel Temple Moline, Illinois Dr. Charles Hollis	1,722	+46	Foursquare Gospel
51	Kansas City Baptist Temple Kansas City, Missouri Rev. Truman Dollar	1,703	-111	Baptist Bible Fellowship
52	Bethany First Church of Nazarene Bethany, Oklahoma Dr. Ponder Gilliland	1,658*	--	Nazarene
53	First Baptist Church San Antonio, Texas Dr. Jimmy Allen	1,650*	--	Southern Baptist
54	Broadway Church of Christ Lubbock, Texas Dr. Joe Barnett	1,616*	--	Church of Christ
55	Bible Baptist Church Savannah, Georgia Dr. Cecil A. Hodges	1,587	+42	Baptist Bible Fellowship
56	First Baptist Church Orlando, Florida Dr. Henry Parker	1,587	+134	Southern Baptist
56	First Baptist Church Long Beach, California Dr. James A. Borror	1,585	-92	Baptist General Conference
58	First Baptist Church Columbia, South Carolina Dr. H. Edwin Young	1,578	-32	Southern Baptist
59	Bethesda Baptist Church Brownsburg, Indiana Rev. Donald Tyler	1,561	+110	Gen'l Ass'n of Regular Baptist Churches
60	Open Door Church Chambersburg, Pennsylvania Rev. Dino Pedrone	1,538	+254	Independent
61	Northwest Baptist Church Miami, Florida Dr. F. William Chapman	1,533	+60	Southern Baptist

Number of Missions	Professions of Faith	Number of Baptisms	Total Income	Number of Buses	Number of Riders	Literature
0	678	234	533,665	20	720	1) Child Evangelism 2) Mile Hi Evangelist Press
0	1,513	365	230,000	20	1,237	1) Child Evangelism 2) Scripture Press
0	301	226	830,000	0	0	Southern Baptist
0	471	59	--	22	500	1) Gospel Light 2) Scripture Press
0	290	235	529,808	14	507	1) Regular Baptist Press 2) Write own.
0	--	--	590,000	3	95	Nazarene Publishing House
6	--	--	886,428	--	--	Southern Baptist
4	--	--	572,211	5	160	1) 20th Century Christian 2) Gospel Light
0	846	472	406,786	19	565	1) Write own. 2) Scripture Press
1	--	108	946,098	5	70	Southern Baptist
--	--	--	560,822	--	--	1) Harvest Publications 2) Scripture Press
7	87	93	909,335	--	--	Southern Baptist
0	--	--	515,439	14	400	Regular Baptist Press
0	--	270	227,000	22	750	Write own.
0	569	193	348,873	18	650	Baptist Publications

Rank	Church City - State Minister	Weekly Attendance	Change in Attendance From Last Year	Denomination
62	Hyde Park Baptist Church Austin, Texas Dr. Ralph Smith	1,523	+50	Southern Baptist
63	Bethany Bible Church Phoenix, Arizona Dr. John Mitchell	1,508	+88	Non-Denominational
64	Calvary Temple Fort Wayne, Indiana Rev. Paul Paino	1,500*	--	Independent
65	First Baptist Church New Castle, Delaware Dr. A. V. Henderson	1,498*	--	Baptist Bible Fellowship
66	Reimer Road Baptist Church Wadsworth, Ohio Rev. John Powell	1,488	+215	Independent Baptist
67	Cottage Hill Baptist Church Mobile, Alabama Rev. Fred Wolfe	1,485	+120	Southern Baptist
68	First Baptist Church Nashville, Tennessee Dr. H. Franklin Paschall	1,481	-147	Southern Baptist
69	Tucson Baptist Temple Tucson, Arizona Dr. Louis Johnson	1,480	+10	Baptist Bible Fellowship
70	First Baptist Church Merritt Island, Florida Dr. Jimmy E. Jackson	1,478	+24	Southern Baptist
71	First Presbyterian Church Colorado Springs, Colorado Rev. John H. Stevens	1,475	+135	United Presbyterian Church USA
72	Calvary Baptist Church Hazel Park, Michigan Dr. David D. Allen	1,473	-71	Independent Baptist
73	First Church of the Nazarene Long Beach, California Rev. Bill Burch	1,458	+53	Church of Nazarene
74	Second Ponce DeLeon Baptist Atlanta, Georgia Dr. Russell Dilday, Jr.	1,453	+51	Southern Baptist
75	Calvary Baptist Church Bellflower, California Dr. Frank Collins	1,453	+53	Baptist Bible Fellowship
76	Assembly of God Tabernacle Atlanta, Georgia Pastor James G. Mayo	1,448	-51	Assembly of God

Number of Missions	Professions of Faith	Number of Baptisms	Total Income	Number of Buses	Number of Riders	Literature
0	168	150	943,946	5	150	Southern Baptist
0	--	--	520,000	--	--	1) Scripture Press 2) Gospel Light
0	--	--	1,300,000	38	650	1) Gospel Light 2) Scripture Press
0	--	--	196,000	15	500	Write own.
0	960	269	204,000	17	687	1) Baptist Publications 2) Regular Baptist Press
0	193	156	518,565	9	350	Southern Baptist
2	79	75	647,143	4	80	Southern Baptist
0	210	125	310,000	8	450	Baptist Publications
1	447	250	641,740	11	200	1) Southern Baptist 2) Gospel Light 3) Union Gospel Press
0	64	52	524,448	1	15	1) Gospel Light 2) David C. Cook
0	101	66	792,003	16	418	1) Scripture Press 2) Gospel Light
6	76	36	365,000	3	185	1) Gospel Light 2) Nazarene Publishing House
0	61	60	825,000	0	0	Southern Baptist
0	--	161	444,578	12	475	1) Gospel Light 2) Write own.
10	300	130	776,000	4	50	1) Gospel Publishing House 2) David C. Cook

Rank	Church City - State Minister	Weekly Attendance	Change in Attendance From Last Year	Denomination
77	First Baptist Church Midland, Texas Dr. Boyd Hunt	1,446	-67	Southern Baptist
78	Canyon Creek Baptist Church Richardson, Texas Dr. Perry D. Purtle	1,428	+858	Independent Baptist
79	Cliff Temple Baptist Church Dallas, Texas Dr. Richard Ivey	1,416*	--	Southern Baptist
80	Broadmoor Baptist Church Shreveport, Louisiana Dr. Scott L. Tatum	1,414*	--	Southern Baptist
81	Limerick Chapel Limerick, Pennsylvania Rev. Richard Gregory	1,412*	--	Independent Fundamental Church of America
82	First Brethren Church Long Beach, California Dr. David L. Hocking	1,405	+135	Nat'l Fellowship of Brethren Churches
83	Briar Lake Baptist Church Decatur, Georgia Rev. J. Hoffman Harris	1,401	+84	Southern Baptist
84	Broadmoor Baptist Church Jackson, Mississippi Dr. David R. Grant	1,395	-8	Southern Baptist
85	Emmanuel Faith Community Church Escondido, California Dr. Richard S. Strauss	1,385	+146	Independent
86	Lima Baptist Temple Lima, Ohio Rev. Ronald Cannon	1,382*	--	Baptist Bible Fellowship
87	First Christian Church Canton, Ohio Dr. E. Richard Crabtree	1,367	-16	Christian Church
88	First Baptist Church Tulsa, Oklahoma Dr. Warren Hultgren	1,367*	--	Southern Baptist
89	Greater First Pentecostal Alexandria, Louisiana Dr. Gerald Mangun	1,365	-163	United Pentecostal
90	North Long Beach Brethren Long Beach, California Dr. Geo. O. Peek	1,364	-24	Grace Brethren
91	Walnut Street Baptist Church Louisville, Kentucky Dr. Wayne DeHoney	1,363	-60	Southern Baptist

Number of Missions	Professions of Faith	Number of Baptisms	Total Income	Number of Buses	Number of Riders	Literature
5	36	36	1,032,082	0	0	Southern Baptist
0	1,000	220	180,000	11	500	1) Gospel Publishing House 2) David C. Cook
0	--	--	750,000	0	0	Southern Baptist
3	--	--	705,414	0	0	Southern Baptist
0	--	--	341,000	7	200	Write own.
0	113	172	464,142	5	117	Child Evangelism
0	112	107	983,618	0	0	Southern Baptist
2	--	104	896,150	6	90	Southern Baptist
0	275	70	743,480	3	50	1) Scripture Press 2) Gospel Light
0	--	--	--	1	40	Baptist Publications
0	38	95	254,912	15	280	Standard Publishing Co.
2	46	37	852,617	0	0	Southern Baptist
1	370	275	326,225	21	475	Pentecostal Publishing House
0	443	98	445,371	6	200	1) Gospel Light 2) David C. Cook
0	--	85	935,289	6	180	Southern Baptist

Rank	Church / City - State / Minister	Weekly Attendance	Change in Attendance From Last Year	Denomination
92	Tabernacle Baptist Church Greenville, South Carolina Dr. Harold B. Sightler	1,360	+17	Independent Baptist
93	Abundant Life Memorial Church Indianapolis, Indiana Rev. T. L. Vibbert	1,353	-154	Assemblies of God
94	First Baptist Church Bossier City, Louisiana Dr. Damon V. Vaughn	1,349	+14	Southern Baptist
95	Mt. Carmel Christian Church Decatur, Georgia Dr. Jack H. Ballard	1,347	+58	Christian Church
96	Woodland Baptist Church Winston-Salem, North Carolina Rev. R. Zeno Groce	1,341	+74	Independent Baptist
97	First Baptist Church Arlington, Texas Dr. Henard E. East	1,339	-5	Southern Baptist
98	Ninth and 0 Baptist Church Louisville, Kentucky Rev. LaVerne Butler	1,317	+93	Southern Baptist
99	Curtis Baptist Church Augusta, Georgia Dr. Lawrence V. Bradley, Jr.	1,313	-78	Southern Baptist
100	Averyville Baptist Church East Peoria, Illinois Rev. Bobby Lounsberry	1,309	+230	Baptist Bible Fellowship

*This figure taken from the last reporting year of the church.

Number of Missions	Professions of Faith	Number of Baptisms	Total Income	Number of Buses	Number of Riders	Literature
4	--	38	404,246	3	45	Baptist Publications
0	5	26	184,981	8	300	Gospel Publishing House
4	443	162	562,609	8	248	Southern Baptist
0	305	147	447,346	0	0	Standard Publishing Company
0	441	54	--	27	552	Union Gospel Press
2	--	52	553,273	0	0	Southern Baptist
0	236	209	450,000	17	575	1) Southern Baptist 2) Scripture Press
18	118	118	469,546	13	170	Southern Baptist
2	708	242	253,930	24	700	Write own.

5

The beautiful thing about the nationwide "50 Fastest Growing Sunday Schools" contest is that anybody can win. This causes excitement to run high!

50 Fastest Growing Sunday Schools

Englishmen went wild 200 years ago when Robert Raikes, editor of the Gloucester Journal, published the results of his experimental school in Sooty Alley. Politicians, ministers and laymen immediately jumped aboard the Sunday School bandwagon. Within five years, there was a Sunday School in every major English town; within 30 years, 1,300,000 (1/3 of the population) were enrolled in Sunday School.

Each year in the U.S., *Christian Life's* listing of fastest growing Sunday Schools brings an almost equally excited response from both pastors and laymen. When the awards are announced during the Mid-America Sunday School Ass'n Convention, delegates cheer the winning Sunday School from each state. The large auditorium is darkened, and spotlights converge on the platform where the representative from each state, including Hawaii and Alaska, receives a 5-foot silk white and red banner. Spontaneous applause breaks out for each of the 50 schools as the crowd recognizes the work of God growing in many denominations and in every state of the Union.

Later, delegates line up at the *Christian Life* booth. Most of them have the same response: "We're going to try to be the fastest-growing Sunday School in our state next year!" And after the convention, letters and phone calls pour into the *Christian Life* office, helping the staff find the fastest-growing Sunday School in each state for the next year.

We discovered some fascinating variables. Some fast-growing Sunday Schools are large, such as First Baptist Church, Hammond, Ind., with a weekly average of 13,561 in 1975 and a 2,258 weekly growth over the previous average. On the other hand, the winning Sunday School in New Hampshire for that year recorded a growth of only 41.

"The beautiful thing about this contest is that anyone can win," says Clate Raymond, executive secretary of MASSA. "A Sunday School doesn't have to be one of the 100 largest to get recognition." Raymond is known for encouraging growth in all Sunday Schools, large or small.

The fastest-growing Sunday School in Texas in 1975 was three-year-old Canyon Creek Baptist Church, Richardson, leaping by 858 over the previous year, an almost unbelievable growth. The Sunday School also won the 1974 award. Dr. Perry Purtle, pastor, wrote *Christian Life* when the Sunday School was six months old.

"Watch for us on the 50 fastest-growing list," he said. He also predicted his church would be one of the "100 Largest" (in 1975 it was number 79 in the nation).

The church has purchased seven acres, has a million dollar facility, and in 1974 had 1,000 professions of faith and 220 baptisms, a stupen-

When awards are announced during the Mid-America Sunday School Ass'n Convention, delegates cheer the winning Sunday School from each state. Rev. Herbert Fitzpatrick received the 1975 award for Maryland.

A Sunday School class listens attentively at Canyon Creek Baptist Church, the fastest-growing Sunday School in Texas. (Canyon Creek Baptist Church, Richardson, TX)

dous record for any Sunday School—even in Texas where they do things "big."

M.C. Johnson, pastor, founded Calvary Temple, Springfield, Ill., in 1968 when *Christian Life* published the first listing of the nation's largest Sunday Schools. He wrote *Christian Life* at that time that his Sunday School planned to be in the "100 Largest" list, as well as to be the fastest-growing Sunday School in

Illinois. They grew by 687 in 1975 with a weekly average of 2,017, and are registered as the 33rd largest in the U.S. (For many years, Johnson did not receive a salary, but put his finances back into the church to help reach Springfield with the Gospel.)

In 1975, 14 churches were repeats from last year's listing, in itself a difficult task. Rapid or exploding growth usually runs out in one year.

Calvary Temple members stage the "Last Supper" on Palm Sunday. Such creative programs help attract visitors to this fast-growing church. (Calvary Temple, Springfield, IL)

Fast growth is comparatively easy at first when a church usually has extra educational space, little indebtedness, trained workers who are not over-involved, and other resources for growth. But it is difficult to continue expansion for two years.

Fast-growing Sunday Schools are not limited to the Baptists, which have 26 on the 1975 list. There are 8 Assembly of God schools, and 2 each from the Pentecostal, Christian, and Church of Christ. Altogether, a total of 12 denominations were scattered among the 50 fastest-growing Sunday Schools in 1975.

Several on the 1975 list are infant churches, while some older churches also captured the award in their state. In the latter category is Bellevue Baptist Church, Memphis, Tenn., which has been called the "mother church" of the Southern Baptist Convention. It was a Sunday School powerhouse under the leadership of Dr. R.G. Lee 25 years ago. Dr. Adrian Rogers, the new aggressive pastor, fired up the trained workers and in 1975 registered a growth of 465 more per week. Another old Southern Baptist church a few miles away has a carbon-copy story. Young Dr. Bobby Moore pushed Broadway Baptist Church upward. They had only five less, or a growth of 460 over their previous year.

What does it take to motivate the Sunday School to become the fastest growing in its state? There is no easy answer, but one of the most important forces seems to be the leader/pastor who has not abdicated his Sunday School responsibilities, but leads his people through the Sunday School. The ministry consumes his life. He is not interested in country club memberships, or a plush pension plan. He is a man of God who attempts to capture his town for Christ. And he is not afraid to publicly announce his goal of building a great church.

Of course, no pastor can do it alone. These fastest-growing Sunday Schools are characterized by teachers who pray, visit and check up on absentees. Other workers drive Sunday School buses, check rolls, lead singing and unselfishly give themselves to the thousands of small jobs that require attention to reach the masses.

Growth never comes naturally to these growing schools. They program for it and plan contests, campaigns and special days. Posters are posted, handbills are handed out and announcements are announced.

Kids love the excitement. "We've got 74!!!" a mop-headed third grader called to his pastor as the Sunday School bus approached the front door at Community Bible Church, fastest growing in Florida. Yet the excitement of the masses does not crowd out the personal touch. A little first-grade girl was among the 74 packed on that bus. She began to cry when she became lost in the crowd on the steps. "I'll help you find your class," a high school bus worker consoled while hugging her.

In a day when main-line denominational churches are dying, these fast-growing Sunday Schools teach the old-fashioned Gospel. They use traditional techniques such as memory work, puppets, flannelgraph, lecture, chorus singing, Bible games, flash cards, pictures and chalk illustrations. It still is important that children learn the Word of God, they insist. These fast-growing Sunday Schools remind us that the Gospel still attracts the masses.

Yet if a church's attendance plateaus, it doesn't mean that God has stopped blessing the congregation. One year the Oakey Street Baptist Church, Las Vegas, was the fastest growing in Nevada, but decreased an average of nine pupils the next year. However, the spiritual growth of the members is increasing. A church, like a growing child, has plateaus where the body prepares for future expansion. These plateaus in growth occur when teaching staff and space is saturated. Before new growth is seen, debts need to be paid off, new space provided, and new converts trained as teachers.

The fastest-growing Sunday School in each state is measured by numerical growth (rate of growth over last year's base figure). Any church can win, large or small. Determine now that next year your church will enter the contest and attempt to be the fastest growing in your state.

Remember: (1) A few concerned people will make a difference. (2) Sustained work at vital areas will cause growth. (3) Constant growth will bring glory to God and salvation to the lost.

Therefore, this is the contest where no one loses.

The "mother church" of the Southern Baptist Convention, Bellevue Baptist in Memphis, has been renewing its reputation for an outstanding Sunday School. (Don Lancaster/Bellevue Baptist, Memphis, TN)

50 Fastest Growing Sunday Schools

STATE	CHURCH	PASTOR	INCREASE	AVERAGE	
				THIS YEAR	LAST YEAR
Alabama	Huffman Assembly of God Birmingham, Ala. 35215	Daniel Ronsisvalle	469	961	492
Alaska	Anchorage Baptist Temple Anchorage, Alaska 99504	Jerry L. Prevo	199	1,134	935
Arizona	Grace Community Church Tempe, Ariz. 85282	Guy A. Davidson	442	1,912	1,470
Arkansas	Victory Baptist Church Pine Bluff, Ark. 71601	J. C. House	117	260	143

STATE	CHURCH	PASTOR	INCREASE	AVERAGE THIS YEAR	LAST YEAR
California	Los Gatos Christian Church Los Gatos, Calif. 95030	Marvin G. Rickard	548	2,089	1,541
Colorado	First Presbyterian Church Colorado Springs, Colo. 80903	John H. Stevens	135	1,475	1,340
Connecticut	Faith Baptist Church Wolcott, Conn. 06716	Dan Souza	41	67	26
Delaware	Concord Baptist Church Wilmington, Delaware 19810	Ted. L. Lilly	152	240	88
Florida	Community Bible Church of Seminole Pinellas Park, Fla. 33565	Mels Carbonell	314	403	89
Georgia	North High Assembly of God Columbus, Ga. 31904	Clyde B. Wasdin	261	1,214	953
Hawaii	Lanakila Baptist Church Waipahu, Hawaii 96797	Robert Knutson	218	898	680
Idaho	First Assembly of God Lewiston, Ida. 83501	Charles L. Mooney	60	494	434
Illinois	Calvary Temple Church Springfield, Ill. 62074	M. C. Johnson	687	2,017	1,330
Indiana	First Conservative Bapt. Church Evansville, Ind. 47708	Maurice R. Melton	207	468	261
Iowa	Westside Assembly of God Davenport, Iowa 52802	Tommy Barnett	618	1,825	1,207
Kentucky	Faith Baptist Temple Louisville, Ky. 40214	Fred N. Lowry	87	415	328
Louisiana	Word of Faith Temple New Orleans, La. 70127	Charles Green	79	498	419
Kansas	Bible Baptist Church Holton, Kans. 66436	Jack Waterman	65	102	37
Maine	Grace Baptist Church Portland, Me. 04104	Harry Boyles	80	300	220
Maryland	First Baptist Church Riverdale, Md. 20840	R. Herbert Fitzpatrick	238	2,546	2,308
Massachusetts	North Baptist Church Brockton, Mass. 02401	F. Gerald Kroll	73	303	230
Michigan	Bethesda Missionary Temple Detroit, Mich. 48234	James Lee Beall	155	2,505	2,350
Minnesota	First Baptist Church Rosemount, Minn. 55068	Ed Johnson	141	851	710

STATE	CHURCH	PASTOR	INCREASE	AVERAGE THIS YEAR	AVERAGE LAST YEAR
Mississippi	Parkway Baptist Church Jackson, Miss. 39209	Bill Causey	63	1,082	1,019
Missouri	Tri-City Baptist Church Kansas City, Mo. 64133	E. Alan Cockrell	571	1,125	554
Montana	Church of God (Sunnyside) Great Falls, Mont. 59405	W. C. Thurman	13	71	58
Nebraska	Bellevue Assembly of God Bellevue, Neb. 68005	Sam Mayo	122	327	205
Nevada	Victory Bible Baptist Sparks, Nev. 89502	Arthur R. Sullivan	33	33	0
New Hampshire	Tri-City Bible Baptist Church Somersworth, N. H. 13878	Ron Welch	41	165	124
New Jersey	Fountain of Life Center Burlington, N. J. 08016	Paul Graban	93	788	695
New Mexico	First Baptist Church Roswell, N. M.	John Murphy	385	1,005	620
New York	Pentecostal Tabernacle Elmira, N. Y. 14904	John Bedzyk	172	1,089	917
North Carolina	Gospel Light Baptist Church Walkertown, N. C. 27051	Bobby Roberson	249	2,058	1,809
North Dakota	Bible Baptist Church Bismarck, N. D. 58501	Roger Bishop	20	110	90
Ohio	Church of Christ in Christian Union Lancaster, Ohio 43140	John Maxwell	298	1,121	823
Oklahoma	First Assembly of God Church Oklahoma City, Okla. 73119	Daniel Sheaffer	441	1,967	1,526
Oregon	Open Bible Standard Church Medford, Ore. 97501	Virgil Harsh	177	381	204
Pennsylvania	The Open Door Church Chambersburg, Pa. 17201	Dino Pedrone	254	1,538	1,284
Rhode Island	Community Baptist Church No. Kingstown, R. I. 02852	James Hoskins	30	130	100
South Carolina	Florence Baptist Temple Florence, S. C. 29501	Bill Monroe	238	1,028	790
South Dakota	East Side Baptist Church Sioux Falls, S. D. 57103	Ralph W. Kennedy	110	280	170
Tennessee	Bellevue Baptist Church Memphis, Tenn. 38104	Adrian Rogers	465	2,301	1,836

STATE	CHURCH	PASTOR	INCREASE	AVERAGE	
				THIS YEAR	LAST YEAR
Texas	Canyon Creek Baptist Church Richardson, Tex. 75080	Perry Purtle	858	1,428	570
Utah	Southeast Christian Church Salt Lake City, Utah 84121	LeRoy Herder	26	238	212
Vermont	Community Bible Church S. Burlington, Vt. 05401	David Siriano	110	160	50
Virginia	Temple Baptist Church Madison Heights, Va. 24572	David Ralston	327	777	450
Washington	Christ Church of Northgate Seattle, Wash. 98125	James Hamann	178	845	667
West Virginia	Shenandoah Bible Baptist Church Martinsburg, W. V. 25401	Donald Smith	160	776	616
Wisconsin	Central Baptist Church Milwaukee, Wis. 53214	James Mastin	116	666	550
Wyoming	Grace Baptist Church Rock Springs, Wyo. 82901	Wallace W. Higgins	90	150	60

6

Here are 50 exciting trends in Sunday Schools today.
How many of these methods is your church employing?

What Lies Ahead?

What is happening to the Sunday School? There are many conflicting reports. Critics who agree that 9:30 Sunday morning is the most wasted hour of the week clap their hands in glee at reports of attendance declines. Fundamentalists shout "Amen" when they hear that the large Sunday Schools are growing and winning scores to Jesus Christ each year.

Some reports claim Sunday Schools are out of date and that teachers conduct classes with methods similar to those used when Robert Raikes began the movement almost 200 years ago. Others see encouraging signs of new life with modern visuals, streamlined quarterlies, and the latest facilities.

The following list of trends for Sunday School are predictive. They are based on recent literature, reports from progressive Sunday Schools, and research at colleges and publishing houses.

Outreach

1. Sunday Schools will continue to emphasize home visitation-evangelism as an extension of Christian education.

2. The Sunday School busing ministry will grow—with emphasis on evangelism to reach children and bring them to church.

Organization and Administration

3. The Board of Christian Education will become a reality for churches up to 600 in attendance. Larger churches will eliminate the Board, delegating the supervision of Christian education to full-time staff members who coordinate the educational activities.

4. Large churches will use mass-data-storage centers (computers), and denominations will make this service available to smaller churches.

5. More special classes for the hard-of-hearing and mentally retarded, and in foreign languages, etc., will meet the needs of various stratas of society.

6. More learning opportunities will be emphasized during the week rather than on Sunday morning. (However, the burden of Bible teaching will continue to be borne by the Sunday School.)

7. The title "Sunday School superintendent" will be dropped in large churches, with the task being shifted to the minister of Christian education or director of Christian education.

8. More men will be used in younger age-group departments, both as teachers and as superintendents.

9. The traditional Sunday School quarter (13 weeks) will be divided into shorter teaching terms.

10. The emphasis of the opening exercise will shift from "getting pupils ready to learn" to being part of the learning process. Just as the closing exercise has been discontinued, there will be no distinctive opening exercise. The entire Sunday School hour will be devoted to

teaching the lesson.

11. Modular time schedules in Sunday School will give opportunity for many learning activities during one morning.

12. More importance will be attached to writing "job descriptions" for each layman involved in a Christian education program in the church.

13. There will be a growing acceptance of the large auditorium Bible class for adults, where the master teacher attracts many who want an excellent coverage of Bible content.

14. Recent trends to institutionalize the Sunday School will be rejected. Less emphasis will be given to organization and administration, with more attention given to Bible teaching.

Methods of Teaching

15. A variety of learning situations will enliven the classroom. Teachers will emphasize more than "memory," and will move to activity and "emotional-outlet" types of learning.

16. Team teaching and team planning will be used more widely in the average Sunday School class.

17. Teaching machines will be incorporated into the Sunday School. This will involve programmed textbooks so that students will receive immediate feedback for correction and evaluation of their performance. We will use machines with buttons; for example, "If you understand, push button 2; if not, button 5."

18. The use of simulation games, especially among the more progressive evangelical churches in urban areas, is inevitable.

19. Eight-millimeter cartridge film will be made available with student workbooks.

20. Dial-access information systems are on the way. Students will be able to "dial-a-lesson" and the teacher will dial for all resource materials needed.

21. Videotapes for EVR in the Sunday School classroom will become popular.

22. Space will be allotted for individual listening posts in certain Sunday School rooms. These listening posts will resemble the library-type electronic posts found at Oral Roberts University.

23. Music will play a bigger role in the learning process.

24. There will be greater use of individual Bible study at the desk during class time. This research-report time will emphasize Biblical interpretation and application.

25. The "code-com" telephone set by Western Electric will be adapted so that deaf and blind pupils will receive the Sunday School materials on Sunday morning.

26. Small groupings within large classes will enable students to discuss/interact with other students. These will be buzz groups, dyads, listening teams, etc.

27. Audio tape cassettes will provide teacher-stimulation and communication, in some places replacing the monthly and/or weekly teachers meeting.

28. Multi-media will be used prominently in Sunday School—i.e., cassette tapes, filmstrips, overhead projectors, records, charts, flannelgraph, banners, inexpensive audiovisuals, and pictures for every classroom situation.

29. Inexpensive banners will become a teaching device.

30. Memory work will continue in many churches but decline in others. The shift away from the King James version to modern translations will cause a de-emphasis of memorization.

31. The "discovery approach" method, with more independent study and learning will pit the student against himself rather than against the class.

32. A teaching kit for each teacher will provide tools such as books, commentaries, filmstrips, records, program materials, and instructional materials.

33. The continued cooperation of evangelical denominations will develop instructional resource materials and make them available to Sunday Schools.

34. The International Uniform Lesson will continue to lose its influence.

35. The popular pocket paperback books and/or workbook-leaflets will replace the traditional quarterly. The leaflets will be distributed weekly, so students can use them in class as a learning aid, then take them home for

The Sunday School busing ministry will grow—with emphasis on evangelism to reach children and bring them to church.

out-of-class resource.

36. There will be an increased use of adult electives over the traditional age-groupings.

37. "Indigenous curriculums," with local Sunday Schools planning their own material from an accumulated study of three or four publishers, will follow patterns set by local public school boards. Many fundamentalists will continue to write Sunday School lessons using the "Bible only," rather than published material. These churches will have a unified lesson.

38. Independent publishers of Sunday School material (such as Scripture Press, Gospel Light Press, David C. Cook, and Baptist Publications of Denver, Colo.) will continue to grow.

39. Sex education will become part of the regular curriculum; however, the term will be changed because of its rejection by many groups.

40. There will be a growth of non-graded curriculum materials and books not produced for Sunday School but used there to meet immediate needs.

41. More non-dated curriculum materials and programs will be used throughout the year.

Aims and Objectives

42. The drift in purpose away from evangelism to education as the major purpose of the Sunday School will continue.

43. The number of large multi-service Sunday Schools, offering more than Bible teaching ministry to the total needs of the person, will grow.

44. Attendance will continue to decline in the mainline denominational Sunday School, while aggressive Sunday Schools among fundamentalists will grow in size.

45. Groups with strong emphasis on evangelism will continue to start new Sunday Schools, while groups interested in social action will not grow but will spend their energy on humanitarian projects.

Facilities

46. Small cubicles (10'x10') will no longer be built for classrooms, but those in existence will continue to be used.

47. New classrooms will have open space—a light and cheerful appearance as in public school classrooms.

48. Large chalkboards, tackboards, maps, and age-graded plastic molded furniture will make rooms appear similar to those in public schools.

49. A number of interest centers will be located in children's rooms—such as play, activity, worship, nature, library and resource centers.

50. Classrooms will have built-in flexibility and expansibility for more-than-Sunday-morning use.

Sunday Schools will continue to use audiovisuals to illustrate Bible lessons. (Emmanuel Lutheran Church, Ft. Wayne, IN)

GREAT SUNDAY SCHOOL "BOOM" AHEAD

by Leon Kilbreth[1]

I predict that we have never seen anything like it! It will far outstrip our great growth in the forties. It's my observation as I travel across America—leading in Sunday School revivals, speaking at Sunday School conventions, assemblies, etc.—that we are entering an era of the greatest Sunday School "boom" that the Christian world has ever seen.

The next five years will bring us into an unprecedented period of gathering people for Bible study. Hundreds of churches will be bursting at the seams. Some of the greatest innovations in outreach methods ever devised will be used and blessed of God. The greatest Sunday School attendances ever recorded will be a part of this "boom." Sunday School enrollment will go to an all-time high. Baptisms and church attendances will soar like the rising flood waters, and multitudes will be added to the Lord's Body.

The Vision

There is a mounting tide of hungering and thirsting among some of God's chosen men. I'm encountering some wonderful men today who are making themselves available to the leadership of the Holy Spirit. Men who are breaking out of a mold they have been in since their seminary days. Men who are tired of trying to run a little weekly program. Men who are tired of the status-quo. Men who no longer have a challenge. Men who have become frustrated and powerless in their preaching and leadership.

These men are moving out with a new hunger for the power of the Holy Spirit in their lives and leadership. They are taking on a new boldness, a new courage, a new determination, a new direction and a new zeal to build a great church for the Lord. And they have come to the realization that building a growing, effective Sunday School is the best way to do it.

The Spark for This Boom

During the last few years we have seen the launching of some of the finest training bases ever developed. These short-term specialized crash courses have been packed full of real helps for starving pastors and church leaders—leaders who have an education, but know nothing about building a great New Testament church; leaders who have been in school all their lives, but know nothing about motivating people, very little about local church leadership and little or nothing of how to give their church a vision.

These training bases—from three to five days in length—have been in the form of growth seminars, leadership conferences, evangelism conferences and specialized training sessions. The teachers, speakers, conference leaders and directors have been men who know what they are doing, men who are doing an outstanding job in the local church day in and day out. They are men who can motivate and inspire; who present simple, practical plans and ways of building a great church; who have a burning desire for reaching people.

These men are "turned-on." They have the freshness of the Holy Spirit upon them and a great *excitement* in their lives and leadership.

With this kind of men leading, teaching and motivating, these specialized training bases have become reservoirs of refreshing mountain streams that have fed and refreshed the souls of dried-up leaders. They have become mountain peaks of new strength. Leaders have stood on these mountains and suddenly have seen a new vision of the Lord's work and their local field. These training opportunities have become classrooms where the Spirit of God walked among the pupils, where men learned not theory only, but began to see that a great church is a philosophy. There, men experienced the new thrill of seeing the Holy Spirit at work in their lives.

From These Training Bases

An army of new leaders—men with new zeal, new purpose, new commitment and a do-or-die spirit of leading their churches—have come from these crash courses to a new height.

These newly motivated, newly equipped and Spirit-filled leaders are the men who now are building the foundations and the launching pads that will usher in this great new Sunday School "boom" that I predict is on its way.

Lift up your eyes and look. You haven't seen anything yet! There are some "giant" leaders getting their churches ready. They are equipping a new army of field hands, training them, motivating them, giving them a new vision, and H-Day (Harvest Day) is just ahead. The white harvest is about ready to be attacked by a group of revived churches who will reach, teach, win and develop great multitudes. Praise God, I can hardly wait!

Denominational labels will not be the determining fact. I see several denominations and their churches involved in this great Sunday School "boom" because some churches in the so-called "dead" denominations have pastors

---

[1] Leon Kilbreth is called "Mr. Sunday School" by Southern Baptists. He is a layman working in Sunday School conferences.

who are far from dead. These pastors are very evangelistic, concerned about reaching people and are "fed-up" with the lack of progress in their denomination. Many of these pastors have become involved in these training bases, and their ministry has been turned around.

But I predict that Baptists will lead in this effort—various groups of Baptists. Southern Baptists have the churches. They have the opportunity, but they also have many difficulties to overcome.

Few Churches Will Be Involved

Only 10 percent of the churches of our land today are considered effective. That means that 10 percent of the churches baptize 90 percent of the converts; 90 percent of the churches baptize only 10 percent of the converts.

I believe that within ten years we will see several hundred huge, "mountain-peak" churches across America—and thousands of small, struggling churches who will have to fight to keep their doors open. The latter will meet on Sunday, but will make no impact on society. These small churches will be killed by a few very aggressive, evangelistic churches which will attract crowds by the thousands, and which will have four or five different services on Sunday, with dual Sunday Schools and dual worship services (already going on). These churches will build great multiple-purpose buildings. They will have large specialized staffs. The quality of lay leadership will be greatly improved. And these churches will have well-rounded programs to meet the needs of the entire family. Many will have their own school systems, radio and TV stations. Their ability to advertise and promote will be fantastic.

My Reason for Saying . . . "A Few Churches"

The building of this kind of a church in our day requires a special kind of pastor/leader—a man completely committed to Christ (many pastors aren't); a man who is willing to pay a high price, a man with unlimited faith and great courage; and a man who refuses to conform to the pressures of society.

This type of man is "on course." He knows where he is going. He doesn't push panic buttons and change his approach and methods every year because someone comes along with a new approach, a new whim or a new gimmick. He operates from a sound foundation. He is open to change, but doesn't change simply because what he is doing may seem to be failing. He simply picks out the best of change to enrich what he already is doing.

It's my observation that most pastors really don't want to reach people in great numbers. It takes too much out of a man; the price is too high. The constant search for new lay leadership and their training, the administering of a staff, the long detailed planning and execution of those plans, the building of new buildings, the acquiring of additional property, the moving to dual Sunday Schools and worship services—all this requires a definite challenge, hard work, personal sacrifice and pressure.

So thousands of churches will remain ordinary. They will continue to remain small—and ordinary.

As for me, I cannot remain silent, neutral, indifferent and see the army of the Lord retreat behind the four walls of a building . . . trying to "hold the fort."

I don't want to be the kind of a leader who is trying to hold the fort . . . I want to help launch an attack. Come, join me!

7

The Sunday School is under attack from many who want to revolutionize its existence and others who want to change its purpose. Sometimes change is proposed merely because of popular—but erroneous—opinions like these.

Answering 10 Criticisms against the Sunday School

The Sunday School movement, which will be 200 years old in 1980, enjoyed general growth until ten years ago. Now attendance is going down in mainline churches, and Sunday Schools are struggling for air. This last decade finds the Sunday School under attack from many who want to revolutionize its existence and others who want to change its purpose. Unfortunately, change sometimes is based merely on opinions. Here are ten popular opinions about Sunday School which are basically wrong. These assumptions hurt the Sunday School and should be corrected.

1. *A good Sunday School is a growing Sunday School.* A rural Sunday School superintendent used a country idiom: "Put the food in the trough and the pigs will come running." He went on to state that if a Sunday School had quality education it would attract the multitudes. However, there are thousands of Sunday Schools that meet the standards of quality, yet their attendance graph line is not going up. In opposite perspective, just because a Sunday School is large, it does not mean that it is doing a good job of teaching the Bible. Some Sunday School leaders have built attendance on gimmicks, promotion and giveaways, yet they have a staggering drop-out rate because the Word of God is not properly taught to keep people returning.

Dr. Jack Hudson, pastor of Northside Baptist Church, Charlotte, N.C., aptly compares promotion to fishing for men. Hudson likens promotion to the bait and Bible teaching to the hook. The bait attracts the fish, but it cannot catch. The hook fastens, but it cannot attract. Hudson indicated he uses promotion to get people to attend Sunday School, and Bible teaching to keep them coming back week after week.

Sunday Schools that emphasize *quality* usually have good Bible teaching. Sunday Schools that emphasize *quantity* usually reflect attendance rises. Therefore, Sunday School leaders should emphasize both growth and Bible teaching.

2. *Contests reflect contemporary advertising techniques and produce superficial Christians.* Robert Raikes, founder of the Sunday School, awarded Testaments, games, shoes, and clothing for good behavior and attendance. During the early days of the American Sunday School Union (founded 1824), children were given a penny to come to Sunday School. Dave Wardle's Master's thesis, *Analysis of Sunday School Attendance Contests* indicated there has never been an age in which leaders did not use contests in Sunday School.

Dr. Greg Dixon, Indianapolis Baptist Temple, claims that "Jesus performed miracles to get people to listen to Him, and since I can't do that, I will use contests and campaigns, and preach to those who come." Contests still can be used to reach the multitudes, as they have been used since the beginning of the movement.

3. *Sunday School attendance is going down.*
A careful analysis of the *American Yearbook of Churches* reveals that Sunday School enrollment doubled in the 15 years between 1945 and 1960 (from 21,426,453 to 40,439,972). After the religious boom immediately following the Second World War, the secular 60s took their toll in churches that had attracted individuals only for social reasons. But those groups that evidenced true spiritual vitality retained membership and others which emphasized evangelism showed growth. According to a 1968 press release, Sunday Schools associated with the National Sunday School Association showed a 3.5 percent numerical increase. Aggressive evangelistic groups such as the Southwide Baptist Fellowship reflected in their yearbook a spectacular gain, growing from 200 churches to more than 1,200, from 1960 to 1970.

4. *Sunday School is for kids.* The Grace Bible Church of Roxanna, Ohio, calls itself "The Family School," a term which fittingly reflects the purpose of Sunday School: to teach the Word of God to every member of the family, including adults. And the Temple Baptist Church, Detroit, Mich., averages approximately 4,000 in Sunday School, half of them adults. The church's $1 million-a-year budget is built on the strength of adults in Sunday School and over half the annual income goes to foreign missions. The strong Sunday School can and does reach adults, along with an outreach to children.

5. *Divide and multiply is the path to growth.*
The Southern Baptist Convention published "The Laws of Sunday School Growth" and concluded that, since new Sunday School classes reach an optimum size in approximately six months, and since every class should have only ten students, growth comes by dividing existing classes into smaller ones and allowing them to expand. This principle appears logical on paper, but in reality usually does not work. New teachers are hard to find, and space seldom is available. The *esprit de corps* of a growing class is killed when a class is divided, in many cases creating stagnation.

Highly motivated teachers who reach pupils and build great classes should be encouraged by being allowed to keep the fruit of the labors. Aggressive teachers who reach boys and girls for Christ will do a better job of keeping them in Sunday School, than will other teachers brought in to work where someone else has "sowed and reaped."

6. *Small classes produce better education.*
Public schools are moving to larger groupings through team teaching. Their first reason for going to larger groups was limited budgets, but now they find that larger classes provide greater motivation—and stimulation—allowing all students to be exposed to the best teachers. More content is communicated and fewer discipline problems result. At the same time, smaller classes allow a greater degree of participation, and permit teachers to concentrate on individual student needs. Sunday School leaders, therefore, should emphasize both large and small classes, not only the latter.

7. *Sunday School should be need-centered.*
Many teachers have fallen into the snare of teaching only that which is practical, believing that "every lesson should be relevant, to keep the interest of the children." Years ago, the Sunday School emphasized the catechism and rote memorization of Bible verses. Children parroted Bible truths without understanding Biblical meaning. As a result, the pendulum swung to the opposite extreme. However, children must know the attributes of God and the truth regarding the Trinity, even though these doctrines may not seem "relevant." Paul exhorted "Put the brethren in remembrance of . . . doctrine" (I Timothy 4:6). Sunday School leaders need to return to teaching Biblical content, yet making it practical for everyday life.

8. *Door-to-door visitation is the most effective way to grow.* A decade ago, most growing Sunday Schools used an organized visitation campaign to reach their neighborhoods. This every-home canvass produced results when people were church-oriented; however, now family schedules are packed. Mobility has put Americans on the move, and a growing emphasis on leisure and entertainment has taken people away from the church. So churches have put visitation on wheels, too. The Rev. Bill Powell, Home Missions Secretary of the Southern Baptist Convention, says, "The Sunday School bus outreach has replaced door-to-door evangelism as the most effective medium for bringing people into the church." The use of Sunday School buses provides the organized program to reach a community, a convenient ride to church, and the technique whereby homes can be reached for Jesus Christ.

The largest Sunday School bus ministry in 1971 was at the Landmark Baptist Temple, Cincinnati, where Dr. John Rawlings sent 120 buses throughout the Greater Cincinnati area, transporting people to Sunday School.

9. *Buildings are needed for expansion.* A typical Sunday School proverb, "You build your Sunday School and it will build your attendance," no longer is true. Many energetic pastors have constructed large buildings but have been disappointed when crowds did not fill them. Empty space does not attract the multitudes; rather, people attract people. When John F. Kennedy ran for President, every press conference was held in a room too small to accommodate the crowd, giving the illusion of a massive following.

Dr. Dallas Billington, minister, Akron Baptist Temple, America's largest Sunday School in 1971, says, "We never constructed a building until after we needed it. Two dozen boys packed into a room tells them our Sunday School is successful and growing."

On the other hand, when a young mother visited United Baptist Church, San Jose, Calif., on Easter Sunday 1971, she would not let her daughter go into the classroom for seven-year-olds. "You don't need more pupils, you need more space," she said to the usher as she returned to her car.

Therefore, a balanced approach to Sunday School construction is needed. Space does not attract more pupils to Sunday School, but you cannot teach in a Sunday School without adequate space.

10. *The well-organized Sunday School will grow.* The fastest growing Sunday School in America in 1972 was the Thomas Road Baptist Church, Lynchburg, Va. It increased from 2,640 to over 6,000 in three years. Yet there is only one committee in the church—the deacons. Little attention is given to job descriptions, reports, organizational charts, committees and accepted business techniques.

"We put emphasis on reaching people and teaching them the Word of God," says Dr. Jerry Falwell, pastor. At the same time, the church is not unorganized. Laymen seem to know what they are doing and quickly do it.

Many Sunday School workers attend conventions and read books, looking for clues to building a large attendance. But the key to growth is not in organization. According to Dr. Harold Henniger, pastor of Canton (Ohio) Baptist Temple, "A church should put emphasis on reaching people and then, when they are present, place emphasis on organization for correct teaching and follow-up."

The Sunday School is in a struggle for its life, as voices demand that it change its form. Sunday School does not need a revolution, only a return to its original foundation. Robert Raikes began the movement by (1) using lay teachers, (2) substituting the Bible for the catechism, (3) centering on the ruffians of the street rather than the children of Christians, and (4) winning people to Christ rather than emphasizing edification.

As the Sunday School has grown, it has become enmeshed in "old wives' tales" and their "sacred cows." Let's do away with the sacred cows of Sunday School so we can return to its original priorities.

section II

Getting the Sunday School Organized

Pastor James Schultz gives a children's sermon at Lennox-Bethany Baptist Church.

8

Pastoral "island hopping" to put out "brush fires" in the various areas of Christian education is weakening churches. Here's how to make your church a true New Testament church.

The Pastor and His Christian Education Program[1]

BY HOWARD G. HENDRICKS

Many a pastor today is an island-hopper. He spends much of his time in his pastoral helicopter as a visiting fireman, moving from one island to another.

After the pastor begins his work at a church, one of the first things his people bring to his attention is the Sunday School. His congregation assumes that if he has been to college or seminary, he is an authority on Sunday School work. And so he seeks to give the Sunday School some motherly inspection. But no sooner does he start to help in the Sunday School than he discovers another problem area—the Sunday evening youth groups. When he begins to work there, he discovers a third area of problems—the weekday clubs. He tries for a period of time to salvage things there and then, much to his surprise, learns about problems in the women's work. By the time he lands on this island and finds that he cannot really do much there, he finds that what he had started to do in the Sunday School is now in need of repair. So he goes back to the Sunday School island and engages in some brush-fire work there.

So the pastor works his way around the various agencies throughout the church. But he discovers that these educational agencies are each vying for the time, attention, money and interest of the children, young people, and adults involved.

[1]Reprinted by permission from Scripture Press Foundation, 1966, world rights reserved.

I believe that in many churches today this is a major problem. And the larger the church, the greater may be the pastoral island-hopping activity. Instead of church activities being correlated, they are often fragmented. How, then, can these component parts of the church program be correlated? How can we float the "islands" together so that we have a concerted program with clear-cut objectives in which all the educational agencies are working together?

To answer these questions I would like to suggest that we think of constructing a building.

I. The first step in correlating your educational program is to check the building code standards.

We are building church programs for the Lord, but many Christians haven't checked the building code standards—in God's Word.

In Acts 2:42-47 we have a portrait of the New Testament church. In this passage are certain clear-cut indications of what constitutes a church with a Bible program.

1. First, a New Testament church must have a program of instruction. "They continued steadfastly in the apostles' doctrine (or teaching)" (Acts 2:42a). In other words, the New Testament church was a teaching church! Christian education is not optional for the church; it is essential. We need to ask ourselves, "Are we really educating the people in our churches?" I believe that one of the

major reasons many evangelical churches are not reaching and holding more people is that they lack a significantly challenging educational program.

During American Education Week I visited the high school my daughter attends. I was profoundly impressed by what's going on in that school, and I was profoundly disturbed by the contrast between education in that school and education in our local churches. What's going on in our churches is often an insult to the intelligence of the people involved. Classes in public schools are *challenging* to teens. These classes have "teen appeal." But what about the classes for young people in your church?

In New York City there are more adults enrolled in some form of adult education than there are children and young people from kindergarten through college! And yet many people say, "You can't teach adults anything. They aren't interested." The usual idea is, "You can't teach an old dog new tricks." Of course this is true if you are teaching dogs and if you are teaching tricks. But frankly, I'm not engaged in either one. Adults *can* learn, *will* learn, and *want* to learn. After an ordination exam in which we drilled a candidate for 3½ hours, a pediatrician, who was attending the ordination examining procedure, turned to me and pointedly asked, "When are our churches going to teach us laymen like that? This young man gave Biblical answers to basic questions that have been clawing at my soul for years. I've been in this church for 20 years, and I haven't learned as much as I learned this morning listening to this young man in this examination."

This illustrates that many Christians are not articulate concerning their faith—largely because of inadequacies in the teaching programs in our churches.

2. *A second characteristic of a New Testament church is worship.* The early church "continued steadfastly . . . in breaking of bread and in *the* prayers" (Acts 2:42). In the original text, a definite article precedes the word "prayers." This may indicate that these were appointed periods of time when the believers assembled for prayer.

Worship is the lost chord of evangelicalism today. Christians attend worship services but many of them do not sincerely worship the Lord. Many people are bored in worship services.

But what is worship? Worship is the personal response of a born-again soul to God's revelation of Himself in His written Word. The moment God says something to us we are obligated to respond, to do something. Are we developing people in our churches who are responding to the Lord in genuine worship? Are our people responding to Him in deep-felt adoration? We need to remember that the New Testament church was a *worshiping* church.

Many people ask me, "Why is it that so many Christians are fed the Word over and over again but show so little evidence of it in their lives?" I believe it's because of failure on the part of Christians to respond in worship to the revelation God has given in His written word.

3. *Another characteristic of a New Testament church is service (or expression).* It's interesting to note in the book of Acts and throughout the entire New Testament that worship always results in service. Did you ever hear someone in your church say, "What we need here is more workers?" In a sense, that's true. Many churches do need more workers. But in another sense, it's not a true analysis. Because first, more *worshipers* are needed!

Why do I say this? Because worshipers make the best workers. I have never found a true worshiper of our Lord who was not a willing worker for our Lord. We have all too many workers who are not worshipers. Consequently, they are working in the energy of the flesh, rather than in the power of the Spirit of God.

The service of the early-church believers was very practical. It took the form of ministering to the material needs of the saints. The Christians "sold their possessions and goods, and parted them to all men, as every man had need" (Acts 2:45). Also this service is evident in their evangelistic outreach. The fact that "the Lord added to the Church daily such as should be saved" (Acts 2:47) implies that the Christians were active in telling others the good news of the Gospel. In the early church Christian service took a variety of forms. But there was always that expression in which the Christians were involved in significant service for the Lord and for fellow saints.

4. *A fourth early-church characteristic was fellowship.* They "continued steadfastly in the apostles' . . . fellowship" (Acts 2:42), and "all that believed were together" (Acts 2:44). The term "fellowship" is often overworked and misunderstood. Christian fellowship doesn't necessarily mean drinking coffee and eating doughnuts. You see, these New Testament saints had fellowship but they never had coffee! You can eat and drink with other Christians, but that doesn't necessarily mean you are having Christian fellowship. In the New Testament, fellowship was a sense of oneness in the Lord's work. It resulted from their being engaged in mutual service. They were bound together as a team. They were working together, employing their spiritual gifts for the building up of the body of Christ.

Check your building code standards. Does your church come up to God's standards for building a New Testament church? To what extent does your church provide adequately for instruction, worship, service, and fellowship for every age level, from the smallest child to the oldest adult? And are instruction, worship, service, and fellowship geared to the pupils' various levels of understanding and spiritual development, so that there is opportunity for them to grow in the Lord? These questions provide a searching test for examining the ministry of your local church. If you do not have these four things in your church, you can hardly say you have a New Testament church.

II. The second step in correlating your educational program is to "inspect the building."

In other words, constantly be evaluating your church program. Take time to ask, "How are we doing? What are our objectives and are we reaching them? Are we getting the job done?" Let's be sure we seek to build a *better* church before we endeavor to build a *bigger* one.

I'd like to suggest four words for you to use when you are inspecting or evaluating the quality of your church's educational ministry.

1. The first word is *reach*. To what extent are you reaching your constituency for Christ? Certainly a weak spot in evangelical churches today is community penetration. Many of our churches are closed clubs for Christians—mutual admiration societies. And, consequently, there is little or no evangelistic dynamic to reach the lost world across the street. Let me ask you this: How many lost people have been in your church in the last 12 months? In some churches it's embarrassing to speak the answer. Let me ask another question: In the last three months, how many Christians in your church have invited non-Christians to their homes? We need more believers who are willing to contact their neighbors, willing to penetrate their neighborhood for Christ, willing to *reach* the lost.

Not long ago a woman told me she was moving.

"Yes, I heard about that," I replied.

"We're thrilled," she said, "because right after we purchased the house we discovered that the people next door to us are Christians."

"That's too bad."

"What do you mean?"

"I mean, isn't it a shame you didn't move into an area where you are the only Christian family on the block?"

"I don't understand. Why do you say that?"

"Because then you'd have to get better acquainted with unsaved families. You'd be less tempted to spend all your spare time with the Christian family next door. You'd see more of the need for reaching your lost neighbors for Christ."

All across the country home Bible classes are being used by the Lord as a means of reaching people for Christ. Briefly, here's how they work: A Christian couple open their home as hosts for a Bible study class for *non-Christian* husbands and wives on a week night. The atmosphere is informal. Thirty minutes are spent in Bible teaching followed by 30 or more minutes in discussion and refreshments. Many have come to know Jesus Christ through these classes!

A Dallas church has a retreat every year for its young people. But in order to go, a Christian teen must bring an unsaved friend. That way 50 percent of the young people are unsaved. What an evangelistic opportunity! This gives a real shot in the arm to these retreats. I've never seen Christian young people get down to business for God quite as much as on these retreats. They begin to realize their own personal responsibility toward the unsaved.

When we lose our community penetration, when we lose our contact with the lost world, we are in a bad way spiritually. Let's *reach* our communities for Christ!

2. The second word is *win*. To what extent are we winning those whom we are reaching? It's one thing to talk with the unsaved and get them to attend church, but it's another thing to win them to the Lord by our witnessing. Evangelism in Sunday School across America has reached a new low. Surprisingly, many teachers say that they don't know how to lead a soul to Christ. You see, an evangelical church is not necessarily an evangelistic church. In one evangelical church I know not one person in

All across the country home Bible classes are reaching people for Christ. (Kenoyer, Selah, WN)

eight years had been won to Christ through the ministry of that church!

How many in your Sunday School met the Lord last year? How many in your Vacation Bible School? How many in your boys' and girls' weekday clubs? Let's reach people, but let's win them, too!

3. The third word by which to test the quality of your church program is *teach*. To what extent are you teaching those you are winning to Christ? We need to discover in our educational programs if we are communicating, if people are learning. Are teachers allowing for feedback discussions in their classes to discover if they are "getting through"? We must not assume that telling is teaching. Of course teaching involves telling, but includes more. If pupils are to learn and live out God's Word, they must interact with it in class in a variety of ways and teaching methods.

4. The fourth word is *train*. To what extent are we training those whom we are teaching? Are we training Christians so that they themselves are "able to teach others also?" (II Timothy 2:2). We are to reach people, win them, teach them, and train them. But to do what? To reach, win, teach, and train others.

Christians *need* training. Take the subject of visitation. The only real way to get Christians to visit is to train them.

If you announce, "Next Tuesday is visitation night; and every one who wants to visit, come out," only a handful of people may show up. Why? Because people don't know how. They are afraid to go knock on a door, for they don't know what to do or say when the door is opened.

This is where training is needed. Tell them what to say, but more than that, show them how to do it. Then have them practice doing it before the group. Send them out as apprentices, in teams of twos—the learner with the more experienced visitation worker. This way the apprentice is being trained. He is learning what to do by getting experience in it, and his fears gradually subside. Let's *train* believers to live for the Lord and serve Him.

A few years ago a man who attended a workshop of mine on visitation asked me if I would stop off at his church the next time I was in his city. I said I would be delighted to. We spent some time evaluating his church. Finally he asked me to talk with his deacons that night. At the meeting he asked me, "Would you suggest we start a visitation program here?" Of course he wanted me to say, "Yes," and to tell the deacons why.

But I answered, "No, I wouldn't."

I would have given anything for a camera to photograph the dropping of his lower jaw. I could almost see what he was thinking. "You *are* the man I heard speak on visitation, aren't you?" He was so flustered, the only thing he could do was repeat the question. "You mean you would not recommend starting a visitation program here?"

"No, I wouldn't," I repeated. Then I continued, "Let me ask you one question: What would you provide for the people when they visit your church?" That precipitated a very interesting discussion among the deacons. In fact, we were there until 1:30 in the morning.

Many times we are so interested in our *outreach* that we forget to examine the quality of our church program. Consequently, *if* visitors come, they may not return.

III. The third step in correlating your educational program is to "draw your blueprint."

In the Word of God *dis*organization is always a mark of carnality. (For example, see I Corinthians 3:1-4.) It is the Holy Spirit who brings order out of chaos (I Corinthians 14:40).

To correlate your educational program, to bring organizational order out of disorder, you need a board or committee of Christian education. The purpose of this policy-forming body is to oversee and correlate the total educational program. Whether you have a small church of 32 people or a large one of 3200, you need some person or a group of persons responsible for coordinating the Sunday School, the Training Hour youth groups, children's church, weekday clubs, Vacation Bible School, camping, and other educational functions such as leadership training, the church library, missionary education, etc. The Board of Christian Education is responsible for the entire educational ministry to children, youth, and adults. It is responsible for seeing that instruction, worship, service, and fellowship are adequately provided in the church program.

The Board of Christian Education should correlate the curriculum. No parent would send his children to a public school where every teacher decides what he wants to teach. But this happens in many evangelical churches. One teacher is interested in teaching one thing, and another teacher wants to teach something else. So you have a "collection"—not a curriculum that is planned, that is correlated, that progresses step by step from department to department.

In your Sunday School and other educational activities you should be teaching all the Bible. "*All* Scripture is given by inspiration of God, and is profitable" (II Timothy 3:16). The Board of Christian Education should also oversee the correlating of various activities, so that unnecessary overlapping and conflict are avoided. In some churches the Sunday School Senior High department plans a hayride for the young people. But unaware of this, the Senior High youth sponsors plan a wiener roast—for the same week! And maybe the Senior High choir plans a social get-together that week, too. Then the young people, because they don't have money or time to go to all of them, must decide which one to attend. Instead of promoting the Sunday School social, a youth group social, and

70

a choir social, you should plan a *social* for Senior Highs. The Christian education board should encourage workers in these various agencies to correlate their activities.

IV. The fourth step in correlating your program in Christian education is to start building with "what you have where you are."

1. *Think and plan long-range.* Too much of our work is sort of a hit-or-miss proposition, in which there's more miss than hit.

Recently I was in a church pastored by a former student of mine. It was a thrilling experience to visit that church. People were responding to the Word—souls were getting saved and people were growing in the Lord. Things were happening; but there's a reason behind it. This pastor has a plan. The church has goals. They haven't reached them yet, but they are in progress.

2. *Educate your leadership with regard to these concepts of Christian education.* How do you do this? By a man-to-man approach. You can never train leaders without personal contact. A pastor in Arizona spends much of his time with individuals, with small groups. For example, he regularly goes out to breakfast with a group of businessmen from his church. As a result, the ministry of that church is becoming *their* vision, *their* burden.

Invite couples to your house for coffee. Get to know them. Share your burdens and concerns. Listen to theirs. Draw them out in discussion over the Word. Pass along ideas. Be enthusiastic about the work of the church. Pray together.

3. *Enlist potential workers.* You can't always enlist already-trained workers, but you can enlist people with potential, people who are willing to be trained. Let's not forget a basic principle of spiritual leadership: God never chooses a man because of what he is, but because of what he is to become.

We often look for "sharp" individuals, and we bypass others whom God wants enlisted and trained for His work. So start where you are with what you have. Start with the people you have and the program you have. Enlist and educate workers and improve the quality of your church's ministry.

Follow these steps and you will be constructing a local-church educational program patterned after New Testament principles!

Awana club tug-of-war. The Christian education board should correlate all church activities, such as this, to prevent schedule conflicts. (Indianapolis Baptist Temple, Indianapolis, IN)

9

The reasons for establishing a local Board of Christian Education might be summed up in one word—*success*.

The Board of Christian Education

The church must teach to win the lost to Christ (Matthew 28:19,20), and to help its constituents grow and mature in the Christian life (Ephesians 4:11-13). As a local church grows, the pastor will need help in coordinating the educational program. Because the church board cannot give adequate time to the church's educational ministry, a Board of Christian Education is necessary for the continued growth and efficiency of the church.

Why Have a Board of Christian Education?

Some question organization asking, "Is it really necessary to build a stronger organizational structure for our educational activities?" The "anti-organization" attitude has tied the hands of many educational leaders in the church. "A stronger organizational structure will sap our spiritual vitality," the argument continues. But once we honestly confront this question, we find that an organized outreach is necessary for a vital evangelistic outreach and to effectively teach God's Word.

The following reasons are offered for organizing the church's educational program under a Board of Christian Education.

1. *To carry out the Great Commission.* The Lord gave His church an explicit commission: "Go and make disciples of all nations . . . *teaching* them to observe everything that I have commanded you" (Matthew 28:19,20 Amplified). The congregation which neglects teaching is stopping short of the very best means of carrying out the Great Commission. To obey His command, we should utilize the very best of communication techniques, personnel and materials. In view of this commission, Christian education in the local church is not an option and cannot be left to chance.

2. *To fulfill the model of representative government in the local church.* The church is made up of the people of God. Every church member has a voice and vote in the direction of his church. As such, every member has an obligation for the spiritual direction of his church. The commission to go, teach and disciple every nation (Matthew 28:18,19) applies to every believer. Therefore, each must be vitally connected to Christian education and have some responsibility in the church. However, since every member cannot serve on the executive board to administer the programs, the congregation must elect members to represent them in matters of Christian education. The Board of Christian Education is called into being to fulfill this task.

3. *To prevent omissions, overlapping and over-emphasis in the local church.* Many agencies operate within the local church—Sunday School, clubs, youth organizations, Vacation Bible School. A student may belong to more than one agency. For example, a Junior High boy may belong to Sunday School, Christian Service Brigade, and the youth group. Without

program coordination, all three might plan a Scripture memorization contest for the same time. Similarly, not one might have a fellowship program to provide the boy with healthy Christian interaction. The Board of Christian Education should plan an educational calendar for the year, making sure that each student has a well-rounded diet of spiritual nourishment.

4. *To provide educated leadership in the local church.* One of the main ministries (but not the only ministry) in the local church is the teaching and training of its members in the Christian faith. The Board of Christian Education reflects this aim through its teacher training program. A teacher training program needs organization and administration, continual evaluation of aims and outcomes, provision for methods and materials for the courses, and incentives for each teacher to carry out the Great Commission.

5. *To effectively correlate and coordinate Christian education.* The Apostle Paul points out that only those holding the necessary spiritual and educational credentials qualify to provide leadership (I Corinthians 16:1,3). Unless we use a coordinated plan to build spiritual truth upon spiritual truth appropriate for each age level, only a few people will grow to Christian maturity—and then only by coincidence. Most will stumble along as ineffective Christians because their church isn't providing solid, well-organized programs.

6. *To avoid duplicating services.* The uncoordinated program which duplicates services wastes human energy. Two people are needed to do the task of one. Those being taught are cheated out of a well-rounded program of learning, and every member suffers from the lack of planning. The remedy usually lies in the establishment of the church's own Board of Christian Education and possibly in the appointment of a Director of Christian Education. The Board of Christian Education consists of people whose experience and knowledge in Christian education equips them to give counsel as to the type of program the church should have. The Director of Christian Education puts that program into operation.

The foregoing reasons for establishing a local Board of Christian Education might be summed up in one word, *success*—reaching the lost and building Christian maturity into individual church members. A board is organized so that, when there is need for improvement in the educational system, capable people will be available to set up a new program.

The local church's educational ministry never stops. The responsibility for continuing its educational ministry is placed upon the Christian Education Board, according to Edward L. Hayes in *The Pastor and His Board of Christian Education* (Scripture Press).

7. *To follow Biblical principles.* Though the Bible does not set down direct instructions about the Board of Christian Education, principles do exist in Scripture which would apply to the establishment of such a Board. Even the apostles sometimes went ahead without a direct command from God. For example they decided that they needed seven men to serve tables (Acts 6:1-7). Since this did not conflict with any Scriptural principle, and was spiritually and practically reasonable, God honored their decision.

In view of the Scriptures which teach the giving of spiritual gifts, an educational program becomes more than a reasonable thing; it becomes a vital necessity. The following quotations tie Christian education to the spiritual gifts:

a) *Gifts to organize and lead:* God gives gifts of leadership to some people for the purpose of building the local church into a mature body. These gifted men must give account of every act they perform, or fail to perform, as leaders of their particular church (I Corinthians 3:1-17; Ephesians 4:1-6).

b) *Gifts to lead and teach:* The spiritual and financial departments are led

Most larger churches have a Board of Christian Education to help the pastor coordinate the educational program. (First Assembly of God, Simi Valley, CA)

by men gifted by God. All churches recognize this. According to the emphasis placed upon the ministry of teaching by the Apostle Paul, it is obvious that this phase of God's overall program should not be ignored. Often in the Bible the ability to lead and teach are considered together. Paul sees Timothy as both a leader and a teacher. Such men in a church today should be recognized and allowed to exercise their gifts (Ephesians 4:11; Timothy 4:10-16).

c) *Purpose of gifts:* The Director of Christian Education and Board of Christian Education form a leadership team. However, it is up to the church to see that these gifted people can use their energies efficiently and effectively. With Christian maturity for every member as a goal, the church must organize to insure the best use of its human resources (Ephesians 4:11,12).

Steps in Setting Up a Board of Christian Education

1. *Appoint an investigating committee.* This committee is responsible for determining the need for a Board of Christian Education. Appointing the investigating committee is the duty of the church board or congregation. This committee serves temporarily and is dissolved when its final recommendations have been presented to the church board. Members of this committee are appointed primarily on the basis of their interest in improving the educational program of the church. They may or may not be leaders. Since they are charged with the responsibility of investigating, they must be given a set of instructions concerning their task. Listed below are three steps which a good investigating committee should take. None is of any real value unless all four are followed.

Establish a Standard.

In the investigation of the educational program of the church, the committee must first learn what is good and efficient educational programming. It is impossible to understand the quality of the program being used if it is not understood what kind of a program is best. There are several ways that a committee can learn this. Here are three:

(a) Contact authorities such as teachers in a Christian education department of a Christian school or Bible college. These individuals usually are willing to be of practical Christian help.

(b) Visit a church that has a good educational program. Most church leaders enjoy sharing ideas about their successful endeavors.

(c) Read articles in books and magazines.

Study the Existing Program.

One of the best ways to understand an existing organization is to draw an organizational chart. This chart should list each person and agency connected with the program and show to whom he is responsible.

Compare Both Programs.

After a complete study has been made concerning the ideal program and the program actually being used at present, then, and only then, can the process of evaluation begin. The committee should write down all the differences between the two programs. This written report should state the entire story as simply as possible, and yet be accurate and complete.

2. *Define the area of responsibility and authority of the Christian Education Board.* This is especially necessary with regard to its relationship to the official church board and the congregation.

3. *Determine the number of people who should be members of the Christian Education Board.* The qualifications required of each member should be determined, along with the procedure for selecting the members.

4. *Seek the congregation's approval.* If the church constitution does not provide for a Board of Christian Education, it would be wise to amend it as required—usually by adding an article concerning it, according to Edward Hayes, cited earlier.

5. *Select members of the Board of Christian Education.* The most practical time of selection is at the annual church meeting, as recommended by a nominating committee. There are several alternatives to this. Some board members may be appointed by the pastor, selected during the worker's conference, or elected by the church executive board and approved by the congregation, suggests Oliver DeWolf Cummings, in *Christian Education in the Local Church* (Judson). However, each of these alternatives detracts from its being a board representative of the congregation. After the Board has been selected, the usual practice is for it to elect its own officers.

Cautions in Organizing the Local Christian Education Program

Churches should observe the previous statement about "needs" very carefully. If the organizational structure outweighs present needs, people will become lost in a maze of offices and duties for which there are really no needs. For example, a small church can entrust educational activities to pastoral direction simply because he will have the necessary overall perspective. Only when the program takes on larger proportions—when increased church attendance calls for more and diversified activities—should the membership establish a Board of Christian Education. Likewise, members of the Board should keep organizational structure simple. If they become entangled in procedures, they may fail their first priority of being leaders (youth sponsors, Sunday School superintendent, etc.). Christian Education Boards in larger churches will, of course, need officers to carry out the paper work.

One final caution: The church must keep its membership informed of the structure and workings of the Christian education program. This kind of information has three purposes: (a) that workers may readily recognize the person to whom they are directly responsible; (b) that members may begin to see possibilities for their own participation in the Christian education program; (c) that new members may immediately discern whether there is an activity or group beneficial to them.

Duties of the Board of Christian Education

Christian education in the local church tends to mushroom as the congregation grows and as leaders begin to assume the outer limits of their responsibilities. The potential for good Christian education depends on how far ahead they are willing to look and plan.

Good Christian education also depends upon a church's willingness to release the pastor to

Good Christian education also depends upon a church's willingness to release the pastor to do his primary job—preaching the Word. (Indianapolis Baptist Temple, Indianapolis, IN)

do his primary job—preaching the Word. Except in the small church, the pastor should not have to activate the educational program. The pastor still fills the role of educator, but in the large church works through others in this area.

Some church members have been so conditioned that when they hire a pastor, they believe he should be the recipient and solver of all problems relating to the congregation, including education. Of course, he does assume congregational problems and, depending upon the size of his church, he may counsel many, along with preaching. But he should not have to spend hours mapping out Sunday School or youth programs, nor be completely up-to-date on the newest methods and materials, nor even be arbitrator of all the interpersonal squabbles. These problems lie somewhere further down the line of Christian education responsibility.

Duties of the Board are:

1. *Establish all policy for the educational programs of the church with respect to materials, personnel, meeting times and meeting places of classes and groups within the program.*

2. *Select and approve all educational literature.* Here are some of the criteria to follow in establishing curriculum (these apply to all segments of the program—Sunday School, VBS, children's church, etc.):

a) Is the curriculum in line with the doctrines which the Bible teaches? The approach which some publishers take may have eye-appeal and attractive presentation, but may lack the spiritual content demanded by Biblical standards.

b) Is the curriculum correlated in content so that students receive a complete program of Bible education beginning with cradle roll and progressing to the home department (shut-ins)? Most companies publishing Christian education materials now offer a curriculum with this built-in asset. This type of well-organized program rarely gives leaders trouble.

c) Is the curriculum up-to-date? Some publishers use pictures taken from the roaring twenties, and their layout seems cluttered and antiquated. Make sure the graphic arts do not convey the message that "Christianity is out of date."

d) Is the curriculum evangelistic? Some literature may be conservative in doctrine without presenting Christ as Savior. Literature should have an evangelistic thrust, reminding workers to win the lost to Christ.

e) Is the curriculum correlated to the age group? Word usage, illustrations, and educational activities should fit the age of the pupils. The spiraling educational requirements of the American public school system demand that the curriculum be reevaluated continually. The same should be true of the Sunday School curriculum.

f) Is the curriculum related to life? Unless the lessons affect the everyday life of the pupils, the whole project is a waste of time. Watch for the practical nature of your curriculum.

The Board of Christian Education should be aware of new trends in materials, and be willing to constantly review the effectiveness of the literature being used. If teachers seem to be unanimous in complaining about curricular sources, the Board should reevaluate that being used.

The Board should appoint a curriculum secretary whose only job is to order all educational materials, distribute those materials before the date needed for use, and keep a file of quarterlies and student books for use by substitute teachers and new students.

3. *Coordinate teaching methods among the various programs, outlining the goals and objectives of those programs.* Each planned activity must be assigned a goal so that materials used will aid in attaining that goal. The following are some possible goals for various agencies:

Sunday School .... evangelism, nurture.
Children's church .... worship, leadership training, nurture.
VBS .... evangelism, nurture.

Weekly clubs ....evangelism, total Christian growth.
Youth meeting ....fellowship, evangelism, leadership training, nurture.
Home department .... nurture, fellowship.

When goals for the various activities have been set, the Board must decide which methods leaders may use. The idea is not to pin leaders into a corner nor to "bottle them up" to certain materials and methods. Rather, this kind of planning insures that the pupils, for whom these programs have been established, will be effectively evangelized and taught the principles of doctrine and Christian maturity through a variety of ways and materials.

What would happen if youth fellowship, girls' club and every other activity were only a carbon copy of Sunday School in methods and goals? What if children were to go to children's church and were expected to enjoy and profit from the experiences, even though no effort were made to change either the routine or the materials used in Sunday School? Under those circumstances, the church has no reason to believe that children or young people would remain in the church, much less grow to Christian maturity. However, the church can hope to hold youngsters and adults alike by diversifying methods and materials.

4. *Select, train and approve leaders and teaching staff.* The criteria for selecting leaders are both tangible and intangible. That is, Christian education training of varying degrees and types can qualify people to teach in the church. This training will range anywhere from a college or Bible school diploma in Christian education to the learning gained in attending courses using the Evangelical Teacher Training Association materials or in studying correspondence courses. Those who show no

The church can hope to hold youngsters and adults alike by diversifying methods and materials.

willingness to train for the job of a teacher probably should be discouraged from joining the staff. Untrained candidates, along with those who have proved to be ineffective teachers, should be eased into other jobs in the church (the Board which drops personnel without consideration for their feelings, can do much harm).

Always make room in the teaching program for the individual who voices the desire to be on the teaching staff. That desire may be God's signal that this person should be given a chance. Unless he is highly qualified and experienced (in other churches), he could be assigned to help in a limited way with a class or group. His performance as a helper will aid the Board in determining his future Christian service.

Some churches conduct an annual talent search through a questionnaire circulated by the Board of Christian Education.

The Board should not depend totally upon outside sources for leadership training, but should itself set up a continuing schedule of courses and activities to train leaders. For help in this area, the Board should contact the Christian Education Department of Christian schools, Bible colleges and larger churches.

The Board should provide each new staff member with a full, written description of the job with which he is being entrusted. Such a job description should be available for everyone from the Director of Christian Education to the teacher's helper and secretary.

5. *Evaluate and plan for future Christian education needs.* The growing church will stop growing unless it has planned ahead to fulfill future needs such children's worship services, additional classroom space, additional qualified teachers, more youth leaders, more personnel for the home department (visitor, teachers), and local summer camps.

Several signs will indicate that growth can be expected in certain areas. For example, a church may have a large primary pupil enrollment. The Board naturally is interested in holding these children and in helping their families, so it begins planning ahead to the time when these children will be eligible for weekday and youth clubs and to when there will be a need for leaders, as well as space, to accommodate these activities. The Board also will need to consider extra teachers for the Sunday School Junior Department. Plans to add new equipment should be made far enough ahead so that these items can be fitted into the budget.

Revised Christian education plans also usually are needed when a community begins changing or when the population increases, decreases or changes its character.

6. *Plan all educational outings and activities.* The church school, like the public school, wants, when possible, to give its students wider experiences than are possible within the confines of the building itself. The possibilities for educational outings are usually greater for a congregation located near a large city than for one in the country. Cities offer more spiritual/intellectual opportunities such as museums, Bible schools and colleges, city missions, headquarters of Christian organizations, and extended youth activities on a weekly basis. However, a church group anywhere can travel to a nearby point of social and spiritual need, such as a children's or senior citizen's home.

7. *Prepare and submit an annual budget for approval by the church.* A Christian education budget is important, for it is a realistic estimate of the projected extent of growth during the coming year. Churches that don't construct a budget usually suffer the following consequences: (1) no objective plans for expansion are made for the coming year, (2) money is spent on pressing needs rather than realistic total church needs (the squeaking wheels get the most grease, rather than careful maintenance to the total machinery), (3) important areas of education are neglected. Usually spending money for the church library is postponed with the excuse, "Buying books is not a crisis need; we will get them later." The Board of Christian Education should construct a budget because the ability and authority to spend money is an instrument to effectively control and administer the program of Christian education. Items which may be included are:

Curriculum (for all programs)
Library - visual aids
        visual aid equipment
        books and magazines
        other library costs

New equipment (used in all activities; this will make up a large portion of the budget).

8. *Appoint the Minister of Christian Education.* How to do this will be discussed in a later chapter.

Qualification for Members of the Board of Christian Education

Positive Qualifications. Perhaps the first desirable personal qualification is the "capacity to grow"—the willingness to continue to study the work, plans, and educational materials of Christian education. The second qualification is a deep interest in the work and a willingness to spend time on the designated responsibility. The third qualification is practical experience in the general field of Christian education. The fourth: the ability to work with others. The fifth is good judgment and intellectual ability.

Coupled with these personal qualifications are professional traits which can be used to God's glory. Executives tend to be more objective in personnel matters because they pay attention to lines of authority. Lawyers look for loopholes and exercise judgment in avoiding trouble. Doctors make good members but tend to assume authority just as they would in the operating room. Finally, teachers and clergymen are usually sensitive to social and moral aspects of problems.

Negative Actions and Attitudes To Avoid. The church should be careful not to staff the Board with learned church members who may be more concerned with theory than with the matter of actually getting the job done. Members must be activists in the most spiritually consecrated and practical sense of the word.

Board members also should avoid riding hobbies and showing favoritism. As has been previously stated, the church establishes a Christian Education Board (rather than a council made up of all Christian education staff members) so that decisions will benefit the entire program and not just certain segments of it. Board members must be spiritual with objectiveness in decision making.

Third, Board members must not let the Christian education staff ignore the line of authority if everyone is to make his maximum contribution. The Sunday School teacher who is unhappy about the location of his class should not complain to the Christian Education Board Chairman. That teacher should be working directly under a department superintendent and should take all his problems to his superior. If he cannot make a satisfactory adjustment, then the problem may have overall implications on the Sunday School, in which case the department superintendent should report to the general superintendent. He in turn may take the problem to the board. In the end, the problem may conceivably be solved with a simple switch of the location of two classes. In this way, the unhappy teacher can be satisfied without involving leaders farther up the line of authority. They remain free for more important duties.

Fourth, the mechanics of Board business must not be ignored. Positively, the Board's monthly meeting should be on a set day at a specified time and place.

Leadership should not be monopolized, either. Since the chairman only moderates the meetings, he and a new secretary ought to be elected every year. In this way, all Board members will be given greater opportunity to concentrate on the Christian education program and problems and to develop their leadership potential.

Some churches hold teachers' and workers' clinics with authorities on the Sunday School as instructors. A 1975 clinic at Indianapolis Baptist Temple drew this large attendance. (Indianapolis Baptist Temple, Indianapolis, IN)

10

The DCE is not the *Christian educator* for the congregation; he is their *director.* The general Sunday School superintendent often is considered second in importance to the pastor. And departmental superintendents can be indispensable.

Administrators

THE DIRECTOR OF CHRISTIAN EDUCATION

When Should a Church Call a Director of Christian Education?

Usually, the need for a Director of Christian Education comes at or near the time when the church is financially able to fill that position. Therefore, as soon as possible, a church should call a Director of Christian Education as the second major step in the process of development. However, the membership must also be spiritually ready to turn the educational leadership over to this person and to accomplish the work of Christian education under his (or her) direction. The DCE is *not the Christian educator* for the congregation; he is their *director* who leads in the work of education.

Paul R. Finlay, Christian educator, has summarized the office beautifully: "the director makes his greatest contribution to the work in the very fact that there is one person, a specialist in the field of Christian education who is coordinating and giving direction and purpose to the church's entire educational program" (in *An Introduction to Christian Education,* ed. by J. Edward Hakes, Moody Press).

How To Go about Calling a Director of Christian Education

Although relatively few churches have a paid Director of Christian Education, it must be noted that the latest trend is for more men than women to enter the field.

According to statistics of the National Association of Directors of Christian Education since it began in 1961, membership has grown to about 200 ... "an unheard of phenomenon 10 or 15 years ago" (Roy B. Zuck, "The Pastor and Trends in Church Education," *Christian Education Monographs,* Scripture Press Foundation). Because of this trend, it would be wise for every church to find the administrative leadership of its educational ministry. The Board of Christian Education and the senior minister should study and evaluate the educational program of the church in its entirety with great care and deliberation. The congregation should then be informed of their findings. The *Board of Christian Education* may then work with the pastor to solve specific problems.

If the need for a Director of Christian Education has been determined, the congregation must be properly informed of his duties and qualifications. By knowing this, the congregation is being prepared for an additional paid staff member. The church must know the status of the Director of Christian Education and his line of authority. Knowing this alone would avoid making the Director of Christian Education an errand boy.

If there is a Director of Christian Education in a neighboring church, it would be wise to invite him to explain his duties to the congregation, says Vernon Kraft in his book, *The Director of Christian Education in the Local Church* (Moody Press).

Usually a church hires a man from its own denomination because it expects him to be in accord with the church's statement of faith and government. Nevertheless, it is a good policy to question the prospective leader concerning his doctrinal position.

Procedure for Calling

After the congregation has been informed about the need for a Director of Christian Education, each prospect should be invited to the church. He should receive a letter outlining the educational needs of the church, the working conditions, financial arrangements, and a complete job description.

The Director of Christian Education, if interested, must interpret his educational training, experience and philosophy in light of the needs of the prospective church.

When the candidate visits the congregation, he should be introduced to the pastor first, the Board of Christian Education next, then the official board, and finally the congregation. The church should underwrite the expenses of the candidate for this visit.

The senior minister and the candidate should spend time in prayer, in fellowship and in talking in detail about duties, working conditions, and financial arrangements. This prevents later difficulties in their relationship. In the final analysis, the Director of Christian Education is hired by and works for the pastor. If both parties feel this is the Lord's leading, then a definite salary offer should be made, required duties outlined, and, in some cases, a plan for retirement mentioned.

The best time for the Director of Christian Education to begin his work is in the summer before secular schools resume classes. Early August is suitable, although earlier in the summer may be even better. The educational program can then be in full swing for fall.

Of course on the first Sunday the Director of Christian Education is on the scene, the senior minister should explain again the educational program to the congregation. The morning service may conclude with an installation or dedication ceremony. Some churches also plan a congregational dinner to welcome the new Director of Christian Education. The evening service might then be given over to the Director of Christian Education, so he could bring a challenging message on the task of Christian education for that local church.

Qualifications

The qualified Director of Christian Education: Who is he? Where is he? These and many other questions face the church which has become aware of its need for a Director of Christian Education. Where does it find the qualified persons from whom to choose? How can it determine qualifications? Are there any standards for such evaluations?

A satisfactory standard will avoid minor con-

The Director of Christian Education should love and understand children. (Scripture Press)

siderations and give way to major principles. Eventually, four major areas for evaluation become apparent. These are character, decorum, training and philosophy. If a prospective Director of Christian Education can qualify in all four areas, the possibility is great that he will prove to be a success, for the personality of a DCE is not nearly as important as his character; his education not nearly as important as his ability.

Character. The first impression, based on personality, is only a hint as to the true nature of the individual. The individual must be examined on the basis of his inner character rather than his outer personality. He must be a born-again believer who is attempting to live a Christian life. The prospective Director of Christian Education must be a true son of God. Beyond this, he must evidence a growing and advanced yieldedness to God. His spiritual maturity will largely determine his success with the entire Christian education staff. Personality traits play a secondary part. These traits must be largely positive. However, in selecting a Director of Christian Education a church cannot afford to concentrate on outer personality and overlook the inner man, the true character of the child of God.

Decorum. This means he uses good taste in his personal conduct. Any person attempting to serve God as a leader of people should be aware of the need to cultivate decorum. It cannot be described only as the presence or absence of any one or more personality traits. Therefore, no prospective Director of Christian Education should overlook the importance of his strengths or underestimate the handicap of his weaknesses. Nor should he fail to cultivate the former or improve the latter. If a man is by nature outstandingly friendly, he should use this ability to relate to people for the glory of God. If bitterness or anger is a weakness, he should exercise constant vigilance to guard against losing his temper.

Beyond personality, decorum enters the realm of habits, mannerisms and cleanliness. A man should survey himself totally for negative points along these lines. By virtue of his office the Director of Christian Education holds a privileged position before God. Any bad habit, distracting mannerism or untidiness may cause this servant of God to be a reproach instead of a blessing. The Christian leader should strive for tasteful conduct of the highest degree.

Training. Some churches have set strict educational standards for a candidate for Director of Christian Education. Most now require a Bachelor's or Master's degree. This is a beginning, but such a standard is by no means an adequate education. A man with a degree is not always a good prospect for Director of Christian Education. He needs training and experience in church education, otherwise he might stress academic teaching over the actual spiritual results of such teaching. Possession of a degree merely means that this individual has been exposed to a certain set of standard requirements and has responded as well as the average student. A college degree alone does not mean that the individual is automatically capable of leading a local church. It is therefore recommended that he be evaluated on the basis of all-around Christian education, training, experience and his past performance as a leader.

Still, the man with an advanced degree in Christian education can legitimately claim that a group of authorities in this field has placed its stamp of approval on him. Remember, God calls the person, not his degree. The prospective Director who has quit school prematurely may also be expected to drop other tasks prematurely.

His career as Director of Christian Education hinges on how well he knows the Lord and the principles by which he is supposed to be living and teaching. His Biblical knowledge will determine the kind of counselor he becomes to his leaders and teachers. It also will help him recognize Biblical preparation in prospective Christian education personnel.

Philosophy. The word which best describes the DCE's total outlook is "philosophy." It refers to mental outlook, ambitions, and presuppositions he brings to his office. His mind must be reconciled to the mental, as well as physical, hardships that await those who dedicate themselves to the work of God. Every Christian worker must face the reality of unpleasant experiences and disappointments. If a man is unwilling to face these circumstances for Christ's sake, there is little chance that he will ever be a successful Director of Christian Education.

Every person naturally has ambitions. The heart of the Director of Christian Education must be ambitious for the work of Christ. If the potential Director of Christian Education has a deep-seated, secret ambition for anything other than serving in the local church, he will have severe problems. Christian joy comes from serving God in the best way possible. If a candidate does not firmly believe that the Director of Christian Education has the greatest opportunity to reach young hearts for Christ, it is doubtful that he should serve in such a capacity. The Director of Christian Education who can visualize a lifetime of service in this field can trust God to supply his need to achieve personal and professional fulfillment. Emotions can lead a person astray in the choice of a career, but God never will.

Duties of the Director of Christian Education

Before we can determine his duties, we must determine the relationship of the Director of Christian Education to the pastor. He is hired by the pastor and receives his direction from him. The pastor is ultimately responsible for the educational program of the church, but delegates this duty to the Director of Christian Education. The Director of Christian Education has not been hired as an assistant minister, although he should be willing to help in every area of the work. He does not usually preach, nor does he make hospital or home calls in a pastoral capacity but should be willing to do so. His time should center on leading the Christian education program of the church.

Specifically, there are seven main duties of the Director of Christian Education.

1. *He counsels and guides the Christian Education Board in much the same manner as the pastor guides the general board.* The Director of Christian Education helps his Board face problems and lends his ability in suggesting how to solve them. He thereby aids in establishing policy for Christian education.

2. *He coordinates the youth program and weekday clubs.* His tasks include:

a) Planning meetings with officers and sponsors.

b) Recruiting sponsors.

c) Providing in-service training.

d) Organizing deputation teams.

e) Planning retreats.

f) Planning for publicity and record keeping.

g) Visiting youth members and prospects.

3. *He recommends sponsors and/or leaders for children's church, local summer camp program, senior citizens' group and the nursery school program.* The appointments come from the Board of Christian Education, but the Director of Christian Education recommends those who are most qualified for these positions. The Director of Christian Education must also coordinate plans for the above named groups.

4. *He gives direction to the Sunday School.*

a) He advises at superintendents' meetings.

b) He assists in recruiting and training teachers (see #5 below).

c) He advises on enlargement of activities such as visitation, contests and publicity.

d) He advises on visual aid selection.

e) He encourages good record keeping and systematic review.

f) He continually reevaluates curriculum materials.

g) He recommends nominees for superintendent.

5. *He is responsible for training leaders.* This duty includes three phases:

a) Location and selection of workers. The Director of Christian Education should list potential leaders and teachers who could fill vacancies. The most consistently successful method of discovering workers is the annual circulation of a service questionnaire.

b) Training. The Director of Christian Education must be able to train new workers and to improve the ability of those already on his staff. The present staff should receive train-

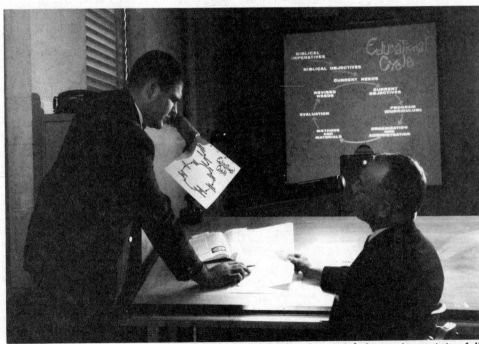

In many churches the responsibility for choosing educational materials for teacher training falls to the Director of Christian Education. (Moody Bible Institute)

ing first, then potential workers. The training process is largely the responsibility of the Director of Christian Education. He should personally supervise the leadership training classes and assist in the instruction of other forms of training. Three major areas of training should be offered:

Leadership Training Classes. These classes should be set up for nine- to twelve-week sessions, with examinations and certificates for those who complete the courses.

Regular Staff Meetings. At each regular meeting of the various teachers and leaders, time should be dedicated to leadership training. Methods and techniques usually are taught at these sessions.

Personal Instruction. A few minutes of personal instruction should never be overlooked as a major phase of leadership training.

c) Encourage spiritual maturity. Teachers sometimes lose sight of this quality in themselves while trying to develop it in their pupils. Since no one is exempt from the pride of the flesh, every one constantly needs to beware of sin in himself and ask God's mercy before trying to help pupils to see their own sinfulness. Therefore, the Director of Christian Education is responsible for the spiritual condition of his staff. He must pray for and counsel with his workers.

6. *He provides vision for the total program of Christian education in the church.* He is responsible for the church's vision in education, then to regulate growth and keep everyone's aim on the ultimate objective.

7. *He teaches the Word of God.* The Director of Christian Education should have the desire, ability and opportunity to teach in several agencies of the local church. He has more educational training than anyone else in the church and should be given the opportunity to use his spiritual gifts. He should teach in Sunday School, teacher training and youth classes.

The Director of Christian Education often vacillates between two extremes. Either he assumes too many teaching posts, not giving adequate attention to organization and administration, or he retreats into his office becoming only an organizer, never using his teaching gifts.

A problem among Directors of Christian Education is the high number of dropouts. Those who begin with a zeal to serve Christ become disillusioned with the role of working with charts, cards and committees. Their mistaken ideas about their role as a Director of Christian Education divorce them from a direct spiritual ministry. Perhaps if more taught classes and exercised their spiritual gifts, they would have greater satisfaction in their ministry. The greatest satisfaction to a man of God is to experience the thrill of leading souls to Christ and of seeing Christians grow through the teaching of the Word of God. This satisfaction might keep more men in the professional ministry.

THE SUPERINTENDENTS

The Role of the General Superintendent

Because of the vital role of the Sunday School in the growth and training of the membership of the church, the general Sunday School superintendent is often considered second in importance to the pastor. Indeed, in some churches the pastor assumes the position of general superintendent of the Sunday School, overseeing its program and personnel. Since the pastor is responsible for leading, feeding and protecting all the flock (Acts 20:28), he has the general administrative oversight of the congregation. This includes the Sunday School. Therefore, the Sunday School Superintendent is the extension of the pastoral responsibility of administration and organization in the life of the Sunday School.

The superintendent is the spiritual leader of the Sunday School, the pacesetter in dedication, faithfulness and zeal.

While his qualifications are generally those for any leader (See Section V-Chapter 24, some factors specific to the Sunday School are:

1. *His calling.* He should view his task as a call to that particular area of service.

2. *Experience.* He should know Sunday School work, from having been a teacher or officer.

3. *Public relations.* He should be able to work with the department superintendents as a team.

The general superintendent should be able to work with the Sunday School staff as a team. (Scripture Press)

4. *Character.* Because of his position and rank in the work of the church, the general superintendent should be of unimpeachable character. He represents the Sunday School.

Department Superintendents

In a large Sunday School, the superintendent of each department will be responsible to the general superintendent, who will work through him with the teachers. In a small school, each individual teacher is responsible to the general superintendent.

The duties of the general superintendent include:

1. *Promotion.* The enthusiasm of the superintendent should be apparent in his effort to make the church and the community aware of the activities and accomplishments of the Sunday School. He will see opportunities for growth through a program of visitation and religious census. He will set the example of concern for the unreached through his own participation in such activities.

2. *Superintend.* His title indicates that he is the person who oversees and directs the work of the teachers and officers of the Sunday School. In consultation with them he evaluates and constantly seeks to improve the program and policies. He maintains careful records of absentees so that concern may be extended. If records show consistent absenteeism, he seeks to determine causes and to make the necessary changes.

3. *Training.* To insure the best possible teaching for maximum results, the superintendent will guide the teachers and officers in maintaining a definite program of in-service training, as well as the training of prospective teachers. He can achieve this through home study, conferences and workshops, weekly teachers and officers' meetings, or a continuing weekly training class.

These age-group specialists will necessarily have qualifications and duties consistent with the needs of their individual departments. At the same time, their spiritual qualifications parallel those of the general superintendent.

1. *Dedication.* He (she) should see the task as a definite call from God.

2. *Training.* He must know the characteristics and needs and how to minister to the age group to which he is called.

3. *Public relations.* He should be a leader, not a driver. The department superintendent needs to be as much aware of the praiseworthy accomplishments of the teachers, as of areas where improvement is needed.

4. *Character.* A genuine Christian character is necessary for one who represents the Lord and His church to a department of teachers and pupils.

In addition, there are additional age-group qualifications.

Cradle Roll Superintendent

1. *Fondness for babies.* While a baby cannot express to its parents its preference in churches, mothers are quick to sense whether baby is contented in the nursery. If unusual crying and fear are manifested, a parent may well try out the nursery of a different church. A worker's love for babies will beget a response of security.

2. *Alertness.* When the baby first arrives, the cradle roll superintendent should visit the home and express the interest of the Sunday School in the new life. Baby's name should be put on the Cradle Roll and an appropriate symbol given to the mother, together with a letter or leaflet explaining the church's concern. There should be an invitation to bring the baby to the church nursery on Sunday, where an adequate staff will take care of it while the mother attends services.

3. *Ability to direct a staff.* Since a baby nursery requires more than one worker, many churches maintain one paid worker, while volunteer ladies rotate in assisting with the care of the babies. The superintendent needs to be a person of tact and discernment in enlisting and selecting mothers.

4. *Hygienic.* Mothers are made aware of the need to protect infants from exposure to germs. The superintendent should be equally aware and take steps to protect all babies from a host of children running in and out of the nursery, or from workers with colds who come to take care of the babies. Laundry and housecleaning will be carefully and regularly accomplished. A plan will be adopted whereby mothers can leave the infant's bottle, with any necessary instructions regarding feeding.

5. *Cheerful.* Babies reflect their environment. Cheerfulness will assure their own pleasantness.

Toddler Department (2's and 3's)

In addition to the considerations listed under Cradle Roll, this superintendent must:

1. *Know toddlers.* She will be aware of abilities and limitations.

2. *Know how to talk.* She will know the difference between talking *down to* them and talking *with* them.

3. *Know methods and materials.* She will be a student as well as a teacher, seeking to do the best job in communicating Bible truth to the little ones. (See Section II-Chapter 12 on the Nursery Department.)

Beginner Superintendent (4's and 5's)

Specialized training for this age group, like that for toddlers, will include:

1. *Knowledge of limitations.* She must know the physical and mental abilities of the age group.

2. *Training in methods.* It is the respon-

Contrary to appearances, the cradle roll superintendent does not spend most of the Sunday morning session sitting in a rocking chair. She only collapses into it in between crises. (Bellevue Baptist Church, Memphis, TN)

sibility of the superintendent to know the best way to reach the hearts of the children, in order to train the teachers. Further study is required in how to pass on her knowledge to the teachers.

3. *Knowledge of how to cope with problems.* Teachers just learning to teach preschoolers often need to refer a crying child or a hyperactive one to an adult who knows how to meet the problem.

4. *Teaching ability.* Often the superintendent serves as the master teacher for worship and story time.

Superintendent of the Primary Department (6's to 8's)

In addition to the qualifications named for preschool superintendents, the primary superintendent should know how to:

1. *Lead a child to Christ.* Primaries readily respond to the invitation for salvation. The superintendent often will be the person to whom he is referred.

2. *Understand needs.* She must know the characteristics of primaries, to guide the teachers in applying lessons to life. Since she herself probably will be the master teacher during worship time, she must know the children. "Be six for a minute," pleaded an advertisement in a public school magazine. Good advice for a church-school teacher also.

Junior Department Superintendent

Special characteristics mark these leaders. They must be:

1. *Flexible in teaching method.* The team teaching approach and the multiple-classes of this department place the superintendent in a teaching position. In the former, she is the master teacher, and in the latter she is usually the one to conduct the worship service.

2. *Wide awake.* To be one up on the Sunday School's most alert and active group, this superintendent needs to be alert and growing.

3. *Active.* To know Juniors on Sunday, the superintendent (as well as the teachers) should be with them in extra-class outings. During a hike, wiener roast, baseball game, or other fun, a Junior often will open up and chat about himself, and his conversation will reveal his philosophy of life and his need.

4. *Soul winner.* Since this age is most responsive to the salvation invitation, the superintendent/teacher should be a soul winner.

Intermediate Department Superintendent

This man or woman must be:

1. *A listener.* Overwhelmed during their changing years, adolescents need adult counselors who will listen to their problems, give advice and help them find solutions.

2. *Innovative.* Feeling themselves superior to preteens, intermediates may affect boredom at presentations where the methods are those used by the Junior Department. The superintendent of teens must master ways to get and hold their attention, or enlist the aid of someone who can.

3. *A learner.* With teens full of doubts and fears, their leader must be able to give them Biblical guidance. He must know where to turn in the Bible for this aid.

4. *Controlled.* Self-control in emotional situations is vital. Shock, anger and tears should be kept in check, though the words and acts of the teens may provoke all three with frequency. This is not the department for a middle-aged, emotional lady to drown every lesson with tears.

Senior High Department Superintendent

Even more than their younger teen friends, the Senior Highs are eager to be led in putting feet to their faith. Therefore their superintendent will need additional qualities:

1. *Need-consciousness.* Searching for ways to involve the teens in service projects, the superintendent will seek out areas where there is need they can meet. He will get acquainted with agencies which make it their business to know such needs, to discover what aid can be extended by the church.

2. *Example.* Idealistic youth seek an example and/or pattern. Besides being able to point them to the Supreme Example, Jesus Christ, the superintendent must himself be a worthy example. Lacking an adult leader in the home, many youth emulate the life of their church teacher.

Adult Department Superintendent

Although the department often is divided into at least three sections—young adult, middle adult, and Golden Age—the superintendent's qualifications for either (or all) will be similar. He may be the director of several teachers in a multiple-department, or he may do the teaching in a smaller group. In either event, his qualifications are similar to those of any superintendent/teacher.

1. *He must know and love his age group.* He must be able to communicate with the students, to meet the specific needs in the lives of each separate group. The responsibility increases if the class includes all ages of adults.

2. *He must know and love the Word.* He must be "ready always to give an answer," for sincere seekers will need untangling from the mass of erroneous ideas. On the other hand, deliberate troublemakers occasionally will seek to lead the class into error. In either situation, the superintendent/teacher must know the Word in order to provide answers.

11

The church must be properly organized for its spiritual thrust, just as the military plans a new thrust into the territory of the opposition.

Organization for Christian Education

The Purpose of Organization

Just as a planned program is necessary to succeed in politics, sports and other phases of life, so it is necessary in the Sunday School. Organization has been defined as "the breaking down of group responsibility into parts which can be assigned to individuals and committees."

A plan requires proper organization. Hit-or-miss work cannot achieve the greatest possible results. Organization assures orderly planning, work and problem solving. Without it, confusion results.

Today's society is highly organized; but organization should be a means to an end. So with the church, organization helps carry out the plan and purpose of the church; presenting the message of Christ to the world in the most effective way.

As the church finds new frontiers for presenting the message of Christ, it must consider the dimensions of the task with its problems, possibilities, needs and means of accomplishment. The church must be properly organized for such a spiritual thrust, just as the military plans a new thrust in the territory of the opposition.

Organization is important for the church because it:

1. *Makes planning possible*. Organization is necessary for planning, evaluation, and revision. In the church things do not just happen. They are more likely to happen when goals are clarified and related to the purposes of the church as a whole, and when procedures have been carefully evaluated and examined in the light of these purposes.

2. *Identifies responsibilities*. These can be allocated among the members of the church.

3. *Identifies problems*. It also helps to solve them.

4. *Charts the future*. It makes possible growth and the formation of policy.

5. *Provides a channel of communication*. This is sometimes referred to as a "chain of command."

6. *Makes for cohesiveness*. It assures a logical approach to all tasks of the church.

The Plan for Organization

God is a God of order and design. Organization is evident in the arrangement of creation, in the created beings, and in the continuing function of that which He created. There is organized arrangement and design even in the minute things God has made. Structure and order are seen in the human body. Just as every living organism requires some form of organization, so the church, which is an organism, requires some form of organization.

There was a method and plan in the ministry of Jesus. Many times in the gospel accounts, organization was demonstrated. When Jesus was preaching and the great crowd became hungry and had to be fed, His disciples waited upon them in an organized plan. When the seventy were sent out to minister, they were sent out two by two in an organized plan. When the Great Commission was given, an organized plan of witnessing was laid out for the disciples for going to Jerusalem, then Judea, then into Samaria, and then to the uttermost parts of the earth with the message.

Organization is demonstrated in the life of the early church. Writing to the Corinthians, Paul says, "God has appointed in the church first apostles, second prophets, third teachers, then workers of miracles, then healers, helpers, administrators, speakers in various kinds of tongues" (I Corinthians 12:28 RSV). Similar references in Romans 12 and Ephesians 4 imply some manner of discovering talents and matching them against the varying needs of the young church.

God also made provision for building up the members of the church through the pattern of organization as given by other New Testament writers.

Principles for Organization in the Church

Some church organizations are maintained for purely sentimental reasons. "This organization has always been in the church, and for that reason it will always continue," is an often-repeated statement. Other organizations are copied from another church or Sunday School. Actually, what works for one church may not work for another. No one specific plan is ordained of God, but it is important that "all things be done decently and in order" (I Corinthians 14:40).

Denominations differ in their patterns of organization; even churches within a denomination differ in some details. There are, however, some basic principles for church

The pastor is the overseer of the entire program of the church. Here Rev. Jerry Falwell poses with some of his young people. (Thomas Road Baptist Church, Lynchburg, VA)

organization.

1. *The pastor.* He is the head of the local church, as Christ's representative, not the errand boy of the congregation. He is the shepherd of his flock, a member of all boards.

2. *Specific objectives.* Each department must have goals to meet specific needs.

3. *Directed functions.* Organizations should be directed and supervised by duly elected officials, all members of the local church.

4. *Coordinated functions.* The different boards should be coordinated in an executive board of the church.

5. *Responsibility to the congregation.* Boards should at specified times report their activities to the general membership.

These principles assure better teamwork among the members and a unifying spirit as they work towards a certain goal together. Good organization places responsibility with those who can assume and provide leadership. Following certain guiding policies for each organization will lay a sound basis for a more efficient program within the church. It will help

The staff at Grace Community Church meets to discuss and pray over the church's various ministries. In place of a Christian Education Director and Board, the church has 10 full-time pastors and 5 part-time pastors. A separate pastor takes charge of each age group in the church, of the tape ministry, the preaching, the Bible study center, the Spanish and hospital ministries, the music, and publications. (Grace Community Church, Sun Valley, CA)

establish a program to reach out and touch more people in the ministry of the church. God channels His power through human instruments.

People must know what their positions and responsibilities are so work can be coordinated and a systematic procedure followed.

The Program of Organizations in the Church

Every denomination has some type of church government which is stated in its constitution. A study of it will show what the local church should follow as its general form of government. The pastor should serve as an ex officio member of all the boards of the church and is responsible for the oversight and welfare of the entire church.

The church board also should include deacons, trustees, church secretary or clerk, treasurer, financial secretary and either a Director of Christian Education or associate pastor, or both if the church is large enough. Other organized boards should be responsible to the official church boards, so the work of the church will be properly coordinated.

The Christian Education Board

1. *Duties.* This board will design the policies and carry out the plans for the entire educational program and work of the church. It will coordinate all the efforts of Christian education with the representatives from the various church groups which are represented on this board. There will be a representative of the church board on the Board of Christian Education to act as liaison between the church and subsidiary organizations. The Christian Education Director will be an ex officio member of this board. The Sunday School superintendent or some other person may be elected or appointed to serve as chairman of the Board of Christian Education.

In some churches the Board of Christian Education is concerned only with the teaching of children. To fulfill its proper ministry, however, it should include Sunday School and Vacation Bible School, youth work, club programs, camps and adult education.

2. *Qualifications of members.* Basic qualifications for those serving on the board are spirituality and capability. They also should have enthusiasm and vision for that work, and an overall program for the church. Someone has said that, "He who has only vision is a dreamer. He who has only a program is a worker. He who has both vision and program is a conqueror!" In addition to spirituality, the chairman should have imagination, initiative and executive ability.

3. *Personnel.* The Board of Christian Education may consist of three, six or nine members, depending upon the size of the church. A three-year term is suggested, with members rotating so there will always be some old, some new members. After the first term

there will never be an altogether new board. This assures continuity of policies and projects.

In addition to the chairman of the Board of Christian Education a vice-chairman should be chosen to serve in the chairman's absence and as a member of the board. A secretary should be chosen from the elected members to keep minutes of meetings and to be responsible for notifying members of the meetings.

Other members will be chosen for their ability and interest in areas concerning the Board of Christian Education. The following would be included: pastor, Director of Christian Education, general superintendent of the Sunday School, department superintendents, representative of the official board, representatives of other church agencies, representative of youth, members at large, and general secretary of the Sunday School.

The Sunday School

The Sunday School is not an agency separate or apart from the church, but is perhaps the best structured agency in the church for carrying out the ministry of Christ most effectively. An organized Sunday School gives responsibility to its workers and effectiveness to its ministry. The Sunday School is evangelistic, missionary and educational.

Realizing the importance of the Sunday School and its place in the church's ministry, the pastor should be closely associated with its entire program. He should be interested in every phase of its work, those who come, its outreach, its leadership, what is being taught in it.

The officers of the Sunday School will be:

1. *The general superintendent.* He will give leadership by promoting the interests of the school; setting an example of Bible study, prayer, vision, enthusiasm, love and devotion to Christ, supervising the general activities of the school; conducting regular conferences of teachers and officers; seeing that proper facilities are provided for classes and teachers; watching the budget closely.

2. *The assistant superintendent.* He should have the same leadership qualifications as the general superintendent and should assist at any time with the general superintendent's duties.

3. *Departmental superintendents.* These leaders should have the same spiritual qualifications as the general superintendent and should be familiar with the characteristics of their age group. They should prepare interesting and effective worship services and activities.

4. *Teachers.* These men and women must be examples in life and testimony; should know the characteristics of the age group assigned; should know and love the Word of God (and people); should have the confidence of the

church members; should be faithful in attendance at the services of the church; and should have the ability to teach with enthusiasm.

Superintendents and teachers in the Sunday School should be:

1. *Consecrated to God.* They also must have an unblemished reputation.

2. *Progressive.* They must be alert to new methods, but should not accept them too readily just because they are new.

3. *Aggressive.* They must be men and women of action, never satisfied with the past and vigorously producing new and greater achievements.

4. *Enthusiastic.* Zealous Christians can inspire a whole corps of other workers. Enthusiasm is contagious.

5. *Devoted to people.* They must maintain a vital interest in people.

The Primary Persons in the Organized Church

1. *The pastor.* He is the overseer of the entire program of the church. He is in this work because he has a special "call" from God and has given himself to full-time service for the Lord Jesus Christ. His duties in the church are many and varied. He is to be a preacher of the Gospel, an administrator of the church, a shepherd of the flock, a priest in the sacred ministry of prayer and intercession, a counselor for the needs and help of the people, a friend to people inside as well as outside the church in time of need. He is a man with a heart sensitive to the needs of men, and yet he must have a tough spirit in the sense that he is not afraid to stand up and speak out for God against the sins of men, regardless of what they may think or say. He is faithful and true to his Lord and to his call, yet becomes "all things to all men" to win those whom he can for the Lord.

The pastor is a member ex officio of all boards and committees in the church. He is interested in the entire program of the church and in the work being done by each committee and board. He is not to be the chairman of these committees, but is to serve as counselor and advisor. He works with people, leading and guiding them, inspiring and encouraging, helping and lifting.

He is the leader of the church program but works closely with his entire staff, realizing that the more they can work together as a "team," the more effective will be their work for Christ. He sees Christian education not only as an important part of the church's ministry but as an agency to aid him in fulfilling of the Great Commission—preaching, teaching and making disciples for Jesus Christ.

2. *The Director of Christian Education*—Like the pastor, the DCE should be qualified and trained for his position and should sense the call of God upon his heart and life. He should have leadership ability, love for the Word and for teaching the Word, and enthusiasm for helping others teach and live the Word. He should be able to lead and inspire others.

His duties are many, for he must work with the entire educational ministry of the church. He must know how to teach; how to analyze the teaching of others and help them; how to organize, evaluate and encourage others in the work of Christian education. He must work to improve the quality and content of Bible teaching and other areas of programming in Christian education. He also must have concern for the souls of men, to properly teach them and to be concerned about reaching those outside the walls and influence of the church. He must be a lover of people, old and young. And he must seek to get the home and church working together—and built upon Christ.

The Director of Christian Education and the pastor must work together as a team, with a reverent respect for each other in their respective fields. The Director of Christian Education is responsible to the pastor and must ever be a faithful and trusted worker who in no way ever tries to work contrary to the wishes of the pastor. He must work closely with the pastor and freely discuss plans that he has for the program of the church. He also must work with the others in the church, never in a dictatorial manner but in a careful, considerate and constructive way. He also must work *with* the other chairmen and superintendents. By precept and example, he should show that he is willing to work hard himself and thus lead the way for others to be willing laborers in the overall program of Christian education. He must see to it that meetings of the various boards and committees are well-planned, duly announced and that all minutes are carefully recorded and filed.

Careful organization in the church will yield effective and acceptable service for the Lord. And the Lord Jesus Christ will reward every man according to the work that has been done, and the way that it has been done, in His name.

Why Have Sunday School Organization?

1. *It is scriptural.* The Lord's work should be done "decently and in order" (I Corinthians 14:40), with thoroughness and conformity. The life of God flows through each member of the Church of Jesus Christ to make it not only an organism, but an organization (I Corinthians 12:12-28).

2. *It is spiritual.* The Sunday School must provide a well-organized body through which the Holy Spirit can work. This provides for unity of purpose and prevents overlapping of programs. It also produces progress in attaining the goals of Sunday School and church.

3. *It is sensible.* Organization is only a means to an end. A structured society meets the needs of a body of people and eliminates confusion and chaos, thereby fulfilling its purpose.

What Are the Precepts of Organization?

The first essential is to determine what the

job is and the areas it will serve. Then, the pastor and church leaders must decide who will do the job—an individual, a group, or a committee. A description of job requirements should be drawn up, to tell the secretary, the teachers, and others what is expected of them.

The following is a suggested guide for Sunday School organization:

1. Establish a goal. Plan everything toward that goal.
2. Develop a spirit of unity.
3. Organize to eliminate duplication.
4. Define duties.
5. Give everyone a responsibility.
6. Make it people-centered, not pastor-centered.
7. Be sure it's flexible enough to adjust to changes brought about by growth.
8. Vary the program continually.
9. Plan toward the future.
10. Keep adequate records and reports to gauge progress or failure and to explain either.

The Plan of Sunday School Organization

There are three organizational divisions of Sunday School work:

1. *Administration.* The primary concern of administration is promotion and Sunday School extension. It also should promote and protect the teaching ministry which needs favorable conditions, proper housing and equipment, and a program of finance that will meet necessary expenses. The administration of the Sunday School should include the important task of enrolling the unreached children of the community. Therefore, it will concern itself with publicity and enlistment that will extend into every home.

2. *Education.* The educational work should be separate from administration, to stress its importance and insure a trained ministry.

Administrators are selected because of executive ability and business training, but educators are chosen because of teaching ability and training. Education concerns itself with a standard of instruction which will accommodate itself to teacher, lesson and pupil.

3. *Evangelism.* Not only are administration and education necessary to the work of the Sunday School, but equally important is the task of evangelism. Seven times as many young people are converted at the age of 16 as at 26. Between the ages of 12 and 16, the Sunday School is the great agency influencing the boy to be a Christian rather than a criminal.

Grading Plans

There are four grading plans for schools of various sizes:

1. *Plan I.* In the smallest schools there are pupils in each division, with a teacher for each group. Each division, therefore, is a department and each teacher a department superintendent, who reports to the general superintendent.

2. *Plan II.* In somewhat larger Sunday Schools the Cradle Roll and Home departments are added. Classes are divided into six groups. In this plan six department superintendents are needed. Some teachers may also serve as department superintendents.

3. *Plan III.* For a still larger school even more classes and departments are needed, with superintendents who are not teachers. There may be several classes in each department.

4. *Plan IV.* A large, closely-graded school has one or more classes for each age group. The departments are headed by superintendents who are not teachers; therefore, at least twelve department superintendents are needed.

Program of Sunday School Organization

1. *The yearly program.* The yearly program should center around the church's objective: to recruit and conserve Christians. The annual program should also include such activities as training leaders, improving equipment, dividing classes, rearranging departments, and financing the school. These are vital steps in the progress of the school and require careful

Evangelism is just as important to the Sunday School as administration and education.

planning.

To keep the year's program moving, a time schedule should be worked out by which the various plans and projects are to be completed. The schedule should include a system for filing, notation and records, and for reminding members of upcoming activities.

2. *The weekly program.* The weekly program is outlined once a year. Each month the school's teachers and officers meet to review the program, make necessary adjustments, and plan specific activities. Every week the superintendent faces the problem of the program for the coming Sunday morning.

There are as many kinds of Sunday morning programs as there are Sunday Schools. Some schools hold the traditional opening assembly, followed by the class sessions and a brief closing session. In others, each department holds its own opening and closing sessions, as well as a teaching period. Many churches provide both departmental and worship services plus teaching sessions on Sunday morning. Certain principles apply to all types of programs. These principles can be summed up in four words: purpose, planning, promptness, participation.

Vary the order of the opening session to stimulate interest, discourage tardiness, and give each service identity.

CORRECTLY GRADING THE SUNDAY SCHOOL FOR GROWTH [1]

In the little red schoolhouse where Granddad went to school, all eight grades were taught in one room. This posed some problems for the schoolmaster as well as the pupils.

When Dad went to school they had closed the little red schoolhouse and built a consolidated building with two rooms. All the younger ones were taught in one room and the older ones in the other. This was a big step in the right direction, for then the teachers could be more specialized in both subject matter and teaching methods.

Today, in a modern school, there is a room for every grade, and the lessons are taught according to the readiness and needs of pupils of each age. The building, the program, and the teaching—all are geared to effect changes in the lives of the pupils.

The same educational growth can be traced in the Sunday School.

In Granddad's day, everybody studied the same lesson in Sunday School. Regardless of age, whatever the subject, something miraculous was supposed to happen as the one lesson was presented to the primary child at the same time it was being given to Granddad. All preschool children were shushed on mother's knee as they "were too infantile to learn anything anyway."

When Dad was a boy, everyone didn't study the same Bible lesson. Pupils were grouped in departments, with three ages studying the same lesson. This was an improvement, but this method, too, posed serious problems. First-graders couldn't read well yet, while third-graders wanted to study much faster. It was easy for both to lose interest. The department lesson theme often was introduced in the opening exercises, and the sharp edge taken off the

[1]Reprinted by permission from *United Evangelical Action*, official publication of the National Association of Evangelicals.

Junior church at Calvary Temple. Many churches provide both departmental and worship services plus teaching sessions on Sunday morning. (Calvary Temple Church, Springfield, IL)

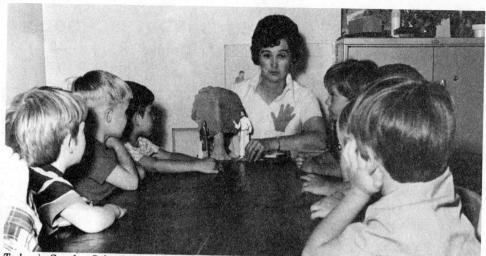

Today in Sunday School there is a class for every age and a Bible study book written especially for each grade. (Standard Publishing)

lesson before the teacher could present it to his class.

Today in Sunday School, there is a class for every age and a Bible study book written especially for each grade, and a worship service at the beginning of the period planned to prepare the hearts of the pupils for the study of God's Word. With this closely-graded system, all that is known about the best teaching methods can be used in the Sunday School and the pupils can be taught the whole Bible systematically and with the greatest degree of understanding. Each teacher now becomes a specialist, teaching one particular age, just as in public school.

Listen to the reaction of a pupil in a closely-graded Sunday School: "We like to study the Bible in our class because we've got a book just for our grade, like in school. It gives us interesting facts about the lesson. It asks questions and then helps us to know where to find the answers right in the Bible. It's a good feeling for a fellow my age to get to know God better. Most of us in our class have Jesus as our Savior and we know we can depend on Him to help us live like a Christian should. And do you know what? The teacher of the next grade has his pupils build a model of the Tabernacle. I'm going to like that!"

Every Sunday School, regardless of its size, should be correctly graded for growth.

Closely-graded material produces positive, consistent results. Patterned after the approach of the public school, it provides an age-graded lesson for each class within a department. The lessons, especially prepared with the age of the pupil in mind, make Bible truths meaningful. Closely-graded lessons should be the goal of every Sunday School.

For the smaller Sunday School, correct grading starts with departmental groups.

The growing Sunday School, however, maintains a planned system for reaching the ideal graded class for every age within the department.

The chart (shown on the next page) for grading Sunday Schools shows how this is done. First, find your Sunday School's enrollment. Then chart your course for growth.

Less Than 100

For Sunday Schools of less than 100, all pre-school pupils are grouped together and the Kindergarten lessons taught. Grades 1, 2 and 3 are grouped and the Combined Primary lessons taught. (There is a special course published for this purpose, whereby the lesson subjects for grades 1, 2 and 3 are given in rotation for the three years, presented on a grade 2 level. Obviously this is intended to be only a temporary measure, and every effort should be made by visitation, follow-up and other means to produce sufficient growth for the grading system to move into its second phase.) Grades 4, 5 and 6 are grouped, and the lessons beginning with the fourth grade rotated through the sixth. The same procedure is followed with grades 7, 8 and 9 and grades 10, 11 and 12. With the Adult class, the Sunday School would have six classes.

For 100 to 150

When the Sunday School reaches 100, the next step should be taken. Preschool pupils are divided. Two- and three-year-olds are taught the Nursery lessons and four-and five-year-olds the Kindergarten lessons. Departmental lessons rotate for two years. In the Primary Department, the first graders are taken from the group, and a separate class formed for them. They will be taught grade 1 lessons, especially geared for beginning readers, from

CHART FOR GRADING SUNDAY SCHOOLS

*Reprinted by permission from United Evangelical Action, *official publication of the National Association of Evangelicals.

CLOSELY GRADED PLAN

Find Your Present Enrollment and Grade to Grow	CRADLE ROLL (TO 2 YEARS)	NURSERY (2-3 YEARS)	KINDERGARTEN (4-5 YEARS)	PRIMARY (AGES 6-7-8)	JUNIOR (AGES 9-10-11)	JUNIOR HIGH (AGES 12-13-14)	HIGH SCHOOL (AGES 15-16-17)	YOUNG PEOPLE (AGES 18-24)	ADULTS (AGES 25-UP)
250 AND UP	USE CRADLE ROLL KIT	USE NURSERY LESSONS	USE KINDERGARTEN LESSONS	GRADE 1 USE FIRST GRADE LESSONS / GRADE 2 USE SECOND GRADE LESSONS / GRADE 3 USE THIRD GRADE LESSONS	GRADE 4 USE FOURTH GRADE LESSONS / GRADE 5 USE FIFTH GRADE LESSONS / GRADE 6 USE SIXTH GRADE LESSONS	GRADE 7 USE SEVENTH GRADE LESSONS / GRADE 8 USE EIGHTH GRADE LESSONS / GRADE 9 USE NINTH GRADE LESSONS	GRADE 10 USE TENTH GRADE LESSONS / GRADE 11 USE ELEVENTH GRADE LESSONS / GRADE 12 USE TWELFTH GRADE LESSONS	COLLEGE YOUNG SINGLE YOUNG MARRIED USE ADULT BIBLE SERIES	GRADED ADULTS WOMEN MEN MIXED USE ADULT BIBLE SERIES
200 TO 250	USE CRADLE ROLL KIT	USE NURSERY LESSONS	USE KINDERGARTEN LESSONS	GRADE 1 USE FIRST GRADE LESSONS / GRADE 2 USE SECOND GRADE LESSONS / GRADE 3 USE THIRD GRADE LESSONS	GRADE 4 USE FOURTH GRADE LESSONS / GRADE 5 USE FIFTH GRADE LESSONS / GRADE 6 USE SIXTH GRADE LESSONS	GRADE 7 USE SEVENTH GRADE LESSONS / GRADE 8 USE EIGHTH GRADE LESSONS / GRADE 9 USE NINTH GRADE LESSONS	GRADE 10 USE TENTH GRADE LESSONS / GRADES 11 and 12 BEGIN WITH ELEVENTH GRADE LESSONS AND ROTATE THROUGH 12TH GRADE	COLLEGE YOUNG SINGLE YOUNG MARRIED USE ADULT BIBLE SERIES	GRADED ADULTS WOMEN MEN MIXED USE ADULT BIBLE SERIES
150 TO 200	USE CRADLE ROLL KIT	USE NURSERY LESSONS	USE KINDERGARTEN LESSONS	GRADE 1 USE FIRST GRADE LESSONS / GRADE 2 USE SECOND GRADE LESSONS / GRADE 3 USE THIRD GRADE LESSONS	GRADE 4 USE FOURTH GRADE LESSONS / GRADE 5 USE FIFTH GRADE LESSONS / GRADE 6 USE SIXTH GRADE LESSONS	GRADE 7 USE SEVENTH GRADE LESSONS / GRADES 8, 9 BEGIN WITH EIGHTH GRADE LESSONS AND ROTATE THROUGH 9TH GRADE	GRADE 10 USE TENTH GRADE LESSONS / GRADES 11 and 12 BEGIN WITH ELEVENTH GRADE LESSONS AND ROTATE THROUGH 12TH GRADE	COLLEGE YOUNG SINGLE YOUNG MARRIED USE ADULT BIBLE SERIES	GRADED ADULTS WOMEN MEN MIXED USE ADULT BIBLE SERIES

DEPARTMENTAL GRADED PLAN

Find Your Present Enrollment and Grade to Grow	CRADLE ROLL (TO 2 YEARS)	NURSERY (2-3 YEARS)	KINDERGARTEN (4-5 YEARS)	PRIMARY (AGES 6-7-8)	JUNIOR (AGES 9-10-11)	JUNIOR HIGH (AGES 12-13-14)	HIGH SCHOOL (AGES 15-16-17)	YOUNG PEOPLE (AGES 18-24)	ADULTS (AGES 25 & OLDER)
100 TO 150	USE CRADLE ROLL KIT	USE NURSERY LESSONS	USE KINDERGARTEN LESSONS	GRADE 1 USE FIRST GRADE LESSONS / GRADES 2, 3 BEGIN WITH 2ND GRADE LESSONS AND ROTATE THROUGH 3RD GRADE	GRADE 4 USE FOURTH GRADE LESSONS / GRADES 5, 6 BEGIN WITH FIFTH GRADE LESSONS AND ROTATE THROUGH 6TH GRADE	GRADE 7 USE SEVENTH GRADE LESSONS / GRADES 8, 9 BEGIN WITH EIGHTH GRADE LESSONS AND ROTATE THROUGH 9TH GRADE	GRADES 10, 11, 12 BEGIN WITH TENTH GRADE LESSONS AND ROTATE THROUGH 11TH and 12TH	ADULT BIBLE SERIES	USE ADULT BIBLE SERIES
LESS THAN 100	USE CRADLE ROLL KIT	PRE-SCHOOL USE KINDERGARTEN LESSONS		COMBINED PRIMARY LESSONS — These books have been especially designed for the smallest church where it is necessary to combine primary grades into one class.	GRADES 4, 5, 6 BEGIN WITH FOURTH GRADE LESSONS AND ROTATE THROUGH 5TH AND 6TH GRADES	GRADES 7, 8, 9 BEGIN WITH SEVENTH GRADE LESSONS AND ROTATE THROUGH 8TH AND 9TH GRADES	GRADES 10, 11, 12 (Or combine 10th with J.H. and 11th and 12th with Young People's Class) BEGIN TENTH GRADE LESSONS. ROTATE THRU 11TH and 12TH	ADULT BIBLE SERIES	USE ADULT BIBLE SERIES

the first quarter book. The rest of the Primaries rotate through the Combined Primary lessons.

In the same way, grade 4 pupils form a separate class and begin with the fourth grade first-quarter book. The remaining Juniors rotate fifth- and sixth-grade lessons. The grade 7 pupils form a new class, studying the seventh-grade first-quarter lessons. The remaining Junior High pupils rotate eighth-and ninth-grade lessons. The Sunday School will have grown to 10 classes.

For 150 to 200

A Sunday School of 150 should operate under the Closely-Graded Plan, with separate classes for all the grades, first through seventh, and the tenth grade. Young people should be separated from the adults. The remaining Junior Highs and Senior Highs continue to rotate lessons.

For 200 to 250

At 200, the Sunday School should have a Junior High Department fully graded. When the attendance reaches 250, the Senior High Department also should be completely graded.

For 250 and UP!

The ideal teaching situation should be reached by the time a Sunday School has 250 pupils in individual age-graded classes. This would include a minimum of 16 classes. (Note: Because the lessons in a graded curriculum are continuous from quarter to quarter, it is best to plan the dividing program for promotion time.)

The best plan for multiplying by dividing in a Sunday School is threefold.

First, divide into departments, by degrees if necessary, because of special or staff problems, preschool from all older. Next divide into grade school, seventh grade through adults; and so on, until the eight basic departments—Nursery, Kindergarten, Primary, Junior, Junior High, Senior High, Young People and Adult—are obtained.

Second, divide departments into grades, as shown above.

Third, divide grades by sex into classes for boys and girls, beginning with the fourth grade.

It is likely that a Sunday School of 150 would have a boys' and a girls' class in each grade in the Junior, Junior High and Senior High departments. It is considered unneccessary to separate boys and girls in the preschool and primary ages, with the possible exception of the third grade. New classes in these departments should be formed of both boys and girls of like age or grade.

As indicated on the chart, the Cradle Roll Department should be a vital part of every Sunday School, no matter how small. The Cradle Roll ministry is conducted without need for space in the church building and therefore does not face the problems of lack of space and equipment. The Cradle Roll ministry, faithfully conducted according to the instructions in the Cradle Roll packet, will bring in the adults and often whole families. Don't overlook its potential when planning your Sunday School for growth.

Each grade in a closely-graded Sunday School should be assigned a substitute teacher. Thus new teachers and workers are enlisted and developed among people who might not at first take a full-time appointment. Having many workers and trainees in a Sunday School usually is a mark of a successful soul-winning church. (To keep a continuous, fresh supply of workers in a growing Sunday School, periodically pass out the Service Enlistment blanks in adult classes or church service or prayer meeting.)

The worship or chapel service in a closely-graded department is a time for creating greater devotion to God. Its purpose is to prepare the hearts for the study of God's Word, not to give time for a review of past lessons or a preview of the coming lesson. (There are available books of Sunday School worship programs for Primaries, Juniors and older, which contain programs for each Sunday and /or season of the year. These are excellent guides for creating the atmosphere of worship in the first part of the Sunday School period.)

CLOSE GRADING is the pedagogical, theological and wise basis on which to organize Sunday Schools. Even the smallest Sunday School with only the minimum of classes should have the closely-graded principle in view and plan toward this goal. Let this chart for grading be a constant reminder of the imperative need for enlargement of your Sunday School to reach more and to teach God's Word better.

VACATION BIBLE SCHOOL AND THE SUNDAY SCHOOL

Vacation Bible School's merits and programs are treated in detail in numerous volumes devoted to that subject. This chapter will simply consider the relationship between Vacation Bible School (hereafter called VBS) and Sunday School.

Someone has defined VBS as "Everyday Sunday School." VBS offers an unequaled opportunity to supplement the Sunday School coverage of Bible subjects. VBS is usually conducted during the morning for one or two weeks during the summer months when the public school is dismissed for vacation. VBS is correlated with the Sunday School in that it continues studies of subjects, characters or passages which strengthen the foundation laid in Sunday School.

VBS Teachers

The main VBS teachers are usually the

regular teachers in the Sunday School. They are best acquainted with the children and the work of the department, so are best qualified. Occasionally, a teacher wants to change her place of service, feeling she might relate better to the pupils of a different group. VBS's brief time with another age group provides a chance to discover whether or not she can work well with the new age level.

Assistants are needed in each department of VBS. The daily teaching periods afford excellent opportunity for willing but untrained workers to become apprentices. Taking a small but regular responsibility, they observe and learn from the teacher. An assistant may take records, take charge of the games at recess, tell the daily missionary story, lead the singing, play the piano, or help with handcrafts. This is a vital and necessary role. At the same time the assistant is preparing for greater service in the Sunday School and in future VBS.

Superintendents in VBS departments have opportunity to see the apprentice teacher in action. At the close of the school they may invite the new worker to become a regular assistant in the department, or they may alert the superintendent and/or the nominating committee that the apprentice is a good worker and should be called upon to serve.

The Pupils

In some church situations, the VBS is announced and opened to boys and girls from any church or no church at all. It is viewed as a missionary opportunity. On the other hand, some churches limit registration to their own members, feeling they cannot afford materials and books for the larger crowd of children.

VSB usually includes children and early teens. Many churches vary the time of the

Refreshment time provides another opportunity for assistants to take responsibility. (Forrest Hills Baptist Church, Decatur, GA)

school, having the teen and even adult classes at night, while the rest of the school meets in the morning. Other churches ask teens to assist in younger classes and do not provide a separate department for them.

Conserving Results

1. *Pupil enrollment cards.* If boys and girls not enrolled in Sunday School come to VBS, their names and addresses should be provided to the proper department superintendent or teacher.

2. *Decisions.* If some children accepted Christ or dedicated their lives for service during VBS, this fact should be passed on to their Sunday School teachers. A home visit may be needed before a child joins the church and is baptized.

3. *Visits.* The Sunday School teacher should follow up on the new boys and girls in VBS, by visiting in the homes. Interest thus expressed may result in a family won for Christ.

4. *Music.* If the regular Sunday School teacher does not work in VBS, she should learn

Children register for VBS in the church parking lot. Information on children not enrolled in Sunday School should be given to the Sunday School staff. (Forrest Hills Baptist Church, Decatur, GA)

and use the new songs taught to her pupils during VBS. Otherwise, the songs may be quickly forgotten. Since songs are carefully correlated with the theme of the school, keeping them in the minds of the pupils will aid their memory of the entire study.

5. *Course of study.* The Sunday School teacher should refer to the characters and stories studied in VBS and build on the new knowledge of her pupils. Play review games concerning the VBS material from time to time, deepening the impressions and aiding in recall.

12

Staff duties, age-group characteristics, materials, suggested sessions, teacher qualifications—all this and more is discussed here.

Departments

THE CRADLE ROLL DEPARTMENT

Definition

In a nutshell, this department literally is the list of babies in the church. "Newborns" are its special outreach, with constant ministry until that baby is transferred to the roll of the Nursery Department.

Why a Cradle Roll?

1. *To reach parents.* Young couples who have given little thought to church or God often have tender hearts after the birth of the new life entrusted to them. The arrival of the baby provides a reason to go to the home and express interest and concern.

2. *To give aid.* More than just adding a baby's name to the ribbon hanging from a cardboard cradle on the wall, the Cradle Roll Department seeks to render aid to the new parents as they begin to train their little one. Through personal visits, printed booklets, and books from the church library, the Cradle Roll visitor can minister to the home.

3. *To reach children.* If the Sunday School waits until babies are large enough to choose to come to Sunday School for Christian instruc-
name on the Cradle Roll is symbolic of the church's concern for that life. It is a reason to keep in touch with the child and encourage his being brought to the Nursery as soon as possible.

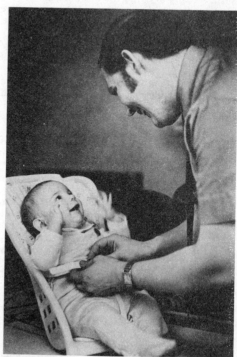

The cradle roll's special outreach is to newborn babies. (Religious News Service Photo)

97

Who Staffs Cradle Roll?

1. *The superintendent.* In a small church, there may be no other person on the Cradle Roll staff besides the superintendent. A lady who is too shy to teach a class may be willing to visit homes and talk with young mothers on a person-to-person basis. A young woman would have much in common with the age-group of Cradle Roll parents; at the same time, an older woman might have more leisure to visit and more experience with which to aid the new parents.

2. *The secretary.* As for any other department, the secretary should keep a record of all the names and addresses and birthdays of the babies on the roll. If a card is kept for each baby, facts should be added after each contact by a visitor. The secretary also will mail birthday cards to the babies each year, until the Nursery Department takes over. Supplies for the department should be ordered by the secretary.

3. *Home visitor.* This may be the superintendent. Or a pair of ladies may like to visit the homes. The more visitors involved (at least one to every eight babies), the more persons will be seeking new babies to visit.

Duties of the Cradle Roll

1. *Visit homes.* As names of new babies or new families are presented to them, visitors should go to those homes and make a friendly visit, seeking to enroll the baby for the Cradle Roll. Leaflets and an appropriate symbol or certificate should be given to the parents to make the event an important one.

2. *Counsel with parents.* While a visitor may not know all the answers, she should be aware of any special needs in the home. If there are questions she cannot answer, she should assure the parent that (1) she will get the answer and report it, or (2) she will refer the question to the church staff member who can provide the needed assistance. Sometimes there are medical or emotional problems, and the pastor would know what professional help is available to the parent.

3. *Provide an adequate church nursery.* The room for bed babies may be one of the most important in the church. Whether or not it is clean, cheerful and well-staffed may determine whether the parents eventually attend church themselves.

4. *Plan a Mothers' Club.* Some mothers may not be able to bring their baby to church and attend themselves. Some kind of meeting with mothers during the week might be the answer to reaching these otherwise unchurched mothers. An informal home meeting would allow discussion of mutual problems and a brief Bible study relating to those needs.

5. *Discover prospects.* In city areas, contact of homes with new babies may be established through regular calls on diaper service firms and/or the corner grocer; the new-comers list

"Grownups may think the nursery is a fine idea, but I'm not so sure." (Don Lancaster/Bellevue Baptist Church, Memphis, TN)

from the welcome wagon; or birth announcements in the newspaper. And if your church has door-to-door visitors, they should report new babies discovered.

6. *Annual Baby Day.* Magnify the importance of the baby in the home and the responsibility of parents during an annual Baby Day emphasis in the church. All the new babies for the year are presented to the church at a special service where a charge is given to the parents by the pastor.

7. *Discover needs.* In the course of a visit, the Cradle Roll workers may find that medical help is needed for parent or child, which the family is unable to get. The worker may (1) refer the problem to an agency of the church to give that aid, or (2) refer the problem to the pastor, who will put the family in touch with a social agency which can provide the aid. A friend in need is a friend indeed. Otherwise disinterested parents may become interested in a church which cares about them. Occasionally the need for clothing or food becomes evident. The visitor may alert a church group to deliver the supplies to the home.

8. *Secure an adult class sponsor.* An adult class may sponsor the Cradle Roll Nursery by providing crib sheets, toys, bottle warmers and other necessary equipment, and by being responsible for washing the linens each week.

This sponsor might also provide emergency babysitting so a parent can go to a doctor or to a revival meeting, maintaining a supply of church-donated used clothing for families, and/ or wash clothes or take food to a mother who has sickness in her home.

THE NURSERY DEPARTMENT

"The handshake of your church" is the Nursery Department. Parents appreciate adequate facilities and specialized care for their children, and show their appreciation by faithful attendance at church.

The Nursery is responsible for children from the time they first come to the church as infants to their third birthday. There are varied needs to be met in these short years.

Crib babies must be attended by a capable and trained person. Confidence is felt by parents who know their child will be safe with the attendants. Ideally, a nurse should be employed to supervise the Nursery Department. Accidents can be prevented, minor injuries treated, and illness recognized.

Toddlers (1-2 years of age) need special attention as they still tire easily. The Walker-Talkers (2-3) will need a room all to themselves as they cannot be trusted near babies and are old enough to be taught definite Bible truths.

Location
The Nursery Department ideally should be on the main floor, near the entrance and, prefer-

ably, close to the Adult Department, where parents will be.

Room
The room should be well ventilated, bright and spacious. Where there is only one large room, it should be partitioned to accommodate the three divisions, as needed.

Personnel

Age Group	Enrollment	Superintendents	Associates
Babies 0-1	13	1	2
Toddlers 1-2	15	1	3
Walker-Talkers 2-3	20	1	4

Materials
1. *Use the Bible.* Have an attractive Bible in the department, with pictures. Keep it in a special place and treat it carefully and reverently. Hold it during the Bible stories and often repeat parts of verses.

2. *Use songs.* For this age, songs should have repetition, a good melody, and be only one or two lines long. Songs may express ideas, provide relaxation and change of position, or help children change from one activity to another. Often it is wise to use a record player rather than have a piano crowd the room.

3. *Use prayer.* Stress one idea at a time. Pray for the children, not about them. Use few names for God, with simple vocabulary.

4. *Use stories.* For these wigglers, stories should be only two or three minutes long, with repetition and simple words. They like rhyme and alliteration.

5. *Use pictures.* Pictures for this age group need a clear outline a few details. Display on their eye level. Pictures gain and hold attention, explain words and ideas, recall stories and verses.

What the Child Can Learn
1. *About God.* The nursery child can comprehend that God made all things, loves everyone, cares for the individual child, hears prayer, knows what is good for each child, is in heaven.

2. *About Jesus.* Even toddlers can grasp that Jesus is God's Son, and that God sent His Son to earth; that Jesus was once a child and grew as other children grow; that Jesus is now in heaven with God; and that Jesus loves me and

is my Friend.

3. *About the Bible*. Little ones are taught by word and example that the Bible is God's Book; the Bible tells about God and Jesus; the Bible is a book of true stories; and the Bible tells us how to do right.

4. *About the church*. Children understand that the church is God's house. They have happy times at church and learn that this is "my" church, and that we learn about God at church.

5. *About his home*. Young children can be taught that God gave him home, parents and brothers and sisters. He can learn to help at home.

6. *About personal development*. Little ones learn basic good behavior by hearing that God wants them to be kind and share toys; to love everyone, and to obey parents.

7. *About missions*. This is the time to help children know that God loves all the children of the world; that some children do not know about God; that they can pray for other boys and girls and for missionaries; and that they can give money to help other children know about God.

How To Teach

Calmness begets calmness. Speak slowly and distinctly, with clear enunciation in a pleasing, well-modulated voice. Show your enthusiasm for the story. Sense the humor and laugh with the children. Display pictures. Make lessons suitable to the level of understanding. Employ frequent repetition.

Suggested One-Hour Session

15-20 minutes.—Arrival, Offering, Activity Centers, and putting away materials.

25-30 minutes.—Songs, welcomes, birthdays, prayer, Bible story and picture study.

15 minutes.—Rest, Bible story activity, handwork, good-byes.

During the first 15 minutes, let a helper at each interest-center guide the children in learning from it: book center, nature center, home living center, blocks and toys and puzzles. Have a bulletin board and suitable pictures at their eye-level.

Space for activities may be made by hinging tables or flannel and chalk boards on a wall.

The Nursery program provides a child's first impression of church, and should encourage an atmosphere of love, security and pleasure. They will associate experiences with God's house. Far from a baby-sitting ministry, it is an opportunity to lay life foundations.

It must provide for activities to stretch restless muscles. Besides games and action centers, use rhythm instruments, such as bells, sticks, detergent bottles with beans to rattle, and oatmeal boxes.

Make the moments count toward impressing one main aim. Use stories, songs, activity games to stress that aim. Teach Christian conduct by inserting a memory verse in stories and activities. Link God's love and care with daily life. This enables tots to sing, give, pray and worship with understanding.

THE BEGINNER DEPARTMENT

This age group cannot be lumped into an "average" or "norm." Some 4's and 5's are nervous and easily overstimulated, while others are quiet and slow to respond. Some appear to have boundless energy, but others are listless. Some have seemingly limitless endurance, while others tire easily.

In the realm of mental capacity and development, a child's vocabulary and reasoning ability depend upon his out-of-church surroundings, experiences and learning stimulation. Some exhibit self-control and self-direction: they control crying and bathroom needs; show patience, courtesy and (usually) kindness. They obey directions.

All normal Beginners can be trained to take off their own coats and hats, put away toys, help take care of equipment, and remember behavior suitable in Sunday School.

Their attention span for a story is only 3 to 4 minutes. They may be interested in a self-chosen activity for 8 or 10 minutes, and in a game much longer. Beginners are interested in the things of God and show remarkable depth of understanding.

1. *Social Behavior*. Beginners may be bossy, "show-offish" or interested in things that belong to others. They need to learn cooperation.

2. *Range of interests*. Restricted to home, Sunday School, natural surroundings.

3. *Curiosity*. They are full of questions: Who? What? Why? Teacher's answers may become their lifelong belief.

4. *Time*. They have a concept of time.

5. *Suggestibility*. While they follow literal suggestions, symbolic expressions have no significance for them.

6. *Imagination*. They are natural mimics, usually with good imaginations.

A beginner can learn that:

1. God shows His love to us by His gifts and care.

2. Jesus is our best Friend.

3. God sent Jesus to die for sin. Jesus is now living.

4. God will forgive sin when we ask Him.

5. God created everything and everyone.

6. God is with us always.

7. The Bible is God's Word. God speaks to us through it.

8. Prayer can be made at any time or place.

9. Jesus helps us to do right things.

10. Jesus is God's own Son; He can do anything.

11. Jesus wants us to love Him.

The Beginner teacher must plan for the short attention span of these youngsters in every activity of the teaching session. (Scripture Press)

The Beginner Teacher's Qualifications:
1. Love for the children.
2. Sympathetic understanding.
3. Happy, child-like spirit.
4. Controlled emotional life.
5. Open-mindedness.
6. Vivid imagination.

The Program for the Teacher

1. *Study the lesson.* See each lesson in relation to the unit, as well as to the one topic, and decide what the lesson ought to accomplish.

2. *Make a list of teaching materials.* Make a check list, so hard-to-get items may be located well in advance of need.

3. *Plan possible activities.* Plan for variety in activities. This will care for each child's individual interests. Be sure all activities relate to the aim of the lesson. Avoid monotony and over-stimulation.

4. *Outline the program.* Have a uniformity in program, for the security it provides. Maintain an atmosphere of freedom and informality. Be orderly, yet have flexibility enough to anticipate interruptions.

5. *Choose songs carefully.* Use songs about their home situations and experiences—glad songs with short sentences. Teach new songs to correlate with the lesson. Singing meets program needs, socializes a group, gives a sense of unity and reinforces Biblical information.

6. *Include essential elements.* Fellowship, learning and worship are important. Use an activity time for friendly greetings, recall of Bible stories, and an activity. Have a group time for songs, birthday recognition, prayer, offering, rest and relaxation, and the Bible story.

Some Suggestions and Ideas

Activity time. Exchange friendly greetings, give needed help with hats and wraps. Recall Bible stories and verses.

Group time. Sing a familiar greeting song, share activity time experiences, and recognize visitors and new members, those with new brothers or sisters, and those with birthdays.

Teach giving. Help children learn to give to the Lord by naming things money will help to buy, singing about it, and praying to God about giving.

Provide rest and relaxation. Take a picture walk. Fly like birds. Skip to rhythm. Sing and march to songs, and/or take a short nap.

Retell the Bible story. Have children repeat the story in their own words, place the story pictures on flannelgraph, draw or show pictures about it, or examine the story in leaflets or story papers.

Classroom Control

Certain principles must be followed if the Beginner class is to be properly controlled and disciplined.

1. *Qualified teachers.* Each teacher must be a consecrated Christian who sets a good example by a separated life. He or she must be a good disciplinarian, be dependable and punctual, be adequately prepared.

2. *Trained teachers.* Each teacher must win the hearts of the children by being sincere and warmhearted. He should be kind and calm at all times. He also should know the background and home situation by contact with parents. He must be specially instructed concerning the needs and goals of that department. He or she should know what is expected, and he should attend workers' meetings which engender unity of purpose among the teachers.

3. *Ideal ratio of teachers.* There should be 1 teacher for 5 to 7 pupils; 2 teachers for 10 pupils; 3 teachers for 11 to 15; 5 teachers for 16 to 20; 7 teachers for 21 to 25; and 8 teachers for 26 to 30 pupils.

Discipline of the Beginner

Establish a pattern of conduct. Set rules that are always followed. This fosters in children a sense of security. Establish set routines for activities.

Make suggestions; don't scold. Don't force children or yell at them. Divert attention by changing interest.

Encourage home cooperation. Parents should instruct children concerning conduct. They should not interfere with the class or stay to watch the children.

Activity Methods to Keep Interest

1. *Have pre-session activities.* When the child arrives, help him choose from available activities.

2. *Provide various interest centers.* Establish a book center, nature center, handwork center, housekeeping center, and others, as room and materials allow.

3. *Make the Bible lesson interesting.* Use slides and filmstrips, drama, puppets, object lessons, pictures, other visual aids, and/or puppets.

4. *Observe special days and occasions.*

5. *Stress Bible memorization through games and drama.*

THE PRIMARY DEPARTMENT

Primaries are beginning to learn by doing. They grow and learn at different rates. Primaries use all their senses in learning; they learn by imitation. Primaries need independence, but they rely on wise, dependable adult guidance. They need to help as well as be helped. They need opportunities for increasing their independence. Wise supervision and a minimum of interference will guide them in getting along with other children.

The teacher must maintain control, but be a genuine friend. While the teacher will respect their ability, they cannot have free rein to do whatever they wish. Limits are set by lesson purpose, abilities, materials, space, time, etc. Teacher must sometimes say a firm no or yes or, "This is what you must do." Do things with the children, not for or to them. Learning results from shared experiences. Plan experiences that involve the whole personality of the primary.

Primary Learning Level

1. The Bible is a very special Book about Jesus and how to please Him.

2. God created all things. Sin spoiled God's perfect creation.

3. All have disobeyed God and need the Savior to take away sin. God will forgive if I am sorry and ask Him.

4. Jesus died to take my punishment for sin. I can receive Him as my Savior. He helps me know how to live right.

5. God is my heavenly Father, who loved me enough to send His Son to earth for me. He is with me and helps me.

6. God's Son never sinned. He did wonderful miracles on earth. He is coming back again.

7. We can talk to God any time. We should thank Him for all His gifts and ask Him for what we need.

8. Church is where we feel God near, but we can worship Him wherever we are.

9. Because God gave His son, we give our time and money to Him.

10. The Lord Jesus wants to save all people everywhere. He wants me to tell others Jesus loves them, too. I can pray and give money to help children in other lands hear about Jesus.

Primaries like action choruses which call for body movements. (Calvary Temple Church, Springfield, IL)

Program

1. *Teaching Bible truths.* Memorizing verses is only one step. Children must understand words and know their meaning. Give them an understanding of the Scriptures to help them develop a proper attitude toward God, Jesus, the Bible, the church, and others.

2. *Activity teaching.* This includes conversation, picture studies, games, visual aids, stories and songs.

3. *Creating mission interest.* Use a globe, exhibits of dolls and/or curios from other countries, mission maps, books; Bible verses which stress God's love for all, questions, friezes showing other races, puppets, and dramatization of missionary work.

4. *Using music.* Words of songs must be understandable to this age group. Avoid symbolic language and abstractions. The melody should be simple, with repetition of phrases. Rhythm should be definite. Songs should be correlated with the lesson theme. Christian character and religious attitudes are formulated by use of songs based on Scripture.

Open Room Teaching

Several factors indicate that it is wise to use open-room teaching for Primaries.

1. Children do not like to be cramped or crowded.

2. Children learn to work, think and plan together, as a group.

3. Much can be learned about children as workers see them work together, expressing themselves in free activity periods.

4. The open room provides opportunities for children to develop plans they and the teachers make.

5. It puts children under the influence of more than one teacher.

6. Small, dark classrooms may dampen the spiritual life of the child.

7. Better and fuller use of materials can be made when all share them in one large classroom.

Suggested Time Schedule

20-30 minutes, activity time. 5 minutes, clean-up time. 25-30 minutes, group time. These periods will include:

1. Sharing experiences through conversation.

2. Worship experiences.

3. Games and activities.

4. Fellowship—recognition of birthdays, etc.

5. Bible story.

6. Planning and practicing ways to put lesson truths into life.

Learning Activities

Types of learning activities include acquiring information, solving problems, appreciation, and handcrafts.

Activities should be chosen because they relate to Bible truths and unit purposes, are appropriate, make best use of resources, provide for best possible teaching, incorporate suggestions of children, and/or provide opportunities for pupil involvement.

Possible activities are:

1. Bible-verse flash cards, verse on one side, reference on the other.

2. Bible-verse jigsaw puzzle.

3. Painting.

4. Matching pictures to stories and characters.

5. Matching pictures to Bible verses.

6. Writing a story about a picture.

7. Drawing reactions to a story or a problem.

8. Dramatization.

9. Tours and field trips.

10. Puppet plays.

THE JUNIOR DEPARTMENT

When a child dedicates his life to Jesus Christ during his Junior years, he forms the basis for the solution of many of the problems of adolescence. Nine-to-eleven-year-olds are most easily won to Christ. They are teachable and ready to form good habits. Juniors want the truth and seek it in the lives of their leaders as well as in their lessons. While preparing to lead the church tomorrow, they are engaged in living *now*.

Juniors are doers. James 1:22 ("But be ye doers of the word, and not hearers only, deceiving your own selves") is aptly called the Junior verse. They also enjoy companionship. They share ideas and fun with their peers. At the same time, they are hero worshippers. Someone has said, "Juniors make you feel they think you are the greatest, even if you are not, while young people make you feel they think you are

Junior-age children are the most easily won to Christ. (Jules Schick)

not great, while they really think you are."

Juniors are in the "golden age of memory." Teachers can take advantage of their interest and ability to memorize by helping them store the Word of God in their hearts for the Spirit to use for the rest of their lives.

Organization

Ideally the Junior Department should be graded according to age, all nine-year-olds in one class, all 10's, all 11's in separate classes. Some leaders also insist the age groups be further separated by having boys in one class and girls in another. In small-church situations, however, where such division is not feasible because of few teachers or few pupils, all three ages and both sexes can and do work together. In fact, they seem to enjoy the competition and interaction possible with the larger group.

Some leaders specify, "Have no more than six or seven Juniors to a teacher." In a sit-down-and-listen situation, such a plan might be interesting. But Juniors are doers, as mentioned above, and drama and contest-games are favorite forms of learning for them. If there is a drama, who will watch if all pupils take part? If two of the six are absent, how much of a contest could take place? Many teachers prefer a class of at least a dozen Juniors. In super-churches, Junior departments use the team teaching method for 25 to 100 boys and girls in one large open-room teaching situation. (See Section VII-Chapter 35).

Whatever the size or division, the Junior class may have officers with regular responsibilities. Officers may be elected every six months, to allow more pupils to serve. Some of these may be:

1. *The missionary chairman.* This person will find and enlist new members, help to keep the "regulars" in Sunday School, visit absentees, and keep a prospect list. He may help develop and work on missionary projects such as making a class map, reading weekly prayer requests for missionaries, making scrapbooks, collecting clothing, and others.

2. *Church attendance chairman.* This person will encourage all to stay for church services and may keep a record of such attendance. He may announce the sermon topic or make posters to encourage interest.

3. *Bible study chairman.* With the help of the teacher, this Junior can create interest in Bible study, in weekly lesson preparation, and in the memory work program.

4. *Room chairman.* This Junior can be responsible for getting assistance in keeping the room clean, neat, and occasionally adorned with flowers and pictures. He can bring supplies for the teacher from the place of storage and return them after use. He also can keep the chalkboard clean and supplied with chalk and eraser.

5. *President.* This person can be called upon to welcome the visitors each Sunday and give them the welcome pin. He should be taught to preside over any class business in an orderly way.

6. *Social chairman.* With guidance from the teacher, this Junior can learn to choose suitable games and plan outings and parties, even directing the games.

Teaching Methods

Select the method according to the lesson content. For ideas on method, refer to the chapter on Visual Aids. No Junior lesson should be without some form of visual aid or action-type presentation. While variety is the keynote for interest, some "skeleton" of a familiar general outline gives security, while the "meat on the bones" provides variety. A successful outline is:

Presession activity. This may take the form of working together on a group project such as a mural, picture map, topographical map, molded waterpots and other Bible-land items, or a sandbox or sandpan scene. It may involve individual solving of a puzzle or coded Bible verse, unscrambling Bible names or verses,

Teachers of Juniors should use visual aids to help hold the attention of the class. (Standard Publishing)

independent sorting of Bible-book cards into divisions. In most groups, some pupils arrive at least half an hour ahead of scheduled starting time. For them, Sunday School should begin when they get there. The presession thus affords that much more teaching time.

Worship service. Suit the choice of songs and Bible reading to the theme of study. Every part of the morning, including the presentation, should stress one chief aim. Limit this worship time to not more than seven minutes. Choose a Bible reading that Juniors can handle from the standpoint of vocabulary and pronunciation. Vary the form of the reading (see Section VII-Chapter 34 on using the Bible). Vary the form in which songs are presented: flannelgraph, flash card, chart, pictures, chalkboard, song sheets.

Review game. Let an assistant teacher lead in a review game such as tic-tac-toe, spelldown, crossword puzzle or other. All questions should aid in recall of the previous lesson, to lay the groundwork for continuation.

Approach. A story, mini-drama, puppet, or personification may lead into the study with a presentation on the Junior level of understanding. The approach should not be a mere review of the two Bible chapters which precede the one being studied. Instead, it should consist of the presentation of a contemporary problem or experience similar to the one being studied in the present lesson.

Bible study. Whether the presentation is via flannelgraph, puppets, chalk or whatever, pupils should have their Bibles open to the selected passage and should be given opportunity to answer questions from time to time. These questions should refer Juniors to the Scripture verse involved and should call for an answer in a student's own words, not the mere reading of the verse. What the pupil says will be remembered by him seven times as long as what the teacher says.

Application. The story, drama or discussion used here should reinforce the aim for the entire period. If, for example, the story of Jacob seeks to emphasize the evil of cheating, let the contemporary application story do likewise. Let discussion prove it to the class. Give an invitation in the brief prayer period, for salvation or dedication.

Memorize a key verse. Again, an assistant teacher can be assigned to teach a memory verse in one of many interesting ways (see chapter on Bible memorization). Vary the method from Sunday to Sunday. Because boys and girls often do not memorize at home, the Sunday School must help them to do so by making it fun. Inexpensive awards, publicly presented, often are sufficient motivation for extra effort.

Announce other Junior weekday activities. Close with a Bible-verse prayer which, because of its weekly repetition, will become hidden in the hearts of all.

Worship
1. *Preparation.* The challenge to the Junior worker is to lead pupils to experience true worship. A "worship service," regardless of how well planned and executed, does not guarantee a worship experience.

The Junior room should have an atmosphere of orderliness. The leader should be prepared, for he cannot lead where he himself has not gone. Leaders must come from "the secret of His presence" if Juniors are to be led into that Presence. All should share in the preparation by participating in the pre-prayer service. Teachers should be seated with their classes before the service begins.

2. *The Junior worship service should contain six basic elements.*

Praise. The call to worship may sound the note of praise with the use of Scripture or poetry. Carefully selected hymns will stimulate such emotions as trust, reverential awe, and joy. Music should be chosen carefully to deepen the thought of the worship theme. Music may be used as a prelude, interlude, offertory, special vocal or intrumental number, during silent prayer, and while marching to classes. The element of praise also may appear in prayer, with emphasis on thanksgiving.

Prayer. Pupils should be led to recognize that prayer is talking to God, having fellowship with Him, not merely a repetition of high-sounding words and phrases. Pupils should be reminded frequently that prayer includes thanking as well as asking; telling God the things that make us happy or sad; telling God we love Him; confessing sin; and talking to Him about others. Prayer time should be brief and reverent, and expressed in a language that is understood by Juniors.

Scripture. The Scripture selection should be prayerfully and carefully chosen to carry out the theme of the service. Frequent use of Scripture which has been memorized is good. Scripture may be read by an adult leader who has practiced reading the passage aloud, or by a pupil, a group, or the entire class. In any event, the passage should be assigned at least a week in advance and drilled by parent, teacher or superintendent. Scripture reading may correlate with the theme of the worship service.

Giving. Juniors may be trained in stewardship through the wise use of the offering. Benevolent impulses will be created as pupils feel financial responsibility for the total program of the church. Juniors may occasionally be given an opportunity to tell how they have earned the money they have brought. Juniors also should be used as ushers for training in churchmanship. And the children should know for what purpose their money is to be used.

Instruction. The time of brief instruction usually is the responsibility of one of the adult leaders. The subjects for instruction in worship may be built around many themes such as

Christ, God's love, God's Word, Bible history, missions, or religious art. This feature should be brief since the class period is for instruction. The material should be selected well in advance to harmonize with the central theme of the worship service. The instruction also should be within the group's experience and comprehension. The methods of presentation may vary: storytelling, talk, object lesson or demonstration.

Fellowship time. Juniors like to show an interest in others. The fellowship period offers opportunity to welcome new members, make announcements of activities, celebrate birthdays, and recognize achievements.

THE JUNIOR HIGH DEPARTMENT

Someone has said that the Junior High Department has more scalps of defeated teachers to its credit than any other department of the Sunday School. While this may be true, it need not be if teachers are dedicated to reaching Junior High pupils for Christ and for eternity.

General Characteristics of Junior High Students

1. *Change.* In body, there is rapid, uneven growth (and girls often outstrip boys in height). In ideals, the young teen is no longer an imitator or hero worshipper, but full of ambitions, with elaborate plans for the future. His ideas are fleeting; his decisions temporary; his disposition changeable. Probably 85 percent of these teens decide on their life's work.

2. *Interest in opposite sex.* Teen boys soon leave the "woman-haters club" of Junior years.

3. *Behavior.* May be silly and flippant, or critical and insensitive. They may ignore friendly gestures.

4. *Independence.* Junior Highs are beginning to establish independence; they want to be grown up.

5. *Activities.* These young people enjoy school and church activities. They incline toward cliques.

6. *Sunday School behavior.* Although they enjoy variety in presentation, Junior Highs may whisper and appear inattentive. They will confide in a teacher they like and who likes them. Approximately 65 percent of the girls and 75 percent of the boys drop out of Sunday School at this critical age.

Needs of the Pupil

Salvation. Needs to recognize his need for a Savior and to have the assurance of salvation.

Dedication. Needs to be challenged to put Bible truths into practice.

Activity. Needs Christian activities in which to use some of his energy.

Friends. Needs someone to depend upon; someone to confide in. Also needs adult guidance which is neither "too late, nor too little."

Aims in Teaching

1. To lead students to a saving knowledge of Jesus Christ.

2. To cause each student to grow and mature in Christ.

3. To show students how God's Word relates to their personal lives.

4. To know each pupil as a friend in order to help him with his problems.

5. To involve each student in the lesson and the class activities.

Principles of Teaching

Because new interests emerge suddenly, and devotion to one study often is short-lived, adolescent education should include a wide variety of subjects.

Stimulate intellectual capacities at this age, for adult life possesses only the improvement of capacities cultivated in early years.

Provide social contacts and development for the youth.

While the last days of childhood present the most promising and practical period for evangelistic effort, the largest number of conversions which "stick" take place during adolescence.

Organized departments should be provided, since the natural social tendency of teens is to form gangs or groups.

Keep open the channels of communication—youth will confide in someone.

Multiply the interests; no real progress can be made until the mental horizon has been widened.

Command by counsel. A young person can be guided even when he cannot be governed; directed when he cannot be driven.

Control by companionship.

Methods for Teaching Junior Highs

1. Have an interesting and challenging presession activity.

2. Have pupils participate by reading from Bibles, pointing out places on maps, discussing clippings and pictures, reviewing the lesson. Junior highs respond more to projected visual aids and discussion than to methods used with younger children.

3. Have a good approach. Never begin with, "Does anyone know what our lesson is about today?" Use thought-provoking questions, a challenge, a brief story, or a visual aid.

4. Let students know you are concerned about them and their problems and are available for help at all times.

5. Give recognition and encouragement to each pupil.

6. Have special projects in which the students can participate.

7. Schedule regular social activities to cultivate and mold Junior Highs into strong Christians.

8. Use a variety of presentations: personal assignments, buzz groups, committee work, storytelling, questions, discussions, circle

Pastor Dick Coleman leads a group of young people in Bible study. (Westside Baptist Church, Leesburg, FL)

conversation, testing, projects, memorization, chalkboard outlines, written reports, testimonies, role play, panels.

Organization

Classes can be divided by age and sex according to the needs of the local church. A class containing six to eight pupils may be ideal for good Bible teaching, but too small for social interaction. (As for other groups, a smaller membership and fewer teachers will make age and sex separation impractical. Too few in a class can be boring and also discouraging.)

The Master Teacher approach is growing in use. All the junior high students are placed in one room and exposed to the teacher best qualified to meet their need. This teacher should be the youth pastor when he is available because he understands adolescents, can com-

municate with them, and has a knowledge of the Scripture.

Class officers may include those named for Juniors, plus a secretary-treasurer, if desired.

THE SENIOR HIGH DEPARTMENT

Characteristics of Seniors

Senior Highs usually have vigor and energy, ambition and enthusiasm. They respond to challenge. They like doing things as a group. As sex interest develops, they enjoy social activities involving the entire department. Like Juniors, they are hero worshippers with more discretion—but like younger teens they need understanding and a confidant.

Creative programs and ministries appeal to senior high pupils. Here the Fabulous Transitions Teen Choir practices for a concert. (Calvary Temple Church, Springfield, IL)

Keeping in mind these particular characteristics, a well-rounded church program for young people should include Bible study, expressional activities (such as Training Union or Christian Endeavor), and social activities.

Officers

Besides president, vice-president and secretary-treasurer, the class needs these committees:

Lookout committee. These young people should lead in contacting absentees and enlisting new members.

Telephone committee. This group should work with the lookout committee. They contact absentees and prospects; give social invitations.

Evangelistic committee. Members should not be afraid to talk to others about Christ; and should have a pleasing personality. It is their responsibility to sponsor a reception each year for all who have committed their lives to Jesus Christ during the year.

Publicity committee. These Seniors make the announcements in Sunday School concerning activities, and are responsible for making posters, getting announcements in the church bulletin, etc.

Reception committee. Members are stationed at the door to welcome new persons to class or to socials.

Sunshine committee. This group looks after class members who are ill, or contacts prospects who are ill.

Social committee. Games, refreshments, programs for dinners, hikes, sports (gymnasium or outdoors), talent night, family night, mother-daughter banquet, father-son banquet, stunt nights—all these and more are the responsibility of this committee.

ADULTS

Young Adults (20-30)

Full grown and in the prime of life, the young marrieds are busy with jobs, homemaking and child-rearing, while singles are career-minded. They are developing hobby skills and abilities.

They are still young enough to recall and relive their youth but old enough to understand life's responsibilities. Because of the drive to succeed, they often are aggressive. They have great reasoning power and desire to feel useful. Most are concerned about others.

Some are inclined toward feelings of failure and unhappiness or pessimism. Some are totally wrapped up in their own pursuits, oblivious to needs or interests of others. In their preoccupation, they are hard to reach.

Because most young adults enjoy social gatherings, they may be enlisted through a social invitation.

Organization

The usual division includes a class for singles, another for the young marrieds. Classes usually consist of a president, vice president and secretary, with social, mission and visitation committees.

Adult classes need to be geared to fellowship and sharing together around God's Word. (Los Gatos Christian Church, Los Gatos, CA)

Aims in Teaching

1. Offer salvation and opportunities for Christian growth.
2. Guide in the development of Christian life and character.
3. Encourage activity in Christian service.
4. Help establish family altars and/or personal devotional periods.
5. Help them adjust to the single life—or to married life, the coming of children, and maintaining a Christian home.
6. Help them grow within the fellowship of the church.

Methods

A good teacher will produce teachers. This class has the greatest potential for producing Sunday School teachers and workers. Therefore, the program should be geared to get these people involved in the study of the Word for themselves. It should help them mature in Christ and form convictions on Christian life and thought, and the Christian home. These convictions should be the result of research, thought and discussion. This group learns through:

Research—Biblical, archaeological, geographical.

Reports—Based on research previously assigned.

Brainstorming—Informal talks on a suggested theme. Each should write down as many ideas as possible in positive statements.

Lectures—Augment with pictures and other aids for interest and retention.

108

Questions and answers—Grab-bag questions encourage participation.

Memorization—Encourage home memory effort via cards or signs.

Discussions—See Section VII-Chapter 37.

Socials—Once-a-month get-togethers as a class brings unity.

Projects—Visitation, transportation assistance to older people, preparation of visual aids for the Sunday School or Vacation Bible School, and ministry to shut-ins are included here.

Teaching attitudes should make students feel wanted and comfortable. Use a vocabulary that students understand. Illustrate lessons with incidents related to the adult's everyday life. Back your teaching with Scripture. Be sincerely enthusiastic. Teach what interests your class, not what you think it needs.

Curriculum

There should be well-balanced Bible study. It may take the form of Bible survey, church history, book study (i.e. Gospel of John), Bible character studies, topical studies (e.g., witnessing, love), Christian living (e.g., personal evangelism, teaching Sunday School, building a Christian home, and training children).

Adults (40-60)

Physically, while adults generally have good health, there is a slight loss of vigor. This is a period of great physical breakdown.

To meet class needs, the teacher should emphasize daily trust in the Lord for strength; should help members utilize their talents with direction; and should encourage them to share resources with those less fortunate. Adults also should be encouraged to use time and energy for God's glory by facing their responsibilities as examples to younger persons. All should participate in the social life of the class, without going to the extremes in sports and vigorous activity.

Mentally, adults of middle years tend to dread the future. Some are disillusioned over failure to achieve their goals. As parents and grandparents they feel multiplied burdens and responsibilities. Their mental powers are keen and productive, and minds are generally mature.

Include positive teaching to counteract the fear of the future. Show the futility of worry, and the power of Christ, the unfailing One. Emphasize the essentials of life. Give Biblical reasons and explanations for assertions. Use members on committees where they can share their mature insights. Encourage discussion, to know their thinking. Foster a reading program to expand their minds. Use capable adults as Sunday School teachers and as teacher-training class teachers.

Socially, middle-agers feel empty when children are grown and gone. Some are burdened by shattered dreams. Others may feel unwanted and unnecessary. Almost all have attained economic and social prestige and security.

Teaching should engage these adults in constructive service, helping them develop interest in new activities. Fellowship will help enlarge their circle of friends. They should be taught God's plan of giving and be guided and challenged to help others. They also should be given opportunity to use their influence in the community. Encourage a Christian stand on social issues.

Spiritually, adults tend to be critical as to morals, though a desire for a "last fling" may be present. Life habits are intensified. The sweet becomes sweeter, the sour more so. Some exhibit spiritual pride.

Teaching should engage these adults in temptation, and the truth of complete spiritual restoration. Reinforce the certainty that Christ is their Anchor, that He can change bad habits. Adults may be won, even at this age, through visitation and church activities. Emphasize the necessity of spiritual growth, for chronological age and spiritual age are not always equal.

Adults (60-on)

Many adults in this age bracket have poor health, with resultant loss of skills and abilities. They need help in transportation and sometimes for comfort in the church.

Intellectual growth may be in spurts. Thinking may become vague and conservative, with reluctance to embrace what is new.

This group needs more short-term studies; meditation and challenge rather than sharp, detailed analysis. Their importance should be recognized at anniversaries. They can help make scrapbooks and visual aids, even equipment. Let them serve on short-term and advisory committees to prevent their feeling slighted and overlooked. Some may be critical of younger people; encourage them to pray instead.

Socially, many older adults are reaping benefits of well-invested money, while others are disillusioned that they can't support themselves on what they've saved. The teacher can inform this over-60 group of Christian trust funds and other resources.

Many need social times to ease the loneliness of friends passing away. Some are shut-ins. An extension department teacher should take them work to do at home, and visit regularly. Also—the church should teach young people the responsibility of supporting and/or visiting their parents so they will not be neglected and lonely.

Spiritually, many elderly members are mature, with a well-rounded outlook on problems. Some tend to live in their spiritual past. Others have become lonely and bitter. Many begin to fear death.

The church can help older members feel needed by asking them to give testimonies of

Each year at Indianapolis Baptist Temple the "Jolly 60's" group elects a King and Queen. (Indianapolis Baptist Temple, Indianapolis, IN)

God's faithfulness in their lives. Activities and programs should foster spiritual friendships. Teaching should prepare them to accept Christ's victory over death and give them hope in His resurrection and second coming.

Methods of Teaching Adults

A method is an orderly procedure or process. Methods of teaching are only tools of instruction to meet needs. True teaching includes telling, showing and doing. Variety also is the spice of adult life.

1. *Lecture method.* This popular method has the advantage of utilizing the least time, being adaptable to large groups, and making lesson preparation easy for the teacher. It allows for illustration, appeals to the emotions, and answers many questions. However, it often becomes monotonous and boring. It discourages student participation, even prompting daydreams. And it prevents discovery of new truth by the student himself.

2. *Question-and-answer method.* Interest-arousing questions (prepared in advance) may be interspersed throughout the lesson, stimulating thought. The questions should teach rather than test. Avoid questions answered by yes or no, or leading questions. Mimeographed questions may be handed out for a month or quarter in advance so that preparation can be made. They may guide the student so he can follow the teacher more easily during the lecture period.

3. *Discussion.* This is effective if well-planned. A few should not be allowed to monopolize the discussion. The leader must be well-informed or well-educated, impartial, patient, and have a sense of humor. All should bear in mind that discussion is not a debate; it is a sharing process. Students should address the class when speaking, not the leader. The teacher must tactfully lead the discussion to the desired goal of the lesson and keep the discussion Bible-centered.

4. *Illustrations.* The teacher may relate experiences, refer to sermons, or include excerpts from periodicals.

5. *Reports.* Topics may be given out in advance. Several members may work together to give a report on a given subject, or one individual may report on a specific subject, contributing toward the main study.

6. *Demonstration or role play.* Occasionally to arouse interest, members may demonstrate a point of the lesson, or introduce a subject, or make application.

7. *Projects.* The group may make models, such as the Tabernacle or a Palestinian village. They may decorate the classroom. They may plan and do group or individual visitation of shut-ins and prospects.

8. *Visual Aids.* See Section VII-Chapter 39. Adults also learn and retain much through the eyegate.

110

13

While it is true that content or experience can be omitted or minimized, one of these must constitute the center around which the other revolves. Three differing views spark this controversy.

Curriculum in Christian Education

Definition

Curriculum has been variously defined:

1. "The sum of all the factors that make for education"—C. Ellis Nelson.

2. "Curriculum is the lesson material through which an educational institution seeks to accomplish its aim"—A.A. Brown.

3. "A course of study to be pursued; an organized plan of study; a grouping of courses included in a specific field; the overall structure or order of a course of study with special reference to subject and content"—Clarence Benson.

4. "Curriculum may be defined as those activities in relation to authoritative content which are guided or employed by Christian leadership in order to bring pupils one step nearer to maturity in Christ"—Lois LeBar.

The Center of the Curriculum

While it is true that content or experience can be omitted or minimized, one of these must constitute the center around which the other revolves, the authority upon which the other depends. Three differing views are held on this controversy:

1. *Poor traditional.* Bible content is the whole curriculum.

2. *Secular and religious liberal.* Only experience-centered curriculum is dynamic. Only relevant content is applied.

3. *Scriptural curriculum.* Curriculum should be Christ-centered rather than Bible-centered, not on sinful human life, but on divine, eternal life—the Living Word.

Scope

1. *Every aspect.* The curriculum should give adequate attention to every aspect of Christian teaching which should be considered by each age group.

2. *Experience.* The curriculum should cover the areas of experience basic and common to each age group. (The experiences of home, community, school, vocation, recreation and others must be presented in the curriculum.)

3. *Objectives.* The curriculum will give attention to the objectives of Christian education for each age group.

4. *Significance.* The curriculum will include all the areas of Bible knowledge which have particular significance and teaching value for each age group.

5. *Specific areas.* The following list indicates specific areas of content which a good curriculum includes. These will be interwoven and given varying amounts of consideration:

a. The Bible, its origin and nature, both Old and New Testaments, and methods of study, devotional use.

b. Faith or beliefs regarding God, Jesus Christ, the nature of man, the meaning of the Church, the Bible as the source of faith, Christianity and world philosophies, the

Christian interpretation of the universe.

c. Personal experiences in Christian living, such as worship, health, stewardship, evangelism, leisure, recreation, vocation, friendship, educational and cultural development.

d. Christian interpretation of sex, preparation for marriage, establishing Christian homes, parenthood, Christian relationships in the home, families in relation to the community.

e. Church life and outreach, including church history, nature and program of the church, church membership, service in and through the church, missionary outreach.

f. Social problems, such as amusements; liquor and other narcotics, gambling, delinquency, and crime; race, group, and interfaith relations; Christian principles in relation to community life, economics, business and labor, government, education and citizenship.

g. World Relations, including world missions, world citizenship, the ecumenical movement.

h. Service and Christian leadership opportunities, measures of preparation, principles and objectives, and skills and methods.

Balance and Correlation

A good curriculum planner determines how much time should be given to each area of study. Some principles for consideration are:

1. The number of sessions assigned to each element and emphasis will reflect the importance of each judged in the light of other elements.

2. The importance of each element will be judged in the light of its most effective contribution to the development of Christian personality and of its importance in the Christian faith.

3. The time assigned to any given emphasis will be consistent with the material available to support and enrich that area of interest.

4. The length of time assigned to any element will be determined by the time needed to initiate and carry through an effective experience.

Sequence

A good curriculum results from carefully planned organization. Care must be given to placing the various elements in the sequence that will contribute most to the development of Christian faith and character.

1. Some progression must be assumed on the part of the learner and teacher. It is not necessary to repeat everything at every stage.

2. The timing of emphases will utilize seasonal interests to the best advantage.

3. The placement of units or courses will observe the need for variety and freshness of approach.

4. Closely related areas of curriculum will be placed to make use of the possibilities of cumulative learning.

5. There will be frequent cumulative learning, providing incentive to commitment and action consistent with the development level of each age group.

Purpose

The purpose of the curriculum is the purpose of Christian education. An effective curriculum:

1. Meets the needs of the church as a whole, as well as individual and personal needs.

2. Corresponds positively to aims and objectives in order that they may be accomplished.

Organizing Principle

The essential function of organization is to bridge the gap between Christian education and the actual learning situation. The curriculum is a plan for communicating the Gospel, based on answers to these questions: (1) To whom are we speaking? (2) Are they good listeners? (3) What do we have to say? (4) Who are we?

Principles in Selection and Evaluation

1. *Guides for selection:*

a. There must be opportunity for the learner to practice the mental responses, actions, and intended behavioral changes.

b. The learning opportunity must be within the comprehension of the learners.

c. The stimulus should be consistent with the likes—not the dislikes—of the learners.

d. The learning content should contribute to instructional objectives.

2. *Guides in evaluation.* There should be:

a. Stipulated courses and/or activities available to pupils (with particular interests and abilities).

b. Adequate time for instructional objectives.

c. Available electives (in varying time allotments).

d. Logical sequence of courses.

e. Coordination of instructional activities.

f. Provision for pupil participation.

g. Remedial or clinical activities.

h. Course arrangement by themes, problems, topics and/or projects.

i. Planning to avoid long gaps.

j. Provision for use of facilities.

k. Allowance for repetition and review.

l. Provision for discontinuance of ineffective activities.

PRINCIPLES OF CURRICULUM BUILDING

Definition

Curriculum is the sum total of the experiences designed to lead the pupil to the realization of a given aim. In the case of Christian education, the primary aim is the growth of the pupil toward Christian maturity.

MODERN CURRICULUM PLANS

UNIFORM GRADING	UNIFIED GRADING	DEPARTMENT GRADING	CLOSE GRADING
The same Bible portion is taught to each age-group.	Different Bible content, related by a single theme, is taught to each age-group.	Different Bible content is provided for each department group (Primary, Junior, etc.).	Different Bible content is provided for pupils in each public school grade.
(1) A small church can unite all pupils in a single lesson-related worship service. (2) All family members can discuss their common lesson at home.	(1) Several age-groups can meet in a single theme-related worship service. (2) At-home discussion of the theme is possible.	(1) All activities are closely related to the Bible lesson in each department group. (2) Lessons can be geared to the social, psychological, emotional and mental level of all pupils.	(1) Curriculum can be planned to fit the stage of development of pupils.
(1) Lessons are repeated on a 5-7 year cycle, provide limited Bible coverage. (2) Bible content often not suitable for pupils of all ages.	(1) Limited number of themes make it difficult to give complete Bible coverage. (2) Lessons taught in each department determined by theme, rather than pupils' developing needs.	(1) Common at-home discussion is limited, since parents and children study different material.	(1) At-home discussion limited. (2) Hard to relate all activities in SS _ hour (songs, worship service, etc.) to theme, since each grade has a different lesson.

Here are the four basic plans evangelical publishers follow in grading their lesson materials. To evaluate curriculum, you need to study the advantages and disadvantages of each curriculum plan when applied to your needs and goals.

Pupil books should be well illustrated, relevant and interesting. (Standard Publishing)

Philosophy

The curriculum of Christian education begins with a Christian purpose. The doctrine of revelation is the foundation of our curriculum. The content of God's revelation to man is found in the Bible. God's personal, direct revelation of Himself is the person of His Son, Jesus the Messiah. The divine element also enters into our curriculum with the illuminating power of the Holy Spirit. The result is a curriculum in Christian education that is supernatural.

Scriptural Principles

1. *Christ-centered.* The basic curriculum of the Christian church at the time of the book of Acts was Christology; the central message of God's Word is still Jesus Christ. The person and work of Jesus Christ must be the core of our curriculum.

2. *Bible-grounded.* Christological speculation apart from the authority of the Scriptures can lead to heresy, as church history will verify. Therefore the curriculum of Christian education must be *Bible-grounded.* Our curriculum

Sunday School Curricula at a Glance

Company Name	Title	Dated Material	Opening Assembly	Age Divisions	Test to Evaluate Pupil Learning	Teacher Helps
Christian Church (Disciples of Christ)	Bethany Uniform Series	Yes	Yes	Grades 1-3, 4-6, 7-12, adult.	Yes	Focus Leader's Foundations for Teaching Church Leaders courses (10 available).
Christian Church (Disciples of Christ)	Perspective Series	No	No	Ages 1-3, 4-5, 6-7-, 8-9, 10-11, 12-13, 14-15, 16-17, 18 and up.	Yes	Teaching kits for grades, except adults Focus Leaders Kit Foundation for Teaching Church Leaders courses (10 available).

must be grounded in the entire Word of God, which we view as the authority of our faith and practice.

3. *Pupil-related.* Jesus Christ Himself was person-centered. He was continually involved in the needs of those around him. Our curriculum cannot operate within a vacuum. The person and work of Jesus Christ as revealed in the Scriptures must be related to the everyday life and needs of individual pupils.

4. *Contemporary.* We teach within the temporal context of the 1970s. Like Jesus, who applied His teachings to His day, we must apply our curriculum to the needs of our contemporaries. Curriculum without practice is dead. Experiences must be provided for the practical outworking of the life of Jesus Christ in today's world.

Factors Involved

1. *Aims and objectives.* The aims and objectives of Christian education must be adjusted to local situations. No doubt there will be some local differences in stated objectives. As long as the objectives are Biblical, involve the primary aim, and are carefully stated, it will be possible to construct a curriculum around them.

2. *Structure of content.* The importance of the structure of the content of Christian education cannot be overemphasized. The fundamentals and principles which make up the Christian world and life view are crucial. Details must be subservient to the structure, for they can be sufficiently reconstructed by pupils who have grasped the structure of God's revelation to us.

3. *Sequential.* Curriculum must take into account the developmental nature of the child.

Content

The entire content of the Scriptures must be included. However, it must be remembered that Scripture is not an end in itself, but a means to knowing Jesus experientially. A systematic treatment of Christian beliefs (encompassing the content of systematic theology and doctrinal distinctives of the local church) also should be covered. Personal experiences in Christian living, such as worship and service, should be included, along with the concept of the Christian family and how to achieve harmony at home. The doctrine and work of the church, a Christian response to social problems, the Christian's response to the larger world, and service and Christian leadership also should be included.

The Curriculum in Use

1. *Adaptation.* Most local churches will be unable to design their own curriculum materials completely. They will, however, be able to design their total curriculum by adapting published materials. Their local church situation will be taken into account when designing the total curriculum.

2. *Unification.* The entire Christian education curriculum must be a unified whole. The curriculum of the various agencies and age groups must be complementary.

3. *Efficient use.* The materials provided for the teachers and leaders must be used with maximum efficiency and effectiveness. This implies that teachers and leaders must be thoroughly equipped to perform their responsibilities.

4. *Involvement.* Maximum involvement in the learning process on the part of pupils should be encouraged by teachers and leaders.

5. *Application.* Opportunity for application must be provided by teachers and leaders to encourage the actual practice of the Christian life.

Multi-Media	Agencies For Which Material is Provided	Cycle	Social Action for Church
No	Sunday Schools.	International Uniform Lessons.	Relates Gospel and life issues, suggests projects.
Teaching kits	Sunday Schools.	Interdenominational Cooperative Curriculum Project Treatment of Scope.	Relates Gospel and life issues as crossing points, suggests projects.

Company Name	Title	Dated Material	Opening Assembly	Age Divisions	Test to Evaluate Pupil Learning	Teacher Helps
Church of the Brethren	Encounter Series	No	No	1-3, 4-5, 6-7, 8-9, 10-11, 12-13, 14-15, 16-17, 18 and up.	Yes	Leadership guide Leadership training.
David C. Cook	Bible in Life Curriculum	Yes	Yes	2-3, 4-5, 6-7, 8-9, 10-11, 12-14, 15-17, 18 and up.	Yes	Teacher guides, teacher-training program, teaching aids.
Free Will Baptist Sunday School Department	Bible-Based Series	Yes	Yes	2-3,4-5,6-8,9-11,12-14, 15-17, 18-24, 25 and up.	No	Teacher guides, visual packets.
Gospel Light Publications	Christ centered Child-concerned Bible-based	No	Yes	By age: cradle roll to adults.	Yes	Multi-media packet, instructor manual, teacher training series.
Gospel Publishing House	Word of Life Curriculum	Yes	Yes	Departmental: nursery, beginner, primary, junior, junior high, high school, adult.	Yes	Teachers quarterlies, Visual aids, pictures.
Nazarene Publishing House	God's Word for All	Yes	Yes	0-2,2-3,4-5, 6-8,9-11,12-14, 15-17, 18 and up.	Yes	Teachers quarterly, magazine, visual resources age-level brochures, age-level filmstrips.
Pathway Press (Church of God)	New Life Curriculum	Yes	Yes	Birth-1,2-3,4-5,6-8, 9-11,12-14,15-17, adult.	No	Teachers quarterlies.
Pentecostal Publishing House	Word Aflame Publications	Yes	Yes	Departmental beginner, 4-5; primary, 6-8; junior high, 12-14; junior, 9-11; senior high, 15-17; adult nursery, 2-3 in Fall '71.	No	Teachers manuals, visual packets, instructions.
Regular Baptist Press	God's Word for the Family	Yes	Yes	Departmental: cradle roll through adults: 0-2,2-3,4-5,6-8,9-11, 12-14,14-18, adult.	Yes	Visual-aid packets instructor manual teacher-training series in instructor manuals.
Scripture Press	The Whole Word for the Whole World	Yes	Yes	0-2,2-3,4-5 6-8,9-11,young teen,high school, adult.	Yes	Teachers manuals, teaching aid packets teaching pictures and other audio visuals.
Standard Publishing House	True to the Bible	Yes	Yes	2-3,4-5,6-8,9-11,12-14, 15-17,18-24, 25 and up.	N.A.	Step-by-step instruction on lesson preparation and presentation.
Union Gospel Press	Christian Life Series	Yes	Yes	Beginner through adult.	No	Teachers quarterlies

Multi-Media	Agencies For Which Material is Provided	Cycle	Social Action for Church
Teaching kits	All needs of denomination.	Developed jointly with American Baptist and Disciples of Christ.	Strong emphasis.
Filmstrips, records, posters, charts, maps, flannelgraph, etc.	Nursery schools, day-care centers, public schools, children's church, youth groups.	Pre-school, 2 yr.; school, 3 yr.; adult, 6 yr.	Social problems are discussed and related to Christianity.
Filmstrips, cassettes, show 'n tell stories.		7 year, age 12 up; 3 year, age 6-11; 2 year, age 2-5.	Application of gospel soul winning.
Filmstrips, posters pictures, charts, flannelgraph, cassettes, etc.	VBS, leader education, children's church, clubs, camp, youth groups.	Cover Bible 4 times from different perspective.	Emphasizes individual and group involvement.
Records, stori-strip, flannelboard, pictures, workbooks, activity packets.	Youth groups, boys and girls groups, missionary groups, VBS, children's camps, youth camps.	Department graded. Also NSSA uniform cycle for adults, youth and junior high.	Urge Christian principles be followed in every facet of society.
Pictures, filmstrips, recordings, charts, maps.	Junior fellowship, young people's society, children's church, VBS, pastor classes, Christian service training, weekday nursery, kindergarten.	International Uniform Lessons high school through adult. Graded curriculum, nursery through junior high.	Encouraged.
No	Family Training Hour.	Prepare own through junior. NSSA, junior high through adult.	Christian helps neighbors, wins community.
Teaching kits, workbooks.	All education needs of denomination.	Nursery-beginner 2 yr. Primary-senior high 3 yr. Adult 7 yr.	Evangelism all inclusive (worldwide).
Pictures, flannelgraph, etc.	Senior high youth hour.	Write own Bible content study.	Stress living in the world according to Biblical teaching.
Teaching aid packets, review-a-packs, tests, charts, maps, filmstrips, etc.	Children's church, VBS, youth programs, camp programs.	All Bible chronological and topical coverage.	Some emphasis on individual social involvement but disavow social gospel.
Varied—depending upon purpose and age group.	VBS, camps, evening youth groups, released time, Christian day schools.	3-year cycle, primary through senior high. International Uniform Lessons, beginner through senior high.	Included where appropriate.
Flannelgraph, workbooks.	Sunday Schools.	International Uniform Lessons.	Emphasizes Christian life with implications.

14

Periodically, a church should determine whether it has the best possible program at the lowest possible unit cost. Here are helpful tips on both financing and budgeting.

Finances and the Church

Biblical Standard for Giving

1. *Old Testament.* In the Old Testament, man acknowledges God's ownership, but within a legalistic system. Man's relation to God there resembles that of a tenant with his landlord. The "first fruits" and tithes are for the acknowledgment of God's gifts.

2. *New Testament.* Ultimate ownership is God's; temporary possession is man's. Possession, the relationship between man and property, is not ownership, but a stewardship relation. Christian giving today involves inquiry or investigation of needs. The immediacy of the need influences distribution of God's property where it is most needed. Since God is the owner, and God is not in need, man is to give from gratitude to acknowledge God's ownership.

Financial Management

1. *Basic Foundational Principles.* It is basic that:

a. A church should have sound financial management to enable it to accomplish its objectives.

b. The management of the church be interested enough in the mission of the church and their own protection to establish a sound financial system.

c. A church should have people with technical competency in accounting matters.

d. A church should organize into a corporation to limit legal liability for the owners and enable the organization to hold title to assets and enter into contracts.

2. *Financial Personnel.* The accounting area includes the pastor, church board, financial committee, church treasurer, and financial secretary.

a. The pastor should present the programs he feels will benefit the church and explain the costs associated with them. He should seek to transfer as many business affairs as possible to the layman, to have more freedom for spiritual guidance of the people.

b. The church board should have direct control over special activities, such as purchasing large assets or obtaining money from an outside source. This will insure a review of all facts and effects of the transaction before its approval. Since the board usually meets only once a month, a special committee should meet more often to discuss and approve the treasurer's actions.

c. The finance committee members have financial background. They oversee the financial record-keeping system, with authorization to make changes as necessary. They take major decisions to the church board, arrange for regular, complete audits by an experienced accountant not involved in financial record-keeping for the congregation, and prepare the annual budget. The chairman should have the

The financial secretary receives, counts, and deposits all contributions. Some other persons should help with the counting. (Luoma Photos, Weirton, WV)

bank statements sent directly to him for reconciliation.

This committee includes all the financial officers, and also other members of the congregation. The congregation's bylaws should spell out the duties and membership requirements.

d. The church treasurer:

(1) Reports to the finance committee and board.

(2) Is responsible for establishing a sound bookkeeping system and insuring its accuracy.

(3) Should set up procedures to safeguard the assets of the church.

(4) Advises the board and membership on financial matters.

(5) May present a forecast of financial plans of the church.

(6) Pays, by check only, all disbursements authorized by the budget or the board. All church officers and committee chairmen ought to understand fully the proper procedures for authorizing payments. A second signature would provide even greater internal control. Pre-numbered checks are used.

(7) Makes no deposits of funds, handles no loose cash, and disassociates himself from responsibility for counting or receiving any of the church's offerings.

(8) Prepares a regular report (monthly or quarterly), including comparisons of expenditures to budgeted amounts.

(9) Keeps a record of checks issued in a cash disbursements journal. No ledger is necessary as regular reports serve the purpose.

(10) Periodically lists assets at cost and replacement values. Lists liabilities and their terms for repayment and interest rates.

e. The financial secretary receives, counts, and deposits all contributions. Some other person should be designated to help with the counting. The financial secretary should give duplicate deposit slips, with adequate notations regarding source and fund, to the treasurer promptly.

He also prepares and forwards to any assistant financial secretary an adequate report of all contributions each week: source, contributor's name, fund, amount, special instructions. The financial secretary keeps a record of all contributions and deposits. No ledger is necessary, as regular reports fulfill this function. He disburses no funds and has no access to the congregation's checking account.

f. The assistant financial secretary keeps the record of each individual's contributions, from whatever source and for whatever purpose. The officer secures this information from offering envelopes or other data provided by the financial secretary. Duplicate deposit slips provide a check on the accuracy of the total entries to all sheets. The assistant financial secretary handles no cash at all; he prepares a regular report of all contributions for each individual contributor.

3. *Church Budget.*

a. It should be practical and reliable, tailored by the administrator to fit the operation of the church.

b. It should eliminate wasteful expenditures, yet it should not promote false economies by failing to provide for minor repairs which soon become costly major repairs.

c. It should be properly constructed to achieve the important Christian goals of the church.

d. The ratio of expenditures to various operations is spelled out and adjustments made from year to year.

e. A projected budget must be based on accurate past financial records.

f. It should be prepared and adopted prior to the end of the fiscal year, to be in effect by the first of the year.

These guidelines will help in financial planning:

a. A church plans on the basis of its continuing existence.

b. Planners must constantly check the financial statement of receipts and disbursements.

c. Planning some portions of the budget may be done on the basis of projected income through pledges.

d. The establishment of a reserve may cause members to reduce their giving, feeling that the church has more money than it can use.

e. Divide an annual budget into monthly or quarterly periods. Analyze actual income and expenses for the last year on a period-to-period basis to see the pattern of income and expense. Make adjustments on this basis.

The Church and Financial Planning

1. *Top-level planning.* Planning should be done at the top level of church management (church board and finance committee).

2. *Planners.* The committee on planning should be composed of those on the official board or boards who have the highest degree of common sense and business acumen.

3. *A flexible plan.* Ensure flexibility of the plan, periodic review, and revision.

4. *Short-range financial planning.* Seasonal influences on financial planning must be taken into account in the areas of program, contribution, and expenditures. This planning is best implemented by a one-year projection of cash contributions and cash requirements.

5. *Long-range financial planning.* Because the long-range goals of a church are spiritual in nature, planning differs from organizations. Three areas must be considered:

a. The goals of a church determine its program. There must be an adequate appraisal of intended functions and goals and a planning of funds to meet these goals.

b. Population movements and the prospect of relocating. The church should be aware of population movements and plan for relocation, if necessary, in order to continue to finance the ongoing ministry.

c. The business cycle and its effects on the community. The planning committee will determine the best time for the church to move, remodel, buy or sell real estate, or build.

6. *Giving potential.* The unit of measurement for operational costs is often average attendance at Sunday morning worship service. Membership requirements vary, but comparisons are made on this basis:

a. National average: $150-$200 (for families with $4,000 to $10,000 income).

b. Urban Protestant churches: $3-$4 per week ($156-$208 per year); $4-plus if the church has a building fund, systematic financial program, or outstanding benevolence giving.

c. Rural Protestant churches: $2-$3 per week ($104-$156 per year).

d. Large churches (attendance over two hundred per Sunday), both rural and urban, usually have a better giving record than small congregations where the average weekly attendance is under one hundred.

In a congregation the special circumstances

Religious News Service Photo

120

that create high incomes for some families will be offset by circumstances which create low incomes for others. The same is true of expenses. By using an average figure, one can establish standards to judge the giving potential. There are various methods of establishing standards:

a. From 70 to 80 percent of the average American family's income before taxes is required for necessary and near-necessary expenses (including taxes). An "improvement factor" of 10 percent is added to the top figure for a growing standard of living. Then the cost of living and improving is 90 percent. The amount remaining suggests that the *giving potential* for a congregation is 10 percent of the total income of all its members.

b. The *actual giving* standard is established by multiplying the per-member gift for the denomination by the number of members in the congregation. The result is a dollar standard based only on the number of members.

c. An *actual giving* standard may also be established with national, regional, or denominational averages per *attender,* multiplied by the average Sunday morning attendance.

d. *Actual giving* based on average contributions in relation to income. To find this standard, first take the per-member gift for a body of churches and divide by the per capita income of the nation for that year. The result is an estimate of the percent of income the average member of the synod or conference actually gives to his church. To convert this percentage figure to a dollar standard for a congregation, first estimate the total income of its members, then multiply. The result is a dollar standard based on the incomes of the parishioners.

e. Estimating the income of a congregation: The income of an American family depends on many things, but two are most important—occupation of the family head and geographic location. National figures must be adjusted to estimate the income at a specific place. The median incomes before taxes of family units by occupational groups should be secured from the *Federal Reserve Bulletin.* To use this information, count the number of units (family heads and unattached individuals) in each occupation. Multiply by the average incomes shown. Then add, and you will have a total income estimate for the congregation. The next step is to adjust the total to the geographic area. Multiply by the figures for the area, as shown on a correction factor map.

7. *Budget Planning.* To keep up with rising unit costs, the church must continue to grow and expand. Periodically, a church should determine whether it ·has the best possible program at the lowest possible unit cost. The smaller the church, the greater is the average "cost" of membership. Churches with fewer than 25 members pay more per member to sustain a meager program. Beyond a certain

minimum size, a substantial proportion of the giving of a local church can go to missions and benevolences without weakening its work.

Families in lower income brackets give the highest percentage of income to the church. After retirement, people in the lower income category continue to give about the same as before.

Membership giving distribution:

4% of the membership gives 1/4 of the money

10% of the membership gives the second 1/4 of the money

20% of the membership gives the third 1/4 of the money

66% of the membership gives the last 1/4 of the money

Therefore: 1/7 of the people give 1/2 of the money

1/3 of the people give 3/4 of the money

If the average giving per attender is less than $150 per year, finances are often the church's biggest problem and the program suffers.

8. *Distribution of funds.* About 80 percent of total gifts are used locally for expenses connected with maintaining buildings, operating expenses, and salaries. About 20 percent goes for home and foreign missions, education, social welfare, world relief, denominational, and interdenominational activities. The music program may use about 10 percent of the total local expense budget.

Accounting Method Principles

1. *Find out what type of financial information is desired.* This information will aid management in making sound decisions.

2. *The method should follow directives.* The church treasurer, denominational headquarters, and auditor have a voice.

3. *The characteristics of any system.* Simplicity, provision for protection of assets, provides a record of transactions, provision for data leading to financial statements, and provision for involving the whole church membership in the financial activities of the church.

4. *Fund accounting.* This is desirable, especially if there is an endowment fund or building program.

Bookkeeping Principles and Procedures

1. *Double entry accounting.* Cash books, ledgers with accounts . well labeled and numbered, and a journal should be used. Trial balances should be taken monthly.

2. *Disbursements.* Vouchers in triplicate should be used rather than checks. The first carbons become the file for entries into the cash book; second carbons should be attached with purchase orders to invoices. Invoices for materials not purchased by the administrator should be approved for payment by the purchaser. Attempt to have all purchases made by the administrator on proper purchase orders,

and avoid payments in cash.

3. *Receipts.* A tally sheet should support every bank deposit. Totals for the Sunday offering should appear on the official tally sheet, identified before deposit is made.

4. *Assets.* The building and equipment assets are shown on the financial statement only if there is an outstanding debt. The value recorded for the asset is the amount of the debt. If the asset is unencumbered by a mortgage, it will normally be shown at a value considerably below the asset's cost, due to its limited utility.

5. *Financial statements.* Any member of the church should be able to understand the statements. They should embrace all activities of the church, such as Sunday School, summer camps, etc. The statement should compare the current financial status with a budget or with figures from the corresponding period last year. The statements should be on time. The longer the delay after the end of the fiscal period, the longer before any needed corrective action can be taken. Statements should be furnished to the minister and church board every month.

Quarterly statements should include a reconciliation with the budget, with all accounts itemized. Annual statements should be complete with details of all income and expense. The treasurer should attach a brief explanation for significant deviations.

Legal Aspects of Financing

1. *Bank.* When choosing a bank, consider its procedures for deposits, use of checks, stop payment orders, reconciling the bank statements, the use of special purpose accounts, supplementary banking services, and the types of accounts it offers.

2. *Wills.* Encourage people to include the church in their will. The church pastor and others should be able to help a person draw up a will. They should know the types of wills, codicils, contesting procedures, and methods for handling the inclusion of a church in a will.

3. *Bequests.* The church should not attempt to promote bequests, but should make materials available to members and friends who might be interested in helping the church in this way after their death.

4. *Trusts.* If an individual wishes to leave a perpetual income to his church he should set up a living trust or a testamentary trust.

5. *Investments and Securities.* The income from church investments normally is not taxable; the church is not usually bound by legal restrictions as to the types of securities it may purchase. The church investment will depend on the objectives and policies of the church investment committee. The six classes of securities are: industrials, U.S. Government securities, public utilities, financials, municipals, and railroad securities.

6. *Credit and Borrowing.* Except when dealing with large banks and/or insurance companies, a church usually has more difficulty borrowing money than a profit-making business. Many firms dislike lending to churches for fear of having to foreclose. Most churches lack good collateral. When borrowing money a church must demonstrate its sincere purpose to repay, its ability to repay, the financial policy of the church that will guarantee repayment, and the plan for repayment.

a. Kinds of borrowing: short-term unsecured loans, secured short-term loans, unsecured long-term loans, and secured long-term loans.

b. Principles of debt financing: Because churches are most vulnerable to downswings in the business cycle, there should be a great deal of restraint during times of prosperity. Most of the church's expenses remain relatively constant during a depression while its income greatly decreases. Ordinarily, no debt should be incurred which cannot be repaid within a 20-year period. Not more than 35 percent of the total budget should be used for debt retirement. The church should insist on the right to pay all or any part of the debt before it is due.

7. *Real estate.* Since real estate and any buildings must be 100 percent financed (paid in full at the time of purchase), equity, types of mortgages, liens, and leases should all be investigated in view of the needs of the church.

8. *Insurance coverage.* Certain types of insurance should be investigated and purchased for adequate coverage.

Finances and the Building Program

1. *Comparisons.* Approximately 30 percent of the Sunday offering in the average Protestant church goes for construction costs, either directly or through interest and principal payments. Most Protestants spend twice as much on local building programs as on outreach through benevolence giving. The giving level in good parishes with a sense of mission and a building fund drive in progress, often averages about $250.

2. *Principles.*

a. Before beginning a building program, determine the giving potential.

b. A building program is an incentive for many to give half again as much as previously.

c. Keep the congregation fully informed of the needs and progress.

d. It is easier to raise money for a building than for missions, staff, or for any other purpose. Therefore, make sure the giving level for missions and for current expenses is up where it should be, before beginning a building fund drive.

e. A church normally begins to develop a building program in response to needs. But the amount of money available often determines the final size and nature of the building.

f. During the first building fund drive anticipate several large cash gifts.

g. It is easiest to raise money for a building under construction, harder to raise money to pay off a mortgage. The older the building, the harder it is; therefore, keep the term of the mortgage as short as possible.

h. Do not bind the hands of the future decision-makers of the church by building more than could be paid off in about five years.

Minister and Staff Support

1. *Principles and suggestions.*

a. Salaries vary by denomination, types of church served, educational preparation, and benefits received.

b. The higher the church membership, the larger the minister's salary; the longer the years of service, the higher the salary.

c. The compensation of a minister should enable him to give full time and energy to his task.

d. The minister should not have to be dependent on ministerial discounts and fees for weddings, baptisms, and funerals.

e. The budget should be arranged in two parts:

Reimbursable expense—funds for all expenses incurred by the minister in travel for the church, including car expense and costs of additional professional training.

Compensation—salary, housing and all utilities, payments toward a pension, and health and accident insurance premiums.

f. As a general rule, to keep abreast of inflation, the minister should have a cash salary at least double that of 1940, and 30 percent more than in 1950.

g. Ministers should keep abreast of the rising costs of Social Security; the church should pay this tax as do other employers.

It is easier to raise money for a building than for missions, staff, or for any other purpose.

15

As you learn to read them, records can be an invaluable aid to measuring the spiritual temperature of your Sunday School—or class!

Records

Reasons for Records

Since "statistics have faces," some teachers describe record-keeping as a "necessary evil" in the Sunday School. A church which is growing and keeping records of that growth often is accused of being "numbers conscious." However, awareness of attendance figures is vital for many reasons.

The church that knows its past has a future. A wise person can "read" tell-tale signs from the records. The average American church member gives approximately $3 each week. Therefore, the offering in average churches should equal $3 per attender (this figure includes dead churches). Growing New Testament churches average at least $4 per attender each week. Other clues of health include looking for 12 percent attendance of the entire Sunday School in the Senior High Department. Anything less reveals spiritual stagnation. Teens don't attend dead churches.

Specific Values (what they accomplish)

1. They challenge the entire Sunday School to work.
2. They provide a complete register of pupils and leaders.
3. They provide a basis for evaluation and measurement.
4. They reveal strengths and weaknesses.
5. They make efficient operation possible.
6. They provide up-to-date statistics for classes, departments and the total school.
7. They provide a list of prospective new pupils.
8. They encourage faithful attendance and membership.
9. They help teachers by revealing spiritual conditions, attendance, study habits, etc.
10. They teach pupils good habits, such as reverence, faithfulness and responsibility.
11. They can be used to guide in curriculum planning.
12. They furnish the key to budget matters.
13. They furnish information for ordering supplies.
14. They motivate people.

Principles for an Efficient Record System

1. *Simplicity.* All workers must be able to operate the record system.
2. *Current.* Records should be kept up-to-date.
3. *System.* Continuity should be maintained, in spite of turnover of workers.
4. *Cumulative.* Records of the past, present and future form a complete picture.
5. *Economy.* Inexpensive blanks, forms and books provide substantial savings over the years.
6. *Permanence.* Books and files should preserve records and materials.
7. *Skill.* A trained and faithful general secretary, along with efficient department and

class secretaries, will save time and energy.

8. *Participation.* All personnel must take part, for greatest effectiveness.

9. *Uniformity.* The same record system should be maintained throughout the whole school, with few adjustments.

10. *Spiritual.* Spiritual conclusions reached after an evaluation of the records should be used to challenge the school, departments and classes to be more like Christ and to serve Him more faithfully.

Records and the Teacher

Records will give the teacher some interesting facts about the pupils and the teaching:

1. *Faithful pupils.* A pupil's presence at every Sunday morning class period reveals faithfulness to God. Hindrances are experienced by most people, but the regular pupils have overcome these hindrances because they wished to do so.

2. *Interested pupils.* Regular pupils are interested pupils. Lack of regular attendance by numbers of pupils points out a lack of interest.

3. *Effective teaching.* The fact that pupils are interested and coming regularly, usually indicates that the teacher's methods and content hold interest and get through to the pupils. When attendance lags and most pupils attend irregularly, a teacher should seek to discover why. The method or content may be at fault with change being necessary.

4. *Financial responsibility.* If a class keeps the six-point record system, a square indicates an "offering brought." Those who contribute regularly may be recognized. A lack of interest in giving will point up need for additional teaching about this Christian responsibility.

5. *Witness.* Most pupils are told that bringing a Bible to class is a silent witness. Again, the six-point record system will reveal whether or not a pupil is consistently bringing his Bible.

6. *New pupils.* Names and addresses of new pupils furnish a teacher with information for follow-up.

Prospects

1. *Visitation.* Prospects discovered during visitation should be recorded. If visiting dates and names of visitors are recorded, duplication of effort will be avoided. Also, lack of concern on the part of some will be revealed.

2. *Class visitors.* Visitors usually enjoy recognition, although shy persons may shrink from the limelight. A general welcome by the class president can suffice—but an assistant should learn the name, address and telephone number of the visitor, so a home visit can be made. Any follow-up should be recorded.

3. *Newcomers.* As class members report newcomers in the community, names and addresses should be recorded for future contacts. Other facts can be added to the record following other visits.

THE
IMPROVED
CLASS-BOOK,
FOR
SUNDAY SCHOOL TEACHERS' MINUTES.

Let all things be done decently and in order.—*Paul.*

KNOWLEDGE OF THE LORD

AMERICAN UNION
SUNDAY SCHOOL

PHILADELPHIA:
Bookstore, No. 146 Chesnut Street.

In the early days of the Sunday School, class rollbooks looked like this. The average size of a Sunday School class was approximately 50 students then. (Museum of Sunday School Heritage, Savannah, GA)

Absentees

1. *Records reveal degree.* A teacher may recall that she has not seen Jimmy in class for a week or two. Careful records will show the actual extent of Jimmy's absence. It may be several weeks, and this absence may call for a visit from the teacher.

2. *Records reveal need.* A pupil's absence several Sundays in a row may indicate there is need to be dealt with. The need may intensify with neglect. If the need is not known, the teacher should discover why absence is frequent. Even though some kind of explanation may be received from class members, the records are sufficient reason for a home visit. The real need may be entirely different from the reported one. (A teacher may learn that Jimmy has moved away, is seriously ill, or even dead.)

3. *Records reveal opportunity.* While faithful pupils often are neglected as far as home visits are concerned, the record of absence provides a teacher with sufficient reason to make the home visits. Without them, teaching cannot be effective.

Kinds of Records

Individual records. The pupil's permanent record should be detailed enough to give an accurate picture of him. Include his name, birthday, address, phone, whether or not he's a Christian, grade, church membership, parent's names and their church relation, occupation, type of home, and last Sunday School attended. Current records will show his punctuality, performance regarding lesson preparation, offering, church attendance, use of Bible, and regularity of attendance.

Records Kept by the Sunday School

1. *Class records.* Enrollment, attendance, information from the six point system (if used), offerings.

2. *Departmental records.* Enrollment, attendance, offering, new members, promotion-day records.

3. *Records for the whole school.* Enrollment, attendance, offering, new members, visitors, number joining the church through the Sunday School.

4. *Staff records.* Qualifications (education and experience); performance (punctuality, visitation, self-improvement).

5. *Prospective teachers.*

6. *Information from surveys.* Information regarding prospective workers, community surveys.

7. *Financial records.* Amounts received, expenditures (gifts and supplies).

8. *Prospect records.* Names of potential Sunday School pupils can be received from community census, pastor, other workers, pupils.

9. *Absentee records.*

10. *Visitors.* Information given to teachers, department secretary and school officers.

11. *Visual records.* These are graphs on attendance, etc.

The success of the record system depends directly on how well the teachers and department workers do their job.

Staff for Keeping Records

1. *General Sunday School secretary.* He or she will compile statistics, keep the record system, train department secretaries, order literature, make periodic progress summaries, supervise record collection and keep records for promotion day.

2. *Registrar.* Records information on individual pupils, keeps enrollment cards and file current, keeps list of teachers, follows up absentees, records and averages monthly grades (6 point system), issues promotion certificates and diplomas, keeps materials and supplies on hand, assists general secretary, makes out permanent record cards, plans Promotion Day program, and cooperates in extension program.

3. *Other possible positions.* (1) Enrollment secretary to enroll new members and keep the list up-to-date; (2) absentee secretary to record and contact absentees; (3) prospect secretary to list prospects and contacts; (4) recording secretary to keep minutes of teachers meetings, etc.; (5) corresponding secretary to keep in touch with outside agencies; and (6) class secretary.

Sunday School record systems have come a long way. Some modern systems contain a master record book, prospect cards, absentee slips, report cards, and other items. (Scripture Press)

16

The key to unlocking the puzzle of how to set up your church library is Rudyard Kipling's "serving men": What, Who, Where, When, How, Why.

The Church Library and the Sunday School

The church library is believed by many to be the storage place for storybooks for boys and girls who have time for reading. The church library is actually one of the most valuable educational resources in the church.

Although the library may be a puzzle to those unacquainted with its treasure, it may be explored with the aid of Rudyard Kipling's "serving men": What, Who, Where, When, How, and Why.

What's in the Library?

1. *Books.* Variety if the key word in selecting books for any library. The reading preferences of Christians vary as much as their tastes in food or clothing.

First, there's fiction. Since Sunday School pupils of all ages can go to the public library and find all manner of fiction books, the church library would do well to major on fiction with a distinctly Christian message. More than one life has been changed and strengthened through the influence of a good book. If in doubt about selections, check the catalogs of Christian publishing houses for titles.

In the nonfiction field, the church should seek out biographies of persons who are recognized for their Christian testimony. Boys and girls of Junior age often prefer biography to fiction and, through it, young people and adults can become acquainted with faithful, outstanding Christians. "Book friends" wield an influence

akin to that of human friends, for they represent the thinking of persons.

In how-to books, pupils of all ages can learn various crafts and perfect their hobbies. This may be the chief reason for a library visit at first. Looking for self-help books, patrons may be attracted to Christian adventure stories or biographies.

Many Christians cannot afford to buy expensive books, but would like to study the Bible in depth. The church library should aid them by having available Bible dictionaries, handbooks, atlases, commentary sets, books for self-study, and books of Bible background. Christian publishers' catalogs list such books.

A Sunday School member should be able to go to the library and select any book there without feeling unsure as to whether the book is reliable and Biblical.

2. *Periodicals.* Magazines of family help as well as Christian magazines for various age levels should be available. Again, people can find secular magazines in the public library. The church can make a greater life investment by assisting people as they become acquainted with the best in Christian literature. Fiction, Bible study, Christian education, and other features are found in *Christian Life, Moody Monthly, Christianity Today, Eternity,* the *Edge, Key to Christian Education,* the *Leader,* and other magazines. (The reference department of a city library should provide ad-

The church library should include children's Bibles in its collection. This six-volume Picture Bible *for* All Ages *appeals greatly to children. (David C. Cook)*

dresses. They have a book in which this information is listed.)

3. *Reference File.* The church librarian should file clippings, stories, articles and poetry by subject. This will aid teachers who seek supplementary material for lessons. Some churches file pictures and maps.

4. *Slides, filmstrips, transparencies.* If the church purchases slides or filmstrips for use in a given class (or department), the visual aids should be placed in the library after use. This allows other teachers to use materials which are too costly for each class to purchase and use only on rare occasions.

Who Uses the Library?

1. *Teachers.* "There is no leading without reading." It is impossible for a stagnant pool to give forth fresh water. A teacher can find enrichment and be revitalized by seeking out study or devotional books in the library. The alphabetical clipping file will aid in lesson preparations, as will the file of slides and filmstrips and other materials.

2. *Officers.* The library should have books and periodicals which will help each Sunday School worker do his best work.

3. *Adults.* Avid readers will explore many types of books. The less eager but willing should be able to find a variety from which to choose. The librarian should have a working knowledge of the shelves and be able to guide persons who come. Many do not know how to use a catalogued library and need help.

4. *Youth.* A well-organized library will have a designated section containing books especially geared for teens. If this is impossible, they may need help finding titles most interesting to and profitable for them.

5. *Juniors.* Often the most prolific readers are in this department. A bright-jacketed book of any level may appeal to them—but they can be guided to the best available at their level of understanding. If the library is attractively arranged with some age-level displays, children will easily find their favorites.

6. *New readers.* Happy is the church family which can find books for their youngest readers. Books with large print and graded vocabulary are carefully maintained in the public school and public library. Church libraries also should stock books for young readers.

7. *Preschoolers.* Visiting the library should be a family affair. Pupils in the youngest classes should be able to find picture books which will increase their Bible knowledge and appreciation for God's knowledge in making His beautiful world. Pictures stimulate thought, leading to questions for which parents can provide Christian answers. Because books of Bible and character stories, to be read aloud by parents, are not found in every home, the Sunday School library should provide them.

Where Is the Library?

This question should not have to be asked —except in large churches where a guided tour is necessary to find any particular section of the church. In average churches, a library display in the foyer should give easy directions for locating the library.

Every teacher and officer in the church should know where the library is in order to direct pupils and newcomers. If the library seems unknown to the majority of the membership, a quarterly (or annual) Library Day might remedy the situation. During the evening service, allow a five-minute announcement of available services. The librarian should mention exciting new books available and call attention to a few old favorites. At the close of the service, he may encourage an open-house visit.

The library goes to Sunday School in some churches. Rolling shelves take appropriate books to each class during the first ten minutes of the session, allowing pupils to return borrowed books and check out new ones. This practice keeps the library's riches in the minds of all. Some who would forget to stop in for a book will borrow one brought to class. Additionally, some church libraries take books to the homes of shut-ins, allowing them to have the pleasure of choosing their favorite reading.

When Should the Library Be Open?

Before or after the regular services, pupils usually find it most convenient to return and borrow books. Some churches, where a staff is present daily, open the library at specified times every day. The schedule should be set by the staff.

How Can a Library Be Started?

1. *Church Budget.* A sum may be allocated annually for the purchase of books and library supplies.

2. *Donations.* Christian families who have outgrown or completed reading some of their books may give them to the library.

3. *Memorial Gifts.* An increasing number of Christian families are specifying memorial gifts of books instead of flowers at their decease.

4. *Special offerings.* In connection with Library Day, the church may receive a special offering for new books and periodicals.

Why a Church Library?

Doesn't the church have enough expense without stocking a library? Can't people go to the public library and find something to read? These questions are answered in the foregoing sections of this chapter. The public library may or may not have suitable books for the Christian family. What they have in their section on "Religion" may or may not be Biblical. Each church therefore is responsible for helping its own people grow and mature in their faith by providing a balanced, nourishing spiritual diet. Reading material is to the mind and heart what food is to the body. Just as the body is weak or strong, depending on the person's diet, so the spiritual life may be weakened or strengthened by the mental diet. The church library can and should be an important source of that strength.

How many more young readers could your church library attract if it added special facilities for them? (Bryce Finch/Baptist Sunday School Board)

section III

Facilities for Learning

17

It is important that, as we think of "equipment" for Christian education, we think of the building in which the work is to be done.

Buildings and Equipment

Christian Education Equipment

The Psalmist wrote, "I was glad when they said unto me, Let us go into the house of the Lord" (Psalm 122:1). Besides the inner strength he received from going, there also must have been something in the appearance of the Temple that made him glad for the opportunity to worship the Lord. It must have been attractive, appealing and inviting.

For years, Christian education's effectiveness was hindered because of limited facilities and equipment. Now we realize that the building sets the pattern for the type and quality of Christian education. It is important that, as we think of "equipment" for Christian education, we think of the building in which the work is to be done.

1. *The Equipped Church Building.* A church must begin its teaching ministry in the existing building, even though facilities may be limited. However, rooms can be clean, neat and attractive. A well-kept building says to outsiders, "This church has vision and is interested in progress." The building indicates that those who attend have spiritual values because they care for the place where they worship God. The world may not know much of the Bible's teaching, but they're acquainted with the axiom, "Cleanliness is next to godliness." A nicely painted building, with shrubs trimmed, grass mowed, and signs properly marked, is a silent sermon. A building with such "appeal" says to some, "Enter in."

The church needs a committee to see that its equipment is kept in good repair. This committee also should see that equipment and facilities are adequate for the growing educational ministry. This indicates vision.

If possible, the pastor's study should be at the church. In addition to the church name sign and schedule of services, there also should be a sign indicating where the pastor's office is located, so visitors, business people, church members and people with problems can locate it.

The pastor's study should have the equipment necessary to carry on the pastor's work. It should be attractive, well-lighted, ventilated, painted, with desks, chairs, filing cabinets, and seating for visitors.

When the church can have a separate church office, this should accommodate visitors so the pastor can have more privacy in his study. This office (with its telephone, desk, chairs, typewriter, and other necessary furniture) may be used for the duplicating work of the church, such as church bulletins.

If the church is large enough to have a Director of Christian Education, a minister of youth, or an associate minister, he should have his own office. It should be equipped with the necessary items to carry on this ministry and perhaps large enough for chairs and a table for conferences with teachers and officers of the church.

The Christian education building should

Pastor Carl Baugh explains the model of the new Calvary Heights Baptist Temple in St. Louis. (Calvary Heights Baptist Temple)

have rooms for the various departments in the Sunday School. These departmental rooms should be accessible for the age groups meeting in them, and well-marked so visitors can be directed or taken to them easily.

In examining the building and equipment, many miscellaneous items should be checked also: coat-racks of various heights, toilet facilities and drinking fountains, chorus and hymn books, pianos, chalkboards and chalk, pulpits, flannelboards, tackboards and other equipment.

While equipment alone is not the answer, it helps produce answers.

2. *The Equipped Administrative Area.* In an effective Christian education ministry the heart and most active area will be the Christian education office and the Christian education director's office.

The church having a Director of Christian Education should provide him with the necessary equipment for his office. The office should be accessible to those who need to visit with him for the work, and should be equipped with a good desk, chairs, adequate lighting, the necessary filing cabinets, and, if there is room, a table for working over plans with leaders in the department as well as for conducting conferences.

If there is only the office for Christian education or the Sunday School—with no particular office for the director—this office should be equipped with the records, the filing cabinet and the other materials necessary for the work. In this office it would be well to store the projectors, screens, tape recorders, record players, and other audiovisual equipment. This office is important and, like the other offices, should be properly marked so people will know where it is. It also should be rather central in its location so the reports on Sunday can be brought there for the tabulating of attendance, etc.

The administration area will be worthy of adequate furnishings: work area, desks, filing cabinet facilities, duplicating facilities and storage. The continued planning for an extended outreach in ministry, as well as the record keeping, is done from the administrative area of the Christian education department. There should be the necessary equipment for this in the well-planned church program.

Building for Team Teaching

Far too often, churches are content to let Christian education people struggle with all but impossible handicaps. If leaders are to cope with changing situations, they must have sound curriculum content, and good teaching facilities and equipment. We need to do some penance for the lack of encouragement given those willing to teach, but whom we needlessly handicap by not providing the tools. The improvement of the educational programs of churches rests upon the parents and the church leaders charged with local church administration.

For those concerned with the educational programs, there should be an immediate evaluation of buildings, equipment, teachers, and the newer methods of teaching suggested by contemporary leaders in the field of religious education. These newer methods envision teachers functioning cooperatively as a team under the direction of an experienced master.

This calls for classrooms considerably larger than those to which many have been accustomed. The number of pupils in each room is considerably greater than that which assembled in the 10- by 12-foot class space. The number of pupils and the size of the classroom should not be determined by an architect, the building committee, or the building budget, but should be designed by those involved in teaching. It should provide the best possible learning situation for the age group involved. The younger the pupils, the more floor space needed to avoid crowding and overstimulation and permit room for activities. The younger the pupils, the fewer to a given classroom, so they may have personal attention and guidance.

The concept of team teaching, unfamiliar to many, often is rejected by Christian education committees which do not understand its purpose or do not visit churches using this method successfully.

This method was evaluated through experiments in our Vacation Bible School years ago. With a good lead teacher and three or four less-experienced persons assisting, there were better results than when pupils went into small classes.

Why not use your vacation school to test group learning? Use two or three trained teachers in each of the various age groups of VBS. Put with them persons with aptitudes for guiding young children.

Such learning procedures do not call for a frightening or drastic revolution in teaching methods. The basic premise is that teachers work cooperatively on a planned program within a given room with a larger number of pupils. Those who have successfully used this method find that the larger room and team of teachers make possible a greater variety of teaching experiences, and that learning can take place in such an environment much more effectively than in a small, crowded room.

This group learning is not restricted to "sitting and telling" but also includes creative, purposeful activities of considerable variety. In all of this, the children learn how to adjust to and appreciate others who come from different backgrounds and who have different tastes and personalities.

During the last 10 or 15 years, there has been a commendable increase in the size of classrooms. However, most rooms still lack inspiration and stimulation. They are devoid of those qualities which evoke a sense of pleasure

During the last 10 or 15 years Sunday School classrooms have been increasing in size, comfort, and versatility. Many offer a colorful decor. (Bible Baptist Church, Savannah, GA)

in their appearance, such as nice furnishings, a good arrangement, lovely colors, etc.

Too many church classrooms offer little beyond four walls and rows of chairs. They are stark, unadorned and "faceless." This need not and should not be. Walls can be made sources of inspiration and can aid in teaching. Make inexpensive display areas of perforated panels with pins or wire brackets for hanging items of interest. Mount pictures with Plasti-tak.

Why should the classroom look the same every Sunday morning? Why not occasionally change the decor, rearrange the furniture, and/or introduce different learning procedures? You cannot find an easy way to good teaching, but you can make it more effective by adding variety, beauty, inspiration and elements of surprise.

"Navy has a saying, 'If it doesn't move, paint it,' " one architect said. School executives now are saying, "If it doesn't move, we don't want it." Generally speaking, this applies to churchschool classrooms, also. Not only are classrooms with large floor areas pleasing and inspiring, but they permit flexibility in teaching methods and the furnishings and equipment can be adjusted to implement those teaching methods.

WHAT TO DO WHEN YOU RUN OUT OF SPACE

Additional space is a crucial factor in Sunday School expansion. Attendance in many growing Sunday Schools has leveled off because the building was inadequate. When there is not additional room for new classes, growth usually stops.

The Bible does not give a blueprint for local churches nor does it contain an organizational chart on how to arrange people in groups.

However, the Bible does tell Christians to gather as a congregation (Hebrews 10:25); to teach (Matthew 28:20); and to preach (II Timothy 4:2). These functions can be carried out only as people congregate. This usually has to be in a specially designed building since most homes are too small. But what happens when the church building is too small? The Gospel is preached, people commit their lives to Jesus and want to join the congregation, but there is no room for expansion.

There are many ways to solve this problem. For example, the United Baptist Church, San Jose, Calif., which increased from 20 to 1,300 in the last six years, rebuilt an old two-story home

To build or not to build, that is the question. This church decided to launch out. (Immanuel Baptist Church, Kenosha, WI)

for the Kindergarten Department. Then they successfully bid on a condemned eight-room modern school building that had to be moved because of a new expressway. Today a number of classes meet on Sunday School buses. According to Pastor Larry Chappell, "We're good at packing."

Here are other solutions to the space problem.

The Master Teacher Plan Allows Expansion

Dr. Jack Hudson began the Northside Baptist Church, Charlotte, N.C., 18 years ago in a small tarpaper-covered building which seated less than 50. Originally, he built small 10-ft. by 10-ft. Sunday School rooms, as he had seen in well-established Southern Baptist churches. To date, the church has built seven times. Each time the Sunday School rooms were made larger. Now Hudson is building a new campus on 156 acres on Interstate 85. All the rooms will be public-school size. The Northside Christian School uses the facilities during the week.

Several years ago, Hudson faced another space problem. The church had a number of small adult classes, but the auditorium was almost empty during Sunday School. He got the adults together.

"The seat you take in Sunday School could hold a child next week," he challenged them.

Hudson then asked the adults to vote to combine all adult classes into an auditorium Bible Class to give space for more children. The vote was unanimous.

Hudson slowly has shifted to the master teacher instructional plan for other classes as well. Two or more teachers now are in one room with 40 or more pupils. According to Hudson, the large open classrooms give expandability and flexibility. When a church grows rapidly, there are not enough teachers for each small classroom; also, the small rooms are expensive to build and maintain, he says.

Second Sunday Schools

The Emmanuel Baptist Church, Marion, Ind., called the Rev. Charles Hand to be pastor when they were averaging less than 300 in Sunday School. Hand had been bus pastor for Dr. Jack Hyles, First Baptist Church, Hammond, Ind., and knew he could build a large Sunday School, but he estimated it would be two years before he ran into space problems at the Marion church. Within six months, however, the Sunday School had doubled.

"We had space for 600, but that's packed out, with chairs to the wall and no room for people to stand," Hand says. He wanted to expand, but was not willing to sacrifice the small Sunday School classes.

"I believe the quality of teaching goes down in large classes; also one teacher can follow up only a certain number of pupils," he says. So expansion plans had to include a number of teachers and a number of small rooms.

Hand went to "two Sunday Schools" with the following schedule:

9:30 - First shift of Sunday School buses arrive.

9:40-10:40 - First regular Sunday School, all ages.

10:40 - Second shift of buses come in and children go to Junior Church.

Churches find varied and ingenius ways to accommodate extra pupils. This tent, erected for the Junior Sunday School classes by the First Freewill Baptist Church, solves the problem temporarily. (First Freewill Baptist Church, Newport News, VA)

10:45	- Church service, all children in age-graded Junior Church.
12:00	- The morning service is over.
12:00-12:45	- Second Sunday School, all ages.

Before the program was begun, Hand talked to the Sunday School teachers and asked which ones would be willing to teach twice. The teachers would not miss the morning service, but would teach before and after.

Next, Hand decided how many pupils he wanted in each Sunday School and divided the buses so there would be an even distribution.

"I didn't want only the poor in my second Sunday School, so we tried to divide the buses economically and socially," he says. "I wanted the middle-class visitor to be able to attend the second Sunday School and not be embarrassed."

Third, Hand wanted only one morning service. "Two preaching services tend to divide a church," he says.

At present, 85 percent of Hand's Sunday School teachers work in both Sunday Schools, but he is aiming for a different staff for each Sunday School. When he began the second Sunday School in November 1971, he had approximately 300 in the second Sunday School and 400 in the first. He reached 913 on the high attendance day the following spring.

Hand admits that for the first six months his second Sunday School did not cause growth.

"If a football team went from a single wing to a split-T, it would take time for the players to adjust," he explains. "The second Sunday School was an innovation. We were bucking the trend, for most people expect Sunday School before preaching." Now, Hand says, people are more willing to work and attend because he has broken down the "traditionalism" of the average Sunday School. The Sunday School averaged more than 800 in the spring of 1972. Last year, the church was tenth in the nation in baptisms (baptized 767), according to a survey published in *The Sword of the Lord*.

The Unified Service

The Ypsilanti (Mich.) Baptist Church averaged 250 in Sunday School during 1960 and was heading toward 1,000; yet space was a factor. The dynamic soul-winning pastor, James Phillips, and a corps of dedicated workers predicted growth success because of the effective evangelistic outreach. Phillips, however, was unwilling to enter a building campaign. The church did not have the money and he did not have the faith to launch out, he says. Then a fire gutted the sanctuary, forcing the small congregation into the basement. Immediately they went into a half-million-dollar expansion for a new auditorium and Sunday School classrooms.

Phillips began preparing the people for radical changes in the Sunday School. The unified service was inaugurated, with Sunday School beginning at 10:00 o'clock, ending at 11:30. The Sunday School and morning services were joined. Attendance jumped 300 to average over 500 in 1971, and jumped 500 in 1972, with an average approaching 1,000. All the Sunday School rooms for adults, college-age students, high schoolers, and junior highs were taken over by the children's division.

Expansion was hectic. Where were these classes to go? There were no buildings in the neighborhood to rent. And the church did not want to go any further into debt. It had just finished a bond program and had secured a loan of $180,000 from the local bank.

To solve the problem, junior high students through adults were placed in the church auditorium, where the pastor taught a 45-minute lesson in addition to announcements, singing, special music, etc.

"It was not best, but the best we could do," Phillips says. Each class, from Junior High through Adults, sits in a designated section of the auditorium. There the teacher is charged with the responsibility of follow-up.

Phillips recognizes that the change allowed him to grow, but admits that attendance has leveled off.

"Our unified Sunday School is working temporarily, but we are not growing in our teenage department, because we can't meet the needs of both teens and adults in the same service," he says. (He teaches the Scriptures verse by verse and appreciates having the teens under his ministry, however.)

Ypsilanti Baptist Church has planned two expansions. Immediately, they are building a two-story, 10,000-square-foot educational wing to take care of current growth. This will also house the Ypsilanti Baptist High School. Within four years, they plan to move several miles away to a 100-acre campus that will accommodate a high school, college, retirement center, and orphanage.

The Indianapolis Baptist Temple also has gone to a unified service. Dr. Greg Dixon, pastor, explains that the average Sunday School has built three spaces for the average pupil. This is uneconomical and impractical, he says. First, space is provided for opening exercises; second, space is provided in the Sunday School class; and third, space is provided in the auditorium for the morning service.

When Dixon dropped the traditional Sunday School organization for the unified service, his Sunday School had 50 percent more space. The following year, attendance jumped from 1,963 to 2,553. Adults are in the auditorium from 10:00 to 11:30 a.m. Also, the children have only one space provided for them on Sunday morning. However, although Children's Church and Sunday School are combined into one service, the functions of teaching and worship are kept separate.

Not only has Dixon eliminated his space problem, but also the duplication of functions

137

such as announcements, singing, worship, and opening prayers; these are done once instead of twice.

Using Old Facilities

Dr. John Rawlings, pastor, Landmark Baptist Temple, Cincinnati, also faced the problem of no room for expansion. He had grown in a few years from 3,540 to 4,715. Heavy mortgages and limited funds kept him from building. Four years before, the church had moved from the Lockland section of Cincinnati to a new 150 acre campus with manicured lawns, woods, lakes, picnic areas and riding fields.

Attendance leveled off at 5,000. However, back in Lockland (a decaying section of the city) stood the old church facilities that had not been sold. Since the church had averaged 2,600 in the old facilities, Rawlings reopened the building for Sunday School and now averages more than 1,000 in attendance there.

Rawlings decided how many Sunday School buses could be routed to the old location and asked that some drivers volunteer to carry their children to that section of the city. He did not want a segregated service of only the poor, but representatives of every segment of society. The Rev. Don Norman now teaches adults at the old Lockland location where he is Sunday School superintendent. The Sunday School has classes for every age level.

According to Rawlings, there is no secret as to what made the Lockland services grow. "We just did there what we are doing at the main location," he says.

Why More Space?

Lack of Sunday School space halts attendance growth for many reasons.

First, you cannot organize new classes for growth if there is no place to put them. Just as a farmer needs additional acreage to harvest a larger crop, so a Sunday School needs more classrooms to expand its ministry.

Second, attendance levels off then begins to decline when too many children are crammed into a classroom. Packed classrooms hinder efficient teaching, and when pupils are "overlooked by the teacher," they become potential dropouts. The farmer knows that planting corn too close together will ruin the crop. In a similar way, an "overcrowded classroom" ultimately stymies growth.

Third, lack of teaching facilities thwarts teacher initiative. When a Sunday School teacher's classroom is overcrowded, he has little incentive to get more pupils, even when exhorted by the superintendent to "go out and

Rooms should be well-lighted, designed to meet pupils' needs, and large enough for activity-centered learning experiences. (Scripture Press)

reach the lost." He realizes it is futile to visit when there is no space for new pupils.

Experts are not agreed on the amount of space needed for Sunday School pupils. A few years ago, Southern Baptist authorities recommended ten square feet per pupil, or small cubicles 10-ft. by 10-ft. (100 square feet) for small classes of ten pupils each. Slightly larger than a walk-in closet, these small classes have been the pattern for many Sunday School buildings throughout the United States.

Today, denominational experts recommend 25 to 35 square feet per pupil.

Rooms should be large enough for activity-centered learning experiences, they say. Classrooms should look like those in public schools. They should be large, light, and geared to meet pupil needs.

Neither theology nor geography seem to affect Sunday School buildings, however. Mainline denominational churches, as well as right-wing fundamentalist churches, have built Sunday School rooms that are well lighted, beautifully decorated, and filled with molded furniture graded to the size of the child. Others still meet in dungeon-like basement rooms where children sit in a circle with Bibles on their laps and listen to the teacher repeat the lesson.

Sometimes lack of space is not the cause of lagging attendance. Instead it is the result of a spiritual problem in the church. The leadership may not have enough faith to organize a campaign to get money to expand. Or the leadership may have a subconscious goal of 100 or 400 in Sunday School. Without ever verbalizing a cut-off level, they may curtail efforts when attendance reaches the desired goal. Then visitation loses its zeal and deterioration sets in.

Buildings cost money and, on occasion, leaders have drawn back in unbelief from progress. They look at the bank balance and decide they can't build. However, a church must look to the command of God to reach the lost (Matthew 28:19), then claim the promise of God (John 14:14), and reach out in evangelism. When lost people are won to Christ and taught to tithe, they will help pay off the mortgage. Leaders must not only trust God for finances but trust God for evangelistic results.

Churches have been constructing buildings since the third century. Some are multi-million-dollar temples for worship; some are crude buildings for preaching. Some were designed by architects as massive monuments to their memory. We should question massive church buildings which are not practical. Sunday School buildings should provide expansion for evangelism and space to teach the Word of God. When a building allows people to carry out the purpose of God, it will have the blessing of God.

18

A good environment for learning is vital to the success of any department. While good work can be done in a room that is less than ideal, a church should strive for the best.

Standards for Equipment

When one looks at Sunday School equipment and buildings, he sees every conceivable type of facilities being used by God. Some Sunday Schools have streamlined buildings of steel, brick, and glass; constructed on a well-landscaped lot. These Sunday Schools are as up-to-date as any public school. On the other end of the spectrum, some Sunday Schools meet in delapidated buildings constructed over one hundred years ago. Children are packed into basements, hallways, and some classes even meet in Sunday School buses. Some Sunday Schools have modern molded plastic chairs in bright colors. Others still use the slat-back folding chairs where children's feet never touch the floor. Some Sunday School rooms have wall-to-wall carpet and indirect lighting. Others have concrete floors. Naked light bulbs hang from the ceilings.

Obviously, the Spirit of God can illuminate the student's heart through the Word of God in any situation. Mark Hopkins said, "Education is the teacher facing the pupil on a log." He was emphasizing the educational relationship between teacher and pupil. But notice there was a log. So there must be a classroom in which learning takes place.

Four principles should be remembered. The first is that Sunday Schools can be effective with any building or equipment. Jesus taught in a boat, on the mountain top, and on the highway. The second principle is that modern facilities and equipment will not guarantee good education. Many Sunday Schools prospered in old facilities yet began to decay when they moved into new buildings. However, it was not the buildings that caused the decay. Beware of claiming, like medieval monks, that comfortable surroundings destroy one's godliness. The third principle is that good facilities will enhance teaching. As a matter of fact, good facilities will become an assistant teacher. The final principle is we should be thankful for the facilities we have, whether they resemble the little red school house out on the prairie or the basement of an inner-city church.

But at the same time, every Sunday School should attempt to upgrade its buildings. We should constantly paint, put down carpeting, or decorate walls to make teaching more effective. Our children live in air-conditioned homes and attend modern public schools with all of their conveniences. The Sunday School should not lag behind. An old building says to the child, "God is out-of-date." A new building will tell the pupil, "Come in and learn."

Buildings and equipment are more than teachers—they advertise our purpose to the world. Outsiders form opinions of the quality of our Sunday Schools by the appearance of our buildings.

We never get a second opportunity to make a good first impression. Therefore, we need the finest possible buildings, equipped with the best possible furniture, to give an opportunity for the best possible teaching. Our aim is to produce the greatest change in the pupils' lives, conformity to the image of Christ.

GENERAL EQUIPMENT STANDARDS *

Department	Chair Height	Chair Rail—floor to top of rail	Table Size*	Storage	Chalkboards in Assembly Rooms	Chalkboards in Classrooms—Height above floor	Tackboards—Height above floor	Piano	Picture Molding (concealed) Height above floor	Picture Rail—Height above floor	Coat Racks—Refer to specific department section
Nursery	10"	—	24"x36"	Cabinets above heads of children	No	—	—	—	—	—	Movable
Beginner	10"–12"	20"	24"x36" and 30"x48"	Cabinets above heads of children	No	—	1'-8" to 2'-0"	Studio	—	2'-0" to 2'-3"	Movable
Primary	12"–14"	24"	38"x48" or 36"x54"	Cabinets above heads of children	Portable	—	2'4"	Studio	7'-0"	2'4" to 2'-8"	Movable
Junior	15"–17"	28"	Trapezoid	Closets or cabinets	Portable	2'-8"	2'-8"	Studio	7'-0"	2'-8"	In assembly
Junior High	16"–18"	32"		Closets or cabinets	Portable	3'-0" to 3'-2"	3'-0"	Studio	7'-0"	No	In assembly
Senior High	18"	32"		Closets	Portable	3'-4"	3'-4"	Regular	7'0"	No	
Adult	18"	32"		Closets	Portable	3'-6"	3'-4"	Regular	7'0"	No	In classroom

*Height of tables should be ten inches above chair height
Coat racks for workers should be at same height as for Adults

141

Every Nursery Department should have a supply of suitable toys. (Scripture Press)

Nursery Department chairs should be about 10 inches high. (Scripture Press)

NURSERY DEPARTMENT STANDARDS

	Babies	Toddlers	Two-Year-Olds	Three-Year-Olds
Baby's Schedule (card)	x			
Babee-Tenda Safety Chair	x	x		
Ball (7" or 9" diameter)	x	x	*	*
Beds (hospital cribs, 27"x42")	x			
Bible (No. 1450 BP)	x	x	x	x
Blockbusters (set of 12)		x	x	*
Blocks			*	x
Blocks (large, wooden, hollow)			*	*
Block accessories			x	x
Books (as recommended)	x	x	x	x
Bookrack (28" long and 27" high)		x	x	x
Cabinet for supplies (on wall, 50" from floor)	x	x	x	x
Chairs (seat 10" from floor)			x	x
Changing diapers, provision for	in bed	x		
Diaper-bag holders (pigeonholes on wall)	x	x		
Dishes (soft plastic)		*	x	x
Doll (rubber, molded head)	x	x	x	x
Doll bed (16" x 28", 16" high)		x	x	x
Easel (for painting)			*	x
Finger paints			*	x
First-aid kit	*	x	x	x
Modeling dough (water clay or homemade dough)			x	x
Nature materials	x	x	x	x
Newsprint paper			*	x
Open shelves (2 sets, 12" deep, 30" long, 26" high; movable, closed back)		x	x	x
Paints and brushes			*	x
Pictures (selected and mounted)	x	x	x	x
Playpen	x	*		
Pull toys		x		
Puzzle rack			x	x
Puzzles (wooden)			x	x
Record albums (Broadman)	x	x	x	x
Record player	x	x	x	x
Resting cots or mats (for extended session)		x		
Rocker (adult)	x			
Rocker (child)		x	x	x
Rocking boat and steps combination		x		
Smocks or uniforms for workers (pastels)	x	*		
Sterilizing solution (Zephiran chloride concentrate, or others)	x	x		
Stove (24" high)			x	x
Sink-refrigerator combination (28"x30", 40" high)	Convenient to all Nursery rooms			
Swing (Cosco)	x			
Table (utility, Cosco)	x			
Table (24"x36", 20" high; usually two)			x	x
Thermometer (room)	x	x	x	x
Toilet (flush bowl or other)	x			
Toilet (juvenile fixtures)		x	x	x
Transportation toys (interlocking trains, boats, cars, trucks)		x	x	x
Wastepaper basket (plastic)	x	x	x	x

*OPTIONAL

SUGGESTED NURSERY ROOM DIAGRAM

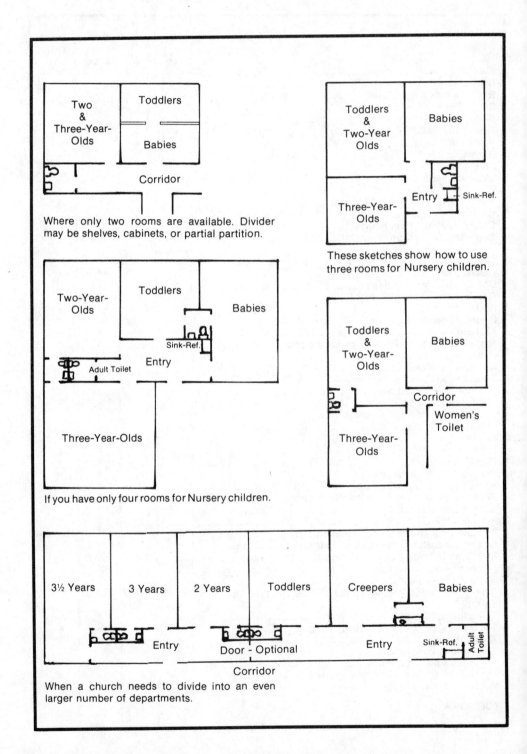

Two & Three-Year-Olds

Toddlers

Babies

Corridor

Where only two rooms are available. Divider may be shelves, cabinets, or partial partition.

Toddlers & Two-Year Olds

Babies

Three-Year-Olds

Entry — Sink-Ref.

These sketches show how to use three rooms for Nursery children.

Two-Year-Olds

Toddlers

Babies

Sink-Ref.

Adult Toilet

Entry

Three-Year-Olds

If you have only four rooms for Nursery children.

Toddlers & Two-Year Olds

Babies

Corridor

Women's Toilet

Three-Year-Olds

3½ Years | 3 Years | 2 Years | Toddlers | Creepers | Babies

Entry

Door - Optional

Entry

Sink-Ref.

Adult Toilet

Corridor

When a church needs to divide into an even larger number of departments.

BEGINNER DEPARTMENT STANDARDS FOR EQUIPMENT

Ample floor space for Beginner children is needed. From 16 square feet to 25 square feet or more is suggested for each child. It is desirable to provide 25 square feet or more per child.

Rooms to accommodate an attendance of up to 25 children in each department are suggested. More than 25 children enrolled would indicate the need for two or more Beginner rooms. A restroom should be accessible, preferably adjoining the room. If there are as many as two Beginner departments, they may be connected by a restroom.

Try to have:

1. Department room off main corridor, entrance at rear of room
2. Located above ground
3. Movable racks for hanging children's wraps and workers' wraps
4. Ample low windows (22″ to 24″ from floor)
5. Floor covering—asphalt tile, rubber tile, or vinyl tile
6. Walls—soundproof, plastered, soft color; acoustical ceiling
7. Picture rail, tackboard(s)
8. Suitable furniture for workers and children
9. Cabinets for storage of:
    Children's books
    Department Bible
    Dolls
    Nature materials such as birds' nests, cotton bolls, seed, flower containers
    Puzzles
    Scissors, crayons, paste, paint, paint brushes, modeling clay
    Smocks for painting
    Drawing paper, construction paper, newsprint paper
    Block accessories
    Record materials
    Record player, recordings
    Musical instruments
    Printed curriculum materials for Sunday School, Beginner music activity, band, kindergarten, etc.

This Beginner plays with the department doll before class starts. (Scripture Press)

A ROOM ARRANGEMENT FOR 4's OR 5's

This room is designed to accommodate 25 children and 5 workers. It will accommodate 20 children for weekday kindergarten.

1. Overhead Storage Cabinet
2. Table for Reports
3. Rack For Children's Wraps
4. Table For Puzzles
5. Table For Art Activities
6. Art Shelves
7. Puzzle Rack on Shelf
8. Table For The "Home"
9. Stove
10. Cabinet-Sink
11. Chest of Drawers
12. Doll Bed
13. Rocking Chair
14. Nature Shelves
15. Bookrack
16. Piano
17. Picture Rail
18. Table-Cabinet and Record Player
19. Block Shelves
20. Tackboard
21. Painting Easel
22. Drying Rack
23. Rack for Adult Wraps
24. Bathroom (connecting another room)

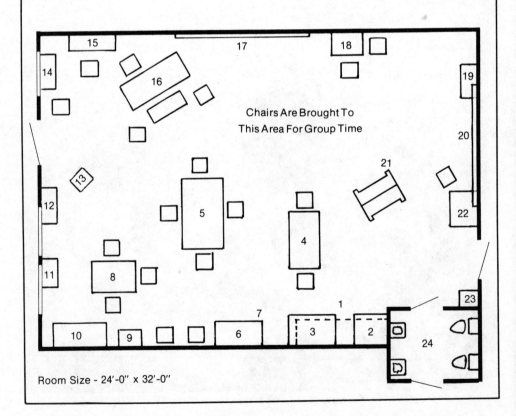

Chairs Are Brought To
This Area For Group Time

Room Size - 24'-0" x 32'-0"

PRIMARY DEPARTMENT
STANDARDS FOR EQUIPMENT

A good environment for learning is vital to the success of a Primary department. Good work can be done in a room that is less than ideal, but a church should strive for the best in space and equipment for its children. A Primary room should be equipped by the church for all the organizations—Sunday School, band and choir.

The following are some recommendations for a good Primary room:

1. Located above ground
2. Planned for 30 to 40 children to be enrolled in the department
3. An open room providing 25 square feet or more per person; 16 square feet to 20 square feet is recommended minimum
4. Ample low windows with clear glass and good screens
5. Asphalt tile, vinyl tile, or rubber tile floor covering
6. Walls that are soundproof, plastered, and painted a soft color
7. Acoustical tile or acoustical plaster ceiling
8. Tackboard (preferably cork) 24 to 30 inches wide, beginning 30 inches from the floor, and as long as space permits; on one or more sides of the room
9. A picture rail 30 inches from the floor, at least 12 feet long, at the front of the room
10. Ample cabinet space—at least 3 separate cabinets, preferably wall hung, 18 inches deep, with locks
11. Rest rooms nearby; a sink in room desirable (29" above floor)

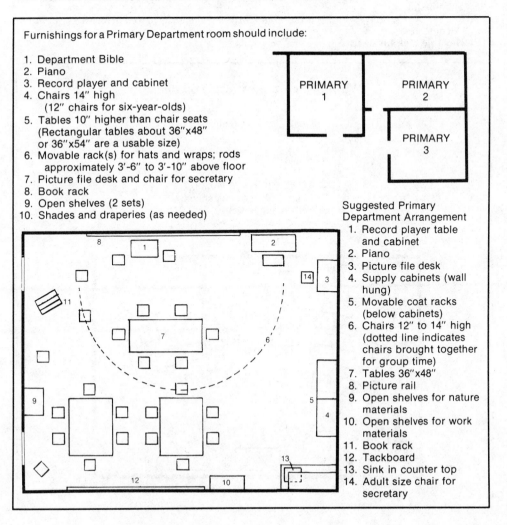

Furnishings for a Primary Department room should include:

1. Department Bible
2. Piano
3. Record player and cabinet
4. Chairs 14" high
   (12" chairs for six-year-olds)
5. Tables 10" higher than chair seats
   (Rectangular tables about 36"x48"
   or 36"x54" are a usable size)
6. Movable rack(s) for hats and wraps; rods
   approximately 3'-6" to 3'-10" above floor
7. Picture file desk and chair for secretary
8. Book rack
9. Open shelves (2 sets)
10. Shades and draperies (as needed)

Suggested Primary Department Arrangement

1. Record player table and cabinet
2. Piano
3. Picture file desk
4. Supply cabinets (wall hung)
5. Movable coat racks (below cabinets)
6. Chairs 12" to 14" high (dotted line indicates chairs brought together for group time)
7. Tables 36"x48"
8. Picture rail
9. Open shelves for nature materials
10. Open shelves for work materials
11. Book rack
12. Tackboard
13. Sink in counter top
14. Adult size chair for secretary

JUNIOR DEPARTMENT STANDARDS FOR EQUIPMENT

Each department should have a large assembly room. It is desirable to provide at least 18 square feet per person (14 square feet per person would be a minimum). A room in proportion of 3 to 4 or 4 to 5 makes a good assembly area.

Most Junior Departments have an average attendance of 40 to 50. When attendance reaches 50, consideration should be given to the creation of two departments. If multiple departments are necessary, they should be in the same area of the building.

Recommendations for Junior Department facilities:
1. Department room off main corridor, entrance at rear of room
2. Located above the ground
3. Classrooms
4. Unbroken wall space at front of assembly room
5. Windows required
6. Floor covering—asphalt tile, rubber tile, vinyl tile, or hardwood
7. Walls—soundproof, soft color; acoustical ceiling
8. Picture mold
9. Combination chalkboard and tackboard
10. Suitable furniture for workers and for boys and girls
11. Storage space, adequate for materials used by all Junior organizations; if desired, this may be divided into separate compartments for each organization; may be closet or wall-hung cabinet(s)
12. Robe storage within assembly area; or use portable robe racks placed in an area adjacent to department
13. Movable rack for wraps

SUGGESTED JUNIOR ROOM DIAGRAM

1. Chairs 15"-17" high
2. Piano
3. Table
4. Music stand
5. Portable chalkboard
6. Tackboard (optional)
7. Record player and cabinet
8. Picture file desk
9. Movable rack for wraps
10. United States and Christian flags

148

JUNIOR HIGH DEPARTMENT STANDARDS FOR EQUIPMENT

This department also should have a large assembly room with at least 18 square feet per person (minimum 14 square feet per person). Like the Junior Department, a room in proportion of 3 to 4 or 4 to 5 is desirable.

No Junior High Department should have more than 64 in average attendance. At that point, consideration should be given to the creation of three departments, one for each age level. Multiple departments should be in the same area of the building. Movable doors between alternate classrooms provide for multiple-use.

Here are some recommendations for Junior High Department facilities:

1. Department room off main corridor, entrance at rear of room
2. Located above the ground
3. Assembly room as a classroom
4. Unbroken wall space at front of assembly room
5. Windows required
6. Floor covering—asphalt tile, rubber tile, vinyl tile, or hardwood
7. Walls—soundproof, soft color; acoustical ceiling
8. Picture mold
9. Combination chalkboard and tackboard up front
10. Suitable furniture for workers and for boys and girls
11. Storage space, adequate for materials used by all Junior High organizations; if desired, this may be divided into separate compartments for each organization; may be closet or wall-hung cabinet(s)
12. Movable rack for wraps

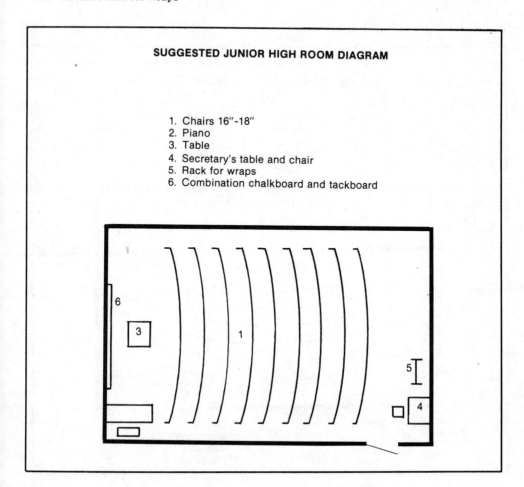

SUGGESTED JUNIOR HIGH ROOM DIAGRAM

1. Chairs 16"-18"
2. Piano
3. Table
4. Secretary's table and chair
5. Rack for wraps
6. Combination chalkboard and tackboard

SENIOR HIGH DEPARTMENT STANDARDS FOR EQUIPMENT

An assembly room will be needed for each Senior High Department, with a minimum of 14 square feet of floor space per person. Movable partitions between alternate classrooms will provide for multiple use.

Basic considerations and/or provisions:

1. Classroom off main corridor, entrance at rear of room
2. May be located on any floor
3. Ample wall space at front of room
4. Windows required
5. Floor covering—asphalt tile, rubber tile, vinyl tile, or hardwood
6. Walls—soundproof, plastered, light color; acoustical ceiling
7. Tackboard near exit door of assembly room; picture mold
8. Combination chalkboard and tackboard at front of classroom; movable chalkboard for extra groups
9. Suitable furniture
10. Storage closets for Sunday School:
    - Record supplies
    - Assembly program properties
    - Erasers, chalk, pencils
    - Posters
    - Free literature
    - Lesson and program periodicals

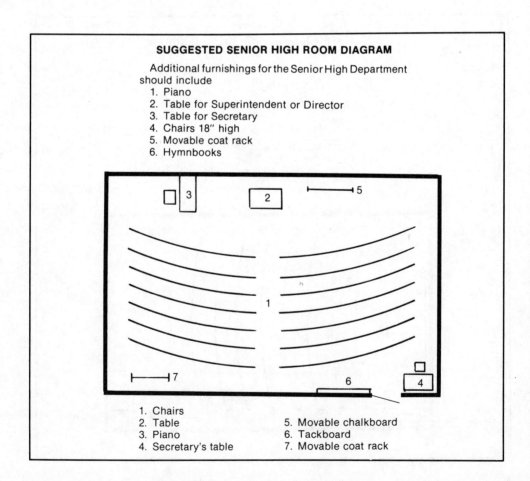

SUGGESTED SENIOR HIGH ROOM DIAGRAM

Additional furnishings for the Senior High Department should include

1. Piano
2. Table for Superintendent or Director
3. Table for Secretary
4. Chairs 18" high
5. Movable coat rack
6. Hymnbooks

1. Chairs
2. Table
3. Piano
4. Secretary's table
5. Movable chalkboard
6. Tackboard
7. Movable coat rack

ADULT DEPARTMENT STANDARDS FOR EQUIPMENT

An assembly room will be needed for each Adult Department. Again, 14 square feet of floor space per person should be provided.

Rooms for classes need not be of uniform size, but it is recommended that each one accommodate from 40 to 50 persons. Separate Adult Department assembly rooms should be provided. Adult Departments prefer the main floor.

Additional suggestions:
1. Department classroom off main corridor; entrance at rear of room
2. Outside window in each room
3. Ample wall space at front of assembly room
4. Floor covering—asphalt tile, rubber tile, vinyl tile, or hardwood
5. Walls—soundproof, light color; acoustical ceiling
6. Suitable furniture
7. Picture mold
8. Bulletin board near exit door of assembly room
9. Separate chalkboard and tackboard in the classroom
10. Storage closets for Sunday School:
    Record supplies
    Program properties
    Erasers, chalk, pencils
    Current posters, charts, other learning aids, curriculum supplements
    Promotional literature
    Lesson and program periodicals

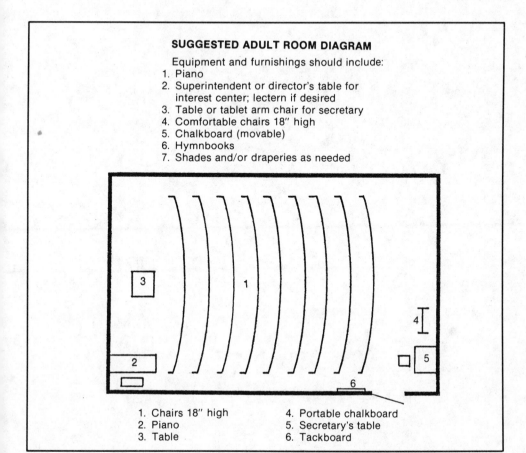

SUGGESTED ADULT ROOM DIAGRAM

Equipment and furnishings should include:
1. Piano
2. Superintendent or director's table for interest center; lectern if desired
3. Table or tablet arm chair for secretary
4. Comfortable chairs 18" high
5. Chalkboard (movable)
6. Hymnbooks
7. Shades and/or draperies as needed

1. Chairs 18" high   4. Portable chalkboard
2. Piano   5. Secretary's table
3. Table   6. Tackboard

section IV

Buses—
One Key to Growth

19

The Sunday School bus ministry operates out of a deep conviction that Jesus commanded His followers to go after the spiritually lost and that He never commanded the unsaved to come to church.

The Indispensable Bus

Explosive church growth—one of the phenomena of our day (see "100 Largest Sunday Schools," October 1975 *Christian Life*)—often stems from extensive use of buses. Where church workers canvass neighborhoods and invite young and old to ride their buses to Sunday School and study the Word of God, church attendance booms.

The Zion Baptist Church in Aurora, Ill., purchased three buses for $1,600 and began their ministry on the first Sunday of March 1970, with 33 riders. The following Sunday buses brought in 105, the next Sunday 141, and on the fourth Sunday, 176. During this time their Sunday School attendance jumped from 243 to 419, and by the end of the year averaged 426.

The Sunday School bus ministry operates out of a deep conviction that Jesus commanded His followers to go after the spiritually lost and that He never commanded the unsaved to come to church.

"People will not come to church—they must be brought. People will not seek Christ—they must be won," says William Powell, associate director, division of evangelism, Southern Baptist Home Mission Board. Powell's strong leadership in Sunday School busing conventions throughout Southern Baptist circles has

All lined up and ready to go—the bus fleet of Landmark Baptist Temple in Cincinnati, Ohio. (Landmark Baptist Temple)

been responsible for renewed aggressive growth in many Southern Baptist churches.

The Sunday School bus ministry is described as the "lost sheep ministry," whereby a church cannot be satisfied with the 99 sheep who are in the fold, but must go out seeking the unsaved. The size of a church seems to have no bearing upon the effectiveness of its church bus ministry.

The First Baptist Church of Jacksonville, Fla., added 800 to its Sunday School within the two years after they added 15 buses for evangelistic outreach.

The Emerton (Md.) Baptist Church, located in a rural area, grew from 227 to 528 in the first 11 months after beginning an aggressive bus ministry down rural lanes.

Most bus ministries are geared to the young because children are responsive to busing. Children like to go places—almost any place—especially with other children. And in public school they learn they can get to those places on buses. Since most parents want their children to receive religious training, they let them ride a bus to church—any church whose bus will stop in front of their house and pick up their children.

Whereas some adults are turned off by the poor or unkempt children often brought by a bus, there are a number of churches with a "Robert Raikes" zeal that have gone after children.

Raikes, as mentioned before, founded the Sunday School by going through Sooty Alley in Gloucester, England, gathering outcast children, and taking them to a kitchen to teach them the Word of God. His modern-day counterparts devote their Saturday mornings to going up and down streets, through playgrounds, gathering children, mindful of the admonition of Jesus, "Suffer the little children to come unto me and forbid them not." These bus workers know that children enjoy contests, awards, treats, socials, activities, singing and laughter; therefore, they provide it.

On their buses they give away McDonald's hamburgers and Kool-Aid, and sometimes stop in local parks on the way home from Sunday School to have a picnic or tug-of-war.

Some churches give away whistles, taffy, or water guns and have "flood the bus Sunday" where kids soak down everyone with a water pistol.

However, frivolity is not all that goes on during the bus ride to Sunday School. Led by bus workers, the children sing choruses, memorize Bible verses, learn lessons and play Bible games. Children are taught concern for others by praying for those who can't come and are taught evangelism by visiting with the bus workers, and inviting their friends to Sunday School.

Every church that goes into a Sunday School bus ministry does not have smooth sailing, however. As attendance grows, many churches experience internal criticism because of the antics of the bus kids. Church members forget that unchurched children act like unchurched children. Other members criticize because of overcrowded conditions and because the organization must be changed and rooms shifted to accommodate a growing attendance. Others criticize the new program, accusing the bus people of being interested only in numbers.

To overcome criticism, Powell recommends that a church educate its members to the benefits of Sunday School busing and point out that a Sunday School bus ministry is a practical application of the Great Commission by taking the Gospel to every creature. Powell also suggests that the deacons, church council, Women's Missionary Union and other key groups be brought in on the ground floor of planning for Sunday School busing. Then he urges that persons from other successful churches experiencing growth with the Sunday School bus ministry be brought in to share with the beginning church.

Many people are willing to serve God in an action-oriented ministry who feel unworthy to teach Sunday School or serve on a church committee. Others are willing to serve when they can see immediate results—a bus full of children the next Sunday. This was the reward of a Bedford County (Va.) farmer who sent his children to Thomas Road Baptist Church. When Jim Vineyard, director of bus ministry, visited in the home, the man received Jesus Christ. He left a spiritually dead church and became a bus worker at the Thomas Road Baptist Church, driving others 30 miles to Sunday School.

A bus ministry also enables a person with little Bible knowledge to begin his Christian service early. Whereas Sunday School teachers must know the Bible and teaching methods, a man can drive a church bus immediately after he is saved or can go house-to-house inviting people to ride a bus to church.

One of the first problems to be resolved is what kind of bus to purchase. Many churches launch their bus programs by buying one good "trip" bus, that is, a new bus in excellent condition able to take long trips. These buses cost $5,000 or more.

Powell, of the Southern Baptist Board, also recommends another type of bus called the "evangelistic bus." This is an older model, usually costing less than $1,000, designed to take a short trip each weekend for the one purpose of transporting children to Sunday School. Some churches are able to purchase a large fleet, using some of the old buses for spare parts, always having five or six available in case of Sunday morning breakdowns.

One denomination recommends that a church rent its bus from a transportation company because there is no large capital investment. Insurance and maintenance are taken care of, and the uniformed driver gives a

A church can turn its buses into rolling advertisements.

sense of security to both parents and children. Then the church needs only a bus captain to solicit riders. The actual maneuvering of the bus is cared for by a paid driver.

On the other side of the coin, a church with a large fleet of buses can paint them the same color and put on as many slogans as it wishes. Then, as the buses sit in a parking lot or are driven through neighborhoods, they advertise the church. Also, these churches argue, the cost is actually half the price of renting buses.

Churches with large bus fleets must provide maintenance. The Indianapolis Baptist Temple recently dedicated a new bus barn with more modern equipment than the Indianapolis Greyhound repair center. The First Baptist Church of Hammond, Ind., provides heated indoor parking for 60 buses and a maintenance shop to handle 5 buses at one time. Their fuel is ordered in bulk. Dr. John Rawlings, Landmark Baptist Temple, Cincinnati, Ohio, claims to save $10,000 a year by purchasing at bulk prices.

Large fleets also experience security problems—broken windows, slashed seats and stolen fuel. The Temple Heights Baptist Church, Tampa, Fla., keeps buses in a yard with a seven-foot chain-link fence, and each night releases two German shepherd dogs. This completely solves their security problem.

However, the advantages of using buses far outweigh the problems involved. So take another look at your rate of Sunday School growth. You may find that, indeed, a bus ministry is indispensable.

Sunday School buses are more important than most people realize. More than one church owns more buses than its city's transportation system. And more churches owe their listing on *Christian Life* magazine's "100 Largest Sun-day Schools" to Sunday School buses than to any other factor. In fact, the church that does not own or rent a fleet of Sunday School buses probably is not a growing church.

Why is the Sunday School bus so important today?

The Sunday School bus ministry was begun prior to World War II when the late Dr. Dallas Billington, former pastor of Akron Baptist Temple, provided a free bus ride to Sunday School for his parishioners who worked in the rubber factory in Akron, Ohio. In those days, many did not have a car, could not afford bus fare, or were not near convenient public transportation. Before this, American churches were founded within walking or buggy-ride distance from homes. Because Billington had used the radio for a city-wide ministry, people from all over wanted to attend his church. Hence the need for transportation. Other churches followed his example, most of them advertising in the newspaper: "Free rides to Sunday School." As a result, the principle became known as *convenience busing.*

During the World War II when an embargo was placed on private busing, Billington went directly to President Franklin D. Roosevelt and got the embargo lifted so he could bring his factory workers to Sunday School. After the war, however, convenience busing declined in effectiveness. Billington saw that many of his members owned first one car, then another, with a resulting decrease in riders on the buses. But the final straw came when the city of Akron upped the price on the buses he was renting from the city transportation company. Billington canceled his bus routes.

At the same time, Dr. Lee Roberson, Highland Park Baptist Church, Chattanooga, Tenn., was using Sunday School buses in a different manner. He appointed bus pastors (also called bus captains) who knocked on doors, inviting people to ride the bus to Sunday School. Many credit Dr. Roberson with being the first to use *evangelistic busing* as a principle.

About the same time Dr. Jack Hyles, First Baptist Church, Hammond, Ind., popularized evangelistic busing. What Roberson began, Hyles amplified throughout southern Chicago and the Calumet district of Indiana, eventually claiming to have more buses than the Hammond Transit Company.

Just as busing has become a big business in the public school system, so it is becoming big business in evangelistic church outreach. The success of the program is seen on Saturday when the bus workers canvass their neighborhoods inviting people to come to Sunday School.

"I'm from First Baptist Church and would like to pick up your children and take them to Sunday School on our bus. We'd come by the front of your house at 8:56 a.m. on Sunday morning," the caller begins.

The secret of Sunday School busing is continual exposure to the program. Bus workers go to every home in their neighborhood, most of them visiting 100 homes each Saturday morning. This takes approximately three hours. Children who miss the previous week are visited the following Saturday. Many of the bus workers go back to the children's homes continually, attempting to reach the parents for Jesus Christ.

On Sunday morning, bus drivers start early—some of them before 8:00—to make their rounds in slums, middle-class neighborhoods, and upper-class neighborhoods. Buses from the Landmark Baptist Temple fan out over the Greater Cincinnati area, some of them going 30 miles in one direction to bring children to Sunday School.

The Sunday School bus ministry is built on the theological principle of reaching people with the Gospel, which is defined as "bringing a man under the sound of the Gospel and motivating him to give sincere attention to the Word of God." The Apostle Paul explains this principle when he says, "I am made all things to all men, that I might by all means save some" (I Corinthians 9:22). Whereas door-to-door evangelism is the first step, getting a person to attend church and listen to an understandable presentation of the Gospel is an even better step of evangelism, authorities say.

A garage mechanic who recently was saved at the Thomas Road Baptist Church, Lynchburg, Va., said, "I don't know nuttin' (sic) so I can't teach Sunday School, but I can drive a bus and bring 75 children for somebody else to teach." He held up his perennially grease-stained hands and added, "God can use these."

The Thomas Road Baptist Church is employing a new thrust in evangelistic busing. Many small rural churches in surrounding counties have closed because preachers are hard to find, people have moved to town, or creeping liberalism has destroyed the evangelistic thrust of the church. As a result, Thomas Road Baptist Church has over 40 routes outside of Lynchburg in rural areas, from which they are experiencing rapid attendance growth through their bus ministry.

Rural children have been conditioned to riding a Sunday School bus. Also, the church brings many rural adults (more than 800) to

"Follow me, third grade boys." Signs direct bus riders to the proper Sunday School classes at Thomas Road Baptist Church. (Thomas Road Baptist Church, Lynchburg, VA)

Sunday School via the buses. According to Marvin Layne, bus coordinator, more than 500 riders come from Bedford County, some 20 miles away, and five buses reach Roanoke, 50 miles away.

One of the criticisms of the Sunday School bus ministry is "proselyting." Should a church send its buses into an area that is considered the parish of another church, especially if the other area has an evangelical church?

Traditionally, ministers have been concerned about proselyting, but two facts in contemporary America have changed the picture. First, the mobility of society and a church's access to mass media make it possible for people to go as far to church as they drive to buy groceries or travel to work. Also, ministers argue, the day of geographic parish ministry is past. If people can drive long distances to church, why not ride a bus?

Recently, the Ministers' Association in Bedford County criticized Dr. Jerry Falwell, Thomas Road's pastor, for running buses in their area.

"We have non-Christian people right here on Thomas Road. If any other church wants to send a bus and reach these people for Jesus Christ, our ushers will help them turn their bus around in our parking lot," Falwell replied.

The Sunday School bus ministry is growing at a phenomenal rate in our nation. When large churches saturate an area with their buses, many smaller churches are forced into the bus ministry as a defensive measure.

Hyles ran Sunday School buses into Hobart, Ind., 25 miles away, and the First Baptist Church, Evergreen Park Baptist Church and Grand Park Baptist Church all began a Sunday School bus ministry. The result: the three smaller churches all experienced growth.

The Southern Baptists were in a Convention-wide attendance slump, when many leaders realized a return to evangelism would cause growth. Therefore, the Convention recently opened a Sunday School Bus Department under its Home Mission Board. The Rev. William

Thomas Road Baptist Church, Lynchburg, VA.

Powell of that department has planned Sunday School bus conventions in every major area of Southern Baptist church influence, to motivate members to build Sunday Schools and reach men, women, young people and children through evangelistic busing.

A number of Sunday School bus clinics are held in churches which have successful bus ministries, such as Trinity Baptist Church, Jacksonville, Fla., and Dayton, (Ohio) Baptist Temple.

In 1972 a Sunday School bus conference at Thomas Road Baptist Church drew more than 2,600 delegates from all over the nation for a three-day seminar on techniques, principles and workshops. It was not the usual "how-to-do-it" seminar, but rather a "how-we-did-it" one. A number of new books on Sunday School busing have been published, such as *Church Bus Evangelism,* by William Powell; *Winning Souls Through Buses,* by Jim Vineyard; and *All about the Bus Ministry,* by Dr. Wally Beebe. Two magazines on busing have been founded: *Bring Them In,* published by Joe R. Sadler, of Nashville, Tenn.; and *Church Bus News,* published by Wally Beebe, full-time Sunday School bus evangelist.

So get on the "bus wagon" and watch your Sunday School and church grow.

20

Establishing and maintaining standard bus routes enables a church to grow as much as desired. Here are 13 factors which will guarantee success.

Essentials for Effective Church Bus Evangelism

BY WILLIAM A. POWELL

Introduction

One of the quickest and surest ways of realizing an immediate and substantial increase in average attendance, annual baptisms, interest, and enthusiasm is launching an aggressive Church Bus Evangelism ministry (CBE) or by revitalizing and expanding an existing one. This has given new direction to many churches.

A standard bus route will average 40 or more riders each week and result in from 10 to 30 baptisms each year. Therefore, establishing and maintaining standard bus routes enables a church to grow as much as desired. This could be referred to as "Controlled Church Growth."

However, some churches will average only 10 to 30 riders per bus and have a relatively small number of baptisms. Oftentimes these bus workers are discouraged and want to quit. On the other hand, some churches will average from 50 to 60 riders per bus and have a large number of baptisms. These bus workers usually are excited, enthusiastic, and willing to give more time to their bus work.

What makes the difference? There is nothing secret or mystical about this. In fact, there are obvious reasons for it. I often go to churches with a sick CBE ministry and find it is because they have neglected one or more of the following 13 items. I know of no church that has an effective CBE ministry without giving special attention to all of these items. Some churches add items to these 13, but all of the most successful churches concur that the following are the essentials.

The first three items and the last are not measurable. They are intangible. It is not always possible for a church to fit exactly into either a "does" or a "does not" category in these four items. But the other nine are measurable. Each church can say yes or no to each of these nine concrete items.

1. *Evangelism.* A church must have a high priority on evangelism and give proper attention to the CBE ministry. The devil sees to it that many problems develop, so this whole effort will fail unless there is a strong commitment to the New Testament priority of evangelism. Many churches say they believe in evangelism but their record of baptisms reveals they have very little commitment to it. And the CBE ministry must not be treated as a stepchild or an in-law. This ministry and its workers should receive consideration equal to that given all other church programs and workers. This includes training, budget, and scheduling. Many believe that a church has no authority to discuss what their top priority will be: Jesus gave explicit instructions to evangelize every person.

2. *Genuine love for children.* A church must have a genuine love for children and a proper concept of the great importance Jesus places upon them. The Gospels carry several sections about Jesus' relationships and experiences

One of the surest ways of increasing attendance, baptisms and enthusiasm is by launching an aggressive bus ministry.

with children. Some of His greatest lessons were taught with a child on His knee or by His side. Some of His followers would often criticize Him for "wasting" His time with children. We must not be guilty of this same attitude. The church must love children rather than just tolerate them. It must recognize that children can and must be saved. My only son was saved at age 5, and last year God used him (he's now 18) to lead more than 200 other persons to accept Christ. We need the "Jesus concept" of children.

3. *A sincere commitment.* A church must have sincere commitment to the leadership of God and complete dependence upon the blessings of God. The church that is committed to the leadership of God does not need to pray a long time to know what He wants them to do—the Bible plainly states that the first priority is to evangelize every person in the area. And God has promised to supply the needs (workers, money, space, etc.) for those who follow His leadership. If you wait until you have all the workers, space and money you think you need before you go out to do His will, then you will never do it. Go ahead and do what He commanded and He has promised to supply the needs. All we have (and all we really need) to depend upon is the blessings of God. The Bible says that it is impossible to please God without faith.

4. *A dedicated, experienced and well-*

qualified CBE director. "Experienced" means that he has "done it himself." It is hard to see how anyone can tell someone else how to do something successfully unless he has done it himself. I do not believe anyone is properly qualified to be a top CBE director unless he personally has started one or more bus routes and has developed them to average 50 or more riders per week for at least one month and has brought in 100 or more riders on his route at least one time.

A person will learn far more about how to direct a successful CBE ministry this way than by reading all the books and attending all the conferences. And the advice and instructions a CBE director of this caliber gives his bus workers carries far more weight. After the decision was made for me to serve as the CBE director for our church, the most important decision that I made was to serve as a bus captain.

A CBE director usually is employed by a church on a part-time basis. Instead of considering him as an added expense, remember that he is one church employee who is a real asset. Not only is he responsible for a great deal of church growth in numbers; church income also will increase.

5. *Visitation.* It is necessary to have dedicated bus captains who will average at least four or five (or more) hours visiting each week. Availability and dependability are the

Children get more out of a service designed for them. When churches begin bus ministries, they may need to make adjustments in their programs and methods.

primary qualifications for bus captains. The hours the captain averages in route visitation to enlist new riders and keep old ones is directly related to the number of riders each week. The rule of thumb is 10 riders for each hour of visitation. That is, the route will average about 10 riders each week for each hour the captain averages visiting each week. Thus, the captain who averages 40 riders or more each week will average four or more hours of visitation each week.

I guess that the second most important decision I made after I became a bus captain was that I would work until five each Saturday afternoon. Up until that decision, I would say each Saturday, "I'll visit as much as I can today." Usually that meant until 1:00 p.m. because I always had many other things to do at home and at the office. So I would usually go home for a late lunch and seldom get back on my route to finish the work. I assume that going home for lunch has ruined more bus captains than anything else (unless it is just plain laziness). But after I decided to be a "five o'clock bus captain" things began to happen.

The last church at which I helped launch a CBE ministry averaged 75 riders per route dur-

ing their second month. And 3 of the 4 bus captains exceeded 100 riders at least once during that second month. And they baptized more converts to Jesus than during the two previous years combined.

6. *Enlistment.* Bus workers must learn (and follow) the best methods of enlisting new riders. Many bus workers go up and down every street, knocking on every door, but this is not the method used by the most successful churches. I know. I used this method my first year until I learned a better one. In about one out of five homes, no one came to the door. And in about one fifth of the homes, there were no children. Then at the homes with children who did not attend church, I had to approach the adults first.

"That is a wonderful thing you are doing but we are not interested. Thank you, anyway," they would most often say.

Thus about half of my efforts were wasted so far as getting a load for Sunday.

Then I learned to go to the children first! Now, for more than two years, I have approached the children as they are out playing. My favorite "first contact" is made with the magic cards. These have Bible verses on one

side and church information on the other, and are available from CBE Supply in Nashville as well as from some Baptist Book Stores and other religious book stores.

I simply ride around in my bus looking for children. When I find them out playing I get out of the bus and ask them if they want to see a magic trick. After I show them the trick and give every child a pair of the cards, I find out which children are not attending church. Then I get them excited about riding "that big bus with all the other boys and girls to my wonderful church." Following this, I fill out a Prospective Bus Riders Card on those not attending any church. Then we go see the parents to make sure it is okay for them to ride my bus the next day.

7. *Program on the bus*. It is essential to have someone to lead a program on each bus. I call them the Teenage Crusaders. They conduct a well-planned program on the bus as the children are being picked up and taken home each Sunday. This consists of good singing, memorizing Bible verses, telling Bible stories, and games.

You can fill a bus by visiting four or more hours each Saturday and using the best meth-

ods of enlisting new riders, but they will not continue riding each week if they have to just sit on the bus and look out the window all the way to church and back. A good program on the bus also helps eliminate most discipline problems—while teaching them some worthwhile things. (Of course most of the formal instruction is planned for the Sunday School itself, but why not use the time they are riding the bus for worthwhile activities?) These programs also help the children enjoy going to church. Personally I feel there is nothing wrong with enjoying going to church. In fact, I do not believe it is wrong to enjoy what happens at church.

8. *Well-prepared Sunday School workers*. Dedicated and well-prepared Sunday School workers are necessary; workers who will capitalize upon their marvelous opportunity of teaching these previously unchurched children and leading them to Christ. There are a few (even one is too many) Sunday School workers who resent the way these children upset well-organized religious activities and necessitate adjustments in normal procedures.

These children know when they are loved or resented. And there must be an adequate number of Sunday School workers to provide good meaningful experiences during the Sunday School hour. The degree of dedication of these workers and the thoroughness of their preparation each week is more valuable than is the worker ratio. And their goal includes leading the children to accept Christ as well as teaching them the Bible.

9. *Children's worship services*. It is necessary to have dedicated and well-prepared leaders of the children's worship services. These unchurched children will not keep coming and receiving maximum benefit from the worship hour if they have to sit through the adult worship service every Sunday.

There are several reasons why many churches have begun church services for children. Space is one—especially when a church engages in an aggressive CBE ministry. But probably the most important reason is that children (whether they came on a bus or in the family car) get much more out of a service designed for them. The music, sermon or Bible story time, terminology, invitation and other elements are all prepared with the children in mind.

This makes the worship hour a meaningful and significant time rather than an "endurance time." Children grow up with favorable attitudes toward church rather than resentment. Another reason is that adults get more out of their church service since there are no squirming children to detract from the worship. Parents can relax, knowing their children are participating in a meaningful worship experience planned for them. These children's church services usually are conducted by volunteer church members who often feel they provide some of their most profitable church experiences.

10. *Qualified counselors.* Qualified counselors are necessary to aid children who respond in a positive way to the Gospel of Christ. Children's worship services consist of three purposes or elements: worship, Bible teaching and evangelism. Many church leaders feel the need for some specific counseling for the children, many of whom have very little church background.

It is wise to select mature Christians and train them for counseling these children. J. B. Waddle outlines a fine plan in his book, *Counseling Children about Conversion and Church Membership.* It involves two or more counseling sessions at church and one or more counseling sessions in the child's home.

11. *Soul winners.* Another essential is a group of dedicated trained soul-winners who contact the parents of these "bused-in" children. In the 25 years I have been a minister, nothing has opened as many doors into the homes and hearts of adults as this bus ministry. I like to think of bus workers as the Green Beret corp of the church, opening up doors and establishing beachheads throughout the unchurched areas of the community. Any church that is alert to its opportunities will be constantly training and developing more soul-winners to go through these open doors with the message of Christ for the adults. The Bible says a child shall lead them. And many adults have followed their children to church and to a conversion experience.

Our Southern Baptist Evangelism Division has some excellent materials, techniques and suggestions for training church members to witness. This includes a week-long lay evangelism school using the WIN materials, and a continuous plan of training these people each week. This is certainly essential to the most successful CBE ministry. We will not win all these parents to Jesus Christ, but we will win far more of the parents whose children ride our buses than we will of the parents whose children do not ride our buses.

As Larry Lewis states, "It is ten times easier to reach a child than it is the parent. But it is ten times easier to reach the parent after we have reached the child."

We want to reach two people in the CBE ministry: the child and the adult. We want to reach the child because we can and should win children to Christ. But even if I did not believe a child could be saved, I would still want to have a CBE ministry because the fastest and surest way of winning parents is through their children. Therefore we must train and develop soul-winners to go through these open doors and lead these adults to Christ.

12. *Special activities.* Also valuable is the special activity bus workers provide for their riders one Sunday each month after church.

This includes picnics, outings, short trips, ballgames, pony rides and/or visiting the zoo or museum.

Although these Sunday afternoon activities require an extra special effort on the part of bus workers, they display love and concern in a way no high sounding sermon ever could.

13. *Willingness of church.* The final essential is the willingness of the church to make whatever changes are necessary in order to evangelize its "Jerusalem." The status quo operation of many churches has them in such a rut that changes are difficult. But the church that never changes will never experience significant growth. Change and growth go hand in hand.

Not all changes produce growth—some changes cause decline. But there will never be any significant growth without appropriate accompanying changes.

Dean Kelley points out in his book *(Why Conservative Churches Are Growing)* that the most popular phrase heard around dying churches is, "But we have never done it that way before." Man, as a creature of habit, is prone to resist change.

Many churches need a major change in priorities. Reconsider and sharpen them. Study your priorities in light of New Testament teachings rather than in light of the current fads in the religious world. Dare to accept the New Testament priority of evangelism. Simply stating or voting on this priority is not adequate. This priority must influence the planning of the annual church budget and the spending of the church income.

This priority also must be reflected in the weekly and monthly schedules of the church. It is a revealing exercise to study the church budget and see how much money is used in evangelizing the area.

Of course there are other things to do than evangelize. But this is the New Testament priority, and most churches have drifted so far away from it that a major operation will be required to bring them back to this basic position.

Many churches also will need to face the question, "Who will lead the church?" The Biblical pattern is for the pastor to lead. But somewhere across the ages an idea has grown up that the pastor is the servant of the church. This is wrong. The New Testament conveys the concept that the pastor is God's under-shepherd to lead the church in its God-given assignment.

Some churches are controlled by small groups or boards made up of a vocal minority. And, tragically, they prefer continuing business-as-usual rather than following the leadership of the pastor.

Another area where change is needed in many churches is in their rededication to the standards of Christ. The call of Christ to rigid discipline and high standards of commitment has been so watered down in some churches that it is hard to distinguish believers from nonbelievers. This is true not only in personal living but also in normal church procedures and operations. Just any old way is okay at most any time.

Some of the "flabby fat cluttering" of church organization and the outmoded haphazard procedures that slow everything down will need to be changed before some churches can carry out their New Testament assignment.

Conclusion

The six words that best describe these thirteen essentials are: commitment, work, problems, changes, results, enthusiasm.

There are many other things that are helpful to a good CBE ministry that are not included in the above essentials. But the most successful churches concur that all 13 are absolutely essential to the most effective CBE ministry. And everything that is essential is included in these 13.

Some will be surprised to see that nothing is mentioned about the size, age or condition of the buses. No mention is made of bubble gum, transistor radios or bicycles. Even the Saturday bus workers' meeting is not included as essential. Population density, racial factors, and income level are not related to the essentials, nor is the age, sex, educational attainments, or native ability of the workers.

All the churches in the world can be put into one of four categories so far as the CBE ministry is concerned. The first and largest group consists of those churches that will never begin this ministry. The second large category (but not nearly as large as the first) consists of churches that begin but fail. Most churches that begin a CBE ministry fail. They do not understand what is involved, get off to a poor start, lack the necessary commitment, never attend a bus clinic, never read the books or listen to the tapes about CBE ministry, never go to a church that is successful, never invite some successful workers to come to their church, etc. They just "give it a little try" to see if it will work—and, sure enough, it does not work for them.

The third category consists of those who start and keep going but at a substandard level. They average from 10 to 30 riders per bus. Only a small number of baptisms result, and nothing unusual happens in their church or community because of this ministry.

The fourth category consists of those averaging 40 or more riders per bus. They are seeing whole families and communities brought to Christ. Bus workers and church members are excited about all the ways God is blessing them because they are majoring on His priority.

Which is your category? How about moving up into category four this year? There are plenty of vacant spaces available.

"Try it—you'll like it."

An outing now and then gives a busing program a special plus. Take the children to the zoo, have a picnic or just go fly a kite. (Religious News Service Photo)

An Effective Organization
for an Aggressive Church
Bus Evangelism Ministry

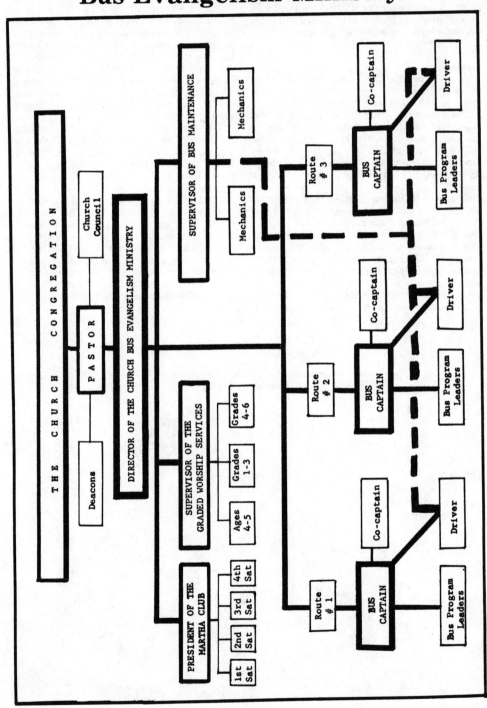

21

Workers are far more important than buses. The pastor who fumbles the ball in this area will lose the game.

Recruiting Workers for the Church Bus Evangelism Ministry

BY WILLIAM A. POWELL

How do you recruit workers at the beginning of a CBE ministry? Here are some tips which can be adapted periodically in lining up additional help.

The recruiting of workers must not be left to chance or to some haphazard spur-of-the-moment thought. An adequate amount of information, inspiration and challenge should be given from the pulpit. Some individuals will respond voluntarily to this public appeal. However, personal contacts should be made with members whom the pastor feels led of God to contact about the CBE ministry.

The pastor of one of the largest and fastest growing churches in America states repeatedly that his one secret to success is his emphasis upon recruiting, training, motivating and supervising workers.

I made a big mistake in my first effort in the CBE ministry many years ago as a pastor in Chicago. I used my thoughts, time and efforts to raise money, find and buy a bus, etc. We obtained a good bus, but I did very little about getting workers. I did not know at that time that workers were far more important than buses. The church finally sold that bus and recovered part of its money. Please do not make the same mistake that I (and many others) did.

Probably the major factor in determining the success of a CBE ministry is the approach used in recruiting, training, motivating and supervising workers.

The pastor who fumbles the ball in this area will lose the game. There are church members who will respond to the pastor's leadership in this who will not respond to any other appeal. The pastor should concentrate upon this and leave some of the related projects for others.

Many churches implement a detailed and well-organized plan of stewardship to meet the church budget each year. This is good. But we all know workers are more important than money. When you get the workers, you also have their money. God has promised to supply all our needs, but He commanded us to pray for workers. So let us pray sincerely for workers and ask God to help us in "calling out the called."

Almost every church has men who can find, buy, renovate, paint, letter and insure buses. But no one in the church can recruit workers as well as the pastor.

Earnest prayer to God for divine leadership and blessing is essential. Jesus commanded the disciples (including us) to pray for workers for the harvest (Matthew 9:38). The obligation to pray for workers is the direct command of Jesus. It is not simply the choice of a pastor who "feels like doing it."

This matter of praying for workers is not optional; it is a Biblical command (Matthew 9:38; Matthew 21:22; Ephesians 3:20).

Every command of Jesus should be diligently heeded. But I know of few, if any, commands of Jesus that more pastors and churches either ignore or treat lightly than this matter of praying for workers. No wonder the crying need of many churches is for more workers. The average church might be a super church if members prayed for workers as much as they prayed for the sick. (However, I favor praying for the sick—especially when I am sick!)

Of course, this also assumes that we believe God answers prayer. If we do not believe that, there is not much use in praying for workers—or even trying to do any church work. James 4:3 points out that we do not have what we want because we do not ask for it.

Praying for workers is better than worrying about workers. This spiritual work requires spiritual people. After all, it is not by might, nor by power, but by God's Spirit (Zechariah 4:6) that His work is accomplished.

There are five pages on recruiting bus workers in my book, *Church Bus Evangelism.*

The pastor should keep in mind that there probably is no group of workers or no church activity that will produce a greater increase in average attendance and annual baptisms than the CBE ministry.

Each standard bus route results in an average attendance of 40 or more each week, and from 10 to 30 baptisms each year. Determine the numerical increase in attendance desired. Then divide the desired increase by 40 to establish how many standard bus routes will be needed. If a church desires to increase its average weekly attendance by 160, and their annual baptisms by 50 or 75, they should establish four routes. Adding 10 standard bus routes will increase the attendance by 400 and the baptisms by 125 to 175 each year.

Thus the pastor who desires a substantial increase in attendance and baptisms will use his time and efforts in recruiting, training, motivating and supervising CBE workers.

A dedicated and qualified CBE director is necessary. Middle-sized and larger churches may employ some experienced person for this position. Other churches may assign this responsibility to one of the current staff members.

In churches where the pastor is the only staff person, he usually should serve as the CBE director until one of the bus captains has obtained adequate experience to enable him to serve until someone is employed for the position. Most churches that begin an effective and aggressive CBE ministry soon will grow to where they will need to employ a CBE director. Some churches would do well to borrow money, if necessary, in order to hire an experienced person to head up this work from the beginning. This person, as I mentioned before, should have served as a bus captain until he built a route average of 50 or more riders each week for a month or longer, until he exceeded 100 riders on at least one Sunday.

Some individual also will be needed to super-vise bus maintenance. There is a two-page job description for this person in my *Church Bus Evangelism* book.

One team will be needed for each bus route. A normal team includes: one captain, one co-captain, one driver, and two Teenage Crusaders. The Personal Commitment Card gives a brief description of these responsibilities. It is available from CBE Supply.

People also will be needed to help renovate, paint and maintain the buses. Cleaning and taping buses in preparation for painting is a major task. Some mechanically oriented person may be recruited to help with the routine maintenance of the buses each week as needed. Of course, some of the renovation, painting and maintenance may be done by paid labor. However, volunteer manpower can reduce costs and provide an excellent opportunity to make a valuable contribution to the church.

Ladies will be needed for the Martha Club, which prepares breakfast each Saturday at 8:45 for the bus workers and serves refreshments to the children between Sunday School and children's church each Sunday. In some churches, the ladies' missionary circles may handle this service.

One team is needed for each age-group unit of the GCS (Graded Church Services). A common practice is to begin with two age-groups: one for preschoolers, another for grades 1-6. It usually becomes necessary to have three or more GCS units as additional bus routes are established. This enables these church services for children to be more closely graded, and, therefore, more beneficial.

The team for each age-group unit of the GCS usually will consist of: the leader, a music director, a pianist, someone to lead in memorizing Bible verses, someone to preach the sermon or tell the Bible story. Of course, it is possible for only two or three persons to handle a large number of children, if necessary, provided they are capable and dedicated enough to make thorough preparation. Even if there is a scarcity of workers, children will receive far more benefit from a service led by two or three dedicated and well-prepared workers than they will from the adult service in the auditorium.

And the Sunday School director will need to recruit and train all these additional Sunday School workers *before the bus routes are begun!*

A nursery also will have to be staffed each Saturday if mothers are enlisted for visitation.

The Commitment Card is excellent for recruiting workers. A list on the front side shows the various workers needed. The other side gives a brief description of the responsibility of each worker. This card is also an excellent aid for raising money to purchase buses.

An adequate quantity of these cards can be ordered from the address shown on the card. (This is usually cheaper than trying to print them locally.) Ushers can distribute these cards

Challenge some of your creative members to join the bus painting crew. They may come up with a design as unique as this church on wheels which travels about Ireland.

to the congregation (above the 6th grade) as they enter the auditorium during the weeks that workers are being recruited.

Each person is then requested to write his name and telephone number on his card and keep it (in Bible or purse) until he is ready to turn it in, indicating how he is willing to help.

Then some well-qualified speaker from another church should be invited to speak to your congregation about the CBE ministry. The purpose: to provide first-hand information, inspiration and challenge. Personal testimonies also are helpful during this effort to recruit workers. These could be given by some of the successful bus workers in your church or from some nearby churches.

Several people may turn in their commitment cards during the first Sunday appeal for workers. This usually will be the day on which the guest speaker is featured. Other members will keep the cards for further consideration of the work—or of the amount of money they can give. Therefore, it is wise to make this appeal on two or three consecutive Sundays. If a guest speaker is brought in for the first appeal, then the pastor definitely should continue the appeal on the other occasions. Perhaps one or two sermons on the need of evangelizing "your Jerusalem and the fields that are white unto harvest" would be in order. Also, a sermon on the value of using one's time for the Kingdom of God instead of for the things of this world

would be valuable, as would one on the teachings and implications of Jesus in Luke 14:15-23.

Put forth an extra effort to help the congregation understand the special place that children and youth occupy in the thoughts, actions and teachings of Jesus. Help the congregation understand that the fastest way of winning a community to Christ and His way of life is to begin with the children.

It is essential that some of the deacons be active bus workers. The deacons should pray earnestly concerning the part each of them will have in the CBE ministry. Some churches feel it is wise to request that every deacon work on a bus route at least one weekend each quarter. This includes route visitation on Saturday as well as picking up riders and taking them home on Sunday. This first-hand experience enables the deacons to have a good concept of what CBE is all about. It also might cause some deacons to become actively involved in the CBE ministry on a regular basis.

The chairman or clerk of the deacons simply assigns each deacon the weekend that is most convenient for him. Then some of the deacons make a brief report on this at the deacons' meetings each month.

New members and new converts often make good bus workers. Some members who are not involved in other church work or who may not be too active in church may be challenged to become bus workers. Some members who already are engaged in other churchwork will get into the CBE ministry as an added area of productive service.

Some members are willing to work in the CBE ministry because they are able to see immediate results. This appeals to them more than the long-range "seed sowing." Other members will agree to serve in the CBE ministry because of a desire to be where the action is—where people are being saved, whole families are being changed, and an entire community is being won to Christ.

All workers should be recruited with the understanding that there is a lot of hard work to be performed and that they will be trained so as to be able to perform well.

The major consideration in selecting workers is availability and dependability. Basic ability, prior experience, formal training, social status, financial standing, and innate talent all added together do not equal the availability/dependability twins.

Workers should be selected for an indefinite period of time rather than on a year-to-year basis. This makes it easy to shift and rotate workers for the greatest efficiency and productivity.

During the recruiting emphasis, the pastor should go through the church membership roll very carefully to consider any possible potential workers who have not already made commitments to the CBE ministry. He should pray for God's leading as he considers possible workers, and that the potential workers will be responsive to His will in this matter.

Oftentimes it is wise to approach individuals and simply request that they pray sincerely for God to show them what He wants them to do in the CBE ministry.

A meeting should conclude the two- or three-week recruiting emphasis. It is good to invite to this meeting interested persons who have not yet made a definite commitment and persons whom the pastor feels God may want to use in this work. This meeting is a good time for sincere soul-searching and prayer.

Some churches like to have a reserve force of bus workers as well as the regulars. These reserves should serve one weekend each month (on Saturday and Sunday), if possible. Also they are on special call in case of needs at other times. This reserve concept is used successfully in our national defense system.

Remember that this is God's work. We are doing it for Him. After you have done your best, prayed sincerely, and acted in faith, God will do the rest. In all of this, do not lose sight of the fact that the bus captains are the key persons. Each bus route will rise or fall upon the bus captain (and the CBE director). Do not entertain hazy ideas or foggy notions as to who spearheads the success or failure for a bus route.

Blessed is the church with a pastor who can see the wisdom of placing great emphasis upon his responsibility for recruiting, training, motivating, and supervising workers.

One man may kill himself trying to do the work of ten men. But the wise man will recruit ten men to do the work of ten men. Then train them. Motivate them. Supervise them.

22

More than two dozen common, human factors often contribute to the failure of a Sunday School bus ministry. Evaluate your program (or proposed program) in light of these factors.

Why Sunday School Buses Fail

BY WILLIAM A. POWELL

Many churches have doubled and tripled their attendance and baptisms with church bus evangelism when following the proper procedures. On the other hand, many churches have experienced disappointments and failures in church bus evangelism. There may be more failures than there are successes. Buying a bus, enlisting a driver, announcing the bus stop schedule, and expecting people to ride it can be the most disappointing mistake that a church has made. Let us see why busing has failed.

You must recognize that the devil will do all he can to cause you to fail in this effort. If there is anyone in your church or community that the devil can influence so as to cause failure, he will do so.

Following are some of the more common human factors contributing to failure. The first category are those I call the nonmeasurable items. These may be a little more abstract than the measurable items. They are listed in the approximate order of importance.

1. Neglecting the final command of Jesus to take the Gospel to every person, beginning in your Jerusalem.

2. Running the church on a "drop in" policy, hoping that lost people will "drop in" and be saved. Permitting this concept to replace the New Testament concepts, "go bring them in" and "compel them to come that my house may be filled."

3. Satisfaction with business as usual procedures and status quo operations. "We're doing about as much good as most of the other churches."

4. A limited vision of the needs and possibilities of church bus evangelism in your area. Thinking too small (Matthew 9:36-38).

5. Failure to see the fields white unto harvest. Failure to recognize that Christ in you is the hope of glory (Colossians 1:27).

6. The belief that "this will not work for us; we have an unusual situation." Almost everyone thinks that his situation is unique.

7. Doubting the proven truth that the number of people attending your church and being baptized is determined by the vision, attitude, and personal commitment of the pastor (and a few key members). (Your average attendance and baptisms are *not* determined by the available space in your buildings, the known workers available, the population density of your area, nor the readily available money. Actually, these factors have very little to do with your attendance and baptisms.)

8. An improper concept of the value of children. A careful study of the Gospels to see what Jesus thought about youth and children, to note the time and attention He devoted to them could revolutionize many churches today. The fastest way to evangelize your community, your city, your county, and your state is to win the children. And the best way to do this is to saturate your area with standard bus routes.

Churches can solve the financial problems presented by the bus ministry. Here Pastor Carl Baugh receives the keys for a bus that has been donated to his church. (Calvary Heights Baptist Temple, St. Louis, MO)

The best way to win adults is to start with the children.

9. Permitting the church to spread so thin in trying to do everything that it accomplishes little of lasting value. Recognize that you cannot do everything. Simply accept the New Testament priority of taking the Gospel to every creature and do it. There are usually other agencies, groups, and persons in the community that can do other things. But there is no one in the community that can evangelize the lost except the church. That is our primary task.

10. Permitting other church activities or circumstances to take priority over evangelism. Remember that we do not need to be victims of circumstances, and we should not permit church activities to interfere with the work of Christ.

11. Lack of faith in God, in His ability to use you and your church, and in His ability to provide for your needs. He has told us to evangelize every person and He will supply our needs (Philippians 4:19, Ephesians 3:30, Matthew 21:22). He will do what He has promised, if we do what He told us to do. It is easier to build buildings, plan budgets, and promote programs than it is to live by faith. But the Bible

says that it is impossible to please God without faith (Hebrews 11:6).

12. A lack of personal commitment that will result in reordering priorities, schedules, and emphases.

13. Failure to prepare for, to expect, and to pray for divine wisdom and strength for the enlarged attacks of the devil upon the church membership and leadership.

14. Waiting for everyone in the church to favor starting church bus evangelism. In fact just one or two key persons can delay or prevent starting. Remember that the majority should determine the action in a church, not a vocal minority.

15. Failure to foresee that a bus program will result in some major changes in your church and in the lives of many people in your church and community.

16. Failure to prepare your church for a large influx of unchurched people, mostly children.

17. Unwillingness to make any major changes necessary to evangelize your area. Unwillingness to recognize that people are more important than rules or procedures. The most common phrase around dying churches is, "But we have never done anything that way

before." And one major reason that many dying churches continue to die is that the leadership is not willing to make necessary changes.

18. Hangups over space and workers. Some church leaders have such fixed ideas on the worker ratio that they almost forget the command of Jesus to take the Gospel to every person. Children of the community stay home and watch TV each Sunday because these leaders cannot adjust organizational structure and personal ideas.

19. Failure to provide an adequate number of Sunday School workers. I do not know what an adequate number is. God may determine that, since He is responsible for providing them. But I do concur with the realization of a growing number of our church leaders that the small class concept is helping to kill some churches. It has come to the place in many churches that class size is more important than the quality of teaching. And this results in the nominating committee just hunting warm bodies to serve as teachers in order to have small classes.

20. Magnifying quality at the expense of quantity. Actually, quality and quantity should go hand in hand—a "both/and" situation rather than "either/or."

21. Excusing feeble efforts in evangelism with the deceptive slogan, "We do not magnify numbers." Numbers may not be so important after we have evangelized every person, as Jesus commanded.

22. Failing to provide adequate support and motivation for your bus workers. Do not treat them as second-class church workers. Provide them their proper share of the budget and attention. Help with adequate motivation.

23. Inadequate organization. Placing the director of the church bus evangelism ministry under the supervision of a committee, a class, or some organization. A lack of proper organizational procedures with the bus workers and the maintenance of buses.

24. The concept that the buses are means of transportation rather than means of evangelism. The concept that the bus ministry is only for poor people. A good church bus evangelism program will work just as well, if not better, in the middle- and upper-income areas.

25. The use of improper methods of evangelizing children. Children can be saved. Children should be saved. And children will be saved if the church follows the command and example of Jesus. Some people get uptight when you talk about winning children to Christ. But about 60 books of the Bible teach that we should guide and direct a child in the way he should go. The devil is so anxious to claim the child for his domain that he has perpetrated some strange ideas about child evangelism.

26. A wrong concept of the use of contests, gifts, awards, and treats.

27. Expecting to have a good bus ministry with leftover workers, and leftover time in the overloaded calendar of church activities.

The second category are the measurable items. These may be a little more concrete and specific than the nonmeasurable items. Actually, they are the visible expressions of most of the nonmeasurable items.

1. Choosing a director of the church bus evangelism ministry who is half-hearted, inadequately trained, inexperienced, unenthusiastic, and uncommitted to this ministry. Each church bus evangelism director should have served successfully as a bus captain. That is, he should have started at least one bus route and built it up to average fifty riders or more a week for at least one month. He should have brought in one hundred or more riders on his route at least one time. *This is very important.* One of the greatest things that could happen in many churches with a sick bus ministry is for the church bus evangelism director to become a bus captain for a few months.

2. Failure of the bus captain to spend an adequate amount of time every Saturday in enlisting new riders, visiting absentees, and contacting known prospects. Each bus captain should average at least four or more hours each week in route visitation with about one and a half hours of this used to enlist new bus riders.

3. Failure to recruit a good team of workers for each bus route. The team should include a competent, safe, and dependable driver; a dedicated, capable, reliable, and committed captain; an enthusiastic and supportive co-captain; and some energetic, dedicated, and dependable teenage bus program leaders.

4. A poor plan of recruiting and training workers. You should study chapters 8 and 9 in my new book entitled *Establishing an Aggressive Bus Ministry.*

5. Failure to provide workers and materials for conducting meaningful church services for children on their level. It is necessary to have a good children's worship program in order to have a successful bus ministry. The workers need to be well-trained and have adequate materials and program helps. The CBE supply in Nashville has the largest collection of books, supplies, and program helps for children's church that I know of anywhere.

6. Failure to provide good programs on the buses enroute to church and back home. The teenagers are usually the bus program leaders. These programs usually consist of singing, memorizing Bible verses, etc.

7. Inadequate training for bus workers. Failure to take them to observe some successful churches. Failure to take them to some good bus clinics.

8. Failure to provide some special activity for the riders after church on Sunday afternoon every few weeks.

9. Failure to train members in the proper counseling of children regarding conversion and church membership. Failure to provide

adequate counseling for the children when they respond to the Gospel. The book by J.B. Waddle entitled *Counseling Children about Conversion and Church Membership* is the best available on this subject. It is practical and helpful.

10. Failure to train members in winning the parents to Christ. The bus workers will open many doors into the homes and hearts of adults. There should be an adequate number of soul winners to go and lead them to Christ.

11. Starting with too few buses. Every church should begin with at least two buses, regardless of how small the church. Churches with a membership of three hundred or more should probably start with more than two buses.

12. Buying just one expensive trip bus as the first bus rather than several evangelism buses.

13. Buying small buses. The buses should be the largest possible—at least 54-passenger capacity or more.

14. Failure to provide adequate Sunday School space. Unwillingness to relocate classes and departments in order to balance the size of the class with the size of the room. Unwillingness to set up two Sunday Schools, if necessary. Unwillingness to rent adjacent space such as school buildings, homes, or public buildings. The final command of Jesus was not to fill your building one Sunday morning but to take the Gospel to every person.

15. Wrong ideas about special high attendance Sundays, as to the value of them, how to plan them, how to promote them, and how to benefit from them.

16. Dependence upon advertising in newspapers, radio, television, or leaflets to secure riders for the buses.

17. Selective evangelism. Passing by certain homes or certain blocks because "that kind of people" are not welcome at your church.

18. Beginning the bus routes too far from the church building. The best place to start is usually right at your church. There is a good chapter in my *Establishing an Aggressive Bus Ministry* on selecting the best areas for the bus routes.

These are only some of the things that can contribute to failure. There are others also. The only thing easy and natural about church bus evangelism is failure. Everything else requires planning and hard work. Perhaps the greatest failure of all is not to begin, if there are many people with transportation needs in your community.

If your church bus evangelism is not succeeding as it should, then consider all of these items. Begin to make improvements in areas of weakness.

section V

Personnel Development

23

What is a Sunday School teacher? Surprisingly, the teacher has a role similar to the pastor's.

The Sunday School Teacher

Inasmuch as there is no institution in the world like Sunday School, we cannot define a Sunday School teacher by comparing him to anyone else. We must go to the Word of God for a description.

The Sunday School teacher has the same responsibility to his class as the pastor has to his flock. We can define a Sunday School teacher as the extension of pastoral ministry into the life of the class. Therefore, to understand the duty of a Sunday School teacher we need to examine the role of the pastor.

God's plan for a pastor is found in Acts

The Sunday School teacher has the same responsibility to his class as the pastor has to his flock. (Canyon Creek Baptist Church, Richardson, TX)

20:28—"Take heed therefore unto yourselves, and to all the flock, over the which the Holy Ghost hath made you overseers, to feed the church of God, which he hath purchased with his own blood."

Notice, the pastor should teach "all the flock," because God has given him responsibility for every person in his congregation.

Technically, the pastor should teach every Sunday School class in the church. But on Sunday morning this is a physical impossibility in a one-hour time span. Also, it is a psychological impossibility, inasmuch as Beginners cannot be taught with young married couples. Therefore, the pastor must delegate his teaching authority to qualified representatives.

Everything a pastor is to his congregation, the Sunday School teacher should be to his class. As the pastor is an example...so the Sunday School teacher is an example. As the pastor must teach the Word of God...so must the Sunday School teacher. As the pastor must visit... so must the Sunday School teacher.

Notice the three responsibilities of the pastor in Acts 20:28-30. These are the responsibilities of a Sunday School teacher.

1. *To lead the flock.* Paul told the elders at Ephesus that they were to take heed to themselves and the flock that God had permitted them to oversee. The leader must lead by example. He must lead by making the correct decisions. He must lead by motivating his people to follow. A Sunday School teacher is first and foremost a spiritual leader.

2. *To feed the flock.* Just as the pastor is to feed all the flock, so the Sunday School teacher should give the Word of God to his pupils. He teaches by lecture, by questions and answers, by visual aids, by repetition, and by explanation. The teacher should use every means possible to reach every pupil.

3. *To protect the flock.* Paul warned the elders that grievous wolves would come from the outside and enter the flock. Therefore they were to be watchful. Also, he warned of some arising from *within* the flock to tear it apart. Just as a shepherd must protect his sheep, so a pastor must protect his congregation. Following this example, the Sunday School teacher must protect his flock. This means visitation. If a young girl is absent two weeks in a row, the teacher should mail a card, contact her by phone, and/or make a personal visit. Some teachers have the mistaken notion that visitation is an American publicity device to balloon attendance. Not so. A teacher visits to

A good Sunday School teacher will visit pupils who are ill, to encourage them in the faith. (Scripture Press)

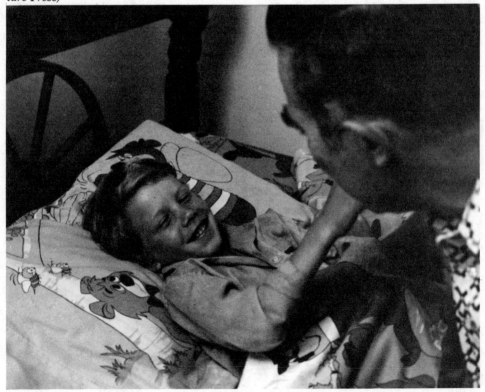

protect straying lambs. Even those who are sick need a "protective call" to encourage them in the faith. The old adage remains true: "A homegoing teacher makes a churchgoing pupil."

Qualifications

A Sunday School teacher not only must be a born-again believer. He must have experienced a spiritual change in his life. To be qualified to present the Gospel of Jesus Christ to the unsaved, he must have the assurance of his own salvation. His spiritual life must be established on a good foundation. He must be wholly separated (set apart) from the lusts of the world.

The Sunday School teacher can maintain a consistent spiritual life by daily yielding himself to the Spirit of God. He must be able to feed himself from the Word of God; to mature in Christ.

The Sunday School teacher must agree with the local church in theology so that there will be no conflict of purposes: pupils will be taught the same Biblical doctrines in both Sunday School and worship services.

A Sunday School teacher must be faithful and regular in church and class attendance, unless ill. If ill, he must inform the superintendent so that he can get a substitute teacher. As a member of the church, he must participate in its activities as well as in the activities of his own class.

A teacher is a builder; each pupil a temple. Therefore the teacher's construction work is most important. First, it consists of leading each pupil to accept Jesus Christ as Lord and Savior. Second, it is building upon that foundation a life free and wholesome—a life which seeks to become everything that God intended, through His grace and power.

Some of the requirements of such a teacher are:

1. *Purpose and perseverance.* The first essential characteristic of any builder is his dedication to his job. Unless personal consecration has been made, it will be impossible to rightly shoulder responsibilities as a Sunday School teacher. There will be no experience to draw upon to help others build their Christian lives.

A teacher must be able to say with Paul, "Brethren, I count not myself to have apprehended: but *this* one thing I *do,* forgetting those things which are behind, and reaching forth unto those things which are before, I press toward the mark for the prize of the high calling of God in Christ Jesus" (Philippians 3:13,14).

A life thus consecrated to the will of God is ready to be used of Him, ready to help build those temples which, for a short while, have been entrusted to his labor. This consecration needs to be daily. It needs to be the prayer before every period of preparation and before entering every class. Only with daily instruction from the Master Builder, can a teacher

rightly build his own temple—and help build someone else's.

2. *Inspiration.* A teacher needs ability to inspire those with whom he works. He can't inspire anyone else unless he is inspired. The teacher who matter-of-factly presents the lesson, with little enthusiasm, will never receive the response from the class that the vibrant, enthusiastic teacher arouses.

There also must be a zest for living in the heart of the teacher, a wholesome interest in life and a sense of wonder.

"It's not the way he teaches—it's the way he lives," one boy said of his teacher.

Vibrant, exuberant Christianity is contagious. Try it on pupils. Take them into God's outdoors. Few children are too young or too old to be awed by the beauties of nature.

Take time to let Psalm 19 sink in. Let childhood wonder take over; let pupils send your spirit soaring. Then bring that wonder and thrill to class. Let pupils know the thrill of trying to behold the love of the Father. If a teacher is completely inspired, captured in mind and spirit, that thrill is transmitted to the class.

3. *Experience.* Another requirement of a builder is experience, for we teach best out of our own experiences.

We may be prone to shrink from experience, not knowing whether or not it will be pleasant. But Jesus never shrank from experience. He welcomed it. He seized all opportunities. He went into the wilderness, knowing He would have to face both physical and spiritual hardships, some new to Him. Yet He went willingly, knowing what He would endure there would equip Him for His ministry.

In our quest to become wise master-builders, we must seek experiences to enrich life and make teaching come alive. Illustrations then will crowd upon us. Extensive research will be unnecessary.

Our experiences may not be sensational, but through them our Christian life will be deepened and our character strengthened. A study of the lives of many great saints also can be of great value, for their problems and experiences parallel contemporary ones.

4. *Knowledge.* A builder also needs to study, to know his materials and tools. A teacher must be a scholar and constant seeker for knowledge even though the field is so great the course cannot be completed in a lifetime.

Many teachers think that with a knowledge of the Bible, they are well-advanced in the field of teaching. True, a Sunday School teacher needs to know what is in the Bible. But he also must know how to interpret those truths and how to translate them into the everyday experiences of his class members, to make them meaningful and significant.

Every teacher needs to know where to find help in understanding difficult portions of Scripture. He or she will seek such aids as pic-

An interested teacher will try to understand each pupil's personal needs and help him adjust to his particular environment. (Scripture Press)

tures, filmstrips, stories, and the like, to make the lesson more vivid and real.

The wise teacher will seek to know the particular needs of the age group with which he is working, to know how best to reach his pupils. He needs to study the psychology of the age group; to understand the children and their reactions. An interested teacher will learn the background of each pupil, understand his personal needs and help him adjust to his particular environment.

5. *Curiosity.* A teacher must possess an inquisitive or exploratory nature. If he doesn't happen to possess this characteristic, it can be developed. One of the first steps in learning is a healthy curiosity. This is true in teaching.

Teaching is both exploration and discovery. The statement in II Corinthians (4:7), "But we have this treasure in earthen vessels, that the excellency of the power may be of God, and not of us," could be interpreted to mean that there is a treasure in every individual, placed there by God. It is the privilege and duty of the teacher to help the pupil find that treasure, that it may be used to the glory of God.

Preparing a Sunday School lesson

1. Start lesson preparation early in the week, so reading and experiences may be incorporated.

2. Have a central aim in your lesson. Observe the unit aim in your quarterly (if any).

3. Read the background Scripture passages from several versions for clarification.

4. Let the passage "soak" into your mind by slow, thoughtful meditation.

5. Use commentaries, Bible dictionaries, and a Bible atlas for additional help.

6. Develop a clear outline for the class to follow. Choose from your teacher's manual what you can fit into the class period, and what you want to emphasize.

7. Arrange time for prayer, review, Bible study (lesson), Bible reading, discussion, pupil's book, memory work, application and closing. Be flexible.

8. Remember the needs of individuals in your class (discovered through visitation). Keep in mind that you are teaching persons and not just lesson content. Know the age group.

9. Develop a file, with a folder for each topic, to add illustrations, outlines and other teaching aids each year you continue to teach.

10. Know the work required in the pupil's book. Determine how to use it in class review, work period, discussion.

11. Plan an interesting approach to capture attention. This may be a question to stimulate thought, a problem to solve, a true-life story to illustrate the lesson, a visual aid to motivate interest in the lesson.

12. Plan variety in methods—visuals, object lessons, drama, stories, sword drills, questions and answers, discussion, writing, buzz groups, problem solving.

13. Plan thoroughly what to say or ask to arouse class participation. Mere "telling is not teaching; listening is not learning!"

14. Develop study questions to cause the pupils to delve into the Bible for themselves—who, what, when, where, why (What does the Bible say? What does it mean? What does it mean to me?).

15. Allow pupils to ask questions. If you don't know the answers, admit it and state you will seek the answer during the week, or assign the question to the class for study.

16. Allow pupils to make applications for themselves. Suggest some applications and let them decide.

17. Prepare the room before the class period,

arranging chairs, visual aid equipment, decorations, objects.

18. Pray for wisdom in preparation, clarity in presentation, and sincerity in application.

Bible Study in Lesson Preparation

The Bible is the Word of God which brings the revelation of God's mind to men. If we are to teach God's message, we must first comprehend what He says. Here are some practical methods for preparing the lesson.

1. *Read the text.* Before reading commentaries in quarterlies or lesson aids, read the Bible lesson passage thoroughly several times. Write down all questions that come to mind. Put yourself in the pupil's place. What does he need to know? What bothers him? Note possible answers.

2. *Read the context.* Read the entire chapter, section, or book of the Bible in which the lesson passage occurs. Some passages of the Bible seem self-contained, but seen in the light of the whole book, they look different. Try to understand the setting by the circumstances under which the passage was written, the line of thought with which it is connected, and the main emphasis of the section where the passage appears.

3. *Study the details.* Who are the persons mentioned? What does this book say about them elsewhere? What does the Bible as a whole teach about them? Use a concordance or Bible dictionary and center references.

Exactly what events occurred? Name them in order. Is there a similar event elsewhere in the Bible? Locate places in an atlas.

4. *What does the text teach?* The teaching of the Bible is called "doctrine." Determine the doctrine by asking, What is the main principle of this text? What do the words mean? How is it illustrated? How is the teaching of this passage linked with the general teaching of the Bible?

5. *How is the teaching applied?* How is this to be applied to the pupil's life? Completion of a Bible story is not the end of a lesson. Its carryover into life must be determined by application.

A SUGGESTED TEACHER'S COVENANT

Recognizing the high privilege that is mine to serve my Lord through our Sunday School, and trusting in the help and guidance of the Holy Spirit, I earnestly pledge myself to this covenant.

1. I will live what I teach about separation from the world and purity of life, "avoiding all appearance of evil," setting an example in dress, conversation, deportment and prayer. Ephesians 4:11.

2. I will be faithful in attendance and make it a practice to be present at least 10 minutes early to welcome each pupil as he arrives. If at any time, through sickness or other emergency, I am unable to teach my class I will notify my

superintendent at the earliest possible moment. I Corinthians 4:2.

3. I will at all times manifest a deep spiritual concern for the members of my class. My first desire shall be to bring about the salvation of each pupil who does not know the Lord Jesus and to encourage the spiritual growth of every Christian. Daniel 12:3.

4. I will carefully prepare my lessons and make each lesson session a matter of earnest prayer. I Thessalonians 5:17.

5. I will regularly attend and urge members of my class to be present at the church services, recognizing that the church and Sunday School are inseparable. Believing in the importance of prayer, I will endeavor to maintain regular attendance at the church services, recognizing that the church and Sunday School are inseparable. Believing in the importance of prayer, I will endeavor to maintain regular attendance at the midweek prayer service, as well as Sunday services.

6. I will teach according to the doctrines of our church, Christ our Savior, Sanctifier and Coming King. Acts 20:27.

7. I will wholeheartedly cooperate with the absentee program of our school and will strive to visit the homes of each pupil at least once a year. Matthew 18:12.

8. I will heartily support the Sunday School program, attending at least nine of the twelve monthly teachers' meetings and the training classes. II Timothy 2:15.

9. I understand that my appointment as a teacher is for the 12-month period beginning the first Sunday in October. Whether my appointment is made then or later in the Sunday School year, I understand that it automatically terminates September 20 and that decisions regarding reappointment are based on my fulfillment of this teacher's covenant. I Corinthians 3:9.

10. I will cheerfully abide by the decisions of my church and Sunday School, cooperating with my fellow workers in bringing our work to the highest possible degree of efficiency as one of the teaching agencies of the church. Matthew 28: 19,20; John 15:16.

The Sunday School teacher has a solemn responsibility before God. (Scripture Press)

24

How can one develop leadership ability?

Leadership

"There go my people. I must hurry and catch up with them, for I am their leader." Ghandi's well-known statement has a certain application to church leadership today. The inability of leaders to lead is a frequent weakness in the volunteer work of the church. Yet while God is the undisputed Leader of His church, He continues to use human instrumentality to accomplish His work.

Leadership is one of the gifts of the Spirit (1 Corinthians 12), and it does not necessarily follow that a given leader is adept in every phase of Sunday School work. One person may have a gift for teaching, another for evangelism, and so on. Few people have all these gifts. Some inept leadership results from the church's tendency to overlook this point and to assume that a leader in one field is suited to lead in any area.

Keeping in mind that specific leaders may be needed for specific areas, examine some of the general qualifications of a leader:

1. *Poise.* Poise is not a "front" or a mask. Poise results when a leader knows his subject and the age group to whom he ministers. Poise comes from relying on the indwelling presence and aid of the Holy Spirit. Thus, one's outer manner reflects his inward faith and assurance.

2. *Bearing.* The leader's bearing further reflects his inner attitude through his posture and walk. While his head is raised in con-

fidence, it is not tilted with pride. While he walks with an air of assurance, it is not a strut of vanity. A leader may be recognized by the pleasure and assurance with which he approaches his task—attitudes, again, born of faith as well as preparation.

3. *Projection.* A leader has eye contact and heart contact with those he leads. He reaches out to his listeners with an interest and concern evident in his words and tone. He knows what he is going to say without having to read it, so his eyes constantly scan the faces of his hearers and note their reactions. He knows enough about his subject to be able to present additional facts if his listeners register lack of comprehension or unrest.

4. *Sharing.* A leader does not attempt to perform all the functions in his given sphere of activity. If, for example, he is the general superintendent of the Sunday School, his function is to share his knowledge and give direction for others to follow. He does not constantly push from behind, saying, "You must do this or that." Rather he shares his own knowledge of how to do it and sets an example through his own performance. The superintendent does not teach, but he usually has the responsibility of training the teachers in his department.

5. *Humility.* Probably this quality differentiates the real leader from the self-styled "big shot." The true leader in God's work has the

Leadership is one of the gifts of the Spirit.

qualification listed by the Lord Jesus Christ, "Whosoever will be chief among you, let him be your servant" (Matthew 20:27). Faithful, willing service commends one for consideration for leadership posts. While some persons seem to have inborn leadership qualities, study and practice can improve this ability. Giving of oneself in service to Christ and His church develops a servant of God. The true leader recognizes his constant dependence upon the wisdom, direction and strength imparted by the Holy Spirit who appointed him to his task.

6. *Followship.* The leader is essentially a follower—of the leadership of the Holy Spirit of God. The Spirit's direction may be extended through the process of open and shut doors, realization of need in a specific area, or a vision of possibilities in a particular field through a message or book.

7. *Example.* The qualities of spiritual devotion that a church has a right to expect from any Christian will be exemplified by the leader. His strength and courage and vision will come from fellowship with God through prayer and Bible study, as well as through service. He has self-discipline. He goes the second mile in unselfish effort. His enthusiasm and other attitudes are contagious. In short, those who look up to him are going to emulate his qualities, so these qualities must be the highest and finest possible.

Characteristics of a Leader
1. *Vision.* He projects into the future, sees ahead.
2. *Commitment.* Our age of tension—with

nuclear warfare, social revolution, population explosion, automation, moral crises, materialism and mobility—breeds rootlessness, lack of identification, alienation, and meaninglessness. Persons who have found the purpose of God in Christ should be able to express their convictions in commitment.

3. *Involvement.* A leader does not just talk about commitment, he does something about commitment. Involvement means concern for life as it is, not what we wish it to be. There is willingness to help solve society's problems.

4. *Positive concept.* A leader has a realistic self-image. He can assess himself objectively, neither being deceived or discouraged by his limitations nor puffed up by his potentialities. He is not overly self-centered or self-concerned. He admits mistakes, but feels competent despite them.

5. *Acceptance.* He feels others are of worth and is supportive, encouraging, helpful, empathic. He cooperates, rather than competes. Feeling that other people are worthwhile, he is apt to feel that their efforts are worthwhile. He finds it difficult to say no when asked to assist in a worthy cause. He is a giving person.

6. *Perception.* The leader is aware of people, circumstances, ideas, attitudes, and the world outside himself. He sees the world in shades of grays, rather than black and white.

7. *Tolerance.* He tolerates ambiguities and uncertainties. He does not jump to conclusions or insist upon immediate action. He may appear to be indecisive, a "middle-of-the-roader." But he is in reality suspending judgment, knowing that there is a time for waiting and a time for action.

8. *Creativity.* The outworking of his unique self. To be creative is to be authentic, original and insightful, rather than imitative.

9. *Interdependence.* He relates to others and recognizes his dependence upon them. Other people's individuality and uniqueness make his own life fuller and more productive. He knows his real strength comes from contacts with others. When he accepts and supports others, he builds a better self. His relationships are not characterized by domination or submission, aggression or appeasement. He is magnanimous and forgiving.

10. *Communication.* The leader is open; he does not wear masks. He listens to others and does not dismiss an idea simply because of its source. He is not as concerned with having people agree with him, as with being understood. In striving to be understood he may try to "get through" the defensive psychological mechanisms of others by couching his ideas in non-threatening terms. This is not compromise, for he is tenacious and vigorous in presenting his beliefs when necessary.

Methods to Improve Leadership
1. *Orientation.* Proper orientation helps a worker do a job better. The first few weeks on

In a team situation members discuss objectives, evaluate experiences and prepare strategy.

the job will be decisive in determining the attitudes and habits of work. Supervisory relationships are best established early.

2. *Job description.* A job description is a useful tool in orientation and supervision. It needs to be flexible but should spell out duties, relationships, available assistance and expectations.

3. *Observation.* Trainees need to observe experienced workers. Observation of the leader in a teaching-learning situation with a chance to discuss the session is helpful to both observer and teacher-leader.

4. *Supervisory conference.* Every worker should have the privilege of reviewing his stewardship of teaching with a qualified supervisor. Evaluation and plans for future emphasis should be discussed.

5. *Workers' conference.* The regularly scheduled conference of workers provides for face to face interchange of view points in a group situation. The conference can be an effective vehicle in keeping spiritual concern before the group, providing training, caring for business that affects the entire group, and in providing fellowship.

6. *Guided reading, listening and seeing.* Church, public and personal libraries contain valuable information that workers can study at their own pace. Much valuable material can be circulated among workers. A growing supply of audio-visual training aids is also available.

7. *Visits with specialists.* Guest lecturers and discussion leaders can meet with your workers and share out of their experience and study.

8. *Delegates to conferences.* Arrange for representatives to attend gatherings that discuss relevant matters and allow them to report back to the group.

9. *Courses of study.* Formal courses of study are a useful means of improving workers. Because they involve a well-trained leader, require attendance and prescribe reading, they are a valuable feature of your leadership training program. Some churches require their leaders to attend improvement sessions.

10. *Apprenticeship.* This ancient method of learning is valuable for moderns. Observing, discussion, attempting, receiving correction and encouragement is a very effective way to learn.

11. *Team teaching and consultation.* In the team situation members of the team discuss objectives, evaluate experiences and prepare strategy. Leadership is shared according to the skills of the team members. Consultation is especially valuable at the beginning of a team experience.

25

In the final analysis, the power and potential of a Sunday School is either generated or dissipated in the teachers' meeting.

The Sunday School Teachers Meeting

The Sunday School teachers' meeting is a tool for leadership education. It brings workers together at regular intervals for conference, study, fellowship, business transactions and inspiration. One leading Christian educator has described it as "an educational session of the school's workers for the purpose of exchanging ideas, receiving inspiration and instruction, and achieving unity in common objectives and programs." Another adds the idea that it is held "with a view to improving (their work)."

It is in the teachers' meeting that: (1) problems are presented and considered, and (2) a solution is sought; (3) new plans of work are talked over; (4) failures are faced and the causes are discovered; (5) successes are reviewed and the reasons found; (6) programs of action are formulated. It is a democratic meeting where each has a voice and all have the common interest of the church and its school at heart.

While the meeting emphasizes teacher improvement, the devotional, educational, and fellowship aspects also are recognized as important. Workers need constant training to keep abreast of the times. They also need incentive and inspiration to accomplish the best results. They grow under the challenge to faithful, sustained effort, brought about by contact with fellow workers under conditions that stimulate and quicken interest, cement friendships, enlarge visions, deepen their sense of responsibility, strengthen loyalty, and motivate them to do the best work possible.

The importance of the teachers' meeting was summarized in the 1960 *Sunday School Encyclopedia:* "In the final analysis, the power and potential of a Sunday School is either generated or dissipated in the teachers' meeting."

Purpose of the Teachers' Meeting

The primary purpose of the teachers' meeting is educational. It is the means whereby workers learn to plan and carry on a better program of teaching. It must be a cooperative study and effort with common understandings about major aims and the elements of a good program. Each worker should examine his own area and recognize the need for improvement. An underlying reason for such a meeting is to provide an opportunity for workers to understand and solve their problems.

The teachers' meeting is not to be confused with the education committee meeting. The purpose of the latter is to give general oversight to the educational work of the church as a whole and to build it into a total comprehensive program. It sets up standards, goals, forms policies, chooses leaders, and sees that the heads of organizations carry out the plans delegated to them.

Not all Sunday Schools teach the lesson to teachers at the weekly meeting. Those who do

The Sunday School teachers' meeting is a tool for leadership education. (Scripture Press)

not should have these goals: (1) fellowship, (2) inspiration, (3) information, (4) instruction (practical messages). Or, stated another way: (1) smooth-running school, (2) spiritual school, (3) evangelistic school, (4) growing school.

1. *To gain a vision of the whole task.* Concentration on the separate details of a picture blurs the effect of the whole. There is a definite need to get a broad view of the work of the Sunday School. The workers should have common understandings about the large general goals, including the elements which make up a comprehensive program. Each worker should know what is being accomplished by the others.

2. *To see the place of one's individual work.* Each worker should see the relationships and interdependence of the various parts. He should also see clearly the true perspective, sense of proportion, and proper relationships of his work to the whole. Lack of cooperation at any point or in any phase of the work weakens the whole program.

3. *To serve as a means for solving problems.* Many problems are best solved through cooperation of the workers. As the adage says, "Many heads are better than one." Ideas will surface in a group that one person alone would not think of.

4. *To reach more with leadership training.* Only a few workers can arrange for trips to teachers institutes, conventions, or meetings, while many can attend a church's once-a-

month meeting.

5. *To make possible democratic planning.* Workers understand more fully those plans they have helped to formulate, and they know better how to put them into effect. They are then more able and willing to carry the work forward.

6. *To keep up-to-date.* The latest educational methods and materials should be explained and/or distributed at the teachers' meeting.

7. *To promote fellowship and deeper consecration.* Thinking together and other teamwork help draw the departments together. Their cooperative worship and prayer brings the blessing of the Lord.

God's Word has all the principles we need to serve Him effectively. In Proverbs 15:22 we read: "Without counsel, purposes are disappointed: but in the multitude of counselors they are established." God's blessing always is on those who obey His word and the advice in it.

Organizing the Teachers' Meeting

1. Although teachers' meetings may be initiated by anyone who has the firm conviction that they really are needed, and who has a knowledge of the purpose of such a program, it is really the pastor's or Sunday School Superintendent's duty to start them. Then it is up to this conscientious "starter" to create interest among teachers and officers.

2. Next, a committee should be appointed to

look into the different aspects of the teachers' meeting, and to list the pros and cons. This committee should report to all the workers and receive approval or disapproval of the program. Teachers and officers must be enthusiastic about such a conference before it is launched, for only as the entire staff works as a unit will the Sunday School operate efficiently.

3. The superintendent of the Sunday School should be responsible for planning and directing the teachers' meeting, although any qualified teacher could handle this position. He should serve as general chairman of the meetings and should conduct the business sessions. However, he should delegate most of the other duties. Wide participation by workers means greater interest and educational growth. He should appoint a committee to plan the program, another to conduct it, and another to put into operation the plans for improvement. The director should give guidance and supply needed materials. He is somewhat like a liaison officer, bringing recommendations of the committee to the conference and taking the problems and requests of the conference to the committee.

4. A secretary should be elected to keep notes of all business and to see that mimeographed copies of the minutes are given to all members, including absentees. A treasurer should be elected to care for all financial matters.

5. To run efficiently, the teachers' meeting should be planned well in advance. It should be organized with a carefully arranged time schedule, to accomplish the maximum results in terms of the total work to be done. Consideration should be given to the following: (a) a theme for each month's meeting, (b) a variety of methods of presentation, (c) items that need to be covered throughout the year, (d) content of the instruction periods, (e) special speakers, and (f) program participation. These meetings can be planned by a committee working with the pastor, the superintendent, and the chairman of the board, or the board can plan the meetings.

Program of the Teachers' Meeting

Many long hours of planning are put into the teachers' meeting to make it interesting and efficient. Therefore, explicit care must be exercised in advertising the meetings. When a meeting is called, every effort should be made to assure attendance.

Since punctuality is vitally important, the meeting should begin promptly at the designated time—and end on time. Also of great importance is the order of the meeting. Many churches find it difficult to plan a specific order, hence the following pattern is suggested:

1. *Devotions.* This includes one or more hymns, Scripture reading, and prayer.
2. *Reports.* Minutes of previous meeting, treasurer's report, and departmental reports.
3. *Unfinished business.* Reports on activities planned at previous meetings.
4. *New business.* Action on recommendations made by departments or committees; also plans for coming events.
5. *Educational feature.* Instruction, various speakers, or films.
6. *Fellowship.* Sometimes the meeting is preceded by a fellowship supper. However, for the best results, a fellowship supper should be given only once a quarter. Some groups serve refreshments during a period of informal fellowship at every meeting.
7. *Departmental meetings.* Some churches have departmental conferences before the fellowship supper. After the supper they present reports and recommendations at the general meeting.

The opening devotional service has a fourfold purpose: (1) to recognize God's presence and guidance, (2) to bring the spirit of worship into the conference, (3) to train the workers in the expression of spiritual aspirations, and (4) to prepare the hearts and minds of those present to get the most out of the session.

In the business session, *Roberts Rules of Order* should be followed. The chairman should be familiar with these rules and should enforce them. Business at the teachers' meeting includes roll call, the reading of the minutes, the attendance report, the treasurer's report and departmental reports. Unfinished business should follow. New business is then considered. Action is taken on requests submitted in the departmental reports.

The educational part of the program is a period of instruction or training. This may effectively be presented by means of reports, visual aids, panel discussion, forums, or demonstrations. (See Section on Methods.)

If the meeting includes a lesson-planning-time, the potential of the lesson can be stressed. The teachers may question some point in the lesson, which then can be explained by an appointed instructor. A speaker who is an authority on a specific subject covered in the lesson would be of great help to the teachers.

After the educational program, points of interest and new ideas should be discussed. The leader should be careful not to let the discussion become irrelevant. If different viewpoints are presented, the leader should give attention to all and bring the group to a definite conclusion.

The social hour should be considered an important fact of the conference, and should be directed by a competent committee, whether there is a fellowship supper or not. A decorated room often adds a desirable atmosphere.

Departmental meetings also are necessary. They should focus on aims, problems, subjects, and methods of special concern to each particular department. The study and planning should be geared to the age group being taught. Lesson applications and teaching methods should be stressed. The superintendent of the specific department should be in charge of the

The educational part of the program may be presented by means of reports, visual aids, panel discussions, or demonstrations. Multimedia learning kits for teacher training are available from various publishers. (David C. Cook)

departmental meetings.

Matters not important enough for the general teachers' meeting can be discussed and settled in departmental meetings. A conclusion should be reached as to recommendations to be submitted to the general meeting or education committee.

The departmental meeting could meet either before or after the general meeting, depending on the needs of the local Sunday School. If the departmental meeting is first, special problems can be brought up later in the general meeting. However, there is some advantage in first meeting together in a large combined group, then planning in detail in separate groups.

If each program is well-planned and interesting, the workers will continue to attend and will receive inestimable help. Some suggested topics for discussion at the teachers' meeting are:

1. How can we increase average attendance?
2. What can be done to make the worship period more meaningful?
3. What can be done to enlist and train more workers?
4. How can we make the visitation program more effective?
5. How can we overcome absenteeism and encourage latecomers to be on time?
6. How should a lesson be prepared?
7. What is the proper use of the Bible in Sunday School?

The sevenfold purpose of the teachers' meetings shows the necessity of continuing such a program after it has been put into operation in order to have a successful, growing Sunday School. Restated, this sevenfold purpose is:

1. Initiate with fellowship.
2. Inspire with worship.
3. Inform with facts.
4. Instruct with practical studies.
5. Involve in departmental groups.
6. Interest with year's program for Sunday School.
7. Intercession through prayer.

A suggested program has been presented incorporating the sevenfold purpose, which may be changed to suit individual needs. Variety is not only good, but essential for worthwhile meetings.

God's Word includes principles regarding every attempt His children make to serve Him. In Proverbs 11:14, we are told, "Where no counsel is, the people fall: but in the multitude of counselors there is safety." And in Proverbs 13:10, God reminds us that "only by pride cometh contention: but with the well-advised is wisdom."

This conclusion may be drawn: "As the teachers' meeting goes, so goes the Sunday School." A successful Sunday School teachers' meeting, supported by hard work and fervent prayer, will help bring about a successful Sunday School to the glory of the Lord Jesus Christ.

26

Your church's ability to maintain an adequate teaching staff depends on its procedures to

Enlist, Train, and Retain Teachers

Enlist

How can a church enlist teachers for the Sunday School? Whose task is it to do the enlisting? From what sources may workers be recruited? Answers include the following:

Source of Prospective Teachers

1. *Churchwide survey.* Discover talents and interests of members. Include questions such as: Have you ever taught Sunday School? If so, what age group? What age group do you prefer to work with? What is your favorite form of recreation: Reading? Music? Sports? Art? Other? Do you play an instrument? Which? File a card for each potential teacher.

2. *Visit.* Call on the persons who show teaching potential. Talk with them and note on their cards any teaching experience, special aptitudes in a craft or profession, or college training in the teaching field.

3. *Observe.* Note the faithful attenders in youth and adult classes. Talk with their teachers about their participation and teaching potential.

4. *Vacation Bible School.* The list of Vacation Bible School workers will turn up names of some who serve regularly as assistants in a department. Their interest and abilities may be further explored.

5. *The invitation.* Those who respond to an invitation for dedication of life for whatever service the Lord opens.

Who Does the Enlisting?

1. *A nominating committee.* Many churches have a nominating committee elected or appointed annually. It is the task of this committee to secure workers for every office and teachers for every department. (Those who have served on the committee often are glad to be released from duty as the year expires, because of the difficulty in getting the consent of persons capable of doing a specific task.)

2. *The Director of Christian Education.* If there is not such a director, the general superintendent of the Sunday School usually is responsible for enlisting workers. During visitation he always should be aware of potential co-laborers in the educational work of the church.

3. *The pastor.* Since he contacts all the membership of the church through home and hospital visits, he is in the best position to know the person behind the face. In the home, he can see the character and personality of the men and women on the roll. He can observe in the lives of the children the type of home training given. Conversation will show him the interests and activities of the people. He can make the initial contact for the nominating committee, or he can refer names to them.

How Can Workers Be Enlisted?

1. *A visit.* This is perhaps the best way to discuss such an important and often life-changing

decision. A casual church hallway chat does not allow for real thought about the seriousness of the request. Time spent in a personal visit emphasizes its importance to the potential teacher.

2. *A letter.* Because a letter may be read and reread, studied and prayed over at leisure, the request for service may be stated on paper. The need often is presented more clearly in writing, and the force of the visitor's personality does not stand between the visitor and the prospect. The force of the request itself makes the impression.

3. *A telephone call.* Again, face-to-face reaction does not distract, and a heart-to-heart call may accomplish what a visit could not. Unable to see the quick negative response often registered at first, a timid superintendent or committee member continues to talk on the telephone without having his enthusiasm dampened. And the prospective teacher cannot see the worried frown of concern on the face of the caller as excuses are given.

4. *A pulpit plea.* Occasionally a pastor feels God would have him give an altar call for a task for which volunteers are needed, leaving it to the Lord—so to speak—to bring forth His chosen workers. A decision made publicly usually proves valid.

Training the Enlisted

"Yes, I'll be glad to do what I can. But I don't know much about teaching," a willing Christian may admit. "I don't know the first thing about standing up there and talking (misconstrued by many as synonymous with *teaching*) or keeping kids quiet." Churches may provide needed guidance to volunteers in a number of ways.

1. *Apprenticeship.* It works in the public school and it works in churches. An inexperienced teacher may be chosen as an assistant in the age-group of expressed interest and preference. Such a person may be of real help to the teacher by arranging chairs, getting out and putting away materials, recording absentees, perhaps playing the piano or leading the singing. The apprentice is in the room to help when a child needs attention (going to the washroom, a slight injury, removing or putting on wraps, misbehavior). At the same time she can observe the regular teacher's methods from week to week. After a time, the apprentice should be asked to be responsible for a specific part of the weekly program: the character or mission story, an object lesson, the songs, a puppet. When she is confident of handling an entire lesson, she should be given additional responsibility.

2. *Training classes.* A continuing training class during the Sunday School hour provides training at the time when the most workers can be present. Some churches have an ongoing training class during the training hour preceding the evening service. This class is not a class in Bible content but a study of teaching methods. Inexperienced teachers (and that, unfortunately, could include a large percentage of

Teaching teams provide excellent opportunities for teacher apprenticeships.

the regular teaching staff of many churches) should attend 8 or 12 weeks of sessions covering various ways of presenting the lesson, maintaining good discipline, capturing and holding attention.

3. *Saturday workshops.* Bring in an outside speaker who can effectively demonstrate a variety of approaches to teaching. Invite all teachers and prospective teachers to come for a Saturday afternoon (or a 10:00 through 2:00 session, including potluck lunch) for training in the use of techniques. This should never be a "sit and listen" affair, where the speaker merely lectures and everyone goes home none the wiser. It should be a demonstration and participation time, when workers are involved in learning by doing.

4. *Workers' banquet.* Prospective workers and regular teachers may be invited to a banquet. The after-dinner program may be a couple of hours of training, discussion and demonstration.

5. *Taped training.* Cassette tapes of teaching motivation and ideas may be circulated individually to new teachers, for their study at home in conjunction with an illustrated manual of instruction. Or the tapes may be enjoyed in a group meeting of all such teachers, followed by demonstration and discussion. (Check Christian supply catalogs for such tapes.)

6. *Books.* Provide each new worker with a good book of many methods of teaching (such as this volume or *Successful Teaching Ideas,*

Standard Publishing, 1975). If this is financially impossible due to large numbers of teachers, secure several copies of such a book for the church library and make it available for new workers for two weeks at a time.

7. *Regular workers' meetings.* Many churches have a weekly meeting of all teachers—including assistants and prospective teachers. A period is devoted to discussion of the Bible content for the forthcoming Sunday, after which individual departments assemble to plan and demonstrate methods on the various levels.

8. *Conventions, conferences.* Arrange for the church to sponsor new teachers as delegates to a statewide or national Sunday School convention, where training in each age group is available. The importance of the task is magnified by the enthusiasm of large numbers of teachers dedicated to the same task.

Retain

The teaching staff of most churches is largely composed of faithful workers who have served in their capacity for many years and have never considered doing anything else. They are dedicated to the Lord as well as to the church, and temporal rewards are not expected. However, even a consecrated teacher succumbs to the temptation to retreat from the firing line occasionally—or permanently. This intent may be due to:

1. *Lack of appreciation.* "I've been teaching in the Junior Department for 15 years and no-

A continuing training class during the Sunday School hour provides training at the time when the most workers can be present. (Scripture Press)

body ever appreciates anything I do," a teacher may complain. And her complaint probably is legitimate. The teacher of children (Juniors and younger) often is the hardest-working, least-appreciated worker in the church. The children themselves rarely say thank you for anything she does—unless prompted—and the parents remain unaware of what goes on in the class, unless a child is displeased with something. The simple device of regular, planned "teacher appreciation" can forestall the retreat of teachers. Teacher Appreciation Day may coincide with the annual Promotion Day. A church gift of a helpful methods or devotional book, public recognition and expressed gratitude, or a workers' banquet are ways to say thank you for long hours spent for the life and souls of children.

2. *Misfits.* Occasionally a volunteer for the teaching corps gets off to a poor start by attempting to serve the wrong age group. Here is a pointed reason for the practice of apprentice teaching. The assistant has opportunity to discover whether or not he can relate to and cope with the students in a given age group.

Some persons are at ease with preschool children, while others only "talk down to them." Some like the challenge of guiding and keeping up with wide-awake Juniors. Others cannot keep them in control and tear their hair out over the mass confusion. Others find the seeming indifference and inattention of teenagers frustrating; or the stoic faces of adults discouraging.

Through discovering their ineptitude with one group, they may be brought to an understanding of their rightful level and be placed where they feel they can do best.

Lack of proper adjustment is not confined to Sunday School teachers. It also happens in the public school. A first-grade teacher once discovered that her young charges "drove her up the wall" to the extent that their talking out of turn made her lose control; she threw a storybook across the room. She resigned from teaching after that first year.

A teacher may not voluntarily come to the superintendent and request a change. For this reason, many churches provide annual opportunities for teachers to answer a questionnaire which asks, "Are you satisfied to work with the age group which you are now serving? Do you want to continue with the same class the coming year? Would you rather serve elsewhere? If so, where?"

3. *Personality clashes.* Not understanding the shyness of a new worker, an experienced teacher may assume responsibilities which could be accomplished by the assistant. The inexperienced one may then feel useless. On the other hand, a new worker may have a spirit of love and enthusiasm which at once endears her to the children who swarm around her to the exclusion of the regular teacher. The result is hurt feelings on the part of the teacher, who may resent the newcomer. Since people sense a feeling of ill will, the new worker may ask for another assignment or may simply resign from teaching. If a superintendent maintains regular department meetings, problems like this can be aired in a Christian manner. Communication often establishes better relationships. If the superintendent cannot change the regular teacher's attitude, and if that established teacher is capable and faithful, he may have to move the assistant to another department for the sake of the future service of the newcomer.

4. *Inadequate classroom and/or equipment.* Having completed a course of instruction in good teaching techniques, some new teachers are shocked when they learn that the classroom where they are expected to teach is not large enough for the recommended activities. He also discovers that the room is next door to "those noisy boys," and the walls are thin. Sometimes he makes a snap judgment that "it can't be done." A more experienced teacher may be able to guide him over the hump, especially if the newcomer has been put in charge of a class by himself. The older teacher can show him how to capture and hold his pupils' attention, even in a noisy situation. The experienced teacher also can suggest substitutions for the plans which had to be abandoned because of over-crowding. For example, a resourceful teacher (old or new) will find ways to enlarge the available space through (1) getting rid of large chairs and using floor mats; (2) hanging chalk and flannel boards on the wall; (3) hinging a work table to the wall, to be pulled down only when needed. Sometimes resourceful teachers will find a junk room in the church which has more space than the assigned room. A simple switch makes everyone happy.

A superintendent or Director of Christian Education should be careful to maintain good relationships and the best possible facilities (however far from ideal) to keep his staff working together in harmony. He knows that it will be harder to get new workers enlisted and trained if he is unable to keep the ones who already are serving.

With teachers, as with business, "a satisfied customer is the best advertisement." The enthusiasm of dedicated teachers makes others willing to try.

CHRISTIAN SERVICE SURVEY

Name _____ Date _____

Residence _____

   (Street - RFD)   (City)   (State or Prov.) (Zip Code)

Occupation _____ Telephone _____ Business Telephone _____

Business Address _____

   (Street - RFD)   (City)   (State or Prov.) (Zip Code)

Age Group Youth ☐ Young Adult ☐ Middle Adult ☐ Older Adult ☐   Special Training _____
   12-24   25-35   35-60   60 plus

Key to Categories: Past (I have served), Present (I am serving), Future (I am willing to serve).

Boards — Committees — Officers	Past	Present	Future
Board of Deacons & Deaconesses	☐	☐	☐
Board of Trustees	☐	☐	☐
Board of Christian Education	☐	☐	☐
Church Moderator	☐	☐	☐
Church Clerk	☐	☐	☐
Church Treasurer	☐	☐	☐
Financial Secretary	☐	☐	☐
Sunday School Superintendent	☐	☐	☐
Sunday School Secretary	☐	☐	☐
Children's Church Director	☐	☐	☐
Training Hour Director	☐	☐	☐
Finance Committee	☐	☐	☐
Music Committee	☐	☐	☐
Visitation Committee	☐	☐	☐
Transportation Committee	☐	☐	☐
Missionary Committee	☐	☐	☐
Ushering Committee	☐	☐	☐
Publicity Committee	☐	☐	☐
Flower Committee	☐	☐	☐
Kitchen Committee	☐	☐	☐
Recreation Committee	☐	☐	☐
Auditing Committee	☐	☐	☐

Services	Past	Present	Future
Prayer Partner	☐	☐	☐
Organist	☐	☐	☐
Pianist	☐	☐	☐
Choir Director	☐	☐	☐
Song Leader	☐	☐	☐
Instrumental Player	☐	☐	☐
Choir Member	☐	☐	☐
Library Worker	☐	☐	☐
Audio Visual Worker	☐	☐	☐
General Office Worker	☐	☐	☐
Typist	☐	☐	☐
Mimeographer	☐	☐	☐
Telephone Caller	☐	☐	☐
Poster Work	☐	☐	☐
Nurse	☐	☐	☐
Recreational Worker	☐	☐	☐
Pageants - Dramatics Worker	☐	☐	☐
Crafts Worker	☐	☐	☐
Painter	☐	☐	☐
Manual Worker	☐	☐	☐
Electrical Worker	☐	☐	☐
Seamstress - Sewer	☐	☐	☐
Others	☐	☐	☐

(continued on next page)

Children's Work

Children's Work	Past	Present	Future
Sunday School:			
Department Supt.	☐	☐	☐
Department Sec.	☐	☐	☐
Department Pianist	☐	☐	☐
Teacher	☐	☐	☐
Children's Church:			
Leader	☐	☐	☐
Pianist	☐	☐	☐
Training Hour:			
Leader	☐	☐	☐
Worker	☐	☐	☐
Pianist	☐	☐	☐
Sponsors	☐	☐	☐
Weekday Club:			
Leader	☐	☐	☐
Worker	☐	☐	☐
Vacation Bible School:			
Dept. Supt.	☐	☐	☐
Dept. Sec.	☐	☐	☐
Dept. Pianist	☐	☐	☐
Teacher	☐	☐	☐

I am especially interested in the
- Cradle Roll, 0-2 yrs. ☐
- Nursery, 2-3 years ☐
- Kindergarten, 4-5 ☐
- Primary, grs. 1-3 ☐
- Junior, grs. 4-6 ☐

Youth Work

Youth Work	Past	Present	Future
Sunday School:			
Department Supt.	☐	☐	☐
Department Sec.	☐	☐	☐
Department Pianist	☐	☐	☐
Teacher	☐	☐	☐
Training Hour:			
Sponsor	☐	☐	☐
Pianist	☐	☐	☐
Officer	☐	☐	☐
Weekday Club:			
Steering Committee	☐	☐	☐
Boys	☐	☐	☐
Girls	☐	☐	☐
Club Leader			
Boys	☐	☐	☐
Girls	☐	☐	☐
Club Helper			
Boys	☐	☐	☐
Girls	☐	☐	☐
Vacation Bible School:			
Dept. Supt.	☐	☐	☐
Dept. Sec.	☐	☐	☐
Pianist	☐	☐	☐
Teacher	☐	☐	☐
Youth Counsellor	☐	☐	

I am especially interested in:
- Jr. Hi's, grs. 7-9 ☐
- Sr. Hi's, grs. 10-12 ☐
- Post High School ☐

Adult Work

Adult Work	Past	Present	Future
Sunday School:			
Department Supt.	☐	☐	☐
Department Sec.	☐	☐	☐
Department Pianist	☐	☐	☐
Teacher	☐	☐	☐
Cradle Roll Visitor	☐	☐	☐
Home Dept. Visitor	☐	☐	☐
Training Union:			
Adult Group Leader	☐	☐	☐
Leadership Education			
Instructor	☐	☐	☐
Group Bible Study			
Leader	☐	☐	☐
Women's Society			
Officer	☐	☐	☐
Group Chairman	☐	☐	☐
Men's Fellowship			
Officer	☐	☐	☐
Family Life Committee	☐	☐	☐
Senior Citizens:			
Leader	☐	☐	☐
Worker	☐	☐	☐

Signature _____

I believe that every church member should share in the church life and work. I intend to serve as I am able when the opportunity is presented to me.

3M–2–67   Printed in U.S.A. by North American Baptists, 7308 Madison Street, Forest Park, Illinois 60130.

section VI

Promotion
and Outreach

OUTREACH

NATURAL

Outreach Necessitates More Leadership

Leadership Sets the Pattern & Provides the Vision

PROGRAM
1. Advertising/Media
2. Canvassing
3. Busing
4. Organized Visitation
5. Psychology
6. Promotional Campaigns

FACTORS

Discipleship Leads to Outreach

Results Motivate Discipleship

A

(See copy below)

SPIRITUAL

FACTORS

LEADERSHIP

NATURAL FACTORS
1. Gifted
2. Multiplication of Ministry
3. "Hot Poker"
4. Formal Training
5. Weekly Interaction
6. Standards

D

CHURCH GROWTH

B

NATURAL MOTIVATION
1. Sense of Accomplishment
2. Recognition
3. Reward
4. Challenge
5. Personal Involvement
6. Competition
7. Exposure

DISCIPLESHIP

CONTRIBUTING

Organization Depends on Leadership

Leadership Values & Promotes Organization

C

TO GROWTH

Needs Necessitate Organization

Organization Promotes Discipleship

CONTRIBUTING

WISE ORGANIZATION
1. For Business Matters
2. For Educational Effectiveness
3. For Building Utilization
4. For Efficiency
5. For Involvement

TO GROWTH

ORGANIZATION

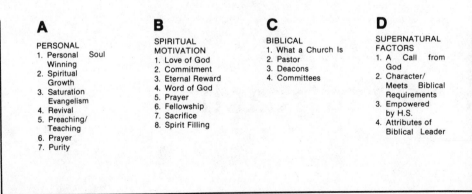

A

PERSONAL
1. Personal Soul Winning
2. Spiritual Growth
3. Saturation Evangelism
4. Revival
5. Preaching/ Teaching
6. Prayer
7. Purity

B

SPIRITUAL MOTIVATION
1. Love of God
2. Commitment
3. Eternal Reward
4. Word of God
5. Prayer
6. Fellowship
7. Sacrifice
8. Spirit Filling

C

BIBLICAL
1. What a Church Is
2. Pastor
3. Deacons
4. Committees

D

SUPERNATURAL FACTORS
1. A Call from God
2. Character/ Meets Biblical Requirements
3. Empowered by H.S.
4. Attributes of Biblical Leader

27

Specific principles seem to characterize growing churches.

Laws of Sunday School Growth

Growth is a dynamic word. Church growth is a dynamic concept. When a young man plants a New Testament church, he expects it to grow just as parents expect their baby to grow. Every pastor called to a new congregation expects results in his ministry. He expects to see people won to the Lord and Christians grow in spiritual stature. This is church growth.

Since church growth is the natural result of a healthy ministry, it is fitting that we define church growth.

First, church growth is numerical growth. However, the record needs to be set straight. No pastor ever aims to have numerical growth for its own sake. To attract a crowd so the church will be the "fastest growing" is not Biblical. The purpose of a church is to carry out the Great Commission: winning the lost to Jesus Christ and teaching them the Word of God (Matthew 28:19,20). When this is done, the congregation will automatically expand. In traditional Sunday Schools, an attendance offering poster was placed where everyone could see it. This made it possible to chart Sunday School growth—and it was an encouragement. The church in Jerusalem grew in numbers (Acts 1:15, 2:41, 4:4, 5:14, 6:1, 7), suggesting that all churches should be growing numerically.

The second area of church growth deals with spiritual maturity. A church should grow in grace, that is, in the total development of its religious life. Just as an individual grows in character, so the church grows in spiritual strength. As individuals within the church yield themselves to God, they grow in spiritual power. As individuals acquire more Bible knowledge, they grow in maturity. As individuals pray and commune with God, they grow in inner character.

Christians make two false assumptions regarding church growth. First, some believe that if the church is growing in spiritual character, an automatic expansion in numbers will result; that quality will lead to quantity. This is not necessarily so. The second false assumption, a reversal of the first, is that churches which are growing in numbers automatically are growing in Biblical maturity. It is possible for a numerically growing church to be superficial. It is also possible for a stagnant congregation to have individuals who are growing in grace and truth. Both congregations are growing, but neither has the full blessing of God.

The diagram at the beginning of this chapter focuses on church growth. The inner circle indicates the priority of growth—spiritual factors. The outer circle indicates the human or numerical aspects of growth. Some pastors give all of their attention to spiritual factors such as prayer, Bible teaching, and holiness, but neglect organization, outreach and wise administration. Other churches give all of their attention to programs, leadership, outreach

199

and attendance campaigns, but they neglect the spiritual dynamics.

Just as the rock thrown into the lake produces the highest waves at the center of impact, the spiritual dynamics of church growth have a greater priority than the natural principles. In the New Testament church, spiritual principles always should override natural principles; human factors should never override the spiritual factors.

The traditional laws of Sunday School growth have concerned themselves with organization and administration. On many occasions, a church has adhered to these "laws" only to stagnate. The churches in the book, *The Ten Largest Sunday Schools,* grew by giant steps, yet broke the traditional laws of Sunday School growth. There were other factors that caused their growth. Some of these were spiritual dynamics and new organizational methods to meet needs and solve problems that prohibited expansion.

The traditional laws of Sunday School growth were not wrong, but not all of them apply today. Many churches applied them and experienced expansion. New laws only add to what has been printed, bringing the Sunday School up to date.

OUTREACH

Spiritual Factors in Outreach

Some churches seem to naturally grow in numbers, reaching the community. These churches do not have organized visitation nor do they use promotional campaigns. Yet visitors come to their services, new members join their rank, offerings climb, and enrollment indicators go up. God has a plan for growing churches. This plan is found in the Word of God. Growing churches in the book of Acts were characterized by the following spiritual factors.

1. *Churches grow when they have New Testament aims.* The aim of the church is to go and "make disciples" of all nations (Matthew 28:19). The early church practiced soul winning, going to every house in Jerusalem (Acts 5:42). Paul went to every home in Ephesus (Acts 20:20) and reached every person in the city (Acts 20:31). God expects a church to grow.

2. *Churches grow best through the Sunday School.* The aims of the church are the aims of Sunday School. The Sunday School does the work of the church in reaching, teaching, winning and training. Some think Sunday School is for kids at 10 a.m., and preaching is for adults at 11 a.m. Both Sunday School and the worship service fulfill the aims of the church.

The Great Commission summarizes the aims of the local church. This is the last command Jesus gave before returning to heaven; this is the strategy of the church which includes preaching and teaching (Sunday School and church): "Go therefore and make disciples of all nations, baptizing them in the name of the Father and the Son and the Holy Spirit, teaching them to observe all that I commanded you; and lo, I am with you always even to the end of the age" (Matthew 28:19-20, New American Standard Bible).

The Great Commission is one command but has three aspects: (1) evangelism, (2) baptism and (3) teaching. Christians cannot choose what aspect of the Great Commission they will obey. A person disobeys the whole command in disobeying part. If a worker emphasizes teaching but neglects evangelism, he is not carrying out the Great Commission. God's strategy is evangelism, baptism and education.

The aspect of the Great Commission found in the word "teach" (verse 19), is better translated "disciple." We are commanded to disciple (evangelize) all nations. Implied in the word "disciple" is reaching the lost, communicating the Gospel to them and leading them to Jesus Christ. When we are discipling (evangelizing), we are helping members follow Jesus Christ and His commands. Therefore, evangelism involves more than presenting the Gospel to the unsaved or sharing salvation with them. We should attempt to persuade them to become Christians; should get people to follow Jesus Christ.

There is no success in the Lord's work without successors. Therefore, we want more than large crowds in Sunday School. We want disciples of Jesus.

Another thrust of the Great Commission is to baptize the new convert after salvation. Baptism is an outer symbol of inner reality. When the new Christian is baptized, he is identified with Christ in His death, burial and resurrected life (Romans 6:4-5). In the New Testament, when the believer was baptized, he also was added to the church (Acts 2:41, 47). Just as baptism symbolizes a Christian being placed in Jesus, so baptism symbolizes being placed in the local body of Christ. Therefore, when Christ commanded the disciples to go and "baptize," He was commanding to go and "church" people, i.e., get them identified with a local church.

The third aspect of the Great Commission is education. The church is given the responsibility of carrying out the example of Jesus the Teacher. He spent time with His disciples. The Sermon on the Mount begins with this observation, His disciples came to Him: and He taught them (Matthew 5:1-2). After He taught the disciples and the multitudes, we find this explanation: "He taught them as one having authority, and not as the scribes" (Matthew 7:29). The content of Christian education is suggested in the Great Commission, "Teaching them to observe all things whatsoever I have commanded you" (Matthew 28:20).

3. *Churches grow when they aim to carry out the Great Commission* (Matthew 28:18-20). They are to: *Make disciples of as many per-*

sons in the world as possible (Matthew 28:18) (a) by showing compassion on the needs of man, (b) by having a vision of what God can do for the lost, (c) by bringing the lost under the hearing of the Gospel, (d) by sharing their Christian experience with the lost, (e) by communicating the Gospel to all men, and (f) by persuading the lost to accept the Gospel.

Identify each Christian with a local church (Matthew 28:19) (a) by getting each Christian under the teaching of the Scriptures, (b) by using the total abilities of each Christian for God's purpose, (c) by encouraging fellowship among Christians so they may strengthen one another, (d) by producing corporate worship and motivating Christians to private worship, (e) by becoming the focus for an organized outreach into the community, (f) by administering the church ordinances.

Teach each Christian to be obedient to the Scriptures (Matthew 28:20) (a) by communicating the content of the Word of God, (b) by training each Christian to use his skills to carry out God's plan for his life, (c) by inculcating Christian values and attitudes in all believers, (d) by motivating Christians to live a godly life as called for in the Scriptures, (e) by supporting the aims and sanctity of the family.

4. *Churches grow by soul winning.* Philip won the Ethiopian eunuch; Peter preached to Cornelius; Paul witnessed to Sergius Paulus. Churches grew through winning souls to Christ. Evangelism is communicating enough of the Gospel so that a man can become saved, then persuading the man to accept Christ. There are two ways of looking at a church's outreach.

First there's *church evangelism*. The examples of the churches in the book of Acts showed congregations that systematically canvassed their communities, reaching lost people with the Gospel. Note the ministry of Paul in Ephesus: "This (ministry) continued by the space of two years; so that all they which dwelt in Asia heard the Word of the Lord Jesus, both Jews and Greeks" (Acts 19:10).

Second, there's *saturation evangelism*. This involves communicating the Gospel by every available means to every available person at every available time. The effect of saturation

Churches grow by soul winning.

evangelism is to completely "immerse" an entire community in the Gospel. In the early church, the disciples had so saturated Jerusalem with the message that the high priest asked, "Did we not ... command you that ye should not teach in this name? And, behold, ye have filled Jerusalem with your doctrine" (Acts 5:28). The result of saturation evangelism was filling Jerusalem with the Gospel.

5. *Churches grow by a program of evangelism.* Saturation evangelism results from an organized program. The city of Jerusalem was filled and every house received the Gospel (Acts 5:42). This was the result of a systematic, comprehensive coverage of the city. In other words, they had a master plan to reach Jerusalem. Today, some suggest that evangelism should be spontaneous, and argue against revival meetings, Sunday School growth campaigns, visitation programs or Sunday School busing. However a master program of outreach is necessary for New Testament evangelism (a) because the church is an organization (plus organism) with a specific goal, i.e., to reach its Jerusalem, (b) because of the evidence of a program in churches in the book of Acts, (c) because the average Christian does not win souls unless motivated, and goals, requirements, examples, and programs will motivate him, and (d) because the Lord is a God of order and rationality. The universe is governed by laws, the spiritual world is governed by laws and the church should have organization, procedure and goals commensurate with the laws of God.

6. *Churches grow through revival.* When the church is in a general state of revival, God blesses its outreach. "If my people, which are called by my name, shall humble themselves, and pray, and seek my face, and turn from their wicked ways; then will I hear from heaven, and will forgive their sin, and will heal their land" (II Chronicles 7:14).

7. *Churches grow through public preaching and teaching.* There is an emphasis in the 20th century on home Bible studies. Evangelistic preaching has been de-emphasized. However, the early church believed in preaching in the open and house-to-house (Acts 2:14-38; 3:12-26; 5:42; 20:20). The Bible is a dynamic book (Hebrews 4:12) and it changes lives. New Christians (II Corinthians 5:17) will attract the interest and attendance of the unsaved. When the Bible is properly preached, the unsaved want to attend and hear its message.

8. *Churches grow by prayer and Biblical conviction.* We do not usually think of prayer as a principle of outreach, at least in a casual manner. However, a praying church is a growing church.

Here are basic prayer concerns:

(a) Pray that the lost will be convicted.

(b) Pray that God will use the preaching of the Word to accomplish His purpose.

(c) Pray for spiritual growth and revival.

(d) Pray for changed lives.

As a result of answered prayer, outsiders will come into the church, producing growth.

Natural Factors in Outreach

God's program for the church to communicate the Gospel does not break the natural laws of communication. As a matter of fact, because all truth flows from God, we can count on Him to bless it no matter what form of communication we use: newspapers, radio, TV, magazines, etc. The natural principles of church growth as well as the spiritual factors of outreach stem from God.

1. *Growing churches project an aggressive image.* A pastor must determine the type of church he believes will best communicate to his community. This will establish an image, which may be defined as "the sum total of the impressions that a church wants to make on the community." Churches may be known as busing churches, youth churches, foreign mission churches, or Bible-teaching churches. When a pastor comes to a community, he should have a clear statement of aims and objectives. He should know what he wants to accomplish. Whether or not these are written down is unimportant. These aims will determine the church's image. The pastor will communicate this image to the entire community.

2. *Growing churches determine what clientele they can reach.* Many "publics" surround a congregation. A clientele is a natural grouping of people with one factor in common. The church can reach them through this common interest.

First, the church must identify these people, determine their need and adapt advertisements to reach them with the Gospel. The following illustration was used by Dr. John Rawlings to determine the type of people who attended his **church. See illustration on page 203.**

Factors which help determine a church's clientele are: (a) the friends of regular attenders, (b) the relatives, (c) neighbors who would not be called their friends, (d) neighbors to the church, (e) those living in the community who are unchurched, (f) unsaved people in other churches, (g) visitors who drive a distance to the church, and (h) new residents to the community. In addition to the above clientele, each of the areas can be further broken down into: (a) new couples, (b) singles, the divorced, (c) servicemen, (e) middle-aged couples, (f) senior citizens, and (g) college students.

No single advertising campaign can reach every clientele. The church must appeal to the needs of each group it wants to reach. Then the church must communicate to each that it is able to meet their needs by its program of ministry.

3. *Growing churches determine to reach every person in the community.* The more persons to whom you present the Gospel, the larger

202

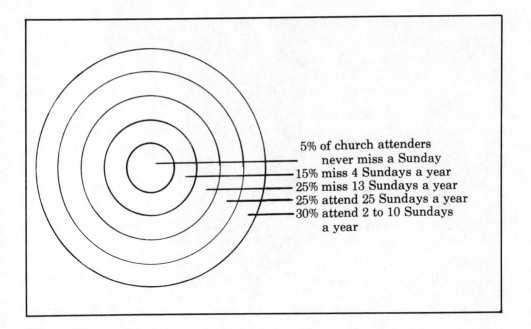

5% of church attenders
  never miss a Sunday
15% miss 4 Sundays a year
25% miss 13 Sundays a year
25% attend 25 Sundays a year
30% attend 2 to 10 Sundays
  a year

the crowd likely to attend the church. This is a principle of sowing and reaping.

Never be satisfied when only one person comes for salvation. Rejoice with those who are saved, but keep seeking others. And don't be discouraged. Some soul winners lose their zeal when their young converts drop out of church.

The more fully a person commits himself to Jesus Christ at the moment of his salvation, the more likelihood of his follow-through in the Christian life. Therefore, preach repentance. Let a new convert know his obligations to the church in witnessing, attendance, tithing, Christian service, baptism, visitation, and prayer meeting.

The secondary motive that often causes a man to make a decision for salvation results in a primary action. Some go to church because they are lonely, others to satisfy parents, others attend because it is the thing to do, or to make business contacts. Some go forward to commit their lives to Jesus because they want to please a wife. Others go because of the pressure of circumstances. However, if they sincerely receive Christ at the altar—they receive eternal life. This principle reveals that people may go to church for secondary reasons; but when the Gospel is preached, their primary need of salvation is met.

4. *Growing churches use every advertising media possible.* The following attitudes toward advertisement will make your Sunday School outreach successful:

Advertise in keeping with your "image."

Make your advertising personal to each different clientele. A general poster or an-nouncement to everyone is not as effective as a "personal announcement" regarding a specific need of a small clientele.

Use advertisements to lead to personal contact. People may not go to church because of impersonal advertisement. They go because of a human contact.

Remember, advertisement begins at home. In a small church situation, spend most of the time and money to reach the officers, the teachers, and the pupils. When these are convinced of the program, they will bring in the outsiders. Advertising is like waves from a splash in a pond; the waves are highest near the splash. Therefore, concentrate your advertisements on those close to home.

Advertising should get everyone involved. If you want to get 500 people to attend Sunday School, try to get 500 people "in" on the special push. This involves contests, delegated work, or other techniques to get them involved.

Use your people to advertise: (a) personal testimony, (b) personal invitation, (c) skits, (d) phoning, (e) distributing handbills, and (f) writing letters.

Use every church resource to advertise special campaigns: (a) church-planning calendar, (b) church bulletins, (c) church newspaper, (d) pastor's newsletter, (e) church bulletin boards, (f) announcements, (g) posters, and (h) announcements on church radio broadcasts.

Advertise through direct mail. God's people should make their advertisements neat, attractive and informative. Most important, use it. Try church newspapers, letters, postcards, even handwritten letters. Mimeographed and/or hastily written newspapers have been

Concentrate your first advertising efforts on those in your own church. (Bethel Community Church)

used effectively by many groups or "movements."

Advertise through communication media: (a) purchased advertisements and press releases in newspapers, (b) radio, church programs, community service programs, (c) community bulletin boards, (d) bumper stickers, (e) billboards, (f) posters in store windows, and (g) church announcement boards.

5. *Growing churches are organized to grow.* Many Sunday Schools do not grow because the leaders plan to keep them small.

Set attendance goals. A church will not grow unless it aims to grow. First, set long-range attendance goals for a period of years. Next, set a yearly goal. A goal will keep vision lifted and a challenge before the people.

A growing Sunday School will have an attendance chart that looks like a two-humped camel. Growth is experienced in the spring and fall, attendance dips in the summer and around Christmas. Since we know when Sunday Schools grow, set attendance goals higher in growth seasons than for other times of the year.

Plan a fall and spring campaign. A Sunday School should schedule its major activities when it will get the greatest results—that is during the fall and spring peak periods. A Sunday School campaign should mobilize the entire energies of the workers to reach the lost, revitalize the Sunday School, and expand attendance. A Sunday School campaign should have the following characteristics: (a) the lesson content should tie to the theme, (b) the

theme should motivate for outreach, (c) the theme should be expressed in a pithy saying, (d) there should be a logo to visualize the campaign, and (e) the campaign should be short enough to sustain interest, but long enough to generate enthusiasm.

Set multiple goals during a Sunday School contest. Usually, one overall attendance goal will not stir all the people. Get several things working. Each of several specific goals will challenge the specific need to which it is tied, and will bring about a specific result. Many goals will create momentum and excitement in the church.

The following may be achieved during a campaign:

(a) An all-time attendance record.

(b) The highest average attendance for the fall/spring.

(c) The highest average attendance for the year.

(d) Class goals.

(e) Departmental goals.

(f) Highest average goals for all the buses.

(g) Highest attendance for an individual bus route.

(h) Greatest number of visitors.

(i) The number of visits made by a worker.

(j) The greatest number of phone calls made.

(k) A goal for the greatest number of postcards written.

The campaign should get as many people as possible involved in outreach. During your fall/spring campaign, plan multiple activities.

Some churches will try one idea to gain attendance such as giving away a Bible, or the reds against the blues.

During a campaign, all of the following might be used:

(a) See section above on multiple records.

(b) A contest of the red against the blue in the adult class.

(c) The one bringing the most visitors is awarded a trip to Disneyworld.

(d) A small gift is given to everyone on certain Sundays.

(e) Certain giveaways are awarded to bus passengers, such as popcorn, watermelon, goldfish, or cotton candy.

(f) Points or prizes are given to those bringing the most visitors.

(g) Your church competes against another church in an attendance contest (such as a church in South Carolina against one in North Carolina—"The Yankees versus the Rebels").

Special personalities or musical groups. A segment of your clientele go to church to hear an outstanding speaker, such as a Christian politician. Others will visit your Sunday School to hear a musical group or soloist. Different kinds of musicians will attract different segments of your clientele to Sunday School.

Multiplied saturation produces explosive attendance. An all-time attendance record can be broken when all of the above are used (goal-setting, campaigns, contests, guest personalities), plus a saturation of total energies by the workers. The people of the church get excited when they experience more on one Sunday than at any other time. Their excitement generates enthusiasm. When the kids feel the momentum of the big day, they bring their friends. When everyone "feels" there will be a big day, the whole project takes on credibility and other advertisement such as handbills, newspapers, radio and letters become more effective.

The high day. The traditional Sunday School celebrated Rally Day on the first Sunday of October. Everyone was "rallied" for the coming Sunday School year and met in the large auditorium for a special program. Today this activity is called "the high day" when a church tries to have one of the largest attendances of the year. If a church uses this strategy every year, an annual expectation is built up. Using the "high day" technique will do the following for your church: (a) it will stir up dead Christians, (b) visitors will see the church at its best and become prospects to be reached for Christ, (c) the faith of the congregation will increase as they expect God to do even greater things in the future.

ORGANIZATION

Most people who want to build a New Testament church give attention to the spiritual growth principles in the Word of God, but neglect the natural factors of good organization and techniques. These principles built on "common sense" cannot be ignored if you want to build a New Testament church. The natural and spiritual factors fit hand in glove. It is possible to get numerical growth by using circuses or Bozo the Clown. This is not "Biblical"—even though the end result has been salvation of souls. Leaders in each church will have to prayerfully consider the "means to the end."

Spiritual Factors of Organization

1. *Churches grow when they meet the Biblical qualifications for a church.* Not every group calling itself a church is in fact a church. Many organizations go by the generic term "church," yet do not meet New Testament criteria. The following principles describe a New Testament church: (a) a church is a group of baptized believers (Acts 2:41, Romans 6:3-6, Ephesians 2:21-22), (b) a church has the presence of Jesus Christ in its midst (Revelation 1:13,20; 2:1,5), (c) a church places itself under the directives of the Word of God (Acts 2:42-43, I Timothy 3:15), (d) a church is organized to carry out the Great Commission (Matthew 28:19-20, Acts 5:42-6:5), (e) a church administers the ordinances, (f) a church is evident when there is a manifestation of the spiritual gifts of leadership and service (Acts 11:22-26).

2. *Churches grow when their leader is truly called and led of God.* Dr. Lee Roberson says, "Everything rises and falls on leadership." The greatest factor in church growth is the leader. The pastor must assume his Biblical position of leadership within the flock (Acts 20:28): (a) the pastor leads by example (I Peter 5:3), (b) the pastor leads by preaching (Hebrews 13:17), (c) the pastor leads by watch-care (Acts 20:29-31), and (d) the pastor leads by wise decision-making (I Peter 5:2).

3. *Churches grow when laymen have their proper places of responsibility.*

Committees, councils and boards are Biblical means of organization. Some fast-growing churches have neglected committees. These churches have strong pastors who make all of the decisions, and while this may be effective, there are liabilities. The church becomes only as stable as the personality of its leader. Only a few leaders are talented enough to become the organizational personification of the church.

A pastor of a growing church needs assistance from his people. Laymen can and should help the pastor in the leadership of the church by serving on organizations such as the finance committee, the Board of Christian Education, building committee, Sunday School council, etc.

The Scripture illustrates organization:
The 12 tribes were organized around the tabernacle. Jesus fed the 5,000 after they were organized into groups of 50. A committee of seven (deacons) were organized to look after

The senior pastor does not make all the decisions at Grace Community Church. A staff of 40, full and part-time pastors and other workers, make most of the decisions together. (Grace Community Church, Sun Valley, CA)

the material needs of widows. Paul organized churches in Asia Minor.

The church was commanded to produce the results of organization: "Let all things be done decently and in order" (I Corinthians 14:40).

The nature of God is consistent and orderly.

The nature of the church demands organization. The church is people, each one working to carry out the Great Commission, not watching from the pews while the pastor performs his ministry. A good pastor leads all the congregation into Christian service. The best way to get everyone involved is through an organized program. When a congregation organizes itself for service, it is carrying out the purpose for which the church was constituted.

Natural Factors of Organization

The Southern Baptists built the largest Protestant denomination in America by organizing their evangelistic outreach. This is still the secret to church growth.

1. *Growing churches allow the pastor to exercise leadership.* These congregations allow their pastors to lead. If a pastor goes in a direction and the people do not follow, he is not a leader. Or, if he runs beyond their ability to follow, he is not a leader. And it must be remembered that the pastor is a leader, not a dictator. There are dangers in a pastor-dominated church, but there also are dangers in a board-dominated church. Dictatorial abuses by pastor and deacons abound. Neither can be successful without the cooperation of the other.

2. *Growing churches have workers who assist the pastor through service, prayer, and encouragement.*

3. *Growing churches are organized to meet the needs of the congregation.* Never organize a

committee or agency before it is needed. And when the organization is no longer serving the needs of its members, disband it.

4. *Growing churches employ qualified people to carry the work forward.* Committees do not get jobs done—people do. Too often committees are regarded as personalities. In fact, a committee is only the sum total of people. The following principles will help solve this point of irritation: (a) never give a job to a committee that can be done by one person; (b) never allow productive people to be tied up in committee work that hinders their leadership or efficiency; (c) committee work is most effective for opinion gathering, policy decisions, and input from the masses; (d) an individual may learn leadership by effectively serving on a committee; (e) excessive committees bog a church down in bureaucracy; (f) the gifted person should be exposed to a great number of people in the largest variety of ministries to accomplish the greatest good for the total church.

This last principle applies to both organization and teaching. The most gifted man might be the Sunday School superintendent and the most gifted woman may teach a large class. People should be used according to their ability. Find your key people and use them.

5. *Growing churches can pinpoint their needs to best solve problems.* The sharper the aim of an organization, the more it can accomplish. As a result of this principle, pupils should be grouped by age in Sunday Schools for efficient teaching.

6. *Growing churches get more people involved in the organization and administration of Sunday School than the average church.* Traditionally, the Sunday School has attempted to get one worker for each ten pupils. This

206

law is still effective when kept in balance with the law of the master teacher. The gifted teacher should be allowed to instruct large classes, but he needs many assistants to take care of follow-up, visitation, record-keeping, and counsel. The master teacher is most effective as a "lecturer." However, it is impossible for him to be a pastor-counselor of a large class. He needs many under-shepherds.

7. *Growing churches build loyalty to the organization on the part of the pupils.* We live in a changing society where people have few loyalties. The one characteristic of change is that it rearranges priorities and disassociates the past. A church should be built on stability, for God does not change. Sunday School organization should be stable to reflect the unchanging God. However, this does not say the organization should be fossilized.

Note the following application of this principle:

(a) Assign a name to each class.

(b) Attempt to develop loyalty to the class.

(c) Try to keep classes in the same room for as long as possible.

(d) Appoint teachers to a class on a permanent basis. The traditional law of Sunday School growth suggested that teachers be appointed on a one-year basis so they would not grow stale. However, teachers can be kept fresh by a consecration service at the beginning of each Sunday School year. Here they are challenged and make a commitment to carry out their responsibilities for the coming year.

(e) Allow a gifted teacher to build the class as large as possible. The traditional law of Sunday School growth maintains that dividing and multiplying is the path of growth, and classes are kept small. This has not always proven effective. Some churches have grown through dividing their classes, while others have been fragmented. The master teacher might build the class from 50 to 400. When the gifted teacher reaches his highest growth potential, then the class should be divided. The highest growth potential is determined by the size of the room, the teacher's ability to communicate, his ability to follow-up, and the logistics of the situation.

8. *Growing churches reflect the normal Sunday attendance curve.* In the area of statistics, there is a bell-shaped curve. Over a period of years, the following curve indicates a healthy Sunday School:

Nursery	7%
Pre-school	8%
Primary	15%
Junior	18%
Junior high and high school	12%
Adults	40%

Some churches with large busing programs have more in the children's program. This often results in an instability of finances and leadership. Many downtown churches on the other hand, have an exorbitant number of people in the adult division, especially senior citizens. If the curve falls off sharply with young adults and correspondingly with small children, the church usually has a leadership problem, although it has little trouble with finances. And without children, a church has no future.

9. *Growing churches are measured by attendance, financial support, and member involvement.* A Sunday School is healthy when people attend, give money, and involve themselves in its service. Therefore, a growing Sunday School ought to incorporate: (a) an active program to foster consistent attendance, (b) an active program to get new attenders, (c) curriculum content to bolster attendance, and (d) external stimulation to encourage attendance.

Many have accused churches of "grabbing money." As a result, some leaders feel "unspiritual" when they talk about money. The opposite is true. When a leader does not mention stewardship, he is not obeying God (Malachi 3:10-11). The average American church-goer gives $157 per year to his church. This averages out to approximately $3 per week per attender. When a church gets more than $3 per person, it is healthy. Therefore, a church ought to: (a) teach stewardship in its curriculum, (b) provide an organizational program for its members to give, (c) motivate everyone to give, and (d) keep careful records of all income.

10. *Growing churches construct buildings and educational space to reflect the purpose of the Sunday School.* The traditional laws of Sunday School growth indicate there must be 10 square feet per pupil. Since it also holds there should be only 10 pupils per class, classrooms were approximately 100 feet square. These classes were ideal for small-group discussion. The trend today is to build classrooms the approximate size of public schoolrooms. These allow larger classes. The advantages of the larger room are: (a) the master teacher can expand attendance, (b) the larger class can provide more motivation to pupils, (c) many adults would rather not visit a small class, but prefer a larger, more impersonal group where they can listen to the Word of God. Keep in mind that the Sunday School is for reaching people and teaching the Word of God. The Sunday School is not a mini-church for liturgy. Neither should the Sunday School be a lounge area with the appearance of a large furniture store. The Sunday School should have rooms constructed for class instruction.

11. *Growing churches use their building as a major means of publicity.* Many people choose a church for its physical facilities.

(a) The church should have visibility in the community. It should be located on a major thoroughfare. Place the building on the property so it can be seen by those passing by. Its prominence in the community will deter-

Growing churches have expandable, convertible educational space. (East Greenich Baptist Church, East Greenich, RI)

mine the likelihood of attendance.

(b) Visitors tend to frequent a church that is convenient, and easily accessible.

(c) Exposure to the masses is also important. Place your church near the shopping center, business district, high school, or some other place where people can easily see the building. The rule of thumb for attracting shoppers is that a store should be seen by the family on their way to work and school in the morning, then again in the evening as they return home. The same rule holds for attracting prospective church members.

12. *Growing churches have expandable, convertible and interchangeable educational space.* A church should get maximum use of its educational space. (a) Rooms should be constructed so they can be expanded when a class grows in size. (b) Next, rooms should be convertible. When the adult class goes from 50 to 100, the children should be able to use the facilities with very little remodeling. (c) Finally, space should be interchangeable for activities. When a gymnasium is built, it should be useable for recreation, education, and banquets, if necessary. Multi-purpose facilities can better serve the congregation, and they cost less.

13. *Growing churches are reflected by expan-*

sion of buildings. If a church never builds or adds to its present facilities, it communicates to the community that it is not growing. Therefore, a pastor is counseled to build a little every few years rather than to initiate a massive construction project every 15 years.

14. *Growing churches economize on building use.* The traditional Sunday School had a "three chair" philosophy. The child was provided a chair and space for the traditional opening exercises. This took approximately 20 minutes. This space had to be heated, cleaned, insured and painted. After opening exercises, the child was sent to a second chair in his small classroom. This space had the same overhead costs as the first. Finally, the child was sent to the sanctuary where a third chair was provided for him, even though this was a pew. Hence, within a three-hour period, the house of God had provided three chairs for the child. This is no longer thought to be a wise use of space.

LEADERSHIP

Numerical growth of a New Testament church begins with the power of God. The leader is the length and shadow of the work he builds for God. Using a clown to draw a crowd is not New Testament growth. New Testament growth does not come from Madison Avenue

208

public relations men, but begins with the man of God. In finding Biblical leadership, the following criteria must be observed.

Spiritual Factors of Leadership

1. *Growing churches have a leader "called" of God.* A person can be assured he is called of God when he meets the following criteria:

(a) He has a burden to serve God. The phrase *burden* was used of the Old Testament prophet (Ezekiel 12:10).

(b) He has a desire to serve God. This is a consuming desire that encompasses all of his perspective.

(c) He has no alternative but to serve God. When God calls a man to serve Him, it is an imperial decree. When God calls a person to teach a Sunday School class, the person may not bargain with God and drive a bus instead. When a person is called of God, 100 percent yieldedness is the only alternative.

2. *Growing churches have an effective leader who displays Biblical spirituality.* A man who is used of God must be filled with the Spirit (Ephesians 5:18). To be filled with the Spirit is to be controlled by the Holy Spirit. God can then put His power through that leader to build a church or to teach a class. The filling of the Spirit leads to soul winning (Acts 2:1-4), answers to prayer (Acts 4:31), joy (Acts 13:52), and fruitfulness (Galatians 5:22-23). To be filled with the Spirit, the church leader must (a) separate himself from all known sin, (b) yield

all conscious endeavors to God, (c) seek the leadership of God in all areas of service, and (d) trust God to work through his service to accomplish the results of the Spirit.

3. *Growing churches see the power of God work through their leader.* There is no formula to secure the empowering of the Holy Spirit. It comes as the leader yields himself to God and exerts every energy in prayer. The leader must be mature and dedicate all of his abilities to serve God. To secure spiritual power, the leader must meet all of the qualifications in the Word of God.

4. *Growing churches share the vision of their leader.* Just as the Old Testament prophet was called a seer (I Samuel 9:9), so the Biblical leader must see first, see farthest, and see most. He must have a vision of what God is going to do with the church. He must have a vision of growth. Then he must inspire his congregation.

5. *Growing churches have a leader with spiritual gifts (Romans 12:3-8, I Corinthians 12:1-27, Ephesians 4:7-13).* A person with a spiritual gift can accomplish spiritual results through the effective use of that gift. (a) Persons with spiritual gifts are relative in their ability to accomplish results. Some with the gift of teaching are more effective than others. (b) Some people have more gifts than others. (c) The gifted man has a combination of intensity and a large number of gifts and is able to accomplish more for God than those with fewer gifts. This accomplishment can be in quantity

The front part of this structure was the first Calvary Temple Church. The back part was a later addition which runs all the way behind the first building. (Calvary Temple Church, Springfield, IL)

or quality (he can produce a depth of spirituality in his followers and/or a large numerical following). (d) A leader's faithful use of his gifts will result in the growth of his abilities. He either accumulates more abilities, or those he already has become more effective.

6. *Growing churches have a leader who aggressively obeys the commands of Christian service.* Some leaders are called of God, have spiritual gifts, and have yielded themselves to God, but they are not effective in their Christian service. They have not been seeking places to serve God. Those who aggressively seek to carry out the New Testament commands concerning service are those who experience the power of God in their lives. The Bible tells us to have a vision (Matthew 10), aggressively reach the lost (Luke 14:23), and preach to as many people as possible (Mark 16:15). Those leaders who actively seek out and obey commands in the Bible are those who have more blessings of God upon their ministry.

7. *Growing churches are the result of the faith of their leader.* Faith usually is considered an intangible quality. Like love, if you have it, you know it. Most people go through life exercising many acts of "faith" every day. We have faith in the chair to hold us, or faith in the airplane to get us to our destination. Biblical faith is centered in Jesus Christ. (a) The more knowledge one has of Jesus Christ, the more he can trust Him. (b) A successful act in trusting God for small things leads to greater spheres of faith. (c) Biblical faith is not wishfully hoping God will bless our endeavors. (d) The closer our project is to the will of God, the more effective our faith will be in trusting God for His blessing upon it. (e) If a service project fails, it is not the leader's lack of faith. Either the project or our service was not in keeping with the will of God.

8. *Growing churches have a leader who is mature.* Spiritual maturity is not an overnight acquisition. Maturity grows through time, successful service and accumulated experiences. Some Sunday School teachers do not have 20 years of experience; rather, they have one year of experience repeated 20 times. That teacher has not grown in maturity. Every time a person trusts God and gets an answer to prayer, he grows in his ability to trust God for bigger things. The same holds true for his spiritual gifts. Every time he stretches his abilities to their ultimate, his ability grows in future potential use. Hence, maturity is acquired as a man walks with God and serves Him for many years. All things being equal, the young man just out of Bible college cannot build a great church as quickly as the seasoned pastor.

9. *Growing churches are built by a leader with resolute determination.* This means he must never give up. When he commits himself to building a church, he is not open to a call from other congregations. He feels the burden of God to reach a community. Therefore, he stays in one place and builds the church. When he meets obstacles, he overcomes them and continues to build.

Natural Factors of Leadership

Leadership has been defined as helping people accomplish the goals of the New Testament church. Therefore, a man who builds a great church will help people accomplish the goals of that church.

1. *Growing churches employ gifted workers to accomplish the most for God.* Every man should be used in the church. However, those who can accomplish the most should be used in strategic places of leadership. The outstanding man, through aggressive outreach, can produce numerical growth. The gifted teacher should be exposed to the maximum number of persons in the largest variety of learning experiences to accomplish the greatest influence in people's lives. This teacher is usually mature, spiritual and trained. He can lead pupils into greater knowledge of the Scripture and their lives can become more Christ-like.

2. *Growing churches realize that effective leadership produces a multiplication of their ministry* (II Timothy 2:2). When the leader properly carries out his duties, he accomplishes two results. First, the work of God prospers. Second, new workers are trained for the ministry. As the leader performs his task, (a) others are inspired to serve, (b) those he reaches grow and want to help in the ministry, and (c) ministry duplicates himself in his people.

3. *Growing churches spawn leadership ability through a "hot poker" approach.* Just as heat transfers from the coals to the poker, so the qualities and attitudes of effective leadership are assimilated. A recruit should spend time with an experienced leader to: (a) gain self-confidence, (b) develop a proper leadership attitude, (c) keep from immature mistakes, (d) acquire a vision of his potential production, and (e) understand the overall strategy of the ministry. The best methods for developing "hot poker" leaders are: (a) by a teaching internship, (b) by bringing great educators to your church, and (c) by taking your staff to seminars, conventions and training sessions outside your church.

4. *Growing churches improve leadership ability through formal training sessions.* A growing Sunday School should plan a program of training. This is effective through: (a) a weekly Sunday School teachers meeting; (b) a specified training class, (c) placing assistants under the master teacher, and (d) providing literature that will increase leadership ability.

5. *Growing churches effectively use leadership by providing a consistent, constant interaction between workers.* No worker can be expected to keep performing at a high level without constant motivation, evaluation and

reward. Most fast-growing Sunday Schools have a weekly Sunday School teachers meeting. Workers are reminded of their task and motivated to better service. Those who have performed well are rewarded. This face-to-face encounter between leader and worker is a necessity for constant growth.

6. *Growing churches give direction to a Sunday School through written standards.* Although most fast-growing Sunday Schools have not written out their standards, this does not mean they do not have standards. Usually, these criteria reside in the heart of the leader. This "personal" method has worked, but growth is limited to the ability of the leader to communicate directly with his staff. When the standards are written, the leader extends his ministry beyond his oral communication. Written standards give: (a) direction for Sunday School growth, (b) a basis for solving problems, (c) cohesiveness to the staff, (d) a basis for determining why the Sunday School is or is not growing, and (e) practical help to another person when the leader leaves the scene.

DISCIPLESHIP

No work is effective for God unless the people are willing to follow God and the leader that He has placed over them. Jesus said, "Whoever does not carry his own cross and come after Me cannot be My disciple" (Luke 14:27). The effectiveness of the church is measured to the degree by which the people follow the Lord. When I was writing the book *The Ten Largest Sunday Schools,* a lady told me, "If my pastor wanted to charge hell with a water bucket, I'd follow him." She had a conviction that her pastor was following God.

Spiritual Factors of Discipleship

1. *Growing churches are characterized by people who love God.* Even though this is an intangible factor, an individual's love will cause him to endure hardships, visit on a bus eight hours on a Saturday, stay up and pray all night, or endure any other hardship for the cross of Christ.

2. *Growing churches are characterized by people with commitment and/or yieldedness.* To be a disciple of Christ, a man must yield himself to do God's will. This involves: (a) a total commitment of one's conscious endeavors and (b) daily yielding of one's self to God.

3. *Growing churches are characterized by people who pray.* The effective disciple spends time: (a) worshiping God (John 9:31), (b) fellowshiping with God, (c) asking for power (Luke 11:13), and (d) praising.

4. *Growing churches are characterized by people who know and live by the Word of God.* A disciple must continue in the Word of God (John 8:31).

5. *Growing churches are characterized by Biblical fellowship among its members.* A disciple must want to fellowship with other disciples. He spends time with them so that he might grow through fellowship.

Growing churches reach people where they are. If a church's music has youth appeal, the church will attract young people. (Living Sound)

Natural Factors of Discipleship

1. *Growing churches reach a man as and where he is.* We cannot expect a lower-class man to attend a church with highbrow music. This man from the housing project cannot "feel affinity" with people who have a different value system. God will reach certain people through a Pentecostal-type church, while others will be reached through a rational Bible study. This principle reflects Genesis 1, "Like produces like."

2. *Growing churches spend time and money on those who will respond most readily.* Jesus taught His disciples that if they were not received in a town, they should shake the dust off their sandals (Luke 9:5). By this, He implied that they should spend time on those who would respond to the message. Therefore, a Sunday School should invest most of its energy on those who will attend rather than those who won't. This does not mean that we should neglect any segment of the population. Sunday School buses are more successful in the slums, housing projects, and among the poor than among the rich. The rich have transportation to bring their children to Sunday School, or won't allow their child to ride a Sunday School bus. The poor are willing to send their children to the church which cares for them.

3. *Growing churches have more people making a profession of faith, hence they have more who can become disciples.* The criticism often is heard that fast-growing churches need a back-door revival. They have many coming down the aisle to receive Christ, yet not everyone continues to grow in faith. However, let us not criticize the churches getting many decisions. Two points should be made, First, we want every person saved that we can possibly reach. Second, we want those saved to go on with Christ. This is discipling. However, emphasizing just discipleship is not the purpose of the church, although the church that has the most professions of faith is most likely to be effective in discipleship.

4. *Growing churches involve new Christians in service.* God wants a new Christian baptized so he feels the obligation of going on with Christ. The outward confession of baptism can be a stimulus to motivate the young Christian to faithfulness. When a person receives Christ, immediately tell the church. Their expectations also motivate him to service.

5. *Growing churches stress salvation of the whole person.* Salvation involves intellect, emotion and will. For a person to be saved, he must *know* the Gospel content, *feel* the conviction of sin and the love of God, then respond by an act of his *will*. This is believing. Since the end product determines the process, plan Sunday School to appeal to the intellect, emotions, and will of the individual. He must know the content of the Gospel, so communicate Bible content. He must feel hatred for sin as well as a love for God. Sing songs to stir emotions and use humor, testimonies, pithy sayings, and activities to motivate pupils. Since salvation involves a decision of the will, get the pupil *doing* things in the class that will immerse him in the Word of God.

6. *Growing churches have disciples that assume the attitudes and practices of their leader.* If the people are not soul winners, it's often because the pastor is ineffective in his outreach. When the people do not sacrifice, it's usually because of their pastor's attitude. Jeremiah the prophet said, "Like priest, like people," meaning the pastor is the length and shadow of the church. He cannot get the people to do what he himself is not willing to do.

7. *Growing churches realize the power of an educated disciple.* The effectiveness of a worker is in direct proportion to his education. Some workers are not successful because they have not been trained. Others fail because they have enough education but don't know the right things (their theology is wrong). Therefore, the leader must reinforce the primacy of the church; this is the cornerstone of Christian education. He also must reinforce the primacy of the church's methods; the disciple must be convinced that the method he uses is the most effective to reach a lost world. And the leader must continually reinforce loyalty to the cause. The rededication service is effective for growth. Workers need to come to the altar and renew their pledge for church growth.

8. *Growing churches realize the power of the motivated worker.* Bus workers without formal education have brought upwards of 500 children to Sunday School. Dwight L. Moody never finished high school but shook two continents for God. Fast-growing Sunday Schools have been built on the shoulders of motivated workers. Therefore, the leader must make the following assumptions: (a) People do not naturally want to serve God, because they are sinners. (b) Because everyone has a gift (ability to serve God), everyone should be serving God. (c) Therefore, the leader should motivate everyone to serve God. To magnify the motivated worker does not lessen our emphasis on the trained worker, for God uses both. But the worker who is trained and motivated is the most effective disciple of all.

Factors That Do Not Affect Church Growth*

Research indicates that no one of the following factors alone has any significant bearing upon church growth. However, clusters of these factors can have a positive or negative effect upon church growth.

1. Location of the church building.
2. Population density of the area.
3. Size and appointments of church buildings.
4. Known workers available.
5. Known financing available.
6. Size of the church.
7. Age of the church.

212

8. Age of the pastor.

9. Size of the church staff.

10. Formal training of the church staff.

11. Hard work—unless it is in the right direction.

12. Denominational affiliation.

13. Organizations within the church.

14. Committees within the church. (Some committees and organizations often prevent growth and even cause decline.)

15. Social, racial and ethnic factors.

16. Economy of the area.

17. Involvement in social matters and benevolence programs.

18. Number and size of other churches in the area.

---

*Reprinted by permission from the Rev. Bill Powell, Southern Baptist Journal.

28

Just follow these five easy steps and watch your Sunday School decrease in attendance and effectiveness.

Why Sunday Schools Decline

Robert Raikes began the Sunday School movement out of evangelistic concern. He observed the vicious juvenile gangs of Gloucester, England, and the evils stemming from the idleness and ignorance of the masses. Guided by the proverb, "Vice can be better prevented than cured," Raikes started a school (1) taught by laymen and not clergymen, (2) with the Bible rather than the catechism for the textbook, (3) geared to youngsters off the streets rather than children of Christians, and (4) designed to win children for Christ. The Sunday School grew so rapidly that 39 years later, when a statue was dedicated to Raikes, 1,300,000 students (one out of every three Englishmen) were enrolled in Sunday School.

In England and America during the last 200 years, Sunday School teachers have invaded saloons, dark alleys and housing projects with the message of Jesus. Sunday School attendance has grown in direct proportion to the dogged determination of teachers who reflect the conviction that students must be reached with the message of the Bible or be eternally lost. But in the last 10 years, Sunday School attendance has been drifting downward because it has been ripped from its moorings.

Originally, the Sunday School was the evangelistic "reaching arm" of the church. Today it is the educational Sesame Street of the congregation.

"When is a school not a school? When it is a

Sunday School," critics have ridiculed. Many contemporary leaders have listened to these opponents and have slowly turned the Sunday School into a fun-loving romper room with Bible stories, rather than into a school with evangelistic zeal.

The following reasons are suggested for Sunday School decline. (No statistical proof is offered to substantiate these reasons for decline. The observations grew out of the author's study of the fast-growing Sunday Schools.)

1. *Evangelism is neglected.* The church boom years immediately after World War II are over. People are no longer pressured by peer status to attend Sunday School. Sunday School is no longer the "in" place to be on Sunday morning. Friendly invitations to "come and hear our pastor" also have lost their appeal. Only 10 percent of Americans attend a Sunday School on an average morning, even though 42 million are on Sunday School rolls. But those Sunday Schools which are growing usually have an aggressive evangelistic approach. Southern Baptists, for example, built the largest Protestant denomination on the premise, "The Sunday School is the evangelistic arm of the church." Three years ago, 92 percent of their church additions came from the Sunday School.

2. *Facilities are inadequate.* Just as a quart of water will not fit into a pint jar, 200 people cannot fit into a Sunday School designed for

214

Southern Baptist home missionary, Chuck Clayton, holds Vacation Bible School in a Lake Tahoe resort area. (Religious News Service Photo)

100. Growing attendance continually needs more space, and if the leadership lacks vision and stops adding educational space, attendance levels off. "Never get out of a building program," Dr. John Rawlings, minister, Landmark Baptist Temple, Cincinnati, Ohio (attendance 4,715), advised a young minister. He explained that physical expansion of church walls reflects inner growth and vitality.

3. *Quality is emphasized to the exclusion of quantity.* Sometimes Sunday Schools stop growing because no emphasis is made on numbers. Spurgeon said more than 100 years ago, "The minister that will not emphasize numbers will not have them."

Many a Sunday School leader follows the unspoken rule, "If we have quality education, we will attract great crowds," but I have observed many outstanding small Sunday Schools that have never grown. Therefore, I believe that quality alone will not lead to a growing attendance. Some hold the opposite opinion, that large Sunday Schools must be good because people are attending. I also have observed crowds flocking to Sunday Schools offering poor education. The conclusion is simple: Quality does not produce quantity or *vice versa.* A Sunday School must work at both quality and quantity to have large crowds and effective education.

4. *Inadequate administration hurts attendance.* Dr. Lee Roberson built the second largest Sunday School in America (attendance 7,453) at Highland Park Baptist Church, Chattanooga, Tenn., on the principle, "The Sunday School rises or falls on leadership." And Dr. Kenneth Connolly, minister of Berean Baptist Church, Orange, Calif., reorganized his Sunday School after hearing a speaker exhort, "Double your teaching staff. Double your room. Most important, double your administrative staff." Connolly followed the formula and leaped from under 200 to an average attendance of 450.

5. *Antiquated educational environment kills growth.* Public school children today are given the finest education in history. It is built on enjoyment, involvement and experience. But a credibility gap can arise when, in Sunday School, they sit in furnace rooms, study from quarterlies with small type and out-of-date pictures, and endure boring lectures.

"The crowds come because we believe in 20th century *saturation evangelism* preaching the Gospel by every available means, to every available person at every available time," Dr. Jerry Falwell, senior minister, Thomas Road Baptist Church, Lynchburg, Va., announced to the record attendance of 10,758 at their 1972 Homecoming.

Complex reasons have caused Sunday School decline in our complex society. There are no simple explanations for the downward spiral. Some Sunday Schools have deteriorated because of the inadequate training of the minister, or because he has ignored the Sunday School. Dr. Jack Hyles, minister, First Baptist Church, Hammond, Ind., blames theological liberalism. Dr. Scott Thompson, minister in the Methodist church, claims his denomination never had the people. Now "roll cleaning" makes their statistics look even worse, he says. Others claim that more long weekends and emphasis on recreation carry parishioners to the lakes rather than to church. Finally, some claim John Dewey's pragmatism in public schools undermined our country's historic Biblical foundation, resulting in less dependence on the church.

Whatever the reasons for decline, the Sunday School can say with Mark Twain, "The rumors of my demise are greatly exaggerated." Even though dwindling in size in mainline churches, Sunday Schools are growing in attendance where there is evangelistic concern.

29

To what human motives do churches appeal when they utilize promotional methods smacking of Barnum and Bailey?

Boost Sunday School Attendance: Yes! But What Are Your Motives?

I believe in Sunday School promotions and contests. But should a mini-bike be ridden down the aisle of a church sanctuary to coax kids to invite their friends to Sunday School? Or should a church set up a shopping-center-style carnival, where children ride with tickets earned by "each one bringing one"?

Many churches have put God in the promotion business and, for the most part, have been successful in attracting masses to their Sunday School; but the nagging question remains, "Are such tactics Biblical?"

"I will do anything to get people to church," one well-known pastor says.

The gimmick trend is not new. During one of *Christian Life* magazine's famous Sunday School contests in the 1950s, Trigger, Roy Rogers' horse, was enrolled in Sunday School at a large California church. And almost 200 years ago, Robert Raikes, founder of Sunday School, gave children money for attendance along with other incentives such as shoes, trousers, books and Bibles.

Some believe we ought to eliminate all Sunday School contests and promotions because they are un-Biblical. But are they? A contest is simply an external stimulus to attract people to hear the Gospel. The miracles performed by Jesus (external stimulus) attracted crowds and caused people to listen to the message. Many times Jesus used miracles as a prelude to His sermons.

The Gospel of salvation never changes, but as the Good News gives a man eternal life, that man must live for God within his culture. Christianity often adapts to the socio-economic society in which it finds itself. In other words, "God meets a man at his own level and lifts him to the divine level." Contests and gimmicks are a way of life for America. The First National Bank gives T-bone steaks to those opening a new account, and gas stations give a free glass or a kite to those who fill-up. Sunday School contests simply are an adaptation of the American way of life.

Six years ago I wrote the book *The Ten Largest Sunday Schools.* Many people criticized this book because America's largest churches used contests and promotions to reach people with the Gospel. I still approve of what these churches did and the way many other churches are reaching unsaved people through Biblical promotions. But the question remains: "Where is the line between a Biblical incentive and a gimmick that smacks of tasteless entrepreneurism?" The following three questions will guide the sincere questioner:

1. *Did the contest accomplish a Biblical aim?* A church invited Bozo the Clown to its Break the Record Day, and counted the largest attendance in its history. The pastor justified his actions by pointing to the fact that more than 100 persons came forward to commit their lives to

Indianapolis Baptist Temple goes in for the spectacular in promotional stunts. The entire Sunday School crowd watches world champion sky diver, Fred Heyenbruck, jump from 5,000 feet to the church parking lot. The event was well-publicized ahead of time. (Indianapolis Baptist Temple, Indianapolis, IN)

Jesus Christ.

An Illinois church promised a free trip to Jamaica to the parishioner who brought the most to Sunday School. The winner had recruited a number of people by giving them $2 each to come to Sunday School. The attendance grew and the head count was accurate.

"You don't have to listen, just come help me win the trip," the winner had told his friends.

Was this contest Biblical? Is a large attendance the only goal of a church?

A Sunday School contest is Biblical when it accomplishes the aims of the Scriptures. The first aim is to reach people with the Gospel—the "good news of salvation" through Jesus Christ. Paul identifies this principle: "And unto the Jews I became as a Jew, that I might gain the Jews . . . to the weak became I as weak, that I might gain the weak: I am made all things to all men, that I might by all means save some" (I Corinthians 9:20-22). The "all things" that Paul

will do to reach people with the Gospel was governed by the phrase *to gain* (or, in our language, *to win*). But before we can win a man to Jesus Christ we must *reach* him; we must "motivate" a man to turn his attention toward the Gospel so that he may give a sincere hearing to the good news.

After a person is brought to church or Sunday School, he must be evangelized. Evangelizing a person is simply giving him an understanding of the plan of salvation, then motivating him to make a decision for God. A Biblical Sunday School contest first gets students "under the sound of the Gospel." Second, it motivates them to give an honest hearing to the Gospel. Finally, it provides an opportunity to properly present the plan of salvation.

A good example of a Biblical campaign is the Twelve Disciples Campaign currently sweeping the country. In most churches, it is successful in swelling attendance. A lesson is

The Apostle Peter visits Bellevue Baptist during its Twelve Disciples campaign for the Sunday School. Each of the twelve disciples were portrayed in this fashion on succeeding Sundays. (Don Lancaster/Bellevue Baptist Church, Memphis, TN)

taught each Sunday on one of the 12 disciples. Those who attend are given a charm likeness of this disciple. If a pupil has perfect attendance for 12 weeks, he will have a completed bracelet with 12 charms. The Calvary Baptist Church, Middletown, Ohio, employed the contest to produce faithful attendance from a vast number of sporadic attenders. The Rev. Jewell Smith, pastor of Temple Baptist Church, Orlando, Fla., says his attendance has gone from 600 to over 2,000 by using the Twelve Disciples Campaign.

Operation Andrew is another successful Sunday School campaign, based on the disciple Andrew's desire to bring his friends to Jesus Christ.

Friend Day, used in many churches, has both a magnetic and Biblical appeal.

"Everyone of you has a friend. Therefore we expect every person to bring a visitor and double our attendance," the Rev. Jack Hudson, pastor of Northside Baptist Church, Charlotte, N.C., announced. They did, reaching over 4,000. But those who came were candidates for the Gospel because the appeal had been, "Because you are my friend, I want you to come and share in my church service."

The Southern Baptists built the largest Protestant movement in America on the adage, "We reach, to teach, to win, to train." If reaching a man is Biblical, then contests that turn an individual's attention to the Gospel should be used.

2. *Did the contest accomplish a Biblical goal?* Educators define a goal as "that outcome by which educational activities are judged." The Biblical goals of Scripture are: building aggressive churches, maturing (completing) saints in Jesus Christ, and bringing glory to God. The goal of evangelism in the New Testament is aimed at gathering people (*ecclesia* means "to assemble") into a New Testament church whether in Thessalonica, Ephesus or St. Louis.

Regrettably, some soldiers of Jesus Christ resort to hit-and-run guerilla warfare. The underground Christian can be a fundamentalist street preacher who buttonholes an individual on the corner and extorts "a decision," or the Jesus freak who pushes his Bible over the counter and manipulates a short-order cook to repeat a religious formula. Neither of these "zealots" is Biblical when he does not attempt to get the newly "professing believer" into a local church.

Another Biblical goal by which to measure Sunday School contests is how the glory of God is communicated. What do people think of God after a contest is completed?

It is possible to give away snow cones and place such emphasis on prizes that the sin-ridden person seeking salvation is "turned off" and leaves church with a bad taste for the Gospel.

3. *Are numbers the mania of your Sunday*

219

School or are numbers the outgrowth of soul winning? There is nothing wrong with numbers. The fourth book in the Bible is called Numbers. Jesus called His early disciples "the twelve," and sent out 70 disciples. There were 120 in the Upper Room, next 3,000 were saved and, finally, 5,000 were in the church. Luke, the historian, said that the number of disciples in Jerusalem multiplied greatly (Acts 6:1). Jesus commanded us to "go and make disciples of all nations" (Matthew 28:19). Making disciples first implies winning people to Christ and, second, getting them to follow Christ. When you have done this, you can count the heads of those who follow Christ.

But Sunday Schools hurt their ministry when they put more emphasis on the *measure* than on the *measured.* The question is not the number *in* Sunday School, but does the Sunday School attendance figure represent (1) souls that are being reached for Christ, (2) people that are studying the Word of God, and (3) individuals who are becoming disciples of Jesus Christ?

When numerical attendance becomes more important than evangelism, a church will spin off into gimmicks or unethical tricks to expand attendance. A Southern Baptist Church in Florida recently jumped 500 in Sunday School attendance by counting a Sunday night Sunday School, Wednesday night Sunday School, convalescent home Sunday School, but no actual growth on Sunday morning.

Another church was caught red-handed by the author when a children's worker reported that the Sunday School attendance represented a double count. Those who remained for children's church were recounted, swelling the attendance by 300.

The prophet Isaiah calls this "lies in the name of the Lord."

I have spoken in 73 of the 100 largest Sunday Schools in the U.S. and, after carefully examining their classes and record books, I find most of them have an accurate count. When a church fudges on its attendance or uses un-Biblical tactics to bolster sagging attendance, it's usually a sign that soul winning is disappearing from its pulpit and pew.

Tricks for boosting attendance in Sunday School are similar to narcotics in an addict—every shot has to have more power or it loses its effect. A pupil is given lifesavers, but they soon lose their appeal. The ante is raised to a candy bar, a helicopter ride, a live pony, a trip to Disneyland and finally a trip to Israel. Faithful attenders someday may have to be promised the moon.

The church that is built on gimmicks must survive on gimmicks. Instead, we should build our churches on soul winning and use promotion and external stimulus to bring pupils under the Gospel.

Some Sunday Schools have confused *means* and *ends.* The end result is winning souls and building strong New Testament churches. The means is an emphasis on numbers. Let us not reverse the two.

There are several advantages to a Biblical emphasis on numbers by churches. First, numbers reflect life and vitality. Dr. W.A. Criswell, First Baptist Church, Dallas, Texas, says, "There is nothing wrong with a small Sunday School but there is something wrong with one that does not grow." The educational statisticians tell us that anything that grows can be measured. Numbers simply tell us if a church is growing or is dead.

A second advantage of numbers is motivation. Attendance graphs and growth charts stimulate workers to dedication and service.

Third, numbers encourage the worker in his faith. When the Grant Memorial Baptist Church, Winnipeg, Canada, dropped three of its bus routes, Pastor David Clink felt a loss of vitality among his members. When the bus ministry was reinstituted, the spiritual temperature rose because, as one deacon stated, "Even though our attendance growth is among children, I feel we are more missionary-minded because we are actually carrying out the Great Commission."

One of the criticisms of an emphasis on numbers is the law of diminishing returns; i.e., a congregation can only grow so large. Ultimately it reaches a saturation point. Logistics make it impossible to preach, teach, counsel and minister to a large multitude.

"Don't emphasize numbers because a church can only get so large," the argument goes.

Granted this argument may become a factor in some churches—but only about 100 churches out of the 334,000 churches in America average over 1,200 in attendance. These are the only ones who would be concerned about this problem.

Let us not bad-mouth those who emphasize numbers, simply because of some abuses. And let us leave the un-Biblical gimmicks on the carnival midway.

Dr. Warren Wiersbe of Moody Memorial Church, Chicago, summed up my feeling: "We count people because people count."

30

Hundreds of teachers have used these principles to double the size of their classes.

20 Ways to Double Your Sunday School Class

You can double the attendance of your Sunday School class. Sound impossible? Well, it isn't. Hundreds of teachers have used the principles I include here, and have had fantastic results. Read all the points carefully—then discuss them with the other teachers in your Sunday School. Think how much could be accomplished for the Lord if *every* class in your school doubled in size this year.

1. *Set an Overall Goal.* If your class has been averaging 15, set a goal of 30. Prepare a poster with a goal of 30. Write 30 on the chalkboard. Saturate your pupils with the goal.

Goal setting works. A junior class in the Florence (S.C.) Baptist Temple hung a large sheet of paper from one wall to another, then had each of the 26 boys write his name on it and sign "52" by his autograph. In that way, each student reinforced the class goal of 52. The total Sunday School set a goal of 1,225. Posters were

This Sunday School has set a goal of breaking its previous record.

put on walls, bulletin boards and doors. Every poster announced the goal of 1,225, but each differently—in German, Spanish, Greek; upper and lower case letters; Gothic and Roman numbers.

2. *Set a Goal for Finding New Prospects.* In order for your class to double, attempt to get twice as many prospects as your average attendance. This means that each member should suggest 2 names. If there are 30 in the class, get 60 names on your prospect list.

An adult class at the Berean Baptist Church, Salem, Va., distributed blank cards to members and asked each to submit names of friends he or she would like to see in the class. After two weeks of listing names, the goal still was not reached. Therefore, three ladies were delegated to phone members of the class and write down the names they suggested. They worked until 100 new names were gathered.

To have a growing Sunday School class, put as much emphasis on finding prospects as on recruiting them.

3. *Assign Prospect Responsibility.* Many growing classes type the names of all prospects on sheets of paper, then distribute photocopies in the class, assigning prospects to be contacted before the next week. The Calvary Baptist Church in Ypsilanti, Mich., printed a motto over its visitation board, "People Expect What You Inspect." Many members work in the automobile assembly plants in Detroit where they are taught by GM that people work according to how closely the foreman supervises them. The same rule applies to Sunday School. Therefore, give each of your class members a prospect to contact, then check up on them the following Sunday to see if they have made the contact.

4. *Phone Every Prospect.* During the fall campaign, phone every prospect on your list ... every week. Extend to each a friendly welcome, giving the time, place and lesson topic.

5. *Send Mail to Every Prospect.* During your campaign, mail every prospect a postcard or letter, inviting him to Sunday School. A housewife can write a personal note to 30 prospective students in 2 hours. A first-class letter to 30 prospects costs less than $5—and eternal benefits will result.

For example, one Sunday several junior boys gathered in the back of a Sunday School room at Calvary Baptist Church, Ypsilanti, Mich., to examine a rolled up piece of paper from the pocket of a 9-year-old. The superintendent, expecting trouble, went back to spy-out the scene. He found the ringleader showing his buddies a postcard he had received from his Sunday School teacher.

"I thought she didn't like you, the way she yells," one of the boys said.

During the pastor's invitation that morning, the teacher walked down the aisle with the boy who said, "I was saved at the end of Sunday School class this morning."

6. *Visit Every Prospect.* Visitation puts the GO in Gospel, carrying the message to every person. After you have phoned every prospect, a visit to his home will convince him of your love. In fact, visit every prospect *every week* during your attendance campaign.

7. *Start a Class Newspaper.* During your campaign, start a one-page (or larger) class newspaper. The junior class at the Crestwicke Baptist Church, Guelph, Ontario, distributes an eight-page paper, *The Roadrunner,* to every junior. Since it is a large class, the teachers spend time writing articles about juniors who recently have committed their lives to Jesus Christ. The paper also includes crossword puzzles, homework, stories, and news about the attendance campaign. The attendance motto and logo also are printed there, reminding the kids of their attendance goals.

The average Sunday School teacher with less than 10 pupils cannot publish a newspaper every week, but he can do it at least twice during each attendance campaign. A newspaper is not hard to prepare. If you've never issued one, simply write a one-page letter giving the news of the class. Then type the letter in two columns to make it look like a newspaper, and put a headline across the top. Fill the newspaper with the names of students, their accomplishments, and what you expect to do for God.

8. *Name Your Class.* Bill Newton took the fourth grade boys class at the Thomas Road Baptist Church, Lynchburg, Va., and called it "The Treehouse Gang." A massive cardboard tree, with a door, was used at the entrance of the room. Two more large trees, reaching from ceiling to floor, covered the inside walls. Later, a stockade was put in the hall surrounding the doors. Bill Newton started his class in September. His goal was to average 54 before the year was out. With enthusiasm, ingenuity, and determination, Newton pushed the average attendance to 94.

9. *Post Attendance.* A junior boys class at the First Baptist Church, Hammond, Ind., called their campaign "Spring Training." A massive box score chart marked hits, runs and errors so that students could follow their progress each week. The class was divided into two sides, and at the beginning of each class they "batted around," adding up visitors, attendance and Bibles.

Since pupils tend to value those things that are important to teachers, make sure to call the roll carefully. This tells each student it's his duty to be in class every Sunday. The extra pressure of some kind of a wall chart gives added motivation.

10. *Get a Motto.* The high school class at the Bible Baptist Church, Savannah, Ga., had a "Fat is Beautiful" campaign. Instead of awarding stars or rockets, or putting names on the wall, they weighed in each week. The

teams began with an equal total weight. Visitors tipped the scales for the winners, while absentees dragged the losers down.

11. *Get a Logo.* The Indianapolis (Ind.) Baptist Temple celebrated its 25th anniversary in 1975. A huge silver seal hung all year in the auditorium with the motto, "The 25th Year of Redemption." Under the motto was their goal, "2,500 Souls Won To Christ in 1975." The entire seal was their logo. They had it fashioned into small silver seals which they affixed to envelopes and letterheads. It was also printed on all the literature of the church.

12. *Give Out Buttons.* Dr. Bob Gray, Trinity Baptist Church, Jacksonville, Fla., set a Florida record of more than 5,000 in Sunday School on the church's 25th anniversary. Each person was given a button ahead of time with the wording "I Am One of 5,000" to remind him to be faithful in attendance.

13. *Stretch Their Faith.* The First Baptist Church, West Hollywood, Fla., planned to beat

pray for 5,000+ every time he ate a meal during the next week. Since most eat three meals a day, every person would pray 21 times for 5,000+. Pastor Verle Ackerman called it, "Fast or Pray," reminding his people that if they didn't pray for 5,000, they should not eat.

The second night, each worker signed a card to pledge, "I will work for 5,000+."

On the third night every teacher made a numerical commitment of a goal for his class on 5,000+ Sunday.

When the tally was in, they had pledged to reach 5,400. Later they reached 5,427, the largest Sunday School in the history of Florida.

14. *Choose a Good Day.* Don't plan a Sunday School campaign for Labor Day weekend, or during the Fourth of July holiday when there is a natural dip in the attendance. The minister who tried to have his largest attendance on Labor Day weekend and the Sunday after Easter, claiming, "Anybody can get a crowd on

Why not ask every Sunday School member to wear a button during the campaign?

the Jacksonville record and have the largest Sunday School in the history of Florida. To do so, attendance had to double from 2,700 to 5,400. In a three-day workers conference, their faith was stretched.

On the first night of the conference, everyone was pinned with a "5,000+" button and asked to

Easter, I want to build an attendance to show our people love God," has missed the whole purpose of an attendance campaign. A high attendance should do more than demonstrate the loyalty of the faithful. It should bring visitors, electrify everyone when the attendance is doubled, and bring men, women and children to a saving faith in Jesus Christ. So plan for Sunday School growth when the best results are possible. Then you will be a good steward of your time, energy and money. Therefore, plan to grow on those days when attendance can be largest.

15. *Remember the Clenched Fist.* A man can keep his fist taut only so long. Then the muscles give out. Likewise, a Sunday School class can pressure itself for expansion for only a short time. Therefore, growing Sunday Schools plan two attendance campaigns for six or seven weeks each spring and fall. They work as hard as they can during a campaign to find prospects, excite students, phone, write and visit. The attendance drive is relaxed during the Christmas holidays, the snows of January, and again during the summer.

16. *Get a Running Start.* Before jumping a creek, a boy runs faster if he has to jump farther. In Sunday School, the larger the goal, the longer it takes to double your class attendance. Plan a six- or seven-week fall campaign with the high Sunday as the last day. Don't read this chapter and plan to double your class next week. Pray to double, plan to double, and promote to double. But remember this: A teacher can't lead if his class won't follow, and pupils won't work to double their class unless their teacher takes the time to convince them it can be done.

17. *Plan a High Day.* Plan a high attendance Sunday on the last Sunday of your campaign. Some criticize this, saying that it only gets a crowd and makes small-class teaching impossible. However, the "high day" really is only a return to the old-fashioned rally day, where all pupils assembled in the auditorium to "rally" enthusiasm for Sunday School. Most teachers need to break lethargy and infuse the pupils with expectation. A "double day" convinces the pupils it can be done again and again, until the class is permanently doubled.

18. *Pray.* A junior boys class at the Forrest Hills Baptist Church, Decatur, Ga., set a goal of 26 in Sunday School. They wanted to double their average attendance of 13. The teacher asked each boy to pray. Several boys promised to bring their buddies. Next Sunday morning they began to fill up the little room...22...23...24...25...26. All the boys cheered. But, the visitors kept coming. Soon they were sitting two to a chair and standing in each row. When the teacher finally counted all the heads, there were 50.

"I can't teach. There are too many in this room," the teacher said apologetically.

A hand went up. "It's my fault," said a tow-headed boy, "I prayed for 50."

God answers the prayer of those who ask for their ministry to be enlarged, but prayer alone cannot build a Sunday School. God will not do what He has commanded us to do. We are to go and reach people. Classes grow when teachers are busy visiting, phoning, mailing and praying all week.

19. *Feed Them the Word.* People go to restaurants where they get good food, then they tell their friends. Books are sold by word of mouth. The satisfied customer is still the best salesman for any product. The basis for growing Sunday School classes is still good Bible teaching which causes students to bring their friends. The Bible must be made interesting, captivating and relevant.

20. *Try Super Saturation.* The disciples went everywhere preaching the Word, reaching all men by all means. A Sunday School teacher should use every technique to excite pupils about coming to Sunday School. Extra promotion, contests, and taking pupils to a ball game show that a teacher cares. Extra preparation, visitation and prayer will get results. The work of God is still spelled W-O-R-K. Any class will grow in direct proportion to the energies expended by the teacher.

Plan a high attendance Sunday for your campaign. "Miracle Day" at Bellevue Baptist brought a record attendance of 4,567 in Sunday School. (Don Lancaster/Bellevue Baptist Church, Memphis)

31

Few Sunday Schools grow without a planned visitation program.

The Visitation Program

Visitation is one area of Sunday School in which it may be said that "everybody's job is nobody's job." Experiments in hit-or-miss visitation compared with an organized plan have proven that a planned program reaches the most people.

Who Visits?

1. *The pastor.* Just as he must set the spiritual pace in other areas of church life, the pastor sets the pace for the visitation program by his own example of regular visitation. Some churches feel they have hired a church visitor when they pay the pastor's salary. Visitation is only one of the pastor's many responsibilities, and it should be shared with others.

2. *The teachers.* Teachers best show their interest and concern when they visit in the home of every pupil at least once during the year. In a very large class, the responsibility may be shared with assistants. There is no substitute for a home visit to help a teacher become really acquainted with the background and the interests, hopes and fears of the pupils—be they young or old. Until something of the spiritual status and needs are known, there cannot be effective ministry.

Not only should a teacher visit those on the roll, but special visits should be made to pupils confined to home or hospital with extended illness. The teacher also should visit homes of new church attenders who have children of her

class's age level.

3. *The deacons.* Deacons usually represent the church rather than the Sunday School when they visit. But they should be interested in the Sunday School to the extent that they will encourage attendance on the part of any who may be lax.

4. *Church officers.* Paid or unpaid workers in the church should visit absentees and prospects, particularly non-Christians in the Sunday School or in the community.

5. *All Sunday School members.* Any Christian should be willing to express interest in an absentee by making a visit. All Christians should be willing to go to the home of newcomers and extend an invitation to Sunday School. Older Christians will seek to win the lost to Christ during such visitation, as the Lord opens the way and reveals the need.

When To Visit

1. *At a designated time.* Set aside a night or afternoon when all visitors meet at the church to pray and to receive visitation assignments. It encourages all present to see that others are concerned.

2. *Whenever possible.* Sometimes employment schedules do not allow some teachers or members to visit at the time set by the church. Their visit at another time may be even more fruitful. Unchurched people in a community often discover the scheduled time

Any Christian should be willing to express interest in an absentee by making a visit. (William A. Painter/Philadelphia College of the Bible)

for church visitation and leave home to avoid the visitors. When an unscheduled visit is made, they are caught by surprise.

3. *At times of special need.* Bereavement or illness in a family may not coincide with the visitation program. Visits at those times are usually opportunities to extend the greatest help because hearts are most "open" to the Word of God.

4. *In case of absence.* When the pupil is absent one Sunday, phone him and let him know he is missed. Everyone likes to know someone cares. When he is absent two Sundays, visit in the home. After he is absent three Sundays, the departmental superintendent should visit in the home. If he is absent four Sundays, the Sunday School superintendent and the pastor should do all they can to solve the problem and to reach this family for Christ. Prayer for the scholar should increase with each absence.

Where To Visit

The answer at first glance would seem to be, "In the immediate area around the church." However, the outlook of most churches has changed regarding this practice. Once a church could say, "This is *my* territory." Now, with church buses often bringing riders from a radius of 25 miles or more, many churches feel that the field is wide open to any and every church, and that any effort is justified.

There are some ethical restrictions to this freedom, however:

1. *Overlapping by Biblical churches.* Some church bus directors have gone overboard for numbers of riders to the extent they visit in the homes of persons who are faithful and regular members of a sister church. They seek to persuade even those faithful workers to change their allegiance and ride the bus to a different church. This has resulted in:

a. Ill will toward fellow Christians. Sheep-stealing is never viewed kindly by another church. Proselyting has been frowned upon since the times of the Galatians. Christians are to love one another; it is difficult to love a Christian who seeks to undermine the work you have done, and many view sheep-stealing in that light.

b. Confused families. In some communities with a multiplicity of church buses covering the territory, the parents may ride to one church, the teenagers to another, and the small children to still a different one. The family is divided and the religious education is haphazard and confused. On a given Sunday, the little children may choose to go with the parents, because of a special program or a special reward. They break the continuity of their lessons and view the Bible as disjointed stories. The teens will be without parental supervision in church. They may feel free to cause disturbance by talking, which they would not do with the parental eye upon them.

2. *Wasted time.* While visitors are spending time calling in homes already reached by a church of like faith and practice, they are using valuable hours needed to go out into an area where no one has visited. Such areas are to be found in nearly every county.

3. *Wasted money.* The car expense of the visitor is wasted when the visit is made to an already churched home. When it is clearly known that the family is regularly attending a church of like faith, it is deliberate waste. Bus drivers who make an effort to secure riders in an area already reached by a sister church waste the Lord's money when they use the bus to pick up a few children from a home where parents already attend a similar church.

4. *Scorn of the unchurched.* Viewing the competition of Christians who pretend to love one another, unbelievers feel their concern is only for members. They may choose to go where they will get the most material gain.

How To Visit

Sometimes new Christians are willing to visit in behalf of the church, but are timid. "I don't know what to say," is their reason for not taking part in the visitation program. Courses discussing soul winning may provide some answers. New Christians may and should visit in the company of an experienced visitor. The visit in behalf of Sunday School (or church) should be viewed as a friendly visit. Going with the hand of friendship extended can put a different light on the conversation. Encourage the one visited to express his interests, views and need, by asking questions, rather than expecting to dominate the conversation. A visit may be opened by:

1. *A leaflet.* A teacher can make friends in a home by taking an absentee member a Sunday School paper or picture card. The small token shows concern and often will open the heart of the recipient.

2. *An illness.* Go to the home to see the sick member. Take a cheery bouquet, a book, magazine or other gift for the one who must spend many days in bed. Expression of interest is all the approach needed. People in the home most often will welcome the friendly overture.

3. *A welcome.* Newcomers are made to feel less lonely when the Sunday School has expressed its interest by a visit—especially if the visitor has brought a plate of cookies, a hot dish or a cake. They are more open to an invitation to services when it is extended by someone who cares.

4. *A spiritual need.* A teacher needs only the knowledge of a sorrow or great problem, to have a reason to make a visit to extend sympathy and offer assistance.

5. *A census.* A visit may be made, stating that the Sunday School is seeking to get acquainted and requests the names and ages and church affiliations of family members. Such a brief visit will open the door for a teacher to call upon children in the age group of her class.

First-time visitors need only introduce themselves, tell what church they represent, state the wish to get acquainted, and record the information. If the family is cordial, they may visit longer.

How Long To Visit

1. *Briefly.* If the family is just arriving home with the week's groceries or from a funeral, it is seldom appropriate to detain them by a long visit. Express interest and concern and depart.

2. *Not at all.* If the person visited is hostile to the church and argumentative, say goodbye quickly. There is nothing to be gained by argument.

3. *A few minutes.* A sick person usually welcomes visitors but may tire quickly. A stay of ten or fifteen minutes usually is sufficient to learn how the person is, to give spiritual comfort and help, and to pray with him.

4. *As long as need be.* Occasionally the Sunday School visitor encounters a spiritual need which cannot be met in a brief conversation. When the needy one expresses a wish for help, sit down with him and open the Bible and stay until the need is met or the person has found the strength and comfort sought.

32

For decades Sunday School contests have generated controversy and packed out church educational facilities.

Promotional Contests

"When many people were little tots they took their castor oil because somebody was going to make animal cookies for them," says Lloyd C. Douglas in *White Banners* (Simon & Schuster). "And then, later on, every time they do something fine and big and nobody comes running up the next minute with animal cookies, they go into tantrums and say, 'Lookit! What's the good of taking nasty medicine if there aren't any animal cookies?'"

Sunday School may not accurately be compared to castor oil—except, hopefully, in isolated instances—but its efforts to widen outreach through the use of contests and/or awards also have been derided. Those who favor expansion via contests often back up their assertions with the logic of the child's mother, who argued, "The cookies at least get the child to take the medicine, and he will benefit by it." Small matter that the medicine was taken originally to get the cookies, for good health was the result.

The Sunday School movement which began in 1780 with Robert Raikes built interest and faithfulness in its scholars with the use of inexpensive and desirable awards. Contests, per se, are known to have been in use for more than 100 years. More recently, controversy took on renewed vigor when *Christian Life* magazine in 1948 instituted an annual enlargement contest which continued in vogue for 11 years, with a cumulative result of almost 1,500,000

persons added to the 5,000 Sunday Schools which participated.

The contests took dozens of forms, each resulting in a prize or award to whoever excelled, or to all who participated. Awards within individual churches varied in value from bubblegum to free gasoline or fishing licenses. For the national winners, prizes supplied by *Christian Life's* advertisers included scholarships, choir robes, projectors and other equipment.

Was the financial investment worthwhile? In spiritual terms, some of the greatly enlarged churches say, "The spiritual effort put forth by the Sunday School workers fired them up to greater vision and dedication and resulted in many souls saved." The unanimous consensus of the winners was that consistent, faithful effort was responsible for the results—not the gimmicks.

Why, then, did the growth not occur before the contest called forth the effort? Roy Garn would have said it was "the magic power of emotional appeal." In his book with that title, Garn details the four basic emotional appeals which break down the sound barrier and provide a hearing for the speaker: self-preservation, money, romance and recognition.

Closely examined, any one of the four could explain the success of a contest. While it might seem that the "money" appeal accounted for the response, it is unlikely that such a small

Church promotion takes many forms. Indianapolis Baptist Temple has used a "Watermelon Day —all you can eat." (Indianapolis Baptist Temple, Indianapolis, IN)

On another occasion the children honey and feather the bus division leaders. (Indianapolis Baptist Temple, Indianapolis, IN)

reward as a pencil or ice cream cone could inspire diligent, time-consuming labor. More likely, the "recognition" the reward represented was responsible. A church's need for "self-preservation" might motivate zeal in the face of growth in surrounding churches. The fourth appeal, "romance," carries the connotation of desire for the "future promise" of a new, improved status. For any or all of these reasons, the contest approach could be considered as a means of pressing toward a high attendance goal.

Working for awards has scriptural foundation. I Corinthians 3:11,14: "For other foundation can no man lay than that which is laid, which is Jesus Christ . . . . If any man's work abide which he hath built thereupon, he shall receive a reward."

But when? The anti-contest camp maintains that future spiritual rewards are forfeited when rewards are handed out in the here-and-now. They cite Matthew 6:2,5,16: "So whenever you do your deeds of charity, never blow your own horn in public, as the hypocrites are in the habit of doing in the synagogues and on the street corners, to be praised by the people. I solemnly say to you, they already have their reward . . . Also, whenever you pray, you must not be like the hypocrites, for they love to pray standing in the synagogues and on the street corners, to attract the attention of people. I solemnly say to you, they already have their reward . . . . Also whenever you fast, you must not look gloomy like the hypocrites, for they put on a gloomy countenance, to let people see them fasting. I solemnly say to you, they already have their reward" (Williams).

Intrinsic (natural) motivation, the contest opposition holds, can be stifled by the substitution of external rewards. A pupil may be attending regularly, for instance, because he likes the teacher and enjoys the lessons and activities. Perhaps his teacher is wise enough to praise his faithfulness or in some way recognize him for it; the pleasure of an interesting class, plus a little praise, makes him eager to repeat his attendance. If, instead, a small gift is handed out impersonally to all who attend X number of times, the inner glow could become a desire for acquisition.

The opposition also claims that rivalry occasioned by rewards defeats the teaching of Christian love and placing others first. The pupil not only hopes to be the winner, he is actually encouraged to hope that others might lose.

Again, critics say, the rewards seem to call forth still greater effort from those who are already strongest, further embarrassing those less able to produce results. And, rewards may be habit-forming.

Regardless of what may be valid reasons for not using contests to encourage church growth and outreach, those who did participate in the aforementioned contests (*Christian Life*),

declare that contests
1. Unify the church.
2. Attract crowds.
3. Get more church members working.
4. Stimulate teachers.
5. Emphasize evangelism.
6. Reach the community.
7. Encourage visitation.
8. Bolster the entire church.
9. Boost attendance permanently.
10. Spur church building and expansion.

Rules for Successful Contests

"We heard about the contest at Brother Hill's church," a neighboring pastor admitted, "so we tried the same thing. Didn't do a thing for us. Can't understand why they got so many new members and we didn't."

Chances are that the would-be imitator failed to imitate the most essential ground rules for successful contests. In a nutshell the "luck" the first church had with their contest was made up of:
1. Labor
2. Untiring effort
3. Careful planning
4. Perseverance

The Rev. Bob Moore, Marietta (Ga.) Baptist Tabernacle, sums up his rules for promotions that bear fruit: (1) maintain high standards for advertising pieces, (2) follow through on what has been announced, (3) do not give awards or rewards that are not earned, (4) use prizes that cannot be gained in any other way, (5) learn the best time to give out promotional items (at the end of the service, he finds), (6) use variety, (7) be willing to invest funds to adequately promote, (8) inspire leaders to *work* the contest, or it will not work.

Successful Contests

1. *Election Campaign.* A strategic time for an election campaign contest is during a political campaign period, when attention is focused on campaigning. The ground rules are based on election procedures:

a. Smaller departments or classes are divided into two "parties" as Amen and Hallelujah parties, and larger departments into four groups, each with a name.

b. Each party selects a candidate, to be elected as class president.

c. Each party selects a secretary, to keep records.

d. Points are earned for the candidate as follows: each person present, 100; each visitor, 150; each new member, 500; and each absentee, -100.

Party members get full credit for bringing visitors to any department of the Sunday School; however, new members get full credit only for joining the sponsoring class.

2. *Goat Contest.* This is one contest where class members work their heads off in order not

to get the award. A farmer may loan or give the Sunday School the goat, which becomes the booby prize. A pen in the backyard of the church will (hopefully) confine the animal for the duration. Such an imprisoned animal needs the "tender loving care" of devoted Sunday School pupils each and every day.

Keeping the goat is a chore to be escaped by working hard. So, each Sunday the class with the lowest percentage of attendance must be responsible for Billy's food and water throughout the ensuing week.

Rules may also include points for such other accomplishments as: present, on time, brought visitor, studied lesson, and so on, or the contest may simply center around attendance. At the end of the contest, Billy may be sold and the proceeds donated to the cause of refreshments for the winner.

3. *Twin Sunday*. This one-Sunday promotional effort is effective as a means of making the church and its ministry known to those who are induced to make a first-time visit. The pastor usually plans to feature the literal twins in the church, or even in the entire community, during the service through special recognition and perhaps an inexpensive gift. This assures the attendance of that many babies, children, and parents, as a starter.

But for this big day, everybody can have a "twin": any visitor brought by a member is considered that person's "twin" for the day. Double cards are provided for each participant. One side of the perforation reads, "I have a Twin," while the other says, "I am a Twin." The member gives the latter to the visitor to wear. Furthermore, a participant may have more than one "twin" on this occasion. He may give out as many twin cards as he is able to bring visitors. Each is his "twin" for the day.

Churches which have used this emphasis report good cooperation on the part of neighbors, friends and relatives who are willing to please someone by coming. Happily, some members of cold, dead churches are exposed to the Word of God through the visit. The

During one Sunday School contest the First Baptist Church of West Hollywood released helium-filled balloons containing invitations to attend Sunday School. (First Baptist Church of West Hollywood, FL)

232

long-range result has been, in some cases, the salvation of souls.

4. *An Everybody-Can-Win Contest.* Motivation determines priorities—even of Sunday School boys and girls. Not all can be expected to respond to an "I Love Jesus" Sunday, and to abandon all other projects for Him, particularly without parental push. So teachers turn to *extrinsic (not inherent) motivation* in various forms:

a. Periodic prizes for each pupil who maintains a specified attendance level for a month. (This may take the form of an award for attendance three out of four Sundays, or perfect attendance may be the standard.)

b. An award or gift for each pupil with perfect attendance for three months, six months, or a year. Graded in value, each lesser prize must be attained before the grand prize for the year can be received.

Does it work? Teachers who have tried attendance recognition have, for the most part, praised the results. Boys and girls from indifferent homes come of their own volition—sometimes with uncombed hair and unwashed face, sometimes having gotten their own breakfast, but they are there, hearing the Word of God. As with adults, some boys and girls are not motivated as much by the monetary value of a gift as by recognition for having had perfect attendance.

Of course, a child's presence in a classroom does not guarantee that the teaching will penetrate the heart. And an attendance habit built on desire for objects may be broken when objects no longer are given. The time to reach the heart and soul is the Sunday that the pupil is sitting in the class, eyes upturned, measuring both teacher and lesson against his home values. Which wins?

5. *March to Sunday School in March.* At least annually comes the month in which the "marching" theme is most appropriate and therefore usually well received and acted upon. To encourage this additional marching to the Sunday School, pastors or educational directors may:

a. Offer a small award or gift to each member who brings a visitor, and each visitor who comes.

b. Offer a small gift to each one who attends on a given Sunday. (One church did this, with an unexpected after-effect. Each person present on the first Sunday of March was given a Bible bookmark with the name of the church and pastor. The only way they could get one was to be there. Many members put them in their Bibles, and one choir member in particular is now glad she did. Ten months after the contest, her Bible—cherished for its long years of use—was stolen from her locked car. The thief decided he could not battle the accusing Book, so dropped it by the roadside. An honest man found it, called the telephone number of the pastor named on the bookmark, and the lady was reunited with her Bible—all because she went to Sunday School the first Sunday in March.)

c. Sponsor a parade the Saturday before the first Sunday, featuring appropriate signs of invitation.

d. Sponsor a churchwide visitation with all classes represented, to meet on the Saturday before the first Sunday, "marching" house to house with invitational handouts.

6. *Fall Roundup.* On a poster for each department in Sunday School draw a cow for each member of every class, with name affixed. In the center of the poster, draw a horse, representing the teacher. As each pupil is signed up, a picture of a cow is pasted over the drawing. When all members have signed, the roundup is completed. (Men's classes use steers instead of cows.)

A big poster in the auditorium will feature a picture of horses with teachers' names, showing they have completed their roundup. Scatter a few cows and steers around the edges.

At the end of the campaign, a picnic may include a pony and wagon for rides for all the children. Toy horses may reward children who brought the most visitors, a radio may reward teenagers, and a Bible may be given to the adult who brought the most visitors.

33

Sunday School programs for special holidays have not outlived their usefulness, not if they are done creatively.

Special Days

Old-time Sunday Schools made much of seasonal and sacred holidays. On these occasions, the entire membership met in the church sanctuary for a program—often featuring every class from toddlers through adults. Few cared whether it was a polished performance—as long as almost everyone had a part.

Those programs probably were remembered longest by the performers themselves. And, because of the seasonal association, the spiritual impact was renewed with each recurrence of the season. There is something to be said against these programs, however. Some child psychology experts believe the system exploited the children, to their emotional and mental detriment. If anyone criticized or laughed at their performance, shy children might become more inhibited. At the same time, if the natural extrovert and leader was too highly praised, he might become vain.

Although in the "good old days," families shared church experiences through these programs, in today's well-organized, departmentalized churches, the spiritual progress of many children goes quietly forward without being noticed by parents or grandparents. In the public school, assembly programs afford more opportunity for family awareness than any activity provided by most churches. Perhaps an occasional unified church assembly for all ages would bridge some generation gaps.

Special-day all-church programs also can bridge a gap between parents and teachers, who, in very large churches, never may meet. As teachers introduce their pupils, Mother and Dad learn for the first time who Bobby's teacher is. (This avoids [hopefully!] the predicament of one preschooler's mother. Jimmy had a new Sunday School teacher, who had been rushed to the hospital. Mother was contacted by a leader who hoped all mothers would send the sick teacher a card. After she hung up, Mother realized she did not know the teacher's name. "Who is your new teacher, Jimmy?" she asked. He thought for awhile, then slowly responded, "I don't know—but I guess she must be Jesus's grandmother, because she's always talking about Him.")

"Isn't Sunday School for the purpose of Bible study?" Curriculum experts protest, "Why have special-day emphases at all? It interrupts our sacred schedule."

However, God interrupted His scheduled programs for special emphases involving the family. In the midst of seeing tens of thousands of His people safely across the Jordan River on their way into the Promised Land, He had General Joshua stop and ask a representative of each tribe to take a large stone and put it on a designated pile. Progress was halted while the special program took place. And progress would thereafter be halted at the place

234

As part of its special day observance, Westside Assembly of God had an Easter egg hunt which created this scene of joyous confusion. (Westside Assembly of God, Davenport, IA)

whenever a family passed by the stones.

"Why is that pile of stones here?" the children would ask. Then, the father would answer their questions, explaining the story.

In Old Testament times, observance of special days included the Passover. Annual pantomime of the event kept the memory fresh in the minds of the delivered. So would the Jews' annual drama of the brave Queen Esther and the hanging of Haman. Doubtless the whole family celebrated the event as a group. Other feasts or celebrations were designated by God to be held with regularity.

In the Christian era, Christmas and Easter became occasions for weeks of rehearsal and preparation for an all-church pageant or drama. Most families were involved as the parent or child had a part or helped with costuming and other duties. Today, there are fewer all-church pageants. Junior has too many other activities, especially at Christmas—the Santa Claus Parade, the school program, television "specials," etc. And Christmas shopping begins before Thanksgiving and continues through the after-Christmas sales.

"People are so busy," say the church leaders, "we don't want to add the burden of rehearsals and programs."

So special-day programs have come to be observed chiefly in the music department of the church. Choirs are going to meet every week anyway, leaders say. They can add the seasonal message to song in their regular practice, and, with no real extra output of time or effort, can produce a special program. But not everyone is qualified to participate in the music. Persons who could give a good account of themselves in a speech or pantomime must be only onlookers. While children's choirs do not exclude monotones, the youth and adult choirs do (if they have a choice), and some who are willing to serve cannot do so when no opportunity is afforded.

A successful program—whether for Mother's Day, Father's Day, Children's Day, Thanksgiving, Christmas, Easter, Promotion Day, or whatever—depends on:

1. *The leader.* Someone must be willing to plan and push the program. Time must be invested in announcing and conducting rehearsals, and in arranging for costumes, decorations, curtains, furniture, etc. This leader need not be the one who accomplishes every task, but the one who directs others to do so.

2. *The participants.* With interest and enthusiasm caught from a dedicated leader, those who take part in a program must be willing to memorize any necessary speeches and to attend rehearsals.

3. *The audience.* The majority of the membership should be willing to attend the final production and encourage those who spent hours preparing the program. While a full

Bellevue Baptist put some creative thought into one of its special days. On "Feeding of the 5,000" Day, 5,400 people attended this out-of-doors Sunday service. A portion of the crowd is shown here. (Bellevue Baptist Church, Memphis, TN)

house may seem frightening, it also is a spur to the participants to do their best. Teachers may prepare children's classes to be good listeners by warning against laughing at performers or attempting to distract them. (There usually is a boy dedicated to this kind of activity.) Sympathy with less-than-perfect performance may help the underachievers try harder next time— or even to attempt a next time.

Where to Find Ideas

1. *Catalogs.* Few teachers have time to spend hours at a bookstore browsing through the program possibilities and making a selection. Catalogs from Christian publishers usually list special-day program collections and describe the contents, so selection may be made by mail.

2. *Publishers of plays.* Three leading publishers of plays for school and community, also publish plays, pantomimes and recitations for church use. They are Baker's Plays, 100 Chauncy Street, Boston, MA 02111; Eldridge Publishing Company, P.O. Drawer 209, Franklin, OH 45005; and T.S. Denison, 5100 West 82nd, Minneapolis, MN 55431.

3. *Other churches' programs.* Visit another church's play or pageant. If it seems a possibility for your group, find out where the script is available.

4. *Write it.* Using musical numbers by regular choir groups, a Sunday School leader can put together a program of recitations and Bible passages in chronological order. (Recitations may be obtained through the catalogs mentioned above.) More often than is supposed possible, a leader who knows the abilities of the children, youth, or adult participants, can plan a better program than a printed one which calls for talents not represented in his group. The fact that it is original also can be emphasized in advertising.

Part of the Christmas program "cast" at Bible Baptist Church poses after the performance. (Bible Baptist Church, Lincoln, NB)

section VII

Class in Session

34

Need some new techniques to liven up your Bible study sessions? Try these.

Using the Bible in Class

Pupils should bring their Bibles not only for points or for a contest, but to use them! Each should be encouraged to own a Bible. If any cannot afford it, the church may provide one. The American Bible Society has one for $1.15. Each age group should use the Bible. Some ideas are:

Age Levels
1. *Preschool.* Teach that the Bible is a special book. It is God's book. It tells about Jesus. It tells what is right and what is wrong. All the stories of the Bible are true stories. Children should see older persons carefully handling the Bible and studying it.

The child should know which stories you tell are from the Bible and which are not. Always hold the Bible when telling a Bible story, but not for other stories. Show Bible pictures. The Bible story for the preschool child should be less than five minutes in length, free from much description, full of repetition, free from fear-producing elements. There should be a Bible in the department.

2. *Primary.* Encourage the child to bring his Bible to use. Point out the difference between the Old and New Testaments. Study the children of the Bible. Help the child locate memory verses and Bible stories in his own Bible. Let the child read carefully selected verses aloud, especially the third-grader. Tell the Bible story from the Bible, not from a quarterly.

3. *Junior.* Teach that the Bible is inspired by God, that it is God's revelation to us, that God expects us to obey its teachings, that the Bible is the final authority in all matters, and that the Bible helps us to solve our everyday problems.

The junior should learn the books of the Bible in order; he should learn the chronology, the history, and the geography of the Bible. He should form the habit of daily reading, and he should memorize Scripture.

Encourage juniors to read their Bibles by having some form of group reading in every class session: unison, responsive, antiphonal (boys vs. girls), by rows. Have sword drills and treasure hunts (references all contain a certain word, the "treasure"), notebooks to copy verses and illustrate. During teaching, pause to ask questions about the Bible passage. To answer, pupils must read verse silently and answer in their own words.

4. *Youth.* Intermediates should be learning to use Bible study helps such as a Bible atlas, dictionary, and harmony of the Gospels. Provide for participation in direct Bible study. Provide a variety of studies—Bible survey, doctrines, the Bible and science, and other topical studies. Allow opportunity for paraphrasing (included in this chapter). See also the section on Bible search.

5. *Adults.* Provide for participation in direct Bible study. Use Bible study guides that can be applied to many passages of Scripture to encourage daily Bible reading. Make use of book

Teach from the Bible, not from an aid.

studies and of topical studies.

Let pupils make their own application when possible. Teach from the Bible, not from an aid. Have an aim for each lesson. Evaluate each lesson.

In all Bible study look for something. Write down what you find. Ask, "What does this mean to me?" Look for answers to the questions:

Is there an example for me to follow?

Is there a command for me to obey?

Is there a sin for me to avoid or forsake?

Is there a promise for me to claim? Are there conditions to that promise?

What does the chapter teach me about God?

What does it teach me about Jesus Christ?

What does it teach me about the Holy Spirit?

What does it teach me about sin?

What does it teach me about Christian living?

What is one practical verse for me to apply to my own life?

Is there anything in this chapter that should be my prayer for today?

Try to think of a song that expresses the teaching of this chapter.

Bible Search

With the presentation of a statement, the class is to search the Scriptures to find the reference and explanation for the statement presented. The following rules should be observed by the class for effective use of Bible search.

1. Each person is to find two references for each statement made.

2. Each person may use all available resource materials to find these Scriptures.

3. Class members may work in pairs, sharing the work and pooling their knowledge. Each pair should present a common conclusion.

4. The conclusions must be written on paper to share with the class.

Have a number of concordances and commentaries available to aid the search for Scripture references. Arrange also for pencils and paper, as well as extra Bibles.

Use a felt-tipped pen to place statements relevant to the topic on a flip chart. Place only one statement on each side of each page of your flip chart. The class should be working on only one assignment at a time. First, show the statement to the class and read it to them. Second, give them about two minutes to search for the scriptural source of each statement. Finally, let the students report on their findings. Be careful that they do not simply read back the phrases of the Scripture verses they have found. Ask them to tell the meaning of the verses. This way, one student teaches the others as he explains and interprets the Word of God. (Note diagram.)

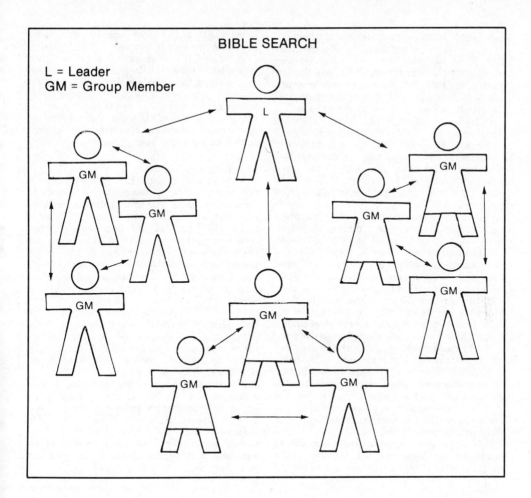

BIBLE SEARCH

L = Leader
GM = Group Member

Paraphrasing

1. *Method.* Many classes have found that restating the truths of Scripture in modern idiom is a helpful learning procedure. A person using this technique rewrites each Scripture verse under consideration. He avoids using the original words of the text; yet the paraphrase must communicate the true meaning of the text. Paraphrasing yields new understanding to adults who are seriously seeking to study the Scriptures.

The student's ability to paraphrase a passage depends upon his grasp of its basic idea. Many times the King James Version expresses thoughts in archaic language. However, any person who honestly seeks to find the true meaning of Scripture can do so. Perhaps the need of twentieth-century Christians is not for modern translations, but for the healing of their own spiritual blindness so that they can understand God's Word. Occasional archaic language is not the main obstacle in understanding God's Word, though modern translations may have a place in the Christian's library.

Paraphrasing as a teaching technique differs from using a modern version. Paraphrasing places emphasis on study by the student. Modern versions are used when emphasis is to be placed on the final product.

Paraphrasing is not an attempt to change the meaning of Scripture. In fact, if students change the meaning of Scripture, they have missed the point of paraphrasing. The purpose is to express the meaning of the Scripture passage in a way that will give a clear understanding to each student.

2. *Room arrangement.* Supply paper and pencils for each student. If possible, provide one or more tables where your students can spread out their Bibles and note paper. Give the group five minutes or so to paraphrase this passage.

3. *Using the paraphrase.* Class members will get more out of the Scripture passage if they are given ample opportunity to discuss their written material. Misunderstanding and lack of clarity in thinking show up quickly in such an exercise. Have several student paraphrases read aloud.

Some of the following questions can help you as a teacher to get the most out of paraphrasing: Which words have been misunderstood by various class members? What are the reasons why different class members interpret words differently? What new insights into the Scripture has the class acquired today?

4. *Tools for paraphrasing.* In paraphrasing Scriptures a variety of tools for Bible study will be helpful. Have several copies of Bible dictionaries on hand. An English dictionary will also be helpful. The dictionary gives good definitions for some archaic words. A book of synonyms and antonyms may also prove useful.

5. *Summary statement.* The class members together should produce a summary statement composed of the best of the students' paraphrased verses. The first step in arriving at a summary statement is to read the verse from the King James Version. Have those students who feel that their contribution will be significant read their paraphrases to the class. The next step is to write the meaning of the verse in one statement. This method, of course, will not give the meaning supplied to the verse by every class member. But perhaps the class can agree to accept one statement as the best.

After the class has agreed upon a paraphrase for each verse, write the finished product on the chalkboard or on a large pad of newsprint. The teacher might appoint a class secretary to do the actual writing so that he himself may continue leading the class.

6. *With prose reproduction.* Appoint a secretary and discussion leader. Rewrite the paraphrase in prose form, making it about the same length as the verse. You may want to put the same message in a totally different setting. (Try to imagine what sort of situation Christ would use if He were telling this parable today.) Avoid using the same key words as are in the original. (Such words as parable, householder, vineyard, servants, etc.) Try to get everyone in the group involved. Discuss the various settings which could be used and the various ways each thought could be expressed.

Role Play and Dialogues

Appoint a group leader. Pick one member of the group to be a news reporter from the *Jerusalem Times.* The front office has received a report that there have been a number of deaths during a feud over the payment of rents on a vineyard outside of town. It is your job to get at the heart of the story by interviewing all the key persons involved. Assign each person a role. You will probably want a representative from the tenant, the servant, eye witnesses, the owner, and anyone else who might have been involved. When roles have been assigned, discuss what each person will say. Everyone in the group should develop an understanding of how the various participants thought and felt. Do not write a script. Just discuss the parts and perform extemporaneously.

Prepare a number of brief extemporaneous dialogues from this scene. Pick as many pairs as you have in your group (one group may have three, if necessary). Assign each pair a different discussion that might have taken place in a certain parable. Try to pick dialogues you think will best portray the thinking and emotion present among the various parties.

35

Some of the nation's largest churches have revolutionized their Sunday Schools by changing to team teaching.

Team Teaching

If one teacher in a Sunday School class is good, two would be better. Agree? Some churches think so. They are using team teaching and master-teaching plans in their Sunday Schools. Vacation Bible School has used team teaching for fifty years, but this technique recently filtered into the Sunday School.

In the master-teacher plan, one teacher teaches large groups of children with the assistance of many helpers. The master-teacher plan has been called modified team teaching.

What Is Team Teaching?

The team approach to teaching calls for two or more persons to guide the learning, growth, cooperation and evaluation of classroom experience. Sharing of responsibility is vital to the team approach.

No one person *can* or *should* be responsible for the spiritual life of a child. In the one-teacher-to-a-classroom approach, the teacher has responsibility for all the praying, teaching, guiding, encouraging and counseling. But every child is different, every class is unique. Needs change from child to child and from age to age. Several teachers should pray, teach, visit, guide and direct the pupil. These teachers form a team.

Team teaching is not entirely new or untried in the Sunday School. For many years the church nursery and kindergarten classes have had two or more teachers. Also, the Vacation Bible School has used teaching teams in beginner and primary classes. Some of the older denominations have been using the team approach in these classes also.

What Are the Advantages of Team Teaching?

Sunday School conventions and Christian education literature have begun stressing the advantages of team teaching.

1. *The emphasis is on the group.* The church has come a long way in understanding how learning takes place. Once people thought that knowledge resided in the adult-teacher, parent, or camp counselor. This knowledge was passed from the adult to the child as apples are passed from one basket to another.

Now educators recognize that the child does his own learning. The teacher only guides the learning experience. We know that boys and girls teach one another through sharing mutual experiences. This interaction has as great an impact on the total learning as the adult teacher. Thus, team teaching emphasizes the group and recognizes the way children learn.

2. *Team teaching increases learning possibilities.* Team teaching permits larger classes because two or more teachers share in the leadership. More children in a group mean more possibilities for rich learning experiences.

3. *Team teaching makes teacher recruitment easier.* People join the teaching staff more

The team in action—fifth grade boys superintendent (left) assists Barbara Durrance remove chalk drawings from the pad while Bob Woodard (right) teaches the lesson. (First Baptist Church of West Hollywood, FL)

readily if they know that the responsibility will be spread around. In a team teaching approach the new teacher is not "on his own." The beginning teacher enters into group planning, sharing and evaluation. He learns from the older, more experienced teachers in the classroom. Still, teaching must be "caught" rather than "taught." New teachers learn to teach by actually teaching with other teachers.

4. *Team teaching offers more possibilities for teachers to grow.* In a team teaching approach several teachers work together in a group. They help one another grow and learn. They share insights from the Scriptures. They encourage one another to try out new ideas. With such support a teacher finds it easier to attempt new methods and try different materials.

When one teacher is isolated in a classroom, outside evaluation is limited. Usually the pupils are the only judge of teaching. Mistakes are perpetuated. Poor teachers do not usually improve their methods except by trial and error. However, the errors have eternal implications. Team teaching helps to minimize mistakes and enrich teaching.

5. *More specialized skills can be utilized.* With more teachers present, more skills are likely to be available for class enrichment. A Sunday School teacher with a specialized skill may join a class for a short time. For instance, the team may feel the need for help with audiovisual aids or a children's choir. A teacher with these special skills may join the team. The new teacher participates in the planning, works in the sessions, and shares in the evaluation. The new teacher's special skills contribute not only to the children but to the other teachers. Thus, every Sunday School classroom can become a training laboratory for teachers. Teachers continue to grow through a team teaching approach.

Who Is on the Team?

Everyone associated with the class is on the team. This includes pianists, class secretary, and others with specialized responsibility. All team members—whether teacher, pianist or superintendent—are thought of as teachers.

The adults are responsible for initial planning and preparation for the learning situation. However, the boys and girls can help plan in the classroom. They can suggest things they want to learn. Especially in the older grades can the pupils share responsibility for what is happening in the classroom. Team teaching means that everyone in a group is teaching!

How Team Teaching Operates

One person on the team should be designated lead teacher. He carries the administrative responsibility—scheduling of the planning meeting, administering the planning, ordering of supplies, caring for some of the details. The lead teacher may serve as chairman of the planning sessions. Or other teachers may serve in this capacity. Some teams rotate the chairmanship of planning, with each teacher in the group taking turns.

How a Team Plans a Lesson

Certain steps should be followed in planning a unit and in carrying out the plans.

1. *All teachers must be fully acquainted with the area of study.* All teachers should read the entire unit—the teachers' manual, the pages in the pupils' quarterly, and other related materials. Each member of the team should make a list of songs, Scripture verses to be used, topics for conversation, activities or projects, handwork, and other suggestions appropriate for the units.

2. *The team must meet for planning.* The planning session should meet at least two weeks before the lesson is taught. The lead teacher schedules the meeting. The chairman for planning presides at the session. Each teacher should share his list of learning materials and activities. Together they may:

a. Think through questions the pupils may raise from the study. Determine how to help the pupils find answers.

b. Consider the aims and purposes of the lesson and make a list of the needs of the pupils. The specific aims should meet immediate needs. However, the pupils may have additional purposes to add.

c. List all possible activities in which their pupils may be engaged for learning and growth.

d. Determine the specific responsibilities for each teacher on the team.

e. Practice the teaching skills each will need during the lesson.

f. Write out a specific lesson plan. Include the sequence of events and persons responsible for each leadership task.

The team makes broad plans. However, the plans should be sufficiently definite so that each teacher can proceed with his individual preparation, yet be flexible enough so that the

The planning session should be held at least two weeks before the lesson is taught.

pupils' ideas can be incorporated.

The success of team teaching depends on team planning. Where all teachers share the planning, all share an equal responsibility for the results. The team should consider the suggestions of each member of the team. No one dominates. No one just listens. All participate.

3. *All members of the team work together during the class.* Even though a teacher may not be in direct command of the class, he should not sit back and take a mental vacation. The silent teacher may be observing the pupil's responses, evaluating an activity, or giving support to the guiding teacher. Each team member, whether teaching or observing, should feel responsible. Then at times the class will be divided into small groups with each teacher working with a group.

4. *Each team member supports the others on the team.* All teachers should help one another to grow and improve. The timid teacher should be encouraged to assume leadership when he is ready. Team members should give and seek constructive suggestions.

5. *The pupils share responsibility.* Pupils of all ages can share responsibility to some extent. All pupils need experience in problem-solving, decision-making, and expressing their own ideas at their own level. All pupils should be able to help choose what they want to learn, under the teacher's guidance, of course.

Younger children can suggest activities or experiences they enjoy. The teacher should listen carefully for the child's questions and comments. Student interest or disinterest will tell a teacher whether he is meeting needs.

Older students can assume more responsibility for helping determine what needs to be learned and how to carry out work. They can help evaluate progress in terms of "how are we doing?"

Members One of Another

One must know a person in order to help him or her. This takes time. Knowing one another means sharing many experiences.

Teachers must know one another well. Informal fellowship among team members is as basic to team teaching as serious planning. This is one reason for regular sessions. One

Even though a teacher may not be in direct command of the class, he should not sit back and take a mental vacation.

246

hour on Sunday morning does not provide sufficient time to know one another. Through-the-week activities make possible a variety of experiences.

Not only must teachers know one another, they must know their pupils. Teachers should phone their pupils, write cards, and make personal visits. Every pupil should be able to say of his class at church, "This is my group. I really belong here; my teacher really cares about me. The other pupils care about me, too. I like my class."

Problems in Team Teaching

Many difficulties beset the forming of a team. The shy, timid teacher may withdraw and not make a contribution to the group. The aggressive teacher may manipulate the other team members. The end product in either case is not a team effort.

Problems in personal relationships may arise. Any time two people work together these difficulties may develop.

Lack of time may be a problem. It takes time for all members of the team to make their suggestions. One or two talkative members may dominate the conversation in the time available. The group needs to take extra time to draw out points from all members. Progress may be slow. However, the team that is willing to move slowly at first in order to be a "team," may later move more rapidly.

Another difficulty in team teaching is personal reticence. "I wouldn't want to tell the story with Mrs. Hesselgrave in the room!" As members of the team support one another, they may overcome this fear.

Misconceptions about Team Teaching

When considering team teaching, people often ask, "If you have thirty-seven children in the room, won't you lose personal contact?" Past experience with team teaching has proven the contrary. Team teachers usually have deeper insight into individual students because of shared observations. In the one-teacher classroom the teacher may overlook Sally because of personal reasons. However, when the team evaluates Sally, three other teachers can share their observations on her progress. "In the multitude of counselors there is safety" (Proverbs 11:14). Also, when more than one teacher is in the room, they can observe Sally in a variety of activities and relationships. Thus they get a better overall understanding of her.

Another misconception relates to teacher recruitment. People often remark, "Team teaching is so difficult, how could we get anyone to serve?" Once again, experience overrules the objection. Teacher recruitment is easier when the candidate knows he will receive in-service training and help in the classroom. The learn-as-you-work approach removes the threatening aspect of teaching. Also, people like the idea that they will not have to assume sole responsibility for the class.

The team teacher is like a member of an orchestra. Each instrument must follow the conductor, be in pitch and on key, able to carry its assignment, and have a knowledge of the responsibilities of others. So in team teaching. Each teacher must come to class prepared, able to carry his assignment, have a knowledge of what other teachers are doing, and work in harmony with others. As the orchestra produces the full and complete symphony, so the team of teachers produce well-rounded, mature students—to the glory of God.

The Master Teacher

The master-teacher method is an innovation used extensively in fast-growing Sunday Schools. Whereas the traditional Sunday School class had the teacher sitting in the center of a small semicircle of pupils, the master teacher leads large groups of students. Some classes have 50 students, others have 200. Whereas past Sunday Schools usually taught Bible content through storytelling and lecturing, the master teacher utilizes emotions, excitement and sensory perception to teach Bible truths.

Churches have usually structured their Sunday Schools to provide one teacher for every 10 pupils. The master-teacher approach exposes all pupils to the most gifted teachers, while other adults assist in the teaching process according to their abilities.

Whereas the Sunday Bible School has met in small, self-contained classrooms about 10 feet square, under the master-teacher approach, classes meet in large, airy, well-lighted rooms and use the total environment for learning. Master teachers use the total room for the entire teaching hour, using every teaching technique available, taking advantage of all avenues of learning.

Oak Forest Baptist Temple's traditional Sunday School averaged 432 in attendance when Pastor William Schroeder changed to the master-teacher approach. At first his teachers were reluctant, but he suggested, "Give it a try." They found the gifted teacher able to motivate all the pupils. The children really enjoyed Sunday School. As a result attendance increased. Also, the group effort by teachers led to more effective teaching, and they won more to the Lord. The church now averages over 1,000. Attendance doubled without providing additional space, although they are now adding more space.

All 10 churches in the book *America's Fastest Growing Churches* use the master-teacher method. The Bible Baptist Church in Savannah, Ga., uses public-school-size rooms, teaching 40 to 60 pupils in each room. In Indianapolis one church uses much larger rooms and teaches 200 pupils in each, one room for each age. All 200 children in the room sit around conference tables (approximately 20

In the small groups pupils ask questions, review the memory verse and do table work.

tables). They listen to the master teacher; then they turn to discuss the lesson around the table with an assistant teacher. The pupils get the motivation of large-group teaching, plus the advantages of discussion in small groups.

In the traditional Sunday School, if the teacher was exceptional, the class got outstanding results. If the teacher was unmotivated and unprepared, everything (and everyone) suffered. Attendance usually dropped off and people were seldom won to Christ. No teacher can do it alone. Every teacher needs assistance, especially in his weak areas. He may need someone to lead singing or to tell the story. Every pupil still needs individual attention, because each one is different, and every situation is unique.

Advantages of Large Group
1. *Motivation.* Built on ability of the teacher to get the pupil excited.
2. *Teacher-centered.* The teacher still sets the pattern of learning.
3. *Application.* By identification with the teacher.

There are three areas for comparison of the master-teacher plan and the small, self-contained classroom. However, the differences are not that distinct, because the master teacher uses both large and small groups.

1. *Communication.* In the traditional classroom communication of Bible content is good where there is an adequate teacher. But there are two problems. First, if the teacher is incompetent, communication is marginal. A small class never guarantees effective teaching, nor does a self-contained classroom assure success. *Good teachers* are the key, not proper size or desirable facilities.

A second problem is dead orthodoxy. Some pupils have learned Bible knowledge but have done nothing with their knowledge. They need motivation or stimulation to apply the Bible to life. Just because a pupil knows the Bible does not guarantee he will live its message. He must be motivated to live for God. When a pupil is excited about the truth, he will learn better and apply more of it to his life. The master-teacher approach should create interest in learning.

2. *Teacher-centered vs. pupil-centered.* Education theory has long discussed the merits of both approaches. Many modern-day pedagogues have swung to the extreme of pupil-centered techniques. Yet the teacher can make a difference when his personality is interjected into the teaching process. "The life of teaching is still the life of the teacher." Learning is significantly enhanced by gifted teachers.

The Sunday School is not an either/or situation. Both teacher-centered and pupil-centered classes should be utilized. The master teacher stands before his pupils (perhaps 60 or more) and communicates the Scriptures; the better his presentation, the more they listen and learn. Then the pupils are divided into small discussion groups. Each teacher-assistant reteaches the same lesson. In the small groups pupils ask questions, review the memory verse, have misunderstandings corrected and receive personal attention. The master-teacher approach takes the best of two worlds. More can be accomplished when the class emphasizes both teacher-centered and pupil-centered learning.

When a church grows rapidly, where does it get additional qualified teachers? The problem is especially acute when Sunday School buses are added and the classes double. Instead of trying to form more small classes, make large ones where your best teachers are in charge and the others assist them. Some churches are forced into the master-teacher approach because of rapid growth; other churches grow because of the advantages of the master-teacher approach.

3. *Application.* Students identify with the master teacher and desire to be like him. Visual and sensory inspiration is necessary; the master teacher can provide a model for their lives. But, at the same time, students learn the most when they rethink and apply truths. As the teacher-assistants discuss the issues at the table, the pupil "tries truth on for size," much as in a self-service shoe department.

The master-teacher approach recognizes that God has gifted certain men and women with the ability to teach—and it seeks to utilize that gift to the fullest extent.

36

Because oral presentation cannot be eliminated, it must be done with an understanding of the teaching-learning process.

The Lecture Method

The lecture method might be better titled "oral presentation by the teacher." It includes all oral presentation by the teacher—remarks made to clarify issues, to elaborate upon pupils' answers to questions, to supplement data already on hand, or to indicate how something is to be done and remarks constituting an extended formal exposition.

Oral presentation is used to a great extent at all levels of instruction. It cannot be avoided, even at the younger ages. It is impossible to eliminate oral presentation, even from methods of instruction that allow greater pupil participation. It must, then, be done effectively and intelligently with an understanding of the laws of the teaching-learning process. Any teacher with a sense of responsibility will wish to master the technique of effective oral presentation.

The Teacher

In the lecture method the success of the educational process lies at the feet of the teacher. He plays a dominant, sometimes exclusive role. He must realize that mere telling is never teaching. The teaching-learning process involves much more than imparting information, more than transferring notes from the teacher's notebook into the student's. The teacher must effectively stimulate the learning process and guide pupil response. He must feel the mental pulse of the students and seek to meet their needs. This can be done by the lecture method to some extent, but it involves real planning and work. The teacher must be well prepared. He must have an over-all view of the subject and its relationships, as well as have a command of the particulars he desires to teach at a given time. In class he must not come across as dogmatic or pushy. The teacher must be a shepherd of thoughts, not one who drives but who leads his pupils to pastures of mental feeding.

The Pupil

The pupil's participation in the lecture method is generally minimal. Yet, there can be active participation, at least mentally. The good teacher can stimulate this kind of interest. The student's mind is not a passive organ, into which the teacher pours predigested materials and thoughts from his notebook. The student must digest and assimilate the material himself if real learning is to take place. Keep in mind that real learning involves changes in beliefs and practices. For this to happen the teacher must set in motion the self-learning process.

The Material

In the lecture method, more than in other methods, the subject determines organization and development of material. The student must be able to follow the presentation. Since the

LECTURE

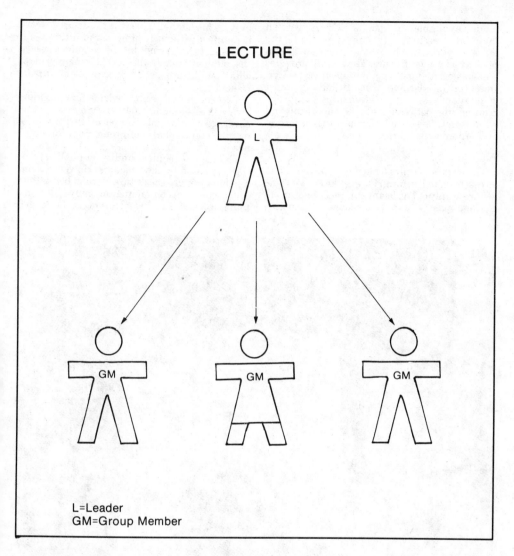

L=Leader
GM=Group Member

intellect functions logically, the subject should be organized logically, one step leading to another, with manifest relationships between parts. In this method the material may be better analyzed, synthesized and balanced.

The lecture method does not exclude variety of presentation or adaptation to the needs of the pupils. The material must be chosen and adapted to meet the needs of the pupils. The aim should be to get the pupil to think along with the instructor in coming to a solution to his problem. Lecturing is not merely covering the material. The teacher must not let the material obstruct his vision for ministry to his pupils.

Advantages

The spoken word can have a strong impact upon an audience. Spoken words communicate more effectively than printed material. Inflection, emphasis and explanation make oral presentation an energetic and dynamic method. The lecture conveys the influence of the teacher's personality. Attractive Christian character means much here. The lecture can arouse interest and motivate pupils. The spoken word has the dynamic qualities which draw men.

The lecture saves time. More ground can be covered by a lecture than by any other method. The lecture can be used with a large group better than any other method. It is easier to lecture than to teach by discussion or question. Since not all teachers are well trained in the more difficult methods of teaching, and since many schools find it difficult to enlist and train enough teachers, the lecture is more popular.

The lecture provides opportunity for use of supplementary material, things that cannot be made available to pupils. Often written material presents only one view while the teacher with much wider experience can present a broader picture. The lecture provides a means of giving the pupil proper perspective. Immature minds have difficulty making proper evaluations, seeing relationships, and discriminating between what is important and what is not. The lecturer can properly interpret and organize the data.

Disadvantages

The lecture permits little pupil participation, so essential to learning. Pupils like activity; the lecture is static. The lecture method tends to encourage passivity and discourage responsi-

bility. This method can stifle the desire to learn if handled without freshness and interest.

The lecture may not be an economical use of the pupil's time. If the teacher merely gives what pupils can get from a text, the time is wasted.

The lecture makes no provision for individual differences among pupils. Selection and coverage of materials, simple or difficult, must be made on the basis of group, not individual, needs.

The lecture requires ability in public speaking possessed by few teachers. However, some teachers can use the lecture method better than any other. Oral communication may be learned and improved. But few lecturers can be at their

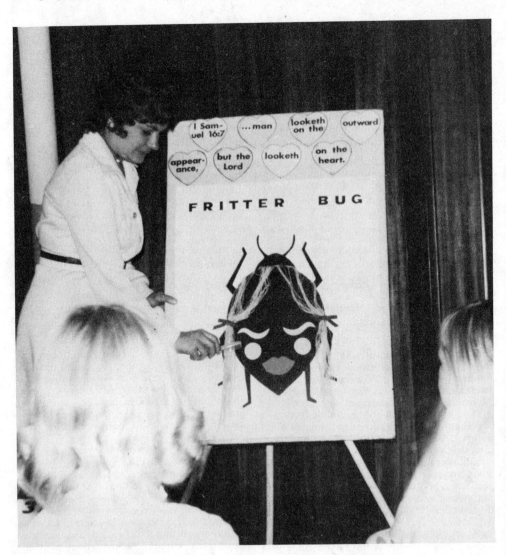

When using the lecture method, plan to have as many teaching aids as possible. (First Baptist Church of West Hollywood, FL)

best constantly.

Teachers are prone to use the lecture method too much. An alert teacher will use more productive methods also.

The lecture may give the pupil more content than he can analyze, understand, or assimilate. The lecture generally gives the pupil only one contact with the material.

Preparing the lecture

1. *Relationship.* Review a brief outline of the whole course. See what part of the course is covered in this lecture and how this lecture relates to the one previous and the one following.

2. *Content.* Study the subject thoroughly. The more details you master, the more confidently you can present the important ones. Study prayerfully. Remember that the Holy Spirit is the only Teacher who can apply this lesson to the students' lives, and He works in answer to prayer. Study selectively. Out of the mass of available information, select the really essential points to get the lesson across. Determine the aim of the lecture. The aim should be threefold, for the whole personality: (1) What do you want the listeners to know (intellect)? (2) What do you want the listeners to feel (sensibility)? (3) What do you want the listeners to do (will)?

3. *Plan.* Select all possible teaching aids and decide when to use them. Write out a complete lesson plan and outline. Assign time limits to each portion of lecture and calculate the time on the clock when you should complete each section. Write these check times prominently on the lesson plan.

Presenting the Lecture

1. *Introduction.* Attract attention of the students, gain their sympathy, and set a friendly tone. Tell what you expect to cover in the lecture—the topic, the main points. Tell your audience why they need to know this information—how they will benefit.

2. *Body.* Present the subject matter logically, clearly, enthusiastically, sincerely, sympathetically, and humorously (when appropriate). Even serious lectures are improved by a chuckle at intervals. Apply the subject specifically to the students. Don't generalize; give concrete suggestions as to how this can work for them. Be personal; remember you are teaching individuals.

Evaluate your communication of ideas as you go along by inviting students to ask questions after each point. Test their grasp of each point by asking them pertinent questions. Be alert to their degree of interest. If interest lags, change your tempo, voice, or method; tell a story; produce an object to see; or otherwise regain attention. They will never learn what they don't hear.

3. *Conclusion.* Review the lesson briefly, summarizing main points. Restate and stress difficult points. When assigning preparation for the next lecture, show how that lecture relates to this one. "Sell it" to them. Challenge the students to make use of this current lesson, beginning now. End on the high note of challenge.

4. *General suggestions.* Observe rules of good homiletics and speech. Speak slowly, distinctly, and audibly, so that students in the back row understand easily. Use visual aids such as the chalkboard, maps, charts, graphs, pictures and objects. Use illustrations such as Bible stories, stories from life, analogies, statistics and testimony from experts or authorities. Set some of your material up as a problem to solve. Unless the students are thinking, they are not learning. Observe the time limits set for each section in your lesson plan. Stop when the time is up. Observe the law of learning readiness. Use varied means of stimulating the pupils' thoughts on the subject to be covered. Arrange the room to suit your purpose. Use a center of attention.

When to Use Lecture

1. When the class is large and pupil participation must be limited.

2. When pupil background and preparation are limited so as to seriously hamper pupil participation.

3. When introducing new or unfamiliar subjects, when giving perspective or summarizing. In the interpretation of difficult material when the students could not be entrusted with the responsibility of coming up with the right answer.

4. When classroom seating arrangements are not conducive to informal discussion.

5. When time is limited. The lecture can be easily altered. When teaching younger children, use the lecture sparingly in conjunction with or in transitions between activities and other methods.

6. When the teacher desires to provoke and guide thinking and stimulate imagination and vision. When students are not accustomed to other methods and reluctant to change.

7. When the material lends itself best to coverage by organized lecture.

When Not to Use Lecture

1. When it is possible to use other methods. When students are eager to participate.

2. When students fall into lazy habits of not preparing for class. Make challenging assignments geared to the life of the pupils.

3. When the class is small and well suited for the use of other methods.

4. When the class is below the senior high level. Use lectures sparingly and wisely.

5. When practice is a necessary factor in the learning process. For example, one must teach, to learn to teach. Practice perfects theory and theory perfects practice. There must be

For adolescents lectures must be made interesting with up-to-date illustrations from real life. (Forrest Hills Baptist Church, Decatur, GA)

demonstration and opportunity to teach.

Use of Lecture with Children

With preschoolers lecture must be interspersed with activities. They have an attention span of 2 to 10 minutes. Avoid extended lecture periods. Lecture must deal with the familiar, making use of the child's vocabulary. Illustrate points with objects and pictures. Lecture must emphasize the present with explanations in terms of the known. Children have a limited concept of space and time.

School-age children must be challenged to think but not overtaxed. Their attention span is about 7 to 15 minutes. Lecture must provide reasonable explanations for everything, coupled with opportunities for making proper behavior choices. Their logic is developing, as well as their awareness of other ideas and beliefs. Lectures must avoid symbolism and abstraction, because children are literalists.

Use of Lecture with Youth

For early adolescents lectures must be made interesting with up-to-date illustrations from real life. Strive for pupil participation. Rapidly growing teens are awkward and restless, unable to find a comfortable position in their chairs. Data in the lecture must be well supported with good authority. Allow the pupils to think for themselves. They want a reason for everything and are beginning to question the validity of presented ideas.

The lecture should make use of the increased ability of middle adolescents to reason. They progress to new concepts with less and less initial review because of an increase in memory span.

Lecture to later adolescents is practical and related to actual problems. They have an insatiable desire for pragmatic knowledge. Lecture must not be dogmatic but should present the rationale behind the argument.

Use of Lecture with Adults

For early adulthood lecture must be used effectively. This audience has reached the peak of intellectual development and reasoning power. They think for themselves and evaluate everything. With this group lecturers must use creative techniques.

The lecture must challenge and motivate those in middle adulthood. Their mental abilities are most productive but will slow down if not used. Lecture must provide a broader outlook because, some adults tend to grow opinionated and shallow with age.

Lecturers to older adults must recognize that their listeners have vast knowledge in many areas, good judgment and many years of experience with life and with the world.

37

Can you involve your Sunday School pupils in a case study? Can you set up a dyad, a symposium, a debate, or a colloquy? Here's how.

Discussion

While discussion may be one of the easiest and most interesting methods of teaching, it holds complications and pitfalls the alert teacher must avoid. Pupils may go off on a tangent and never get back to the original subject. The conversation will take off wildly once they hit on "last night's game" or "Mary and Bill are going steady." The teacher must keep a firm hand to maintain control of the discussion.

Preparation for discussion cannot be too extensive. The teacher needs preparation for starting the discussion. Once discussion is underway, the teacher must guide it constantly toward its goal. The teacher should set up a *definite* goal, propose a way to get there, and give guidance on that way.

There are two particular difficulties with discussion, one of which the teacher will be sure to encounter in almost any discussion. First, "No one will talk; I can't get anyone to discuss." By introducing the subject in terms interesting to the group and using some incident pertinent to their experiences, a teacher can stimulate almost any group to participate in a discussion. Give pupils opportunity to get used to each other, to know each other. If they are accustomed to lectures on Sunday morning, begin by asking questions you know they can answer, to gradually break the ice.

Second, "Everyone wants to talk at once, and I can hardly control them." This is probably not as common a difficulty as the first, but will be

found in junior high and high school groups. These pupils are getting a first taste of freedom in class. A firm hand will be needed. Don't be afraid to teach a few lessons in common courtesy. The teacher will even need to take over the discussion at times, to keep it in hand. But this is better than letting it run wild. A mixture of diplomacy and a knowledge of the subject and of human nature will usually overcome the difficulties.

The buzz session.

One of the favorite kinds of discussion for young people and adults, buzz sessions not only give more people opportunity to take part, but also provide for an introductory presentation of the subject by someone well-versed on it. (See diagram.) The advantage of small-group discussion is that each participant has a chance to test his thoughts in an informal and unthreatening atmosphere. Ideas unworthy of presentation before the entire group are weeded out in the buzz group. This saves valuable time. Also, when a group of 60 is divided into 10 buzz groups, 10 people can speak at once. During these sessions surveys of the different opinions within the group can be taken quickly by the recorders. The result is a multiplication of information on a particular topic. This method of group involvement taps the resources of everyone present.

Another advantage of the buzz group is that it allows for the spotting and utilizing of leadership within the group. Those who contribute new ideas to the group can be consulted in the future as resource persons. The contributions of these people would have been forever lost under the traditional speaker-listener method. The buzz group has proved itself a highly effective tool for communication within a group and can be counted on to stimulate creative and purposeful activity in any gathering.

The buzz group also has disadvantages or problems. The first problem can result from the method used to organize the buzz group within the meeting. If done improperly, the meeting can dissolve into mass confusion. Then, too, this teaching technique seldom works with younger age groups. Their attention span is short and their ability to grasp concepts has not developed. Even the junior high student sometimes has difficulty in the buzz group

because the internal authority of the group is not strong enough to maintain purposeful activity. When the leader is working with these younger age groups, he should be certain no one is left out of a buzz group and that each group understands what is required.

Another problem is repetition in the reporting sessions. If the scope of the subject has been too narrow, the various groups will overlap. This results in a boring report session, because all the reporters say the same things. Give each buzz group a particular phase of the problem or topic and have them focus attention only in this area.

Even if the previous dangers are avoided, it is still possible to over-use this valuable teaching technique. Every situation does not call for buzz groups. This teaching technique and instrument of communication should be used economically, not as a quick substitute for an unplanned and unorganized meeting. Success

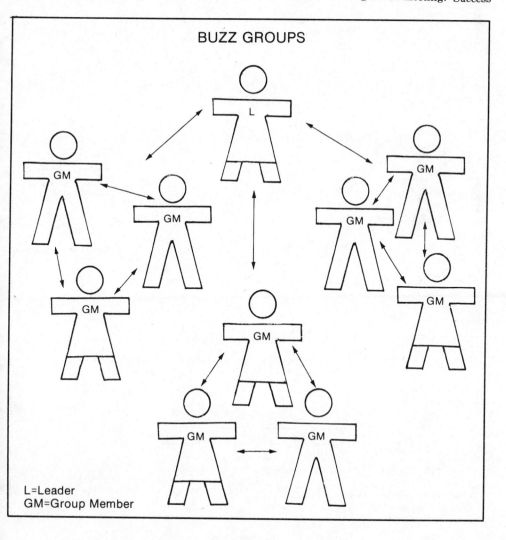

BUZZ GROUPS

L=Leader
GM=Group Member

with buzz groups requires organized leaders, adequate time for completion and mature groups.

1. *How to use buzz groups.* Buzz groups can be effectively used to stimulate discussion and enhance the learning process in a variety of situations. For example, if a group is assembled to listen to a lecture, they may break into small groups to list questions they would like the speaker to answer. After he has spoken they may reassemble to the small groups for further discussion.

Buzz groups can be used to start a meeting. For example, suppose a speaker does not show up in time. Those who come can informally be put into small groups to discuss the topic of the speaker. By the time the speaker arrives, they will be warmed up on the subject and may have listed points they desire the speaker to cover.

In a small group studying the Bible, each group may read the passage silently and dis-

cuss findings. Their findings may later be compared with other group discoveries, resulting in the pooling of many individuals' efforts.

Buzz groups may be employed to overcome people's feelings of apathy or helplessness and to redirect a group toward action. A good preliminary for buzz groups is role play, where the audience has opportunity to see the problem and gain the facts. When they break into small groups, they can act as a team, often simply blowing off steam. Yet here they reassure each other through discussion that something can be done about the problem. People get involved when the groups are small.

Divide the class into groups of three to six persons. Give the groups a brief time to discuss assigned questions. Write out questions on file cards and give one to the leader of each buzz group, so the members can refer to the questions at any time. Ask each group to appoint a representative to report the findings to the en-

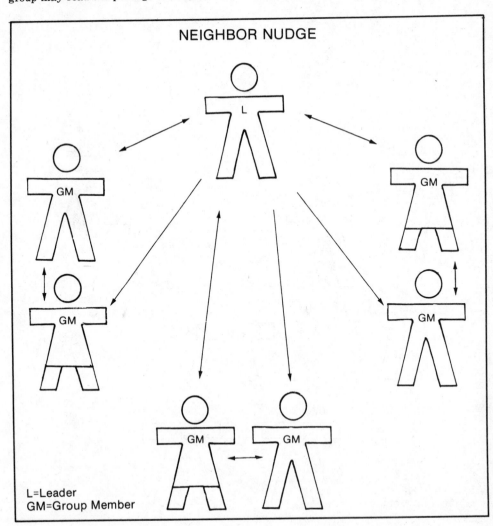

NEIGHBOR NUDGE

L=Leader
GM=Group Member

tire class. Direct the groups to different sections of the classroom. No group needs to leave the room, for the voices of each group will merely add to the background hum.

Give a two-minute warning signal for termination of discussion, and then direct the class to reassemble. After all groups have reported, the teacher is responsible for summarizing the findings and concluding the lesson.

Dyad or Neighbor Nudge.

Divide the class into pairs. Start at the left side of each row, and have the students number off for discussion. If the room is crowded, have the partners turn their chairs toward each other. This will help to minimize the sound of the discussions. Set aside approximately three minutes for the activity. Have each individual share with his partner one particular practical application of material just presented to the group. Remind students that every person should contribute to the discussion. (See diagram.)

Listening Team

Each listening team should have from four to six people on it; four groups are ideal. In each team appoint a team captain to make a report to the entire class after the lecture. Divide the class into teams by number and instruct them to sit together according to their numbers. This way, teams are not made up of social cliques, and there can be more interaction in the group. If the class is small and cannot have four teams, assign a question to each individual in the class. (See diagram.)

Each team is given a listening assignment on a file card before the lecture begins. The value of a listening team is that *all* of the class gives close attention to *all* of the lecture because a person doesn't know when information about

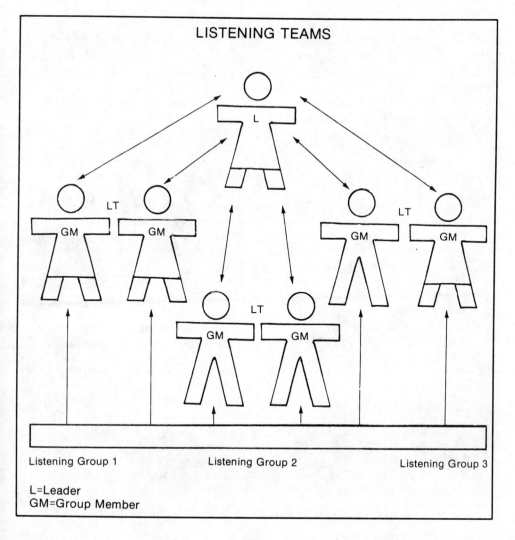

LISTENING TEAMS

L

LT
GM GM

LT
GM GM

LT
GM GM

GM

Listening Group 1   Listening Group 2   Listening Group 3

L=Leader
GM=Group Member

his assignment will be given.

Be sure to leave time for student discussion, or class members will feel cheated. They will conclude, rightly, that you are just presenting another lecture. Give the listening teams five or six minutes to discuss the answers to their assigned questions. Someone in each team should write a summary of the discussion. As the small groups discuss, write the four questions on the chalkboard. When each listening team is making its report, the other students in the class can see the question toward which the discussion is directed. Let the spokesman from each team report. Others on the team may like to amplify what the spokesman has said. A discussion can edify the whole class. Divide discussion time into fourths, allowing equal time for each team.

The Panel Discussion.

The panel is a much-used form of discussion and has both advantages and disadvantages.

Its greatest advantage is that the various members of the panel do a great amount of preparation and study on the subject to be discussed. They must do some thorough thinking on the matter, both pro and con. The panel discussion usually deals with subjects that have two sides. One half of the panel will speak for the matter and the other half against it. Its greatest disadvantage is that the thorough thinking and discussing will be done only by those on the panel, while the rest of the class will merely listen. (See diagram.)

A panel discussion usually begins with the leader presenting the problem, showing both sides of the issue. The various members of both sides, in no particular order, present their arguments for and against the issue. The other members of the panel, however, may feel free to question or to answer any point given by the member speaking. Following the presentation by the panel members, the discussion may or

A good panel discussion depends on the preparation beforehand. (Seattle Pacific College)

may not be opened to the other members of the group. It is, of course, of more value to the class as a whole if they are permitted to ask questions or give opinions. Naturally, if more take part, more will have been stimulated to do real thinking in the matter.

Circular Response

Some teachers feel that circular response merely consumes class time. They believe students are not learning because specific lesson content is not being presented. However, teachers should think in terms of meeting the needs of students. Discussion and involvement by individual members of the class may provide just the needed motivation for serious consideration of the Christian faith. Student involvement in the class is the key to personal growth.

If possible, have the class seated in a semicircle. Go around the group clockwise, giving each person an opportunity to contribute. If the class is seated auditorium style, have each one in a row contribute, going from left to right, through all the rows. (See diagram on next page.)

Ask each student to contribute the first thing that comes to his mind on the topic. His contribution may be an illustration from life, a question, a fact from the Bible, a question based on a previous contribution by another member, or a personal insight regarding the topic. Do not evaluate contributions made, or the shy person who only asked a question or read a verse of Scripture may be embarrassed. Stand by the chalkboard and be prepared to write down questions the students ask during the response. Do not try to answer the questions at this time. After each has contributed, stop and discuss the questions.

Brainstorm

Give each student a three-by-five-inch card

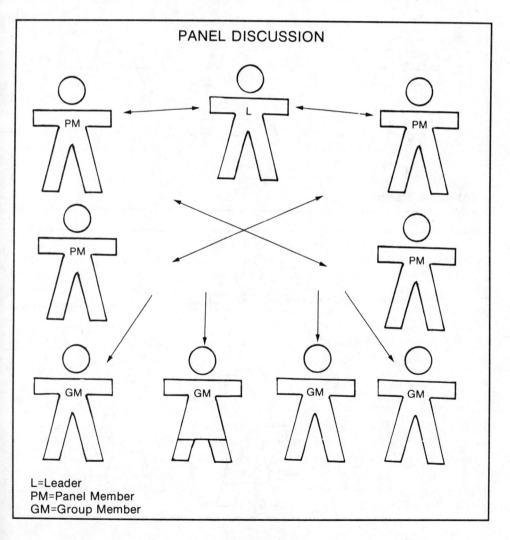

PANEL DISCUSSION

L=Leader
PM=Panel Member
GM=Group Member

CIRCULAR RESPONSE

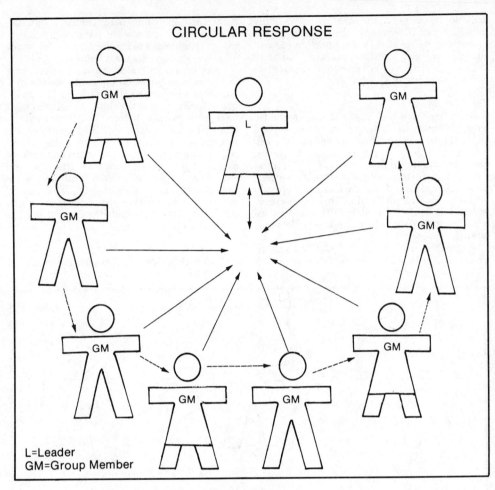

L=Leader
GM=Group Member

BRAINSTORM

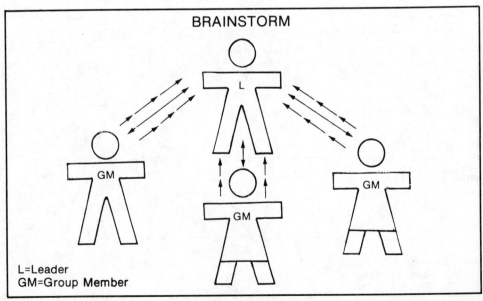

L=Leader
GM=Group Member

SYMPOSIUM

L=Leader
S=Speaker
GM=Group Member

on which you have written a word to be discussed. Have each write down the first thing that comes to mind concerning the word. Discuss contributions later. Right now, get students to think creatively. After each has written something on the card, give opportunity to share the ideas. The ground rules for brainstorming are simple. Each person says what is on his card or whatever comes to mind that he may not have written down. As he reacts to what is said by others, he should not question the validity of their contributions. When such questioning and refutation begin, creativity generally stops. The aim of brainstorming is creativity.

Encourage members to amplify what is said by other students. This is called "hitchhiking" on someone else's thoughts. The contribution of one student may bring to another person's mind a further thought on the topic. This person shares his new or expanded thought. (See diagram.)

The symposium

This method of discussion is not often used, as it is even more limiting than the panel discussion. As a general rule, it consists of three or more members of the class, each discussing some point of the problem. Generally, the problem is not controversial. In other words, the symposium is usually a lecture broken up into several small sections, a different class member giving each section. (See diagram.)

Debate

The debate is a teaching technique that is seldom used in the church to communicate the Word of God. However, it can be effectively used. A debate can engender objective thinking. It can cause students to compare scriptural truth with man's ideas.

Print on the chalkboard: "Resolved, that Jesus offered the Davidic kingdom to Israel, but the nation rejected Him in unbelief." Several days before the debate assign two students to

263

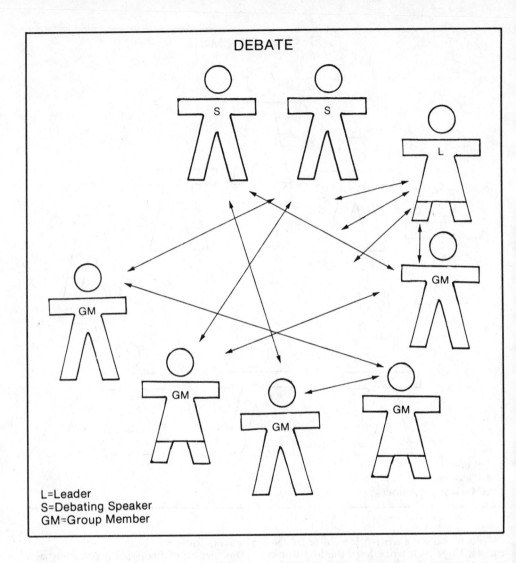

DEBATE

L=Leader
S=Debating Speaker
GM=Group Member

study the Scripture portion and defend the resolution, and two students to oppose the resolution. Debate demands thorough knowledge of the subject. Preparation should include analysis of the topic from opposing points of view. The teacher should help the students prepare by making research material available to both sides. Arguments for and against Jesus' offer of the kingdom should be shared with the debaters. Type these reasons out and give them to the four debaters. Challenge those helping in the debate to find true solutions to the problem. They should do more than attempt to win the debate; they should also try to find the correct answer to the question. Ask each debater to continually prove his point by Scripture reference.

Before the debate begins read the Scripture portion for the lesson to the class. Ask them to look up and read each Scripture reference made by those taking part in the debate. Ask them to analyze Scripture used by debaters to determine whether the speakers have interpreted correctly. The class should see the full implication of the problem if the debate is properly done. But do not be alarmed if some members are left in doubt, because a debate is a factual presentation *with persuasion*. If there are questions in the minds of some class members, clear them up in summary.

Each speaker should be given three minutes to make his first presentation. A timer should be appointed and provided with a bell. Remind debaters they will be interrupted if they run overtime.

Use the following sequence of presentation:
1. First affirmative speaker
2. First negative speaker
3. Second affirmative speaker
4. Second negative speaker

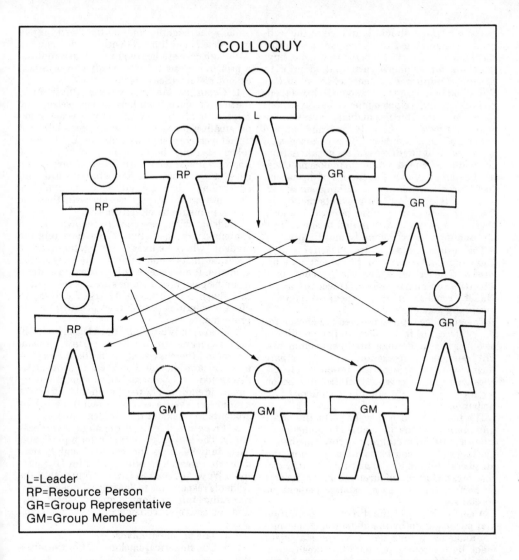

COLLOQUY

L=Leader
RP=Resource Person
GR=Group Representative
GM=Group Member

During the rebuttal use the reverse order:
1. First negative speaker
2. First affirmative speaker
3. Second negative speaker
4. Second affirmative speaker

Allow each person in the debate two minutes for rebuttal.

Arrange for two tables at the front of the class, two affirmative speakers at one and two negative speakers at the other. Prepare a large name card to identify each speaker to the class. Ask each debater to stand and address the class when speaking. The teacher presides over the debate at a small table between the two larger tables.

At the close, ask the class for a vote on the conclusions. If the class is given opportunity to vote on the winners of the debate, use the following criteria for declaring the winners: (1) the presentation of facts or content; (2) the

substantiation or proof of their statements; (3) ability to answer (the rebuttal). There may be danger in voting on winners in a Sunday School class. This added pressure may motivate a debater to try to win, rather than to present the facts. (See diagram.)

Colloquy

A colloquy is a modification of the panel discussion. Less formal, the colloquy utilizes several representatives from the audience and several resource persons familiar with the problem. The audience representatives present the problem, and the resource persons comment on various aspects of it. The audience and its representatives participate under the guidance of the moderator. The moderator (M) develops the discussion of the resource persons (RP), audience or group representatives (GR), and the audience. (See diagram.)

The moderator should be skilled in the techniques of handling discussions. The moderator (1) plans with panel members prior to meeting; (2) plans for audience participation prior to meeting; (3) informs audience of the nature of the colloquy and of their responsibility; (4) encourages and develops audience participation; (5) restates and clarifies audience questions to panel; (6) develops friendly, informal atmosphere, controls tempers; (7) keeps discussion within time limit; (8) recognizes speakers from the audience, one at a time; (9) makes practical application; (10) changes tactics of discussion to fit problem; (11) avoids taking sides; (12) avoids talking a lot; (13) prevents monopoly; (14) keeps discussion on the point; (15) allows those who haven't participated to speak first; (16) summarizes occasionally and finally.

The resource persons are chosen for their knowledge and interest in the subject to be discussed. The resource persons (1) contribute when their opinion is needed; (2) keep to subject; (3) keep remarks short; (4) speak in nontechnical language.

The audience representatives are chosen for their interest in the subject and the ability to ask questions and make intelligent comments. The audience representatives (1) prepare themselves; (2) present the problem; (3) ask questions of the experts; (4) clarify discussion for the audience; (5) stimulate audience participation.

The topic should be chosen to fit the needs and interests of the audience. The audience (1) studies material pertaining to the topic before meeting; (2) is courteous to moderator and members of colloquy; (3) arranges further discussion and future action; (4) recognizes its part as participants; (5) uses resource persons as specialists.

A colloquy (1) permits direct representation and participation by the audience; (2) permits the audience to question a vague statement made by a resource person; (3) makes the experts consider more closely the needs of the audience; (4) stimulates the audience through those representing it to listen more carefully and participate more freely; (5) offers an opportunity for those audience representatives to challenge the resource persons; (6) provides the stimulus for the resource persons to get accurate information; (7) gives the audience an intimate feeling of association with the members on the platform.

On the other hand, a colloquy (1) often does not allow sufficient time to present; (2) requires a skillful moderator; (3) may let resource persons assume a dominant role; (4) is most effective for a controversial issue.

Case Study

The aim of the case study, like that of all teaching methods, is to stimulate learning. Its value as a teaching method has been largely overlooked or limited within the church. Although case studies require skill in handling, a properly presented case study can bring excellent results. (See diagram.)

1. *Choosing the proper case study.* As a matter of good common sense, select one familiar to all. If one wanted to do a case study on stealing for second graders, he would not depict teenagers stealing hubcaps. By the same token, stealing chocolate pie would hardly be appropriate for teenagers. The teacher using a case study must consider the cultural and educational background of his students. Students must identify closely with the case study, to insure its effectiveness.

Students will more readily identify with a contemporary case study. This type hits the student "where he lives." It must, however, be accurate in its application to the lives of the students. If a teacher wants to use a case study from the past, he should be sure it is relevant to the students. In this type of study the class can observe solutions people have already found to problems.

The case study is usually not a lesson in itself, but a means to teach a certain lesson. Therefore, the case study must be interesting and relevant enough to evoke an enthusiastic discussion at its conclusion. It should have a climactic ending. The teacher should not offer a solution or even a choice of solutions. Allow students to work out the problem themselves.

2. *Preparation in the use of a particular case study.* The bulk of preparation for a particular case study lies upon the leader, though he may delegate research to others. Martha Leypoldt, in *40 Ways to Teach in Groups,* states that the leader is responsible to "prepare the case study, recording information factually, accurately, and objectively, considering the following facts:

    a. The people involved

    b. The historical background of the situation

    c. The relationships between persons or groups involved

    d. The religious background and perspective of the situation

    e. The sociological factors involved

    f. The economic factors involved

    g. The educational backgrounds of persons involved

    h. The ethnic origins of persons involved

    i. The tensions causing the problem."

Once the leader has researched the subject thoroughly, he then has to organize his material. Matters superfluous to solving the problem should be eliminated. The remaining information is then organized to arouse the interest of the group, reveal the importance of the problem, and show the relevance of the problem to life. The leader is then ready to begin the case study itself.

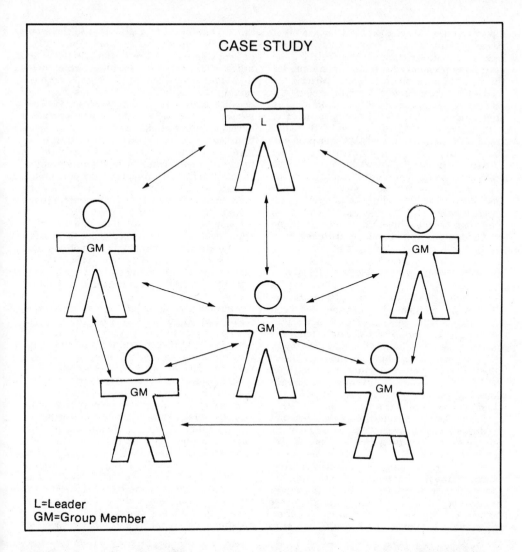

CASE STUDY

L=Leader
GM=Group Member

3. *Presenting the case study.* If the case study is presented at the beginning of the lesson, it is the focal point of the whole lesson. Or a case study can be presented after the aim of the lesson is clear, in order to make the lesson personal. The case study is not an illustration, since the group discusses the aspects of the case and makes a decision as to the outcome.

The teacher presents the case study by relating the essential facts. If he gives no conclusion, he leads the students to pull the facts together and come up with a solution. If he gives a conclusion, he leads the students to discuss its value and tell how they would have decided. Either way, the case study involves presentation and discussion.

4. *Discussing and applying the case study.* The key question in a case study is, "What would you do?" The teacher should be thoroughly acquainted with all the facts and should have answered the key question for himself. The purposes of the discussion are to accomplish the aim of the lesson plan and to apply the lesson to the students' lives. The application is inherent in the key question, "What would you do?" The closer the case study is to the students' lives, the more clearly do the students apply the solutions to themselves. If the case study deals with a problem which the students have not as yet seriously considered, they should be led to exercise empathy, forcing them to consider the new situation or problem.

5. *Values of the case study as a teaching method.* A notable value of the case study is that it allows the student to involve himself in a real-life situation without really ever taking part in it. A student can imagine, through the case study, being confronted with an "honest versus dishonest" decision. The case study is a sort of "on the job training." Secondly, since

most everyone likes a good story (especially if he can identify with it), the case study is an excellent attention-getting device. Thirdly, the case study prompts discussion and stimulates thinking. Finally, the case study permits the student to take an active part in the class.

6. *Some weaknesses of case studies.* The student may not be able to identify sufficiently with the case. He might tell himself, "That could never happen to me." Another problem, the students might tend to give "the proper Christian answer," rather than their true feelings. The students may simply not be interested in the problem which a particular case study presents. The case study cannot succeed without a good discussion. The group may not solve the problem, or it may lead some students into wrong actions or attitudes.

QUESTION AND ANSWER METHOD

Throughout history the value of the question-and-answer method in education has been recognized. While questioning was used in teaching long before Socrates' day, he made the question method famous. The question lay at the heart of the teaching methods of Jesus Christ. The Gospels record more than one hundred of His questions. Today, much teaching is done by means of the question, either as the chief method, or as a component part of other methods. The use of questions alone does not produce effective teaching, but proper use of the question-answer method greatly aids effective teaching.

Why are questions so effective? They stimulate the natural tendency of the mind to inquire into the unknown. They test the pupil's understanding of the facts and his ability to use facts in a fruitful way. Questions arouse curiosity, stimulate interest and cause the pupil to think. Questions bring problems to the attention of the hearer and create a desire to find answers. Questions direct attention to the significant elements in a situation, which helps to divide major from minor factors. By questioning the teacher gets and holds attention, because questions require a response. They allow the pupil to express his own thoughts and develop appreciations and attitudes. Questions draw out quieter members. Questions give the teacher information concerning his teaching, reveal whether pupils are learning. If not, then the teaching plan must be changed. Questions have value for use in drill and review, for deepening impressions, and for fixing facts in the memory of the pupil.

Properly directed questions can ascertain what the pupils have learned, guide them in further learning, correct misconceptions and imperfect understanding, help them to see interrelationships among facts, aid in organizing thinking, and lead to fruitful expression of learning.

What makes a good question? A teacher who would teach well must develop ability to ask good questions in the right way, and to answer both good and bad questions in the right way. Good questions are logical and developmental. All questions on a given subject should be related. Questions should be full and complete, not merely leading questions with yes or no answers. Good questions help pupils learn, keep the whole class actively interested, and give insights. A good question should help pupils see how facts fit together. Questions should be a two-way device. A pupil's question may even further learning better than a teacher's. Learn to say, "I don't know " to some questions. Make your questions brief, clear, and direct. Address them to the whole class before calling on one pupil. If a teacher addresses a question to one pupil, he may lose the class.

Proper use of the question-answer method greatly aids effective teaching. (Canyon Creek Baptist Church)

38

People will remember a story when they have forgotten everything else.

Storytelling

Storytelling is effective from the beginning stages of learning to the adult level, although its greatest value may be with teaching children. Stories can usually be used anytime and anywhere. They can be used as a part of a lecture, as illustrations during discussion, as a part of worship, or as "filler material" if the lesson is too short. Choose stories carefully. Make them an integral part of the lesson or worship. Because everyone loves stories, *use them well!*

A story may be used to present salvation, create and hold interest, introduce new ideas, or enable listeners to put themselves into real-life situations. A story can help to clarify wrong ideas, give solutions for existing problems, and train in moral conduct. It can create desirable attitudes or receptivity to new truth and experiences. A story develops the imagination, cultivates a sense of humor, and tends to relax the listeners. People will remember a story when they have forgotten everything else. A story wraps up abstract truth in life experiences which are easily understood.

A story is a narrative about persons or events. Their progress arouses interest from the start and sustains it through the climax. A story is not a report, a series of descriptions or a succession of events. A story has an introduction which captures interest and establishes the problem. Stories have a logical order of events, a climax, and a conclusion which leaves no questions or loose ends.

Choosing a story

1. *Occasion.* When choosing a story, keep the occasion in mind. For example, do not choose one of the hair-raising Old Testament battle tales for a worship period. If the story is a part of a lesson, be sure the point of the story is the same as that of the lesson. Some stories can be used to illustrate more than one type of lesson, but don't stretch the application too far.

2. *Length.* Keep in mind the length of the story. Be guided by the amount of time for a lesson. You would not want to take the whole period in telling just the story. If you don't know how much time you will have, choose a story which can be easily lengthened or shortened in the telling. The age group will help determine the length of the story. Very small children would usually rather hear two or three short stories than one long one. The interest span of a four-year-old is much shorter than that of a ten-year-old.

3. *Age group.* The age of the listeners will also determine many other factors. For very small children choose stories within their sphere of experience. The details should not be lengthy, and there should be a minimum of description. Juniors and intermediates love "hero" stories and a great deal of action. Teenagers and grownups alike want details, realism, little repetition, and a strong climax. Perhaps one exception to the limit on repetition is the story of

269

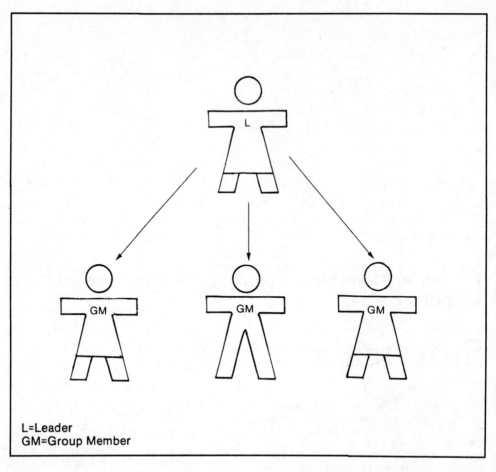

L=Leader
GM=Group Member

"Tiki-tiki-tembo," where the repetition of the long name becomes an integral part of the plot. Use vocabulary suitable to the audience. Big words only bore children, and impress few teenagers. Moreover, if listeners do not understand the words, they lose some of the story. The continuity is broken.

Preparing the story

1. *Read it.* Read it through several times to acquaint yourself thoroughly with it, until all names and places are familiar. If there are unusual names, check pronunciation in a dictionary. Practice saying them aloud until they give no trouble. Stumbling on words causes children to giggle or become annoyed.

2. *Outline it.* When you are well acquainted with the story, outline it on paper. Beginning with the first incident, number the incidents in order and then learn the outline thoroughly. There is nothing that can throw you off more quickly than to forget an incident, only to discover later that you have no explanation for some result! Children sense this quickly and are puzzled. The same holds true for characters in

the story. Suddenly to have some unknown and unmentioned person figure in the climax can throw the listener off the track, and lessen the effect of the climax.

3. *Find the climax.* Find the climax of the story, and let all that comes before build toward that climax. When the climax has been reached, draw the story to a quick end. Dragging a story out leads to moralizing, which simply bores the listener.

4. *Fill in the details.* Color and suspense depend on the details. Too many will deaden your story, but the right amount will help listeners picture the scenes and will add to the suspense. Times and places are important, as are names and relationships.

5. *Practice your story.* Always practice your story before you tell it. It is easy to think it through and decide you know it, but it is something else to get up and tell it. Listen to your tone patterns. A singsong voice annoys a listener as much as a dead voice! Practice in front of a mirror, to see how you will appear to your audience. Check nervous habits. For example, if you sway from one foot to the other, you will make your listeners dizzy! Or you may

A good visual aid can add to the sense of reality of the story a teacher tells. (Indianapolis Baptist Temple, Indianapolis, IN)

have a furious scowl on your face as the action becomes more intense! If some youngster is handy, practice the story on him. His reaction will reveal the success you are likely to have on a group of children of the same age. If he becomes bored, check the story for action. If he loves it, leave it alone!

Telling the Story

1. *Be natural.* Be relaxed at all times, and do not be afraid to use motions to illustrate the action. To point "far down the road" helps children sense distance; but to stomp your feet for "the sound of many feet passing by" will probably disturb the listeners, or set off little feet stomping with you! Action is one of the best tools in storytelling. To say someone is coming, running or walking is far more interesting than merely to say someone is there. To put the stone into David's slingshot, whirl the sling, and let the stone fly will set children on the edge of their seats. But merely telling them David killed the giant with his slingshot may seem funny or even impossible to them.

2. *Speak directly to the audience.* If you look at them as you speak, they will respond more than if you gaze at the ceiling or the back wall. If you look in one direction for a long time, children may turn and look in that direction. Look at the audience; be interested in their reactions. They will, in turn, be more interested in you and your story.

3. *Use color and action when you tell a story.* A certain amount of description is good, but too much can deaden the story. For example, the description of the court in the story of Queen Esther will fire the imagination of any child. Giving the color of objects in the story stimulates the imagination of the listener and heightens his interest.

4. *Be enthusiastic.* The persuaded persuade. Your own interest in the story and the way you tell it determines how it will be received. If you are enthusiastic, the listeners will be enthusiastic, for enthusiasm is contagious. Your tone of voice will indicate your interest. A period or question mark where an exclamation belongs will not inspire your audience. Check tonal habits again. Use the range of your natural voice—loud or soft for emotional variations, rising or falling at the right places!

39

Visual aids greatly enhance learning, but aids vary in quality. This chapter will help the Sunday School teacher select and use visual aids more effectively.

Visual Aids

Visual aids may be defined as objects, symbols, materials and methods that appeal to the sense of sight. Their purpose is to clarify thought by making the abstract concrete. Visual aids are valuable in the teaching-learning process. Proper use of visual aids will help clarify the material, illustrate difficult points, make learning more lasting since a child remembers 50 percent of what he sees, complement other teaching methods, motivate change, speed learning, get attention, improve behavior, make learning more enjoyable, and provide eye appeal as an avenue to the soul.

1. *Problems of visual aids.* Use of visual aids can be a hindrance to good teaching if:

a. They become lessons in themselves.

b. They become a substitute for traditional teaching methods.

c. They are limited to one kind.

d. They become mere entertainment.

e. The instructor is not fully versed in the use of the aid.

There are some disadvantages and limitations to the use of visual aids:

a. The cost of some visual aids makes use prohibitive.

b. Some upkeep of mechanical aids and replacement of materials is expensive.

c. Storage space is required for large mechanical aids.

d. Small-size visual aids may only be viewed by a small group.

e. Projected visual aids require room space for seating, good acoustics, and good lighting.

f. It takes time to set up and take down visual aids, write script for them, and train people in their use.

g. Packaged visual aids are not always edited and may be inappropriate.

2. *Principles for visual aids.* Some guidelines in selection and use are:

a. Be familiar with the field, especially the latest developments in methods and effective uses. A teacher should read periodical reviews of literature in the field, invite resource experts in the field to demonstrate use of an aid, have group discussion and periodic reports on the subject, offer courses in the effective use of visual aids, and secure catalogs or price lists from many companies.

b. Be careful in selecting your visual aids. Select the aids requested by the teacher who will use them. Select aids in your price range and with which you are familiar—or become familiar. Choose aids which are durable, attractive, professionally made, and which present an effective message. Select the aids you know how to operate or those with clear instructions for use. Check to be sure the aids are free from false doctrine or undesirable elements.

c. Choose aids appropriate to your teaching situation. Use aids that are interesting and understandable to each age level, accurate,

273

authentic, realistic, educative rather than entertaining, able to accomplish the desired purpose, stimulating, and easily transported.

d. Be intelligent and efficient in use of visual aids. Have all equipment set up and tested beforehand. Plan and practice all mechanical procedures thoroughly. Be sure of visibility of the aids from all parts of the room. Plan a smooth transition into use of the visual aid. Apply the lesson of the visual aid to the lives of the students.

Specific Visual Aids, Non-projected

1. *Chalkboard.* A chalkboard has a dark, waterproof surface, smooth enough to mark with chalk without distortion, grainy enough to hold chalk. Chalkboards may be composed of slate, glass, porcelain, or several types of wood and paper materials. The most practical type is a green composition board with a dull green finish. (The change from the previous "black" boards resulted in the present term, "chalk" boards). Chalkboards may be made by applying a special type of paint, made up of ground slate and iron oxides, to any paintable surface. The size of the board usually depends on its purpose and the size and shape of the area where it will be used. Some special boards are permanently marked with grids, staff lines for music or with some other feature for specific purposes. Chalkboards may be movable or stationary, but should always be clearly visible to all students.

The chalkboard is one of the most accessible visual aids. (Geneva College)

274

The chalkboard has a number of advantages:

a. Uses both verbal and visual communication

b. Accessibility

c. Economical (inexpensive, easy to use, reusable, minimum space needed)

d. Versatility

e. Allows for group participation and involvement

f. Allows for closely supervised instruction and evaluation

g. Makes learning more accurate

h. Speeds learning

i. Makes learning more enjoyable than verbal method alone

j. Acquaints pupils and professor with each other

k. Motivates action and interest

l. Stimulates creative thinking

m. Deepens understanding

n. Aids memory

o. Focuses attention and provides summary reference

p. Aids vocabulary growth

q. Teaches organization and leadership

r. Can help develop stronger personalities and overcome fears

s. Changes attitudes and opinions

t. Provides relief from looking at the teacher's features

u. Can reproduce material not presented in textbooks—illustrations, etc.

v. Can serve as a bulletin board, projection screen, etc.

The chalkboard also has disadvantages:

a. Its usefulness may be overlooked because it is "common."

b. Usage often ignores proper techniques.

c. It may be made a substitute for preparation.

d. Lesson may be made to fit board, not vice versa.

e. Size of board may limit application before erasure.

f. Material on board is not permanent.

g. Board may become cluttered or may not be cleaned properly.

h. Teacher or students' poor writing may confuse others.

i. Poor chalk detracts.

j. Boards may adversely affect acoustics.

k. It has limitations caused by size, location or material.

l. Pupils may have to change positions to see.

m. Time may be wasted when students travel to and from board.

n. Error may be permanently impressed on students' minds.

o. Material may be obscured by someone standing in front.

p. Chalk dust may cause throat, skin, or clothes irritations.

How do you use a chalkboard?

a. Use clear, firm lines.

b. Put work high enough for everyone to see.

c. Write largely.

d. Organize work.

e. Erase the board after use.

f. Keep the lines horizontal when writing.

g. Stand sideways when writing.

h. Hold chalk between thumb and forefinger and write at a 30 degree angle to prevent squeaking.

i. In lecturing write difficult names, formulas, and dates to be remembered and copied.

j. In discussions put the subject clearly and inescapably in front of the eyes of the class. Write down the problem. Write down the partial solutions as suggested. Modify and rephrase as necessary. Be careful to arrange problem and solution in clear and forcible logic, listing conclusions.

k. In drawing use match-stick men rather than full-bodied ones.

l. In outlining use little detail.

m. In geometric drawings use colored chalk for overlapping lines.

n. Label all diagrams clearly.

o. Use perforated paper to draw maps and other sketches. Trace the pattern on a large sheet of drawing paper. Punch holes along the outlines. Tape the paper on the chalkboard and rub or pat a chalky eraser over the holes several times. Remove the paper and the outline of the drawing remains on the board. Fill in the outline with chalk.

p. Put meaningful and important vocabulary words on the board.

q. Permit children to use the board, for it enhances learning.

r. Create suspense by placing a series of drawings or ideas on the board and covering with paper. Uncover each as it is discussed.

s. Using chalkboard wax to stick paper and other materials to the board will prevent damage to the board.

t. Do not use chalkboards to the exclusion of other visual aids.

2. *Maps.* It is better to draw a map than to use a ready-constructed one. Maps come in many forms—outline, wall, slide, globe, or a collection in a book. They may be topographical, political, commercial, economic, or a combination. Globes give a more accurate impression of distances and directions, but are limited to use in small groups.

To be effective maps should be free from unnecessary detail, should highlight the major emphasis of your lesson, should be readable, must be properly mounted, and must be large enough to be seen easily.

Class use of maps may include these variations:

a. Call on pupils to come and point out a city or river location.

b. Put plastic over the map and let pupils use a grease pencil to trace the movements of story characters.

c. Trace a large map onto corrugated board. Let pupils color the map. Punch a hole and put a paper fastener at each city location. From week to week pupils may move yarn from one location to the next. For several routes use different colors of yarn.

d. Make a picture map. Instead of paper fasteners and yarn, let the pupils mark city locations with objects symbolic of events. Stick these in place with tape or Plasti-tak. For example, use a water jar where water was turned to wine.

e. Make a parable map following directions in number three. A picture at each parable location will trace the progress of Jesus' ministry.

f. After a series of studies, provide pupils with unlabeled maps with dots for cities. The class should identify cities, countries and bodies of water.

g. Let pupils make a relief (topographical) map, working on it from week to week.

When using the sandtable, you should dampen the sand. Use a topographical map as a guide and shape hills and valleys; put down foil for seas and rivers.

When making a papier mache map, one may obtain a "mix" at a hobby shop or start from scratch. Mache is made by tearing newsprint paper into bits and soaking them in hot water. Stir with the hands until paper disintegrates. Strain through cloth to remove excess moisture.

Pictures can be used to start discussion, recapture straying attention, or review a lesson. (Standard Publishing)

Mix paper with a pint of wheat paste. Add flour or starch until thick enough to retain shape. After shaping map, you should allow it to dry at least a week. Let pupils paint or spray it the next session. It may be sprayed with hair spray.

Maps can also be modeled from homemade compounds. Use a mixture of one part salt, two parts flour, and one part water for a molding clay. Or make a sawdust compound by adding wallpaper paste to two quarts of sawdust. Add enough water to achieve the right consistency. Trace a large map, or enlarge one, onto a cardboard background. Insert a finishing nail at the location of each city. Pupils should shape mountains with their hands and carefully scrape clay from the area which will be the sea or a river. The following week let several pupils paint the provinces, seas, etc. Others may make a label for each nail and tape it on.

3. *Flat pictures.* These include photographs, clippings, paintings, prints, cartoons, drawings—any picture not projected. They may be obtained from Sunday School magazines and/or papers, publishing houses, calendars, greeting cards, even catalogs. School supply house catalogs list art pictures.

Pictures may be used with posters, charts, maps, dioramas, flash cards for teaching songs and verses, homemade flannelgraph lessons, review games, Bible-verse matching games, puzzles in presession or review, story-wheels and rebus stories.

Flat pictures are easy to use, carry, and store. (Scripture Press)

4. *Bulletin boards.* These may be used for both promotion and education. The materials should be attractive and relevant to the needs and interests of the group. Bulletin boards in classrooms, assembly rooms, or central places in the church can provide valuable training and teaching aids or be used for advertising. To be effective, longer-term displays must be attractive, neatly arranged, changed often. During a teaching session a bulletin board might hold a time line of yarn and thumbtacks.

5. *Posters.* Making attractive posters can be a good project for a class. Posters can create a desired atmosphere, teach a new idea, or announce and advertise important events. In an effective poster the message is obvious at a glance, simple and to the point, and large enough to be seen from the farthest possible viewing position. Words, symbols and pictures are large and familiar. The poster has eye appeal.

6. *Graphs.* Graphs are excellent for making contrasts and comparisons, or presenting complicated facts and statistics. Graphs which are involved and difficult are worthless. The graph should tell the story at a glance, with little explanation needed.

Types of graphs include:

a. Bar graph—bars arranged horizontally or vertically.

b. "Pie" graph—resembles a pie and is useful for presenting a breakdown or distribution.

c. Line graph—useful to depict trends.

d. Pictorial graph—tells the story by illustrations; more difficult to produce, but more effective.

7. *Flash cards.* Large cards, usually in a sequence, are flashed one at a time for review and drill, storytelling and memory work teaching. They may be used in combination with other aids such as posters, charts, maps, graphs and diagrams.

Effective cards should have large lettering

Bulletin boards can be used for both promotion and education. (Dianne Phelps/NSSA, Detroit, MI)

for easy reading, be held high enough for everyone to see, be flashed at the right moment, be kept in proper order for easy presentation, be exposed long enough for clear comprehension, and be as brief as possible.

8. *Charts.* These are chiefly analytical and show proper sequence. Titles, labels, columns, lines, arrows, numerals, colors, varied type, diagrams, illustrations, pictures, maps, notes, and other devices help clarify the material and make it more readable and meaningful. Charts are less flexible than chalkboards. Once a chart is finished, you can highlight it or add to it, but you cannot change that which is already written on it. Charts require some skill in preparation.

Charts have many advantages:

a. Charts attract attention and communicate to the eye.

b. Charts can be prepared in advance and are easy to use in teaching.

c. Charts help to make the lesson clear to the student. What may be confusing after an explanation becomes understandable after it is seen on a chart.

d. Charts save teaching time and enable the teacher to give more time to group discussion.

e. Charts add variety to a lesson and increase retention by students.

f. Most charts are inexpensive and may be used repeatedly.

Kinds of charts include flash (several charts in sequence), flip, pocket (as for memory work), strip (cover certain words with a taped-on strip and remove at proper time), sleeve (slide a paper "sleeve" over words to cover those not under discussion), shaped (a question-shaped chart to ask a question), link (sectional, linked with paper clips as discussed).

9. *Flannelgraph.* Flannelgraph, intriguing as it may be, if used invariably, becomes monotonous. It can be repeated more often in preschool classes, because younger children

Many publishing houses include visual aids in their instructional materials. (David C. Cook Publishing Co.)

Flannelgraph has such a variety of uses that no teacher should be without it. (Scripture Press)

like repetition.

a. *Board.* A simple board may be made from the side of a large corrugated box. Cut out two boards 2 x 3 feet and hinge in the center, or make one large board and fold, if desired. Reinforce the fold with heavy tape. Staple blue outing flannel on the board and tape around the edges. Or the teacher could make one board in a chart combination a flannelgraph by covering it with blue flannel. Some teachers of preschoolers wear a "story apron" with flannel pockets. Figures are kept in the pocket and removed as used. If classroom space does allow room for an easel or table, hang a lightweight flannelboard on the wall, at pupil eye-level, tilted slightly forward at bottom.

b. *Backgrounds.* While these may be purchased ready-made, they may also be easily and inexpensively made by hand. With light blue outing flannel as a neutral background, sketch the desired indoor or outdoor scene in colored chalk. Fill in the details with more chalk. Spray the finished scene with hairspray as a fixative.

Some oil stick products, which are brighter, are available at school supply houses. Markal and Sanford's Cra-pas Payons are obtainable at Christian supply stores. If crayolas are used, the finished scene should be ironed on the reverse side, to cause the color to penetrate the material and become indelible. Artists may complete a crayon scene with touches of oil paint.

Many Christian publishers' catalogs list both figures and backgrounds. They are also obtainable at Christian bookstores.

c. *Figures.* There are several kinds available:

Pictograph - Suedegraph. On heavy stock vello paper, one of the earliest producers of flannelgraph (Scripture Press - See publisher list.) has dozens of stories now available.

Child Evangelism. A complete catalog of stories is available on request. (See publisher list.)

Other publishers. Check all catalogs received.

World Wide Visuals. Write for descriptive, illustrated price list. Address is World Wide Visual Aids, P.O. Box 1226, National City, California 92050.

Scene-O-Felt. Address is Munn Art Studio, P.O. Box 204, Hillsdale, Michigan 49242.

Magazines. Back the pictures cut from magazines with vello paper or flannel and use them to illustrate stories.

d. *Using the flannelgraph.* Most commercial flannelgraph sets include the story. The teacher may substitute words that are natural to him. If no suggestions are available, tell the story with enthusiasm and expression, standing at one side of the board with Bible in hand. The figures then may be used in review. Even preschoolers like to place figures on the board,

even though a "man" may float in the sky or fall into the sea. They happily place the leading character of the story or a star in the sky. Allow pupils to take turns, if the class is large. At the second retelling, pupils may tell their part of the story as they place the picture on the board.

Object lessons may also be presented on the flannelgraph. Whole books of object lessons are available. Ready-made object lessons for flannelgraph may also be obtained. (Check catalogs for books and lessons.) Then, too, such lessons may easily be made by the teacher, using felt, flannel, double knit or construction paper backed with vello paper.

e. *Memory drill.* Refer to the section on memory work for use of scrambled verses.

Tic-tac-toe may be played on a yarn chart on flannelgraph. As questions are answered, put the symbol in the spaces with squares of flannel.

f. *Story outlines.* Place a few words on each point in a story or lesson on the board as each point is begun. Points covered may be removed.

10. *Exhibits.* Bible stories frequently refer to objects and clothing unfamiliar to hearers. Pictures aid understanding but "realia" is best. If the objects are available from Holy Land tourists, display them. If the "widow's mite" is mentioned, show one. If you refer to the Kaffia headdress, exhibit one—preferably *on* someone. If flowers are mentioned, show a flower card of pressed flowers from Bethlehem. Missionary stories are often clarified by exhibits of realia from the land under study.

11. *Models.* Older primaries and juniors can learn the boxlike architecture of the Palestinian house by making a village of such houses. A 16-square-fold of an 8 x 12 inch square of heavy brown sack paper is a simple basic pattern. Add a paper "fence" around the roof; cut a door and a window. Accordion-fold stairs may be added at the side.

12. *Sandtable.* Dampen sand and shape rolling hills and a river or lake. Let primaries or juniors make trees (construction paper or cardboard) and houses (see models) or tents (as for Abram) and place as desired. Add water jars and other accessories. Clothespins or chenille-wire figures may be draped with a square of cloth with a neck-hole, and tied on with a yarn belt. Construction paper animals such as donkeys and camels may be scattered about.

13. *Object Lessons.* Simple object lessons are effective teaching tools. They focus attention and aid memory. The object should be familiar, and the illustration drawn from the object must be simple and easy to understand. Many simple object lessons use everyday objects such as a hammer, pen, pins, potatoes and others. (Check catalogs.)

The object should be secondary. Unless the object brings out the point of the lesson, it has no teaching value. An object unrelated to the story only scatters the lesson's impact. Use only one object to teach one truth, for more may confuse. One lesson should have one chief aim, toward which the whole presentation is geared. For younger children use objects that are not symbolic and whose value is real. Children who are early juniors and under do not understand symbolic lessons.

Trick object lessons and many chemical object lessons are not usually effective in teaching a truth because attention may center on the trick. These are most useful as entertainment. Evaluate the effectiveness of a magic lesson by recall the following week. Note which points are recalled—the trick or the message of the application.

PUPPETS

A few years ago puppets were thought to be only a game. They were not considered educational. Modern educators claimed that children learned best by their experiences, rather than watching the teacher perform with aids such as puppets. But a revolution has occurred. Sesame Street has used puppets, and it has been proved that children who watch Sesame Street learn better and faster. As a result, a puppet revival has come in American education.

The face of any story character can be painted on the puppet. Papier mache, styrofoam ball, or a stuffed sock are popular and simple bases for a head. The clothing should be colorful and easily changed. Clothing can be made with a basic puppet dress pattern. (See *You Can Be A Puppeteer* by London.)

The teacher may operate the puppet and then allow the children an opportunity, thus reinforcing the learning experience. On the other hand, the child can make up his own actions and words.

Aims
1. To dramatize truth, enabling the child to remember much better.
2. To present information in an indirect, but understandable form.
3. To call forth ingenuity and resources at little cost, on the part of both teacher and pupil.
4. To encourage participation from all class members, even those too shy to become active in other areas.
5. To encourage creativity.
6. To give a child opportunity to be involved in a role-playing situation. This is a wonderful way for a child to see his own problems and often recognize the answers without a teacher's suggestions. In this type of situation teacher also benefits by glimpsing the child's feelings, emotions and outlook on life. This enables the teacher to deal directly with the actual needs of this child, rather than with what she simply thinks are needs.
7. To provide positive reinforcement to attract the pupil to continue attending Sunday School.
8. To discipline indirectly yet effectively. In a puppet presentation use an actual situation where the children see their own actions reflected, causing no hard feelings toward the teacher for correcting them.

Advantages
1. Puppets provide anonymity. Many children do not like to display themselves in front of their peers. Puppets allow them to be creative and expressive without embarrassment.
2. Puppets eliminate the need for body movements in drama. Since the child does not need to think about facial expression, gesturing and stage position, he can better concentrate on the spoken lines that have been assigned to him.
3. Television has made puppets popular and familiar to children. They will be enthusiastic about imitating something they have seen on TV.
4. Using puppets provides in-depth study of a passage or story. By the time the children have made the puppets, studied their lines and put on the performance, they will be thoroughly familiar with the passage.
5. Making and using puppets may stimulate a reticent child to take part in informal drama later.
6. Use of puppets by the teacher gains the pupils' attention and keeps it throughout the story, whether the class is large or small.
7. Memory retention by the child is far greater when he sees the story, than when he simply hears it.

Disadvantages
1. Puppets are time-consuming and require talent to create and decorate.
2. The eager actor is denied opportunity to experiment with body movements.
3. The more advanced form of puppetry, such as marionettes, requires handling in a professional manner. Most Sunday School teachers do not have these skills.

Types
1. *Paper bag.* There are two forms of this most elementary kind of hand puppet. In one the bag fits over the entire hand. The face is glued on the bottom of the unopened bag. The top half of the mouth is level with the end of the flap, and the bottom half is glued on the side of the sack. "Wave" the fingers to simulate talking as the story is narrated. This kind of puppet is often included in teaching aid packets from Sunday School suppliers. For the second type of puppet, the bag fits over the operator's first

As a result of "Sesame Street" a puppet revival has hit American education.

Gayle Godwin talks to Willy and Whacky at the Vacation Bible School opening assembly. (Bible Baptist Church, Lincoln, NB)

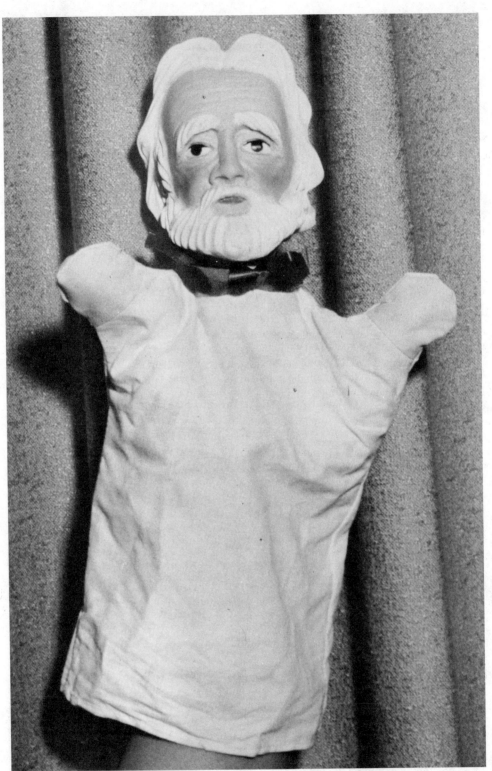

This puppet is one of the many types available commercially.

three fingers and is tied, leaving the thumb and fifth finger for the puppet's arms. The three fingers move the mouth part up and down for speech.

2. *Mitten.* This uses a mitten instead of the bag, giving the appearance of clothing.

3. *Stick.* The head (or whole figure) is on a stick which the operator manipulates. Cloth or a sock may cover the operator's hand.

4. *Spool.* A spool or similar object is used as the foundation of the head and a sock again covers the hand.

5. *Finger.* This is usually on a tiny glove-finger end which fits on one finger. Usually it is just the head. Being small, several may be used at once, to have interaction.

6. *Shadow.* The puppet is silhouetted on a screen, making clothes and distinct facial features unnecessary.

7. *Marionettes.* Advanced puppetry, using puppets manipulated with strings attached to all movable parts of the body. The operator is not seen; only his voice is heard. This usually demands a set of well-made puppets. Much action can be presented with these.

Principles

1. Keep puppet actions geared to the age level. The younger the children, the simpler the action.

2. Keep the situations familiar to the children.

3. Make sure the situations are true-to-life, not abstract, since younger children cannot identify with abstract ideas.

4. The teacher must be fully prepared. He must have definite goals in mind and procedures to attain his goals. He should also exercise his creative and imaginative ability, at the same time adhering to the theme of the lesson.

5. The type of puppet should be geared to the age level of the class.

6. Begin with simple puppetry. As you become more experienced, branch out into more advanced and complex forms.

7. While puppets have their greatest value with younger children, other age groups also enjoy them. Their use will require more exper-
tise under the scrutiny of older pupils, however. Of course, a polished performance of puppetry will hold the attention of any age.

Effectiveness

1. Puppets are a refreshing change from regular storytelling.

2. Puppets are enjoyable and intriguing for the children, thus encouraging attendance in Sunday School.

3. Puppets give the children a better method of interacting with the subject of the lesson, thus learning the lesson better.

4. Discipline is less of a problem, resulting in fewer dropouts due to hurt pride over correction.

5. Puppet role-play for children can be very effective. The puppets act out what goes on at a church service, or in other life situations, showing the children what is expected of them. When they are confident and willing to participate, the learning situation occurs.

RESOURCES FOR FURTHER READING

Cassell, Sylvia. *Fun with Puppets.* Nashville: Broadman Press, 1956.

Cully, Iris. *Children in the Church.* Philadelphia: Westminster Press.

DeKieffer, Robert, and Cochran, Lee W. *Manual of Audio-Visual Techniques.* Englewood Cliffs: Prentice-Hall, 1955.

Filkin, W. *Basic Teacher Training Course.* Elgin: David C. Cook Pub., 1964

Haas, Kenneth B., and Packer, Harry Q. *Preparation and Use of Visual Aids.* New York: Prentice-Hall, 1955.

London, Carolyn. *You Can Be a Puppeteer* Chicago: Moody Press, 1972.

Manson, Olive Holmes. *Visualize, Vitalize Christian Teaching.* Los Angeles: Cowman Publications, 1959.

Morrison, Eleanor Shelton, and Foster, Virgil E. *Creative Teaching in the Church.* Englewood Cliffs: Prentice-Hall, 1963.

Sapp, Phyllis Woodruff. *Creative Teaching in the Church School.* Nashville: Broadman Press, 1967.

40

Here are some tips for using these valuable media effectively in the classroom.

Slides, Filmstrips, Motion Pictures

Slides, filmstrips and motion pictures are excellent media to teach Bible stories; teach Bible background, customs, and geography; teach practical Christian principles through real-life situations; train teachers and leaders; educate in crafts, first aid, safety, special skills, etc. in club programs; show Bible scenes as background to narration; teach missions (slides and tape recordings from the field); teach new songs by visualizing them; use for special programs, as Christmas or Easter. (Take slides of costumed members acting out the Christmas story; make tape recording to fit the pictures and show at Christmas.)

Principles for Use
1. Select filmstrips which fit the age level.
2. Select materials which serve a definite purpose in the class session; projected material should supplement teaching.
3. Preview the film or filmstrip before using.
4. Know how to operate the equipment.
5. Arrive early to set up equipment and check room arrangement.
6. Set up and focus the film before the audience arrives.
7. Make the mechanical operation of the showing as inconspicuous as possible.
8. Remember a take-up reel; be sure it is in gear; don't pick up film on the floor; wind it slowly.
9. Have tape available to splice film if it

should break.
10. Don't force filmstrip; sprocket holes are easily damaged.
11. Don't put your fingers on the surface of the slides or filmstrip.
12. Don't place screen too high for children, but put it high enough so they can easily see over heads.
13. Adjust size of image to size of audience. The image should be no larger than necessary for good viewing by those farthest away from the screen. The smaller the image, the brighter it will be.
14. The sound speaker should be placed a little above heads of the group and pointed toward the middle of the last three rows of seats.
15. Check volume from several spots in the room.
16. Direct attention to the special point of view with which the film is to be watched. Raise questions to be answered in the film; suggest points to watch for and discuss at finish.
17. Follow up film with discussion and action, if appropriate.
18. You can use just the audio to vary the presentation of a Bible or character story. Tape the story to play in class. This device is useful when a moving story must be told and the teacher may dissolve in tears. Use some of the excellent children's story of "Bible in Living Sound" records to present the story with sound effects and drama. Discuss the material after it

An occasional filmstrip will add interest to junior church sessions. (Calvary Temple Church, Springfield, IL)

is presented. Prepare the listeners by listing on the chalkboard some questions to be answered by the recorded story.

19. For story sequence and sound effects, tape-recorded sound may be correlated with slides. Practice the production to get it synchronized correctly. (i.e., if the slide calls for a lion roaring, tape enough roars from a sound-effects record to cover the time needed to describe the beast's place in the story.)

20. You may wish to make a tape to go with a filmstrip. The Dukane Projector (see catalog) uses both, simultaneously. Two machines also may be correlated, as for slides (above).

Overhead Projectors

1. *Purpose of using the overhead.* The overhead projector aids in teaching because it increases understanding by adding the visual element, adds interest, lengthens retention by causing students to use the eyes as well as the ears, and makes teaching more effective. The overhead projector offers a learning experience not easily gained otherwise.

2. *Advantages*

a. The teacher can face the class while making presentation.

b. Overhead projectors may be used without turning out lights.

c. Overhead projectors may be used with large audiences.

d. Overhead projectors contribute to clearer and more effective communication by using vision as well as hearing.

e. Other visual aids may be used simultaneously.

f. The instructor may prepare his own materials. Anything that can be traced, photographed, drawn, printed or typed may be placed on transparency.

g. Materials may be pointed out or added to the transparency while it is being used.

h. Two or more transparencies may be overlaid to give perspective or to superimpose charts, drawings or maps.

3. *Weaknesses.* The chief disadvantage of this aid is its cost, especially for a small school or church. However, if a school or church can purchase a projector and the materials, transparencies may be made on the premises for the occasion. It is not advisable, however, unless the machine will be used regularly. If the church or small school uses visual aids consistently, it would soon absorb the cost of a projector.

4. *Technique for using.* Prepared materials or instructor-made transparencies can be made for practically every teaching situation. The following is a general procedure for making transparencies:

a. Mark on tracing paper the general outlines of the projection area. Then sketch the drawing or words you wish to reproduce.

b. Place a piece of clear acetate (the transparency-pressure-sensitive film) over the "master" and trace it.

c. Color or accent the drawing in the desired colors, with felt pens, color tape, drawing pens, or suitable acetate inks.

d. If all the information is on one sheet, mount it with pressure sensitive tapes.

e. If the transparency is to be used frequently, it may be sprayed with clear plastic to seal the drawings or letters and prevent running and fading. It may also be mounted in a cardboard frame for easy storage.

f. Overlay films (transparencies) can be added to the basic picture or frame by making a hinge of pressure sensitive tape on the face of the mount.

g. Duplicates may be handed out on regular mimeo paper for note-taking by students. Use pointers or felt-tip pens to add outline or drawing as the presentation proceeds. Other visual aids such as a slide projector, maps, 3-D models and the like, can be used simultaneously.

h. Plan a follow-up exercise to insure understanding of the material presented. This can be in the form of a quiz, discussion, prepared questions, summary.

i. Evaluate the presentation afterward; write comments or note changes needed in presentation to take into account when the material is next presented.

j. An outline should be written beforehand to insure coherent and reasonable progress and development of thought.

Sources of Audiovisuals

Audio Visual Service, 2445 Park Avenue South, Minneapolis. Films and filmstrips for rent.

Augsburg Publishing House, 426 South 5th Street, Minneapolis. Films and filmstrips for rent.

Beacon Films and Filmstrips, 1515 E. 66th Street, Minneapolis. Films and filmstrips for rent; many are good for teacher training.

Cathedral Filmstrips. "Passion Story" Five filmstrips and records on the arrest, trial, death

Preschoolers listen to a cassette recording of "Little Marcy" at the listening center. (First Baptist Church of West Hollywood, FL)

and resurrection of Christ.

"Parables from Nature" Twelve filmstrips and records on the parables Jesus told; very good for preschool and primary departments.

Eldridge Publishing Co., P. O. Drawer 209, Franklin, Ohio 45005—sound effects.

GAF Corporation, Portland, Oregon 97207—slides.

Gospel Films Library, 5105 Nicollet Avenue South, Minneapolis. Films for youth for rent.

Mid-West Audio Visual, 10 West 25th Street, Minneapolis. Films for rent; filmstrips for sale; handle Moody Filmstrips.

Sentinel Records, Simi, California, has "The Bible in Living Sound" recordings.

Singspiration, Zondervan, 1415 Lake Drive S.E., Grand Rapids, Michigan 49506. Has a wide variety of children's records—Bible character and missionary stories and songs.

Word of Truth Productions, Box 2, Burnt Hills, New York 12027—slides.

World Wide Pictures, 1313 Hennepin Avenue, Minneapolis. Films by Billy Graham team for rent.

"Your Story Hour," Berrien Springs, Michigan, has recorded Bible and contemporary plays.

Many church and school publishing house catalogs list tape recorders, record players, and projectors and screens, as well as the various materials which can be projected.

41

Handcrafts are not busy work. They should make the
lesson truths more meaningful to pupils.

Correlated Handcrafts

Correlated handcrafts reinforce the truths of
the lesson. These handcrafts are distinguished
from busy work by this correlation with the lesson emphasis. Correlated handwork should be
creative. The student should be able to detect its
purpose. Handwork may include a great variety of things, from drawing to constructing
models or keeping notebooks.

Handcrafts should make the truth of the lesson more vivid. It should accomplish this more
economically than another technique. It should
clarify concepts for the pupil in a way that
stories alone could not do.

Advantages of Handcrafts

1. Handcrafts develop mental coordination,
manual agility, problem-solving skills, and
ability to follow directions.

2. The process promotes unity within the
group, yet leaves room for creativity.

3. Completing a craft provides a sense of accomplishment and feelings of confidence.
Crafts could open areas of hobby interest for
further pursuit.

4. Handcrafts clarify concepts for pupils and
make truth more vivid and real.

5. Handling objects helps to establish a
sense of chronology or historical sequence difficult to achieve through storytelling alone.

Weaknesses of Handcrafts

1. Since people work at different rates, some
finish before others and become bored. Also,
people are gifted with various abilities. All
people are not equally adept at any given project.

2. Most leather and plastic crafts are expensive and materials cannot be procured easily.

3. Not all crafts are adaptable for all age
levels.

4. While handcrafts should be utilized with a
definite purpose in mind, often they are merely
time-fillers.

5. It is often difficult to relate handcrafts to
theology, except through relating them to
stories.

6. Handcrafts require a lot of working room
and storage and display space.

7. Some handcrafts are messy, and unsuited
for Sunday attire.

Principles for Use of Handcrafts

1. Provide situations and experiences so that
each child grows in creative ability and learns
how to work well with a group.

2. Guard against the tendency to make
handwork an end in itself. Be sure the activity
helps achieve the purposes of the unit of study.
Handwork is justified only as it contributes to
learning.

3. Handwork should, if possible, be interspersed with mental activities, to make a
total learning situation. Handcrafts should be

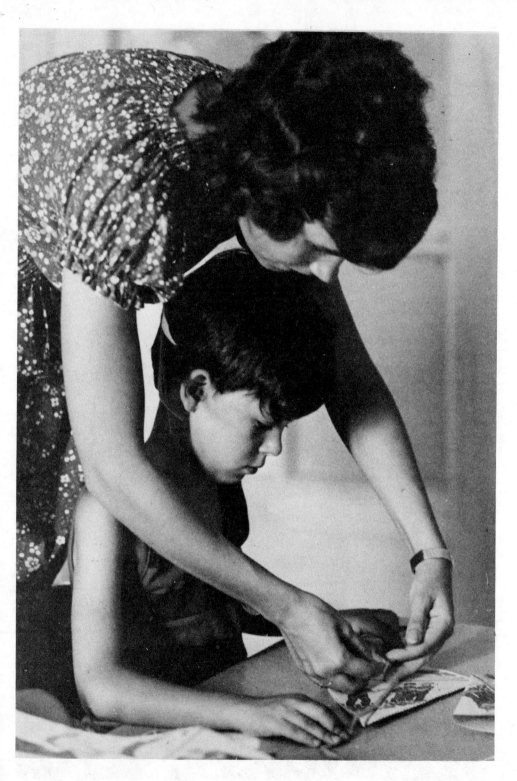

Handcrafts should make the truths of the lesson more vivid.

a necessary and component part of the most effective teaching, not something tacked onto the lesson period.

4. The handwork activity should teach something of value that could not be taught more effectively another way.

5. Choose activities suited to the age of the boys and girls and that arouse a desire to discover, to learn, to work in the group, and to share.

6. Motivate expressional activities by using poetry, hymns, Bible verses, pictures, and conversation.

7. Avoid asking the pupils to do something too difficult or too simple. To encourage originality the work should be within the range of the pupils' abilities.

8. Quality of product should never take precedence over teaching value. Yet the pupil should think well enough of his project to put forth his best effort.

9. Recognize the child's efforts to create and help him learn how to improve. Maintain proper balance between the pupil's initiative and teacher help.

10. The teacher is the guide and must make adequate and careful preparation to see that the work accomplishes its purposes.

11. Provide opportunities for constructive criticism so that each child may improve what he does.

12. Give definite directions on how to use materials for the first time, such as how to wipe a paint brush to avoid dripping.

13. Avoid undertaking to guide pupils in that which you do not know how to do.

14. Prepare and provide all the necessary materials, supplies, and equipment.

15. The pupil should see the value in the work. He should recognize how the handwork furthers the lessons's objectives.

16. Clarify the spiritual values to be realized.

17. Evaluate what has been done in the light of the purpose.

The story seems more real if the preschool child has something to see, hear or feel. (Scripture Press)

Effectiveness

Whether behavior problems result from poor teaching or from poor child-training by parents, the proper use of handwork may eliminate behavioral problems. A teacher noted that the troublemaker in his class was a caricaturist. The child had made a drawing on the chalkboard before class. The drawing depicted the teacher holding the pupils with chains. In the discussion that followed the students complained that they had heard the Bible stories before and that they were never allowed to express themselves. One pupil suggested making a mural like they did in public school. The teacher suggested a mural of the life of David which they were studying. The troublemaker was appointed advisor of the project. Today he is a dependable layman in the church.

Some pupils make trouble. Others are simply bored. With the proper use of handcrafts both will respond, become involved and committed.

They may even show enthusiasm!

Use According to Age Level

The question is not so much what kind of handcrafts should be used for each age level, but rather what use can any particular handcraft have with the age in question. Some things, like models, can be adapted to any age level. The important factors are physical and mental abilities. These vary with the person as well as with the age. The interest of the student is a vital factor in using handcrafts.

1. *Preschool*—The child is not expected to "make something" according to adult standards. He should experience freedom and satisfying activity. The child mostly plays, and toys are important at this stage. He draws or models life as he sees it, thus revealing much about himself.

2. *Grades one and two*—The child can now draw pictures and is proud of his ability to write. He likes to build models, although he is

293

Even primary children can undertake simple murals.

just beginning. Puppets are popular. He needs much guidance. The home is the center of his life, and projects should be related to this subject.

3. *Grades three and four*—Because they need to develop skills, making things is important in their learning process. They need to gain confidence, make something worthwhile, gain a feeling of achievement, and recognize their ability to contribute to a group. They are able to do basic research.

4. *Grades five and six*—The teacher ought to think in terms of projects such as notebooks, collections, or writing an artistic work within the scope of a project. The junior can make useful things.

5. *Junior High*—Projects create interest; however, free choice must be given to the student so he can pursue his own interests. Intermediates can take on responsibility and are very capable. Charts, displays, notebooks and more complex projects are possible.

6. *High School*—Service projects can be exploited, for the high school student would be more inclined to make something for someone. Creative writing or artistic expression connected with worship symbols are possibilities. Teenagers are capable of complex projects.

Resources for Further Reading

Doan, Eleanor. *Handcrafts Encyclopedia.* Glendale: Gospel Light Publications, 1961.

Eckgren, Betty Lois and Fishel, Vivian. *500 Live Ideas for the Grade Teacher.* Evanston: Row, Peterson, 1952.

Keiser, Armilda B., *Here's How and When.* New York: Friendship Press, 1952.

Lobingier, John Leslie. *If Teaching Is Your Job.* Boston: Pilgrim Press, 1956. pp. 74-78.

Morrison, Eleanor Shelton, and Foster, Virgil E. *Creative Teaching in the Church.* Englewood Cliffs, New Jersey: Prentice-Hall, 1963. pp. 207-222.

Parkhill, Martha, and Spoeth, Dorothy. *It's Fun to Make Things.* New York: A.S. Barnes and Co., 1941.

Roorbach, Rosemary K. *Teaching Children in the Church.* New York-Nashville: Abingdon Press, 1959. pp. 84-102.

Sapp, Phyllis Woodruff. *Creative Teaching in the Church School.* Nashville: Broadman Press, 1967. pp. 26-41.

Torrance, Ellis Paul. *Rewarding Creative Behavior.* Englewood Cliffs, New Jersey: Prentice-Hall, 1965.

Junior High pupils usually pitch in to a project with enthusiasm. These Seattle youngsters sort seeds for Food for the Hungry. The seeds went to Bangladesh and Panama.

DIORAMAS

A diorama is a three-dimensional scene which tells a story. It is adaptable to any age level and almost any subject. Students can build dioramas in any box or frame—a shoe box or corrugated carton, a window sill, a bookcase shelf, a mantel, or a sandbox or sandpan.

Suitable Subjects

1. A scene from a Bible story, such as Andrew bringing Peter to Jesus.
2. Bible customs; a diorama of a woman getting water from a well.
3. Illustrations of Christian growth and conduct.
4. Missions, with a scene from a mission field.
5. Church history, depicting an early church scene or event.

Advantages for the Students

1. Affords benefits of learning cooperation, sharing, friendliness.
2. Offers opportunity for the shy person to participate and the aggressive one to use his energy constructively.
3. Gives opportunity for class members to do research and use information.
4. Teachers discover understandings, feelings, and skills of the group. This knowledge enables teachers to guide the class to better knowledge, attitudes, and habits by further conversation and aids during a project.

Materials

1. *Permanent box frame.* This can be reused by placing in it new figures and scenes. May be a wood or corrugated cardboard carton.
2. *A three-part cardboard background.* Cut three pieces of heavy cardboard, the middle about two feet long and a foot high, side pieces about one foot square. Hinge together with tape or lacing. Cover with shelf or wrapping paper, on which background scenery is drawn. Reuse by making new background covers.
3. *Figures.* Wind two pipe cleaners together by using a third. Glue or tape on a construction paper head. Add facial features. Dress the figure to fit the character. Place feet of figure in clay to make figure stand up. Or use clothespins and dress as above. Other figures may be drawn on cardboard and cut out, made of plywood, papier mache, or modeling clay.
4. *Palm Trees.* Palm trees may be made by rolling brown construction paper into a tube the desired height and diameter for the scene. Glue. Fold 9 × 12 inch green crepe paper fanwise, about an inch for each fold, then fold in half. Draw pattern of palm leaf on folded fan, with base of frond on the fold. Cut out and arrange leaves in a bunch. Tie with thread or string. Glue leaves inside the top of the brown paper tube. Cut up the base of the tube a half inch in four places; fold back to make the tree stand up.

Apple trees may be made by hole-punching colored tissue paper and gluing the resulting "confetti" to the stems of twigs. Use spools for trunk. Large weeds with small dried flowers or pods painted green will resemble trees. Live evergreens will serve as pine trees.

5. *Oriental houses.* Use brown construction paper with a 16-square fold. Cut and paste as for a box. Invert, making open side down. Add a railing around the flat top, and accordion-fold stairs leading to the roof. Cut out a window and door.

6. *Variations.* Curtains across the front of the scene may be used as a screen for shadow pictures. Flashlights may light interior through holes in each side of box. Cellophane in front will give an unusual and beautiful effect. Make a peep show with a scene inside of shoe box. Slit an end of the box through which to view the scene. Cut a rectangular opening in the top cover of the box to let in enough light to see the three-dimensional scene.

Procedure

1. Tell the story.
2. Discuss the subject with your class.
3. Smaller children may each draw a picture to illustrate the theme. Comment on good points of each and hang up *all* pictures.
4. Let class choose scene for illustration.
5. Plan together, with reference materials on hand—pictures, books, maps, handwork books on dioramas.
6. Divide class into committees, each to work on certain aspects. One may decide upon box or frame. A second might make the background and fit it into place. The third would work on the "floor" of the box to simulate the interior of a building, or the trees, roads, water, and hills of the outdoors. Another committee could make the figures.
7. Arrange and rearrange figures and background to best advantage. Display most important figures and objects in foreground.
8. Retell the story, using the diorama, with group participation.
9. Evaluate the project.

42

Every member of your youth group can participate in role play.

Psycho-drama, Field Trips

A role is the way one behaves in a given situation. When people role play, they assume roles in a situation and act them out, hopefully reaching a constructive conclusion. Role playing is a method of developing more desirable behavior in real-life situations.

When people role play, they assume roles in a situation and act them out, hopefully reaching a constructive conclusion. Role playing is a method of developing more desirable behavior in real-life situations.

It is important to distinguish psycho-drama or role play from conventional drama. Role play is not an artistic performance based on a literary text, but an extemporaneous activity in which participants "feel their way through" the situation. Observers question the participants and arrive at an interpretation.

Role play takes various forms. It may seek to apply principles to a hypothetical problem, with an open-ended solution. It may follow historical and literary texts with known outcomes. The first form would apply a Bible passage to a contemporary situation. The second form would involve role-playing a biblical narrative. Among other variants are experimental role play, where the reactions of players to the unexpected are tested, and case analysis, an attempt to act out all important aspects of a large-scale problem over an extended period of time.

Aims of Role Play

1. *Stimulate discussion.* When a group does not care or know much about a topic, it is hard to get a discussion going on the subject. To overcome this problem we often use a speaker to start the process, followed by a good discussion leader. Role play can also serve this purpose. It brings members of a group directly into a situation. Every member has a chance to share in the group feeling, just as an audience reacts at a play. Role play will prompt people to speak spontaneously and stimulate active discussion.

2. *Release emotions.* Some people are reluctant to discuss personal feelings. They do not know how others will react. If the class is to deal with the problems that really trouble members, feelings must be expressed. Emotions need to be dealt with if attitudes are to be affected and learning is to take place.

3. *Bring the problem to life.* At times a group thinks a topic is academic or hypothetical. It may have been put on the agenda by a planning committee or a leader and the group considers it unimportant or unreal. Sometimes the members see the importance, but deal with the situation in a theoretical way. Role playing brings it to life dramatically.

4. *Train in leadership skills.* An important function of a group leader is helping the group to solve problems. The most significant aspect is giving procedural help—guiding the group to approach a problem systematically. In such an approach the group examines the problem, investigates the information and draws conclusions. Any group can engage in problem-solving, with different members alternately playing the leader. In this way the skills involved in helping a group to approach a

297

Role play brings members of a group directly into a situation. (Ed Deringer)

problem systematically can be studied and practiced. In problem-solving sessions the person in the leadership role can practice other skills as well.

5. *Other reasons for role playing.* To encourage readiness to learn, lessen anxiety by anticipatory rehearsal, provide cross-cultural skill practice, report on a topic and improve group functioning.

Strengths of the Technique

1. In historical or Biblical role playing, figures from the past come to life and their problems seem more real.

2. The players often identify with the roles being portrayed, learning to look at a given situation from a different point of view.

3. Their sensitivities are developed because they learn how it feels to be in someone else's position.

4. Team members with special problems, experiences, or competencies can brief the others on particular problems.

5. Role play is flexible and can be tailored to the problem the group is concerned about.

6. It is especially good as an exploratory device when a group is beginning a study.

7. Participants remember the material because they experience it.

8. Role play leads the class to discuss attitudes they would not normally express with

traditional methods.

9. Class members can experiment with new or different responses without suffering consequences that might be experienced in life.

Weaknesses of the Technique

1. Inexperienced teachers could lose effective control of the class, so new teachers will avoid using role play.

2. Teachers must be oriented to the subject matter and methods.

3. A teacher might lack ingenuity.

4. Dealing with the emotional reactions of participants unknown to the teacher can be dangerous.

5. Undesirable effects can come from putting unpopular people in certain roles.

6. A poorly supervised class may engage in idle, useless discussion. Only superficial opinions and prejudices may be aired if discussion is not well controlled.

7. The class may view role play as a game, rather than an educational experience.

8. Older people tend to laugh and be self-conscious. They may be unable to identify with their assigned roles. Shyness and hesitancy may develop at any age level.

Principles for Use of Technique

1. First, the teacher must present the essential situation to be role played, including the characters, the setting, the situation or problem, the Biblical and/or literary text.

2. If in the role play a small group acts before a large group of observers, participants should be volunteers with a choice of roles. Time limitations may prevent this for younger pupils.

3. A short briefing session is essential to coach participants on their specific roles. Those who will add the element of surprise should have special briefing unknown to the observers or to other players.

4. The number of characters involved should be limited, to prevent confusion.

5. When possible, provide an open-ended situation where role players must discover solutions.

6. In role playing a complex problem, the teacher may act as a clarifier by interrupting the action for brief commentary.

7. The observers should evaluate the action at its conclusion, discussing the validity of the emotions portrayed, the facts cited, and the consequences of possible actions.

Examples of Effective Use

1. Bible truths such as the religious and civil trials of Christ are well-suited to role play.

2. Selected students could role play the meeting of a student with a friend he is trying to win to Christ. The class would then evaluate the visit in terms of its effectiveness.

3. A pastor can deal with problems of adolescents in this framework, giving them a chance to see the problem from two points of view.

4. Role play can be used in teacher training. Effective and ineffective teaching methods may be enacted before the class.

5. The rights and wrongs of church ushering, song leading and other services could be taught in this way.

6. Visitation procedure can be effectively taught through a role play situation.

Usefulness at Various Age Levels

1. *Primary.* The uninhibited primary child gives an honest reaction to the situation being portrayed. He thinks literally and simply, so the teacher must choose material which is concrete rather than symbolic. It must be easy to understand. The primary child has a short interest span (20 minutes); therefore, the role play must be short and interesting. He is concerned about group acceptance, so as many children as possible should be used in the role play.

2. *Junior.* The junior child loves to *do* things, and the role play gives him a chance to take an active role. He loves true stories. The content can often be historical. Since the junior is a hero worshipper, choose a hero with whom he can identify. The junior still does not understand symbols, so make the content explicit.

3. *Junior High.* The junior high student is starting to be interested in others and their opinions. For this reason role play is excellent at this age. As the young teen's decision-making power grows, role play can turn him to consideration of Christ's claims. The young teen is beginning to grasp symbols, so include more of the abstract. He is interested in morality, and role play is related to moral issues. Since puberty comes at this time, the psychodrama can take up the problems of sexual awareness.

4. *High School.* High schoolers begin to encounter antichristian views, and role play can give advance preparation.

By the middle teens a person has formed prejudices, but role play can help him see the other person's view on race, culture, or faith. The high schooler can plan role play.

5. *Adults.* Adults have developed a capacity for abstraction. They vary greatly, so role play can be flexible. With adults role play is a good "starter" in a new area of study, as it undermines the copious inhibitions of adults. However, they may have to be sold on role play as a learning technique because of their greater self-consciousness and inability to identify.

FIELD TRIPS

Field trips capitalize educationally on the wandering and exploring instinct. They acquaint the pupil with his environment and

Children remember a Bible story much longer if they have an opportunity to act it out. (Scripture Press)

interpret, supplement, and enrich curricular experiences. Before going on any trip, plan what to observe and have definite questions in mind. The teacher should visit the place beforehand to be well-informed as to what the pupils will see. At the destination, the teacher should wait till all are assembled and should speak so that all can hear (always difficult in a large group, but absolutely necessary to effective learning). On return to class, ideas learned should be reviewed.

1. *Local trips.* Simplest type, in which the group visits points, parts, or sections of its own building and grounds. Primaries or beginners may visit the church sanctuary to learn the meaning of the "pulpit," "pew," and "organ."

2. *Community trip.* This is the usual field trip to some point of interest outside the local place of teaching, such as when the high school class visits a college or the college class visits a Jewish synagogue to observe worship. A class of prospective Sunday School teachers may visit and observe public school classes. Or the Sunday School staff may visit another church to observe architecture, planning of space, furnishings and equipment.

3. *Tour.* The tour or journey is a trip lasting several days, a month, or even longer.

4. *The imaginary tour.* All the details of the trip are investigated, studied and planned, just as though the group were actually going. This is an excellent technique for missionary programs.

5. *The individual trip.* The pupil may take a trip by himself because of an assignment of some particular responsibility in connection with curricular work or because of his own specialized interests.

43

Many youth groups are experimenting with multi-media presentations to communicate the Gospel. Here's how to do it.

Multi-Media

A slide production project takes advantage of the current interest in photography, media and sense perception. Usually young people undertake this kind of project with the aim of describing the Gospel to their non-Christian friends. Music and the media tell the story. Because the medium stimulates thought and involves the viewer visually and audibly, it has great impact. The slides may have familiar scenes of the community, with youth involved in different activities. The slides flash on to screens in sequence. Contemporary music blares from speakers. A discussion and question time follows the slides.

The group effort tends to knit the young people together. The youth group should strive to involve the whole group by using each individual's talents. Some can write and others handle the technical aspects of the production. They will see how the church can use everyone's talent in expressing the Gospel to the world. If the youth can view the project as an expression of their own lives and faith, it will build unity in the group. They may begin to think in terms of new and creative ways to tell the Good News.

Personnel

Each aspect of the project demands special talents and interests. For this reason each young person's abilities should be explored and utilized. The project does not require profes-

sionally trained people to be a success. Sometimes inexperienced youth come up with creative and effective ideas. This is an expression of the youth group, not a professional movie studio. Do not be surprised at the finished product, however. It may look quite professional, even though you thought it would never work.

1. *Cameramen.* Almost anyone can take slide pictures. Choose one or two persons in the group who can take good pictures to head this committee. Anyone in the group can submit pictures taken on vacations or at school. Get casual and real-life pictures which best tell the message.

2. *Script men.* Selection of this committee should be based on the interests and talents of the group. Select youth who are creative and able to write well. This committee determines the application of the message to the medium. The committee should not have more than four or five members. Too many ideas make for disharmony and confusion.

3. *Music editors.* This committee should not have more than two or three members. They should select music with a direct relationship to the message. Music editors should know both popular and good Christian music. They should look for music and words to reflect the script.

4. *Sound and lighting crew.* This committee should have members who know how to tape record and to wire the speakers for effective

sound. Two or three people are usually sufficient. If few youth have such talents, ask those who have an interest in this aspect to work with an experienced advisor or parent.

5. *Projector crew.* Members of this committee do the actual showing of the slides. The number on this crew depends on the number of projectors used. The projectors must be coordinated with each other and with the music and script. One member serves as coach to help each person running a projector. The coach directs the slide sequences to begin and end at the proper place in the script.

6. *Ushers.* This committee plans arrangement of chairs and helps coordinate the program activities. They usher the audience into the rows, making sure all are in the best positions to see all the screens and hear the music. If tickets are used, they can take these also.

Materials

One important feature of this project is that most materials are common both to the church and the home. It is not necessary to have the most modern and expensive equipment. Usually equipment used in church or home is adequate.

1. *Camera.* Most cameras take slide pictures. A camera with a wide-angle lens or telephoto lens will improve the quality. Since film is expensive, it is important to make sure the camera works and the flashbulbs ignite correctly. Film should have 20 or more exposures, to take sequential pictures. Ask parents and photographers to get film developed inexpensively.

2. *Script materials.* Material used depends on the theme or script idea. If the group wants to base the production around a Biblical portion or character, then information may be needed from a Bible dictionary or from the Bible itself. The group may desire to select reading material expressing thoughts of young persons today. Magazine, newspaper and editorial articles may provide suitable material. The committee should look for pictures in magazines and newspapers, as well as posters hanging in shops and coffee houses.

3. *Records, tape recorders, speakers.* Electrical equipment, properly used, gives a professional touch. Select records on the basis of their message and sound quality. Good speakers can make the music sound alive. Usually the young people have good stereo records and tape recorders in their homes.

4. *Projectors and screens.* Most slide projectors work well for this project. The number of pictures taken and the number of screens used determine how many projectors will be needed. In beginning it is advisable to have no more than three projectors. Each projector can use different types of trays or carousels. The bigger the carousel, the more slides it will hold. Large carousels reduce or eliminate the need for changing during performance. The projectors should not skip slides or stick. Make sure there are plenty of outlets for the cords. Bring extension cords, if necessary. Provide an extra projector bulb for each machine. An extra projector is advisable for emergencies.

Production

1. Determine the theme or message. This becomes the basis for the whole slide presentation. Music and script are selected to convey this message. Music can be used as the basic script. The message would then be in the music, and the slides would be coordinated with the music. In many ways this type of production is easiest, since the words to the music help determine the type of pictures needed.

Another alternative to script writing is to find a Bible verse or portion which could be used for the theme. Music would be selected as background or to further the story. Slides can be taken in contemporary situations to help the audience visualize the meaning of the Scripture. The Scripture can be read phrase by phrase with a few minutes between readings.

Some groups find it difficult to decide on one theme. In this case, a more unstructured script may be written. Music with a message would be selected. Random photos taken to present important thoughts would be shown in series while the music plays, without relationship between music and slides. Slides of captions or signs could be taken. The script could be woven around these visual readings without narration.

2. Determine the kind of pictures needed to illustrate the script. The script writers should list ideas or places to go for each record or for the theme. This also will aid in taking good and relevant pictures.

3. Collect relevant magazine pictures and captions. Many times the pictures found in magazines can be photographed and shown on slides. There is opportunity for creative work with sayings or titles. This is a great source for theme material.

4. Actually begin to take pictures. Unposed action shots are best. Individuals in the youth group can be the subjects. Sometimes pictures of crowds or buildings add a special dimension. It is good to try and take photographs of everyone in the group. Pictures should be taken everywhere the group goes. Variety makes for interesting photographs. While the script is the guide for taking pictures, always have a camera ready to capture that unusual picture.

Approximately 75 to 100 slides are needed for three projectors. The amount will vary, depending on the capacity of each projector. Usually the older projectors will hold 25 slides. Newer equipment sometimes can show 75 slides with one carousel.

If the pictures were taken with the script in mind, editing the slides will be simplified.

Group pictures first into themes, according to the script. Then place the groups in order of presentation. Words of the music or script should be studied by the script committee as they choose slides for the presentation.

After groups of slides are arranged according to theme and sequence in the script, divide each group between the three projectors to be used. Put one picture from the group into the tray or carousel of each projector. The idea is to have each projector showing part of the same theme in sequence. This enables the three projectors to show a panorama of thought, much like a film.

Once the slides have been placed in the projectors, the basic work is done. The next step is to show the slides on the screen without music, in order to make final arrangements of the slides, to be sure pictures are right-side-up and words and captions readable.

After checking out the slides in the projectors, add the music. It is best to start the tape recorder and play just one song or theme. A system of alternating the projectors should be determined. For example, projector #1 shows

The photographer should watch for unposed action shots, especially of young people.

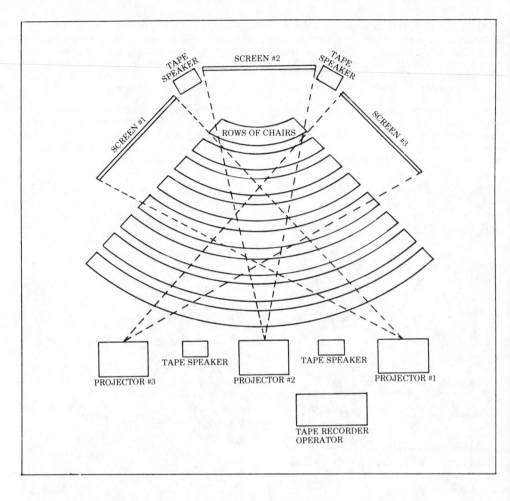

the first slide. Projector #2 waits for the right time and then shows a slide. There are now two pictures on two different screens. Projector #3 adds a picture to the third screen. Once all screens are filled, the projectors can follow the same system to progress the theme. The system of showing slides can be varied so the sequence is not so noticeable. Someone should direct the three projectors, much like a music director. It is best to stay with an easy system at first.

If each song or theme can be worked on separately, the projector operators can decide how fast to change the slides. They must complete each song or theme without running out of slides or having slides left over when the music ends. Much practice and coordination are needed. A director or sponsor could help in directing the slide timing and changing. Gradually the presentation will look more like a motion picture than a slide presentation. Because of the limitations of conventional equipment it is not possible to change the slides in rapid sequence. As a matter of fact, with three screens to look at, the audience will need

to think about each picture and why that particular slide was included.

Performance

To make the performance run smoothly, it is essential to go through the whole production. Usually the production will run 15 to 25 minutes, depending on the number of pictures taken and songs recorded. Last minute adjustments should be made before the showing, rather than have embarrassing incidents in the final performance.

The diagram below will help with room arrangements. Size of the room and facilities will dictate the precise arrangement needed. The sound should not be too loud nor too soft. The media of sound and slides should not compete for attention, but should combine for the total experience. Since the projectors are behind the audience, they must be elevated above the heads of the audience. Any kind of platform or elevated table will raise the projector to the desired height.

44

How can you set up a filing system that will save you time in your Sunday School work? How can you include missions education in your class work? What is the best way to plan a lesson? Here are some helpful suggestions.

Helpful Hints

HOW TO PLAN A LESSON

This chapter deals with planning a Sunday School lesson without a quarterly. In case of emergency, a teacher may be called on to plan a Sunday School lesson, with only a Scripture passage as a guide. Some churches provide little more than the basic Scripture, with perhaps a few notes for adults, and expect their preschool and elementary teachers to teach with no other assistance. Actually, no one in possession of this volume will be in that helpless a situation. Its many resources will be pointed out in this chapter.

To illustrate the planning process, let us follow through with a specific Scripture passage and discover how the lesson goes together. Because of the selectivity possible in 2 Kings 5:1-16, the story of Naaman, the leper, we will use this passage.

The Aim

1. *Consider the age group.* Very small children cannot grasp the symbolism of comparing leprosy to sin in the life. Neither have they arrived at the place where they see their sins in need of cleansing. They *can* understand the concept of obeying God, so the aim for their lesson could be to teach that God's Word must be obeyed if we are to receive blessing.

In primary and junior classes most pupils have a realization of sin. They can relate to the aim of teaching that salvation must be obtained in God's way. Furthermore, they can understand the need for witnessing. Another aim for them might be to teach the importance of telling others the good news of Jesus. Or, the aim may stress the rewards of witnessing. This division of possibilities extends throughout adult classes.

2. *Consider the needs.* The aim will be chosen, not only in the light of the pupils' level of understanding, but also on the basis of need. If a class of any age is composed almost entirely of professing Christians and church members, the aim need not be to teach salvation but to teach the importance and joys of witnessing. Consider the spiritual level of the class in choosing the aim.

3. *Consider the text.* The Scripture lesson is not a departing point for the teacher to ride his hobby horses. "No Scripture is of any private interpretation." God had rather specific points in mind when He guided writers to put down the facts in a given passage. It is possible to so spiritualize almost any passage that its actual teaching is obscured.

The Naaman passage shows clearly that Naaman was cured only when he did exactly what God's man instructed. Salvation is obtained only when a man comes in God's way and completely obeys. The passage at the same time clearly teaches that Naaman found out about God's man because a believer spoke up

305

and told Mrs. Naaman about him.

"Chasing rabbits" in the passage could lead a class far afield—divine healing, the importance of listening to the advice of friends, and probably a dozen other side issues. Hitting too many points like a shotgun lessens the impact.

The Memory Verse

1. *Consider the age group.* While even preschoolers can and do memorize John 3:16, a long verse is less likely to be meaningful to them. A short verse can be repeated over and over by them in connection with role play, and be easily learned in its context. Select a verse with words within the understanding of the age group. Juniors and up may use Acts 1:8 for this passage, while preschoolers can say, "Ye shall be witnesses unto me," only a part of the verse.

2. *Consider the aim.* The memory verse must correlate with the aim. If the emphasis is on witnessing, the above choices are appropriate. If, instead, salvation is stressed, then a verse like Acts 16:31 would be good.

The Approach

1. *Consider the age group.* If a contemporary story is the type of introduction used, be sure it is on the level of understanding of the class. A class of juniors can relate to an account of an adult sports incident, but adults will not respond as readily to a child-level story of a behavior problem. Nor will juniors understand a political illustration or problem. Preschoolers like to hear about children their own age.

2. *Use variety.* One teacher used an object lesson to start every teaching period. "The worst method of teaching is the one that is used all the time." When possible, take advantage of new ways to capture and hold interest, without which there is no learning. Let a hand puppet tell the introductory story. Or tell a contemporary story. In a lesson on Naaman refer to *Ben Hur*, which recalls the horrors of leprosy. Or let two or three students role play a problem relating to the theme (again the horror and isolation of leprosy may be stressed). One could use a picture, Biblical or contemporary, to stress an unusual fact in the story or Scripture passage to follow. Play a record or a cassette tape with a song that expresses the theme or aim, or tells a story of similar emphasis. Show slides or filmstrips clarifying customs, costumes or geography.

3. *Build on the everyday knowledge of the pupil.* Jesus, who knew man's mind because He made it, used stories of everyday events and objects to interest His listeners in spiritual truth. He then moved from the earthly to the heavenly.

Presentation

Use variety in presenting the Bible lesson. This book suggests many techniques in Section VII. Some possibilities are visual aids, discussion, recordings, role play and puppets.

At the end of the lesson the teacher must carefully apply the Bible truths to the students' lives. The application can take different forms:

1. *Open-end story.* Let the students decide how to complete the lesson story in harmony with the aim of the lesson.

2. *Drama.* A few students may role play the problem and its solution.

3. *A story.* The story should include characters and action which further the lesson aim.

4. *Chalkboard.* Comparisons may be made on the board, or conclusions stated.

5. *A question.* A question may call for a decision.

6. *A role-play game.* Preschoolers and primaries may play a game in which they act out the virtue being taught. Following a lesson on Naaman with emphasis on witnessing, they may play, "How am I telling somebody about Jesus?" One may knock on the door and pretend to talk. Another may sing, and so on.

HOW TO FILE LESSON MATERIALS

Some persons are "string savers," "squirrels," or "pack rats," by nature. They store every article they feel might have some future use. The practice is not without merit, depending on the place and manner of storage. Probably everyone at some time experiences the frustration of "carefully putting away" a clipping, a picture, an article deemed of value, only to forget where it was placed. Or one spends an hour searching for it in a miscellaneous collection in a drawer. The simple expedient of an alphabetical file will save valuable hours of fruitless searching.

*How Can a Christian Education
File Be Organized?*

1. *Biblically.* The best way for a beginning Sunday School teacher to start a file is by Bible reference. Secure 66 file folders, then place the name of each book of the Bible on a folder. At first, file lessons by Bible books. After all, Sunday School lessons should be based on Scripture.

One can supplement this file by taking notes in Bible conferences, teacher training classes, and during the pastor's weekly sermon. These notes can be filed along with the Sunday School lessons for future reference.

As the file grows larger, add file folders for individual chapters of a book. This will force one to center Sunday School teaching on the Bible. Also, for future lessons a teacher can quickly refer to previous research on a given topic. (Note: Illustrations, teaching aids, pictures and materials used in teaching should not be filed under the Biblical file. These should go in the alphabetical file.)

2. *Alphabetically.* Initially, a file may fit into a single drawer. (A transfer file box or a corrugated packing box accommodating letter-size file folders may be used). Folders may be labeled as needed, depending on the teacher's personal collection of material. Possible subjects include Bible studies, archaeology, Easter, Christmas, poetry, puppets, animals, visual aids. These should be arranged alphabetically.

3. *By subject.* The file remains alphabetical, but subdivisions are made according to subject within the alphabetical frame, instead of filing by names, as in the case of business correspondence or student files. For example, a teacher may have a special interest in archaeology. Under the *A* division, a divider will be labeled *Archaeology.* Folders alphabetized behind that divider may include Africa, books, Holy Land, Indian, marine—and any other aspects of archaeology on which the teacher has collected information. When a file is first organized, ample space may allow filing of entire copies of magazines with significant articles. As space fills up, clipping will be necessary, or a magazine shelf-file.

4. *Numerical.* Some teachers and Bible students prefer to number their subjects and file according to number. Only the person filing the material will know the key, and quick reference is difficult by anybody else.

What Goes in the File?

The answer is, everything a teacher wishes to keep—everything which has potential value for teaching or personal study. The variety is as great as the teacher's personal interest. Some useful subjects include teaching methods (separate folders on each method on which information has been collected), Bible studies, Bible background (archaeology and history), Bible geography, cults, Vacation Bible School, teacher training, church history, special days (Easter, Mother's Day, etc.), recreation and social activities, publicity, pedagogy, psychology, stories, quotations, biography, handwork ideas, patterns.

1. *The picture file.* Pictures can be filed by subject or by size. When filing by subject, alphabetize carefully for quick location—animals, children, family, friends, life of Christ, missionary, nature, Old Testament—whatever subjects are necessary for the teacher's regular use.

The size of pictures varies according to their source. Teaching pictures purchased regularly with the lesson study aids may be filed in a special drawer which accommodates their larger size. They should be filed according to subjects and/or unit of study. Extremely small pictures (useful in scrapbooks and with an opaque projector) may be filed in folders according to the quantity—one folder for Old

Testament, one for New Testament, one for children (or whatever the age group taught).

2. *The flannelgraph file.* Flannelgraph materials may be filed alphabetically or by type. If the stories are labeled according to character or subject, alphabetize in filing: Abraham, Creation, Daniel, Easter, etc. When filing by type, use separate divisions for Bible stories, missionary stories, character stories, or Bible verses or songs. Alphabetize the folders or titles under each category.

3. *Catalogs.* Request and file catalogs from Christian publishing houses, for reference when materials are needed. A large accumulation can overflow a filing cabinet. They may be filed on book shelves in files made by covering detergent boxes with Contact paper and labeling the back.

Maintaining Your File

Occasionally, an article you want to keep will appear on the reverse side of another subject equally valuable. In this case, you should cross reference the articles. The paper may be placed under one title, but a plain white sheet of paper should be filed under the other title, telling where the article is to be found. When an article is temporarily removed from the file and placed elsewhere, the fact may be noted on a sheet of paper and placed in the folder.

From time to time your file will need weeding. This doesn't have to be a big project. A home owner may run across a weed when he is on the way to pick peas. So he pulls it up. As a teacher searches for an item in the file, he may run across an article about a method or fact which is obsolete; so he discards the article. If the file drawer is getting too full for easy filing, time should be taken to check several folders to find items which have served their purpose and are no longer useful. They may be removed to make room for more current material.

TEACHING FOREIGN MISSIONS IN THE SUNDAY SCHOOL

Why are there not enough volunteers to fill the openings on the various mission fields? Certainly, it is because young people are not being faced with the challenge of giving themselves in service in a faraway and often difficult place. If they do not belong to a special missionary organization, many Sunday School pupils—young or old—do not receive specific information on missions.

Begin Missions Teaching

The logical place for Sunday School members to learn about missions is the Sunday School.

1. *Have a plan.* Unless missions teaching is incorporated in the regular curriculum of a denomination or church, there must be a definite plan to include it on a regular basis.

These youngsters learn about another culture by building a replica of a Zaire hut. (First Baptist Church, Calimesa, CA)

What is left to hit-or-miss will be missed.

a. Appoint an assistant teacher within each department to be responsible for the missionary teaching.

b. Choose a regular time—weekly or monthly—when the missionary story or facts will be presented.

c. Choose specific mission fields for study, to be sure the teaching is thorough, rather than presenting sketchy information about many places and people.

2. *Have a program.* Suggest that the missionary chairman select others to serve as a committee to build a definite program.

a. Select the fields for study.

b. Find books, pictures, maps, filmstrips and other necessary materials on those fields.

c. Have pictures of the missionaries on those fields for the pupils to "meet" during the study.

d. Have songs or games and occasionally a food typical of the land being studied.

e. Use the national costume during presentation of the material, if possible.

f. Display articles from the land under study.

3. *Develop missionary projects.*

a. Let the pupils work on a missionary map. Some who are artistic can enlarge a map of the area being studied. Let pupils add the names of towns, using the small map as a guide. From time to time (weekly or monthly), let a small representative picture be placed on the map at the location discussed in class.

b. Prepare a missionary box. Fill the box with pictures, books, games or puzzles that missionaries can use in their teaching. Missionaries find Sunday School paper pictures useful as awards to boys and girls who otherwise would never see such a picture. Classes may prepare scrapbooks of Bible pictures and stories for the missionaries. Adult classes may make garments to send to hospitals for new babies, or supply other medical needs.

c. Make a class scrapbook. While all pupils may contribute pictures and write articles to go in the scrapbook, have a committee responsible for planning and arrangement of the contents.

d. Write to the missionary. Appoint a committee of pupils to correspond with boys and girls on the mission field. Letters from the missionaries may be added to the scrapbook.

e. Make teaching devices for missionaries. Classes of juniors through adults can make object lessons, posters, puppets, charts, story wheels and other aids to use in teaching. Such aids are expensive to take in a missionary's luggage and hard to make from materials available on the field.

f. Have a systematic missionary offering. Pupils often give with more concern to those with whom they are acquainted. While the church may have a missionary budget, pupils will feel more personally involved in giving if an occasional special offering is received for missionaries about whom they have studied.

4. *Extend the missionary challenge.* After a missionary presentation, opportunity should be given for pupils to make a definite commitment to service, if God has laid it on their hearts. A public acknowledgment of dedication increases the responsibility of the pupil making the decision.

45

"Music hath charms to soothe the savage breast," observed an English dramatist. Wise Christian workers will likewise recognize the power of music and utilize it in Christian education.

Music in the Sunday School

Music used to be the means of occupying the punctual Sunday School scholars while they waited for the tardy superintendent. It didn't matter what songs were chosen—just as long as the pianist could play them and the often-unwilling pinch-hitter could sing them. But today's leaders are aware of music's contribution to learning.

1. The melody often makes the message memorable. Television commercials usually are tuneful. The youngest members of the family can at least hum the tune, and may even lisp the words, heedless of any unworthy message. This should be true of Sunday School tunes also.

2. The correlated message of the song should add to the total impact of the aim.

3. An appropriate tune should set the mood for the lesson.

What Type Music?

1. Graded. Not every song is suitable for every age level. Little children would have difficulty relating to the message of "How Firm a Foundation," while teenagers could not be bribed to sing "Jesus Loves the Little Ones Like Me." With many fine compilations of songs for each age level, there is little reason for errors in judgment along that line. With songs, as with teaching or stories, children are literalists. As a rule, pre-teens do not readily grasp symbolism. While preschoolers may enjoy the lilt and

motions of "Deep and Wide," its meaning is lost to them. (On the other hand, there sometimes are surprising responses to symbol songs. For example, all the members of a family were singing "When the Roll Is Called Up Yonder, I'll Be there" as they rode to church one Sunday morning. Five-year-old Shawn soloed after the others finished: "When the roll is called up Yonder, I *won't* be there, because I've never seen saved." She was promptly led to Jesus.)

2. Correlated. Besides singing "with understanding," pupils should sing words that emphasize the theme of study for the day. If the Good Samaritan is the story for Juniors, a song like "Help Somebody Today" is reinforcing. This technique can provide adequate expression for teens and adults, too. If preschoolers through primaries are learning how God made everything, they can carry away the message of God's power in the singing of "God Can Do Everything." "The Wonder Song," which can be used with motions, is even more memorable.

3. Suitable Melody. Slow tempo and low volume should be appropriate for a sad or warning song, while a faster rhythm and loud tone would express a militant song. Though the author may have exclaimed with joy and gratitude, "What a Friend We Have in Jesus!" many churches tend to make it more of a question, by dragging it in sorrow. It would be equally unsuitable to rush through an invitational number such as "Just As I Am," when words and tune show that it is expressing deep contrition and humility. Occasionally so-called "children's choruses" have unscriptural words added to peppy tunes, rendering them popular with boys and girls—particularly when the leaders have not analyzed the words nor explained them.

When To Use Songs

1. *In worship.* The term *worship* is a misnomer for in many services two or three songs are hurried through, supplemented by a few unrelated verses of Scripture and a prayer. **Well-chosen songs** *can* **help to set the at-** mosphere of worship, but it is not accidental. With the aid of a topical index or the leader's knowledge and discretion, songs should be chosen which will draw the class or department into prayer and praise.

2. *In Approaching the Lesson.* During the time immediately before the lesson, a song may be used to introduce the theme. If the lesson stresses obedience, for example, the message of "Trust and Obey" would be excellent. If the theme is on the power of the tongue, "Angry Words, O Let Them Never" has appropriate words.

3. *To Emphasize.* More than once during the

If your church does not use songbooks especially prepared for children, be careful to select hymns children can understand.

preschool class period, a song can and should be inserted. Not only will it aid the understanding of both story and song, it will afford a time to stretch cramped muscles and enable pupils to give better attention to what follows.

4. *In Making the Application.* A song can allow a class to express thanksgiving, praise, faith, dedication or other decisions, through its well-chosen words. Many young people have dedicated their lives while singing "Living for Jesus" or "Wherever He Leads, I'll Go." Others have volunteered for missionary service through "I'll Go Where You Want Me To Go."

How Many Songs?

The answer to this question depends on:

1. *Time available.* If the worship or lesson preparation period is brief, limit the songs accordingly. Usually one or two stanzas from several songs are better than five stanzas from only one. Variety allows more worshipers to respond. Words and melodies that appeal to one person may not appeal to another.

2. *Choice available.* Some doctrines have not been expressed often in music. There may be only one song available which really expresses the truth that needs to be reinforced. In such case, a group may sing the first stanza before the Bible reading and prayer, and intersperse another stanza before a brief story or object lesson or whatever. The class period may then be closed by singing the last stanza.

3. *Singers available.* In small classes, the assembled group may have so few who can sing at all that a prolonged song service proves embarrassing. On some occasions it may even be preferable for the group to read aloud the words of two or three stanzas, instead of attempting to sing them. Those who feel unqualified to sing will thus have opportunity to express the message aloud.

Special Music

Should solos, duets and other ensembles or instrumental numbers be used in Sunday School? There are several reasons for an affirmative answer:

1. *The singer will remember.* A young person given opportunity to sing a solo will remember the message—much longer than anyone listening. (The same is true for participants in ensembles.)

2. *Participants will use talents.* Allowing musical youth to render a service to the Sunday School through song is a means of encouraging them to develop their God-given talents and use them for His glory. These same youth are freely called on by the public school and expected to give their time in rehearsals and performance. The Sunday School should expect them to do as much for the church. It often is true that boys and girls do for the church just what is expected of them. If nothing is expected, little is volunteered.

3. *It is Scriptural.* While some church groups have felt that the use of instruments in a church is not fitting, there are Scripture passages which show otherwise. Psalm 150 exhorts that many different kinds of instruments be used in praise of God. It adds, "Let everything that hath breath praise the Lord." Young people learn to play instruments in a school band, and may never be invited to dedicate that talent to God. It is not strange that they may form "combos" to play for parties and dances. Their gifts

The Acts High School class listens to music composed and played by one of its own members. (Grace Community Church, Sun Valley, CA)

313

and training are not appreciated nor claimed by the church. Instruments dedicated to God and His service are not so likely to be given to worldly entertainment.

The Song Leader

While smaller churches may consider themselves fortunate if anyone at all is willing to stand up and announce the songs, there are qualifications for this important person which should be considered when a choice is possible.

1. *Consistent Christian testimony.* Anyone in a position of leadership is a reflection of the church and the Savior. If the witness is negative, the work is hurt.

2. *Enthusiasm.* This trait in a person of minor talent can render leadership more effective than a gifted person lacking enthusiasm. Knowledge of the words of the song and the value of the song, added to the leader's joy in the Lord, can produce enthusiasm. "Like leader, like people." The response will be enthusiastic.

3. *Good musicianship.* While the need for enthusiasm remains true, a leader should have knowledge of the correct tune of the song and should know how to keep time—whether or not he knows how to "wave his arms" correctly. If the pianist is capable of maintaining good speed and rhythm, a less efficient song director can (and usually does) follow the lead of the piano. Given a place of musical responsibility, the lay leader always can improve his knowledge and ability by seeking out instruction. School musicians are willing to instruct them, if assistance cannot be found in another church. Instead of doing only "the best he can with what he has," the church musician should seek to improve in order to serve better.

46

The discipline problems of the past were simple compared to those of today.

How to Discipline

A new problem is erupting in Sunday Schools. It's discipline—on a larger, more frightening scale than ever before.

Pupils "shake down" offering money from other pupils in the washroom; slash cushioned pews when ushers aren't looking. They slap around younger children when bus workers aren't present, and they rip from Sunday School rooms anything that is not nailed down.

The discipline problems of the past—when pupils wouldn't share crayons, or found it hard to keep still while waiting in line—were simple compared to those of today. The exasperating new tensions come from children who throw around four-letter words, use their fists, spit, bite and/or defiantly "stare down" meek teachers.

How have teachers reacted? Some have whipped inner-city boys, but striking a child is against the law. Some teachers yell at pupils, who only yell back. Other teachers grit their teeth, cry or quit.

What causes this severe disorderly behavior? For one thing, permissive public school behavior is spilling over into the Sunday School, but this is not the whole problem. Children from Christian families usually are better behaved than their public school counterparts, so it's more than just the influence of our society on Sunday School scholars. A second factor is that the explosive growth of the bus ministry has brought children primarily from

Discipline problems are increasing in the Sunday Schools of today. (Scripture Press)

housing projects, slums, and low-rent apartments. Often undisciplined, these children have been dumped into traditional Sunday School classes, creating a conflict of cultures.

What can be done? Teachers are finding that gimmicks can't keep a 20th-century student quiet. In the past, teachers have awarded prizes for the quietest or used the mystery chair. But that doesn't always work. Today's pupils are involved in the learning process, and most Sunday School teachers are not ready or equipped to share classroom control. At school, pupils have a voice in disciplining fellow students. Should they have the same authority in the house of God?

The authority of Sunday School is the Word of God, whereas the authority of public school is the democratic process. Therefore, teachers should handle problems differently on Sunday. Since God is love, teachers must communicate love. Since the Bible upholds what is "right," teachers can't let pupils continue in wrong behavior. Since the Ten Commandments prohibit taking God's name in vain, teachers can't allow cursing.

What can teachers do? Good class discipline begins with self-discipline. Teachers must prepare well, plan class activities, master content and give attention to interesting teaching techniques. They must remember that listening is not learning, therefore teaching is not telling. Pupils must stand, s-t-r-e-t-c-h, yell, march and act out Bible stories. The primary department at Welsch Avenue Free Will Baptist Church, Columbus, Ohio, directs the little ones in spontaneous calisthenics at the beginning of class. They are able to jump all over the place. "It's getting the wiggles out," explains the teacher.

Sometimes students are disruptive because of room conditions. The room is too crowded, too stuffy, too cluttered, too hot or too dark. Adequate facilities won't guarantee good behavior, but poor facilities will produce the opposite.

Attractive visual aids hold the pupils' attention and help cut down on discipline problems. (Scripture Press)

Teachers can unfuse class explosions by getting to know their students, walking the bus route on Saturday morning, then coming early on Sunday to talk with them before class. When a child is rebellious, ask him "Why?" and remind him Sunday School is a place to learn about Jesus Christ. By sharing love and attention a teacher may meet the very need that causes the child to rebel in class.

A classroom is a threatening situation to many pupils, therefore they retaliate and strike out at the teacher. Remove some of the threat by giving instructions carefully. Pupils will respond better when they know what is expected of the entire class. Next, when they are asked to participate, clearly tell what is expected of each individual.

Don't respond to your students out of bias or prejudice. Some teachers don't like long hair, chicanos, dirty dresses, runny noses or laughing, pushy girls. If a teacher reacts personally, behavior degenerates to a shouting match. When a teacher corrects a disruptive student, it's an argument, even though the teacher is in the place of authority. Make sure that student discipline is the result of broken rules, not personality dislike.

Other positive steps toward getting good discipline include praise for good behavior, employing enough helpers, teachers sitting among pupils, attractive visuals, and concentrated prayer for problem students.

However, in certain cases, negative steps can be in order. Some excellent teachers have captivated the interest of all the juniors but one. A rebellious boy laughs as the flannelgraph story is told. Good teachers have followed every suggestion only to be thwarted by a pseudo-delinquent who curses, laughs at the things of Christ and mocks prayer. The majority of the class who want to hear the lesson should not be sacrificed to one lawless pupil.

Remove the belligerent student from the class. Put him in the secretary's office or sit him in a chair in the hall. In doing so, he loses his platform to perform for the kids, you reduce pressure on him, and when he is out of the room you can counsel him individually. (Some of you may remember being sent to the principal's office because of bad behavior.) First, let him sit quietly and wait. This gives him a chance to think.

Gayle McKinney, teacher of 4th and 5th grade children at First Baptist Church, Hammond, Ind., has a large class meeting in an old furniture display store. When a child disrupts her class of inner-city students, an assistant takes the offender to the hall, decorated in rose-patterned wallpaper, where he is instructed, "Put your nose on that rose."

After assembly, Gayle talks with each offender individually, using an approach every Sunday School teacher could follow. "Your teacher has spent over two hours preparing a lesson. He has prayed. And we have Sunday School so that boys and girls may learn about Jesus. You cut up and kept the class from listening, so we had to bring you out here. We want you to learn about Jesus. When you tell me you're ready to listen to the teacher, we'll take you back inside."

This approach appeals to proper motives and places responsibility back on the pupils. It is love in action. According to Gayle, who has taken knives and an assortment of other destructive instruments from her pupils, "It works 99 percent of the time. If they don't behave, we leave them in the hall."

Several weeks ago Gayle had a 9-year-old girl standing with her nose against the wall.

"What is your name?" Gayle asked the little girl, who wore a dirty, wrinkled dress.

"None of your business."

"Where do you live?" Gayle persisted.

"None of your business."

"How old are you?" Gayle knelt beside the girl and put her arm around her shoulder.

She shrugged the arm away. "None of your business."

Finally the little girl blurted out, "I hate Sunday School; I hate you; and I'm not coming back."

"Good." Gayle put her arm around the girl again. "You are wasting your time, your teacher's time and hurting other boys and girls. But I love you."

The little girl stayed with her nose on the flower. "I felt terrible," confessed Gayle. The next Sunday, the little girl ran up and grabbed Gayle around the knees.

"Hi, teacher," she said, her attitude reversed.

When asked why, she explained, "I got saved in Junior church last week."

"What's your name?" Gayle asked.

"Barbara."

For Christmas, little Barbara brought an apple perfume bottle and announced, "An apple for my favorite teacher."

Teacher attitude toward behavior is important. Always keep the goal of good behavior before the class. Dianne Phelps uses a large picture of Senor B. Havior to remind her primary pupils constantly how they are doing. During their missions emphasis at Ward United Presbyterian Church, Livonia, Mich., Dianne turns the Latin American Senor's mouth up (smiling). If pupils "cut up" Dianne turns his mouth down (frowning). According to her, the visual reminder is better than a finger at the mouth with a hissing, *Shhhhhh*.

Dianne corrected little Joe Barnett several times for talking. Finally, she turned Senor B. Havior's mouth down stating that Joe was the cause. After class, Joe was penitent.

"Tell God I'm sorry," he told Dianne.

This is the response we should aim for.

47

The Word of God, hidden in a child's heart, can become the means God uses to keep that individual in His kingdom throughout a lifetime.

Remembering

BIBLE MEMORIZATION

Some teachers hold that what is memorized in early years is never really understood and, therefore, unnecessary. They say it is foolish to learn something that cannot be understood, and the result of such learning is merely parrot-like repetition. On the other side of the question, some argue that it is not necessary for children to understand all they memorize. What children learn in early years they will remember longest in life. Understanding will come later and will benefit them then. Further, memorization is good mental exercise!

There is some truth to both sides of the question. Too much memory work in the Sunday School can bore the children. For children who do not memorize easily, it can become a mental block. Because of the embarrassment they feel over their inability to keep up, they stay home on Sunday morning. Too much time spent on memory work takes precious time from the lesson period, often too short anyway.

Arguments in favor of memorization are more numerous and more convincing than those against it. Memorization for memorization's sake may not be of much value, but memorization with a purpose, as a means to an end, is good. Public schools provide motives for memorization. One country schoolteacher required every pupil to learn and recite Edgar

Allen Poe's "The Raven" in its entirety. They did it to keep from failing in seventh grade.

What motives can Sunday Schools offer young people for learning God's Word?

1. *To know what they believe.* Untaught Christians are easy victims for false cults and perverters of Scripture. Christians need to know the Scripture to refute the lies.

2. *To have a pattern for Christian living.* In a world of television and movie idols, young people need a safe and sure guide. Should a Christian be different? How different? "Let no man despise thy youth," Paul advised. "Be thou an example of the believers." With the aid of a concordance, help the class select passages which answer questions about dress and conduct. A notebook or poster project would focus the points and aid memorization of them.

3. *To help them win others.* A youth became a Christian at the age of 16. He and two pals bought a set of Scripture memory cards and carried them constantly, to learn passages answering excuses and problems of the unsaved. They started young to win souls. After the war the youth barely finished college before he was called to be a pilot of a missionary plane. He won many to Christ before his plane crashed against the mountains of Maracaibo, Venezuela.

4. *To comfort others, and to be prepared for sorrow.* Everyone is eventually called upon to comfort a weeping friend, or to face the death of

Jo Taylor at Bible Baptist Church teaches memory work by means of a visual aid. (Bible Baptist Church, Lincoln, NB)

a loved one. Knowledge of God's Word will help one "over the hump" when the time comes. If students are forearmed by the Word of God, they will be able to put up a better fight against the temptation to despair. Dramatize in class the use of these Scriptures. Let someone be the representative of a false cult, and let a Christian answer his arguments by Scripture he has memorized. Role play grief, doubt, or soul-winning in the same way.

5. *To know the Lord Jesus Christ more fully.* Christ Himself knew the Scriptures. He quoted from them constantly in His earthly ministry, using them as absolute and final authority, showing thus their divine origin. A lesson on how He used the Scriptures will emphasize the need for His children to know how and when to use them. The Lord Jesus used the Scriptures in defense and as a weapon against Satan and His enemies. And, finally, He laid down His life in fulfillment of the Scriptures (Matthew 26:53,54).

6. *External motivation.* A reward can spell the difference between successful memorization and complete indifference to it. The reward may be an award to each one who completes a given passage. Or the teacher might have a 100 percent box, where memory work counts a certain percent and those who qualify reach into the box and "grab" a wrapped, inexpensive gift. A party or an outing might reward all who complete memory work. A pupil might receive recognition through a symbolic trophy.

Motivation could come from a multiple-part weekly award, as a shoe bag of construction paper with a shoe for each verse for each pupil. As each verse is learned, that "shoe" is placed in the bag; bags are taken home at the end of the quarter. Another multiple-part award might be a Holy Land village. Each pupil has a typical Israeli landscape scene. A small square house for each verse is attached to the scene with double-faced tape as a verse is learned. The village scene is carried home when completed. Other multiple-part objects are chains, a verse per link; fans, a verse per section, fastened with a brad; key rings of construction paper keys with imprinted reference, fastened by yarn or ribbon.

How to Drill in Class

Many pupils will not memorize at home. The following drill games make them eager to learn in class.

1. *Hangman.* On chalkboard or newsprint make a horizontal dash for each letter of each word in a verse, dividing words by vertical lines. Draw a scaffold at the end. As pupils name a letter of the alphabet, in turn, the teacher writes that letter in each blank where it goes. If a named letter is not in the verse, draw a circle for the head of the victim (the class or the devil). Each unused letter adds another part of

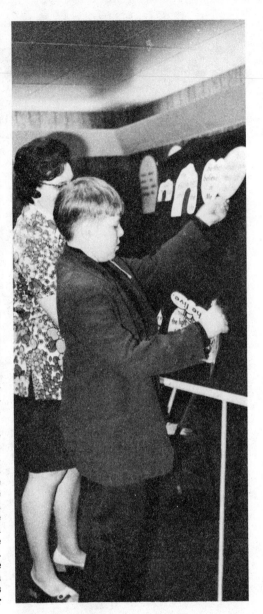

A pupil unscrambles the words of a verse on the flannelgraph board. (Indianapolis Baptist Temple, Indianapolis, IN)

the body. When someone recognizes the verse, complete it and read it together. Then the teacher may erase a few words as pupils shut their eyes. They open their eyes and read the verse again. Repeat the procedure till all is erased and they "read" from memory.

2. *Spelldown.* The old spelling-bee method is useful with juniors and older classes. Sides alternate in reciting verses or names of Bible books. When a pupil misses, he sits down.

3. *Scrambled verses.* On squares of felt, blotter paper, or vello, print the words of a Scripture verse and place them on the flannelgraph in jumbled order. Let pupils rearrange correctly. Vary by letting one group scramble, the next straighten. Each time a verse is corrected, let the entire group repeat it together.

4. *Magnet board.* Back card rectangles with tiny magnets. Print on each card a word of the verse. Scramble on magnet board and play as flannelgraph game.

5. *Dramatization.* Simple motions portray action of a verse.

6. *Role play and repetition.* Use with preschoolers and young primaries. Climax each dramatization with the correlated memory verse. The action associates the words with their meaning.

7. *Pocket chart.* Cut two-inch strips of cardboard into rectangles. On the top half of each print a word of the memory verse. Make or buy a chart with a number of pockets. Give each word to a pupil to place in a pocket in the order in which the word appears in the verse. When completed, all read the verse together. Chart may be bought at a school supply store or made of heavy wrapping paper.

8. *Bible baseball.* Questions "batted" are limited during memory drill to statements such as, "Repeat a verse which begins, 'Abstain from . . .' " Or if the drill is on Bible books, use questions such as, "What book comes after Judges?"

9. *Choral reading.* If the group is large, divide into two sides, with solo, duet, etc., for each side. Choose from each group a soloist, quartet, duet, indicating with raised fingers which is to read. The entire hand indicates all should read. Read the memory passage several times, directing as a choir. Each rereading for improvement impresses the memory.

10. *Progressive recitation.* Let each pupil in turn read one word of the verse. Then each remembers his one word and repeats it from memory the next time around. At each round, increase speed. Finally, all repeat each word together.

11. *Clothesline drill.* Attach one-word paper strips to a rope by clothespins, scrambling the order of a verse. Let pupils unscramble.

12. *Flash cards.* On cardboard rectangles print the first half of each verse. Flash the cards one at a time before the class. Whoever finishes the verse first may hold the card; the one with the most cards wins.

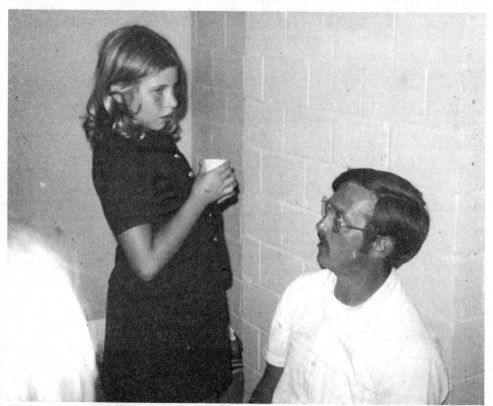

A junior girl at Bible Baptist Church recites a memory verse to helper, Randy Zachry. (Bible Baptist Church, Lincoln, NB)

13. *Key-word cards*. A flash-card drill, printing only the key word on the card.

14. *Singing Scripture*. Use choruses which are Scripture set to music. (John 3:16 fits into "Silent Night." "John 3:16, John 3:16, For God so loved the world that he . . ." etc.)

15. *King on the throne*. One student on a chair-throne wears a construction paper crown, as king (or queen). Others ask questions limited to memory verses. "What verse ends with *all?*" If the king cannot answer, but the questioner can, the questioner becomes king.

16. *Musical grab bag*. Print on strips of paper the references for verses learned. (Or print the words of verses, minus references.) Place in a paper bag, which is passed while piano or record player plays. As music stops, player with the bag must fish out a strip of paper. If a reference, he recites verse. If verse, he recites reference.

17. *Fishing*. On fish-shaped pieces of construction paper, print memory verse references. Place on each a paper clip. Put all in a bowl for a "pond." Attach a small magnet to a string tied to a dowel stick for a pole. Pupil casts line into the "pond." For whatever "fish" he catches, he recites the verse.

18. *Matching hide-and-seek*. Print memory verses on paper hearts at Valentine's Day, eggs at Easter, trees at Christmas, and so on. Cut the paper in half and hide the pieces. Pupils must find and match the halves, then partners recite verse together.

REVIEW GAMES

"Review" provides another look at stories and lessons to insure longer retention by pupils. Old-time teaching majored in the playback of facts drawn out by questions at the close of each lesson. Sometimes the teacher's confidence was bolstered by the expedient of yes or no questions.

Review games accomplish the same purpose as drill, with the added factor of interest. They review the previous lesson and lay again the groundwork on which the new lesson may be built. The introductory moments of a teaching session should allow five to seven minutes for a review game.

The following review games will recall the previous lesson and also reveal to the teacher where the class needs more instruction.

1. *Soldier game*. Put on a table a pile of from five to ten question cards concerning the past lesson for each child. The children are soldiers who, at the teacher's command, march around the table. At the order, "halt," each child draws a card. If the child correctly answers the question, he keeps the card. Any incorrectly answered cards are given to the teacher. The object is not to let the teacher get more cards than a soldier has. Primaries and juniors like

this game.

2. *Classroom basketball*. Make a hoop by attaching a rounded wire coat hanger to posterboard. A pair of socks or wadded-up paper can be the "ball." Prepare questions on recent stories. Divide the group into two teams. Each in turn tries a "foul shot" at the hoop-basket. If he makes a score, he gets to answer a question. He gets 5 points if he answers correctly. Then the other team has a turn. The team reaching 50 points wins.

3. *Question spinner*. Make a large posterboard circle. The "pointer" should be attached with a paper fastener, with a small circle of cardboard cut like a "washer." Make slits around the edge in which to insert small tabbed cards of questions about the previous lesson. (This would also be a good review during the last month of the quarter.) A pupil gives the spinner a whirl. When the pointer stops on a question, he answers. Allow 5 points for a correct answer. If the class is divided into two or more teams, the first to reach 50 points is the winner. Awards are optional.

4. *Magic pencil*. Make an oversize pencil from an empty cardboard roll with a thumbtack box at the eraser end and a pointed drinking cup as the point. Cover with bright contact paper or construction paper. Put on a label, "Magic pencil." Remove "eraser." Inside have slips of paper with names of Bible stories or characters. The game may be played by individual pupils. If a pupil draws the name of a character, he may act out or tell of an accomplishment of the character for the class to guess. If played by teams, Bible story names may be listed. A team must act out the story it draws, for the other team to guess.

5. *King on the throne*. Confining the questions to lessons studied during the past quarter, select one pupil as "king," seating him on the "throne" in the middle of the room. A construction paper crown will set him apart and add importance to his position. The others question the king concerning the lessons. As long as he can answer correctly, he stays on the throne. When he cannot answer a question, the one asking it may take his place, provided the questioner knows the answer.

6. *Picture map*. After studying events which took place in Bible lands, place a large outline map of this area at the front of the room. Small pictures identified with each lesson should be cut out or drawn for use. Teacher holds up picture and identifies it. She asks, "Who can pin this picture on the map where the story took place?" Scotch tape may be used instead of pins to make an attractive picture map for future reference.

7. *Pass the basket*. Let each pupil in turn select a folded question from a basket, read it aloud, and give his answer, if possible. Each time he answers correctly, he keeps the question slip. The basket is passed several times,

Puppets can provide a unique way to teach memory verses, give announcements or review lessons. Gil Gilmore uses a paper bag for his puppet stage. (First Baptist Church of West Hollywood, FL)

and the one who has been able to keep the most question slips is declared winner.

8. *Spelldown.* As in an old-fashioned spelling bee, pupils line up in even sides facing each other. When individuals correctly answer a question asked by the teacher, they remain in line. When they fail to answer, they must sit down. The winning side is the one with the largest number of players standing at the end of a given time.

9. *Wrong word story.* For each pupil make a copy of the story of the last lesson. Intentionally, insert wrong statements. Ask the pupils to underline each incorrect statement. The following is an example.

Underline the wrong statements in this story. There are six.

A young man who was rich came to Jesus one day to ask Him a question. It was the most important question anyone could ever ask. It was, "How can I *become very wise?*"

The man who asked the question was a good man. He kept God's laws. But he was not good enough. He loved the *Temple* more than he loved Jesus.

Jesus said, "Go and sell *half* of everything you own and come and give it *to Me.*"

The *old man* was very sad. He could not have eternal life because *he did not have enough money.*

10. *Riddle cards.* On one side of 3 × 5 cards print "Who am I," "What am I?" or "Who said?" questions. For example: "I was one of Peter's helpers. I was a lady. I was kind to

people. I sewed clothes for people who needed them. Who am I?" On the back of the card print the answer (Dorcas). You can use the riddle cards during presession or during review time.

11. *Twenty questions—or less.* List on chalkboard names of ten characters recently studied. Ask one pupil to stand up while the other pupils ask him questions about the character he secretly chooses to be. In one class a boy chose to be Peter. The pupils quickly caught on and fired questions. Some were off base, but when one boy established that the subject had once been nicknamed "The Rock," half a dozen youngsters guessed, "Peter!" It took five questions.

The question, "Were you a short man?" identified Zaccheus.

If some children have trouble selecting anyone to impersonate, write after each name a short Bible reference they may look up.

12. *A matching test.* Write on the chalkboard questions based on the quarter's work. Put the answers on the board, but not in the same order. Pupils then choose the right answers for the questions. Number both lists, so pupils need only write the number of the correct answer beside the number of the question.

13. *Multiple-choice questions.* Compile questions, each with several answers. Give each student a sheet of paper and a pencil and read each question and its possible answers. Students write down the number of the right answer. Or they may be given a paper with questions printed and be asked to underline the correct answer.

14. *Object box.* An "object box" provides intriguing review for juniors. In a shoe box put objects representing facts in stories. At the close of a study on the journeys of Paul, for instance, objects would represent his experiences. Have an opening large enough for the child's hand to reach in easily and pull out a small article, without exposing the entire contents. Suggested objects are a small boat (the shipwreck), a stone (stoning of Stephen which resulted in Paul's conversion), a purple crayon (the meeting with Lydia, seller of purple), a piece of chain (prison, or imprisoning of Christians), a silver object (Diana of the Ephesians), a small basket (Paul's escape in a basket let down over the wall), a light bulb or a flashlight (the light that blinded him at conversion), flowers or a wreath (Paul and Barnabas being worshipped at Lystra).

15. *A take-home test.* At the close of a lesson give each pupil a paper with a puzzle, sentences with blanks to fill in, or multiple-choice questions. At the top put the Bible references where answers are found. Ask pupils to write the answers down and bring them back the next Sunday. Urging students to keep the papers in their Bibles may prevent the papers from getting lost or misplaced at home.

16. *Build the church.* Draw and cut from heavy paper a large church with two windows and a door. Cut out the windows and door. Cut the church into pieces as follows: left section of church, right section of church, steeple, window, window, and door. Write a question about the last lesson on the back of each part.

Give the sections of the church building to six members. They may ask the questions of other members. As the questions are answered, let pupils construct the church building by placing the sections on the wall or tackboard, using Plasti-Tak, Scotch tape, or thumbtacks. Bibles may be used, if needed, to answer the questions.

Any large object may be similarly cut up and reconstructed—piano, house, car, etc.

17. *Scrambled puzzles.* Jumble and print letters of a Bible name on a sheet of paper. Put a clue at the bottom. Give one puzzle to each class member and allow time to unscramble the name. Use several different names. Discuss answers.

18. *Grab bag.* Put questions into a paper sack and let each pupil reach in and grab a question. Competition may be individual or team. On teams, members may consult with each other or may be individually responsible for the answers. Play musical grab bag by passing the sack while music continues. When music stops, the one who holds the bag takes out a question and answers or refers it to the class.

19. *Charades.* This old party game may be given a Sunday School twist. Teams of pupils take turns representing briefly an incident or story in past lessons and the others guess which one it is.

20. *Matching words.* In one column on the chalkboard put a list of towns, people, mountains, etc., covered in recent lessons. In another column put the event or the name of another person connected with each item in the first column. Jumble the order and let pupils come, one at a time, and draw a line from a name to the correct event or place.

21. *Rhyming review.* Draw on the chalkboard two long lines, with rhyming words at the end, such as *boy* and *joy.* Ask what phrase ending with boy will describe something in the last lesson. ("A small lunch in the hands of a little boy") Do the same for the next line (something like "was used by Jesus to bring a crowd joy.")

22. *Rebus puzzle.* Draw on chalkboard simple pictures of objects. Under each picture, put a blank for each letter of the name of the object. Lead the class in filling in the blanks. Show how to cross out letters of words after a minus sign. For young primaries or a class new to the game, make the puzzle only four pictures at first, as: picture one, plus picture two, minus picture three equals picture four. (Example: PLANT + SKATE - TANK = PLATES.)

48

The retarded, the deaf, the handicapped, shut-ins—these neglected people can be reached with the Gospel by churches which have the vision and are willing to learn how.

Special Ministries

MINISTRY TO THE RETARDED

"Preach the Gospel to every creature" must be construed to mean all persons, in all circumstances. Therefore, the Great Commission must include a Sunday School class for the mentally retarded.

There are many misconceptions regarding the mentally retarded. The most erroneous judgment is that he is insane—i.e., that he has mental illness. This is not so. The mentally retarded person has not grown at the expected rate of development or has not completed the growth cycle. There are two classes of the "exceptional" people: (1) The trainable has an IQ of 30-55 and (2) the educable has an IQ of 55-80. The public schools usually have special education classes for the educable. At times the educable are found in regular public school classes. If they attend Sunday School, they are usually enrolled in the regular age-level class. Most trainables, however, do not go to school, except in a few cases where there are institutional schools. Only a few churches have classes for the trainable.

Mental retardation is usually the result of a brain injury at birth or serious illness. In this broad classification are mongolism, cerebral palsy, retarded emotional growth, and such physical complications as sight and hearing handicaps, slow and incomplete motor-ability development, and mild forms of epilepsy.

The Sunday School is lagging behind in reaching and teaching the mentally retarded even though attempts now are being made to rectify the situation. There are several reasons why the Sunday School has done so little in this area.

1. *Confused parents.* Some parents may shut their eyes to the facts of their child's learning ability. They are so eager to believe the child is normal they will not face the fact that he needs a special kind of teaching. Therefore they subject him to the disadvantage of being placed with others his age, with whom he cannot keep up.

2. *Lack of teachers.* Many Sunday Schools find it hard to secure enough teachers to staff all classes in the regular age-group divisions. Even if they are aware of the need for a special education class, there is no one to teach it.

3. *Lack of training.* As with other forms of Sunday School teaching, there may be some who are willing to serve as teachers in a special education class, perhaps out of compassion for the retarded ones. But because of their inability to express Bible truths on a level where they may be grasped, their efforts are of no avail.

4. *Unkind teasing by other children.* "He's a dummy" may be bluntly stated by a child who sees the slow comprehension of a retardate. Unfortunately, the slow one often fully comprehends that he is the object of ridicule. He may shrink from going again to the Sunday School where he was embarrassed.

Remedies

The attitudes can be corrected. Sometimes it is the parents who must make the first move.

1. *Accept the child for what he is.* When parents accept the limitations of their retarded child and love him and make him part of the family's experiences, they go far toward assuring his acceptance by their church friends.

2. *Pastoral influence.* Special recognition may be given to the progress of mentally retarded pupils in the Sunday School. When appropriate, the pastor can go far toward reinforcing their self-confidence by a word of praise—publicly as well as privately. Because he is usually the one who enlists workers for the various classes in the Sunday School, he should also be quick to praise the faithful ministry of the teachers of the mentally retarded.

3. *Training.* A willing Christian may be unable to attend a university for special training in teaching the retarded. She will find much valuable guidance in the book by this author and Roberta Groff, *Successful Ministry to the Retarded.* Suggestions are drawn from its pages.

4. *Compassionate teachers of other classes.* An observant teacher usually has opportunity to learn of the taunting of a slow learner. It is not amiss for the teacher to illustrate this unfairness through a lesson on kindness and Christian love. Telling a story of a similar problem, he can point out the hurt and tell his pupils to avoid being cruel and to use their influence to stop others from unkindness.

Problems of the Mentally Retarded

While generalizations cannot be made, researchers have found that the chief problems of the trainable retarded are due to the fact that they have one or more of these groups of characteristics:

1. Shy, fearful, tense.
2. Hyperactive, nervous.
3. Attention-seekers.
4. Short in attention span.
5. Stubborn, obstinate.
6. Poor in communication.
7. Poor in motor ability.
8. Mischievous, destructive.
9. Aggressive.
10. Emotionally unstable.
11. Withdrawn.
12. Infantile, immature.

With this imposing list, the question comes, "Who would want to cope with children with these traits?" The answer—"A teacher who realizes that they have eternal souls, and that many of them can choose between right and wrong."

The Teacher

All the qualifications stated for any Sunday School teacher are required by the teacher of the mentally retarded, plus a double portion of some, such as:

1. *Love.* The retarded one, sometimes unwanted in his own family or perhaps institutionalized, may never have known the touch of Christian love before he came to Sunday School. He is most responsive.

2. *Wisdom.* "Let him (her) ask of God," for the child with the crippled mind reacts to social contacts in an unorthodox manner. Discipline requires knowledge of how to avoid causing frustration, when and how to offer reinforcing praise, even how to cope with a destructive temper tantrum.

3. *Patience.* There is no doubt that patience must be the end product of meeting the challenge of children with multiplied problems. It is also prerequisite from the start.

The Lessons

1. *Literal.* Like the normal toddler or preschooler, the trainable retarded can grasp the truths of God's greatness in Creation, His love expressed through His gifts, His desire for obedience through the experiences of Bible characters. However, since the retarded child does not reason, he cannot comprehend the idea of an object representing a truth.

2. *Visualized.* Even more than the normal learner, the retarded needs visuals as an aid to understanding and to strengthen memory retention.

3. *Undistracted.* Because his attention span is minimal, the retarded pupil should be in a classroom with the least interruptions. Quiet, neat and attractive surroundings have a soothing effect. Too much brilliance in color could prove distracting. A carpeted floor would help muffle some of the sound of feet during activities. And the classroom for the special education class should not be in a department area where other children's classes are in session and where voices carry.

Activities

1. *Music.* The alert teacher will carefully watch the effects of certain songs on her class. If overexcitement propels pupils towards hyperactivity, the tune must be changed. This group of pupils likes music and is responsive. Wise selection of songs can set the tone for a good lesson period.

2. *Handwork.* The criteria for appropriate handwork for these slow learners are (a) simplicity, (b) usefulness, and (c) interest. Great care must be exercised to guide in the making of any article. Much encouragement and praise are needed for children who may have extreme insecurity. Criticism should be positive, rather than negative. "Let's do it this way," instead of, "Don't do it that way" is the proper way to correct.

3. *Role play.* Like normal 4s and 5s, the trainables enjoy simultaneous role play, when

all in the group perform an action in the story. For example, all can stand as angels, arms extended, saying, "Fear not," to the women at the empty tomb of Jesus. All can walk (in a circle) the long road to Jerusalem with the 12-year-old Jesus. Familiar with make-believe, one child alone often will become brave enough to take a part by himself.

4. *Puppets.* Shy retarded children will find in puppets the same security other children find. They can express their feelings and reactions through the actions and speech of puppets, thereby revealing much about themselves to the teacher.

Can the Retarded Be Saved?

While the theological implications of the question have been argued pro and con by church leaders through the centuries, their teachers have found that the trainable as well as the educable usually have a sense of right and wrong. They feel the need of God. Because their understanding is childlike, the Gospel must be presented to them as to a very small child. They can be shown that "all have sinned" (Romans 3:23); that "The wages of sin is death but the gift of God is eternal life through Jesus Christ our Lord" (Romans 6:23); and that "Christ died for our sins" (Romans 5:8).

While some may not understand the way of salvation, all should be given the opportunity of a careful, clear explanation.

MINISTRY TO THE DEAF

"There are not enough deaf people in our community to have a class for them," a church sometimes excuses its lack of ministry. How many constitute enough for a class? Recall that Mark Hopkins' definition of a school was "the teacher at one end of a log and the student at the other."

Let's consider first the church where several deaf attend.

The Class for Deaf

1. *Equipment.* The usual comfortable, lighted, ventilated room is necessary. Furnishings should include a chalkboard, an easel for flannelgraph and/or charts, Bibles, pencils and paper, pictures.

2. *Curriculum.* Teaching materials to be read by the deaf in preparation for their lesson should be written especially for them. Their language is less complex at the same age and grade level than that of hearing persons. Denominational publications often make provision for such literature. If a church writes its own materials, a deaf Christian or one who understands their language limitations should prepare it.

This class for the retarded encourages its members to develop their musical talent. (Indianapolis Baptist Temple, Indianapolis)

Subject matter will depend upon the spiritual and Biblical progress of the deaf person. Some deaf are not exposed to Christian teaching at an early age in the home. They may come to church with no understanding of stories and truths that other children absorb without effort. A good place to begin is where Paul began in dealing with the people of Athens: "God who made heaven and earth and everything also made you. And He has a plan for you."

3. *Procedure.* "Use the deaf sign language" may seem to be a simple description of procedure. Those who teach the deaf regularly have discovered it is not simple. There sometimes are distractions. Since the deaf hear with their eyes, when their attention is distracted for any reason, they miss what the teacher is "saying" with signs. Also, among the deaf as among the hearing, there may be boredom. If a deaf person wants to turn off the teacher and the teaching, he needs only to lower his eyes. This shuts out communication.

The concerned teacher of the deaf will not be content with merely using the sign language. To enliven interest and clarify difficult points he will use:

a. Chalkboard. "I use the chalkboard to write a question for the class to think about, or a Bible verse to be stressed or learned," said Mrs. Pepper Moore, for many years interpreter and teacher of the deaf at First Baptist Church, Nashville, Tenn.

b. Flannelgraph. The intrigue of pictures adhering to the board will capture attention and focus eyes on the explaining signs.

c. Drama. Signs may spell out words for which the deaf have no basis on which to build understanding. "David hit Goliath with a stone from his slingshot and the giant fell down." The teacher may state the facts with signs and then literally act out the facts. (Actions are the oldest international sign language.)

d. Puppets. With interpretation, the deaf can and do follow the meaning of a Bible puppet presentation.

e. Charts. A chart may hold the outline of the principle points of a lesson. For greatest attention, the strip chart or link chart, revealing one point at a time, will be most effective.

f. In more advanced classes, the deaf can participate in role play. The entire drama may be pantomimed without the need for sign language.

A Class with One or Two Deaf

Should the deaf child who comes home from a school for the deaf be ignored in a Sunday School class? Should he be treated as though he were hearing? The problem is not one to be ignored. Ministering to the spiritual needs of a deaf child may mean winning a family.

1. *A church class in sign language.* In areas where deaf children are present occasionally in

classes, a church may form a Sunday nignt class in sign language, taught by an interpreter from a church which has a deaf ministry.

2. *Seat the child with interpreter.* When the deaf child is present in class, allow space beside him for the interpreter. This helps him understand what is going on, even though the interpreter may not be an expert.

3. *Use visual aids.* Use the chalkboard to write out unusual names, places, Bible references. Show pictures that tell the essence of the story.

4. *Encourage participation.* In playing review games, allow the deaf child to respond, through the interpreter. Let him feel he is part of the class. He will enjoy participating in role play.

Special Services to Deaf

Often a teacher of the deaf will discover he is the only link between the deaf and the complicated world about him. He will have occasion to render him many special services, such as:

1. *Medical.* Few doctors are prepared to understand the symptoms of the deaf. An interpreter is necessary to help the medical man know what is needed and to help the patient understand the treatment prescribed and be able to follow it. In some cases he will also have to interpret to the patient's family.

2. *Legal.* A deaf person may need to draw up a will, to buy a house or a car, or face some other legal problem with which he cannot cope. A Christian teacher-friend who is concerned about him can make sure those involved have full and correct understanding of the case.

3. *Emotional.* Deaf persons meet problems of

The class for the deaf at Indianapolis Baptist Temple has a large attendance. (Indianapolis Baptist Temple, Indianapolis, IN)

life, just as hearing persons do. In case of serious illness, death in the family, grave injustice, lies, or other hurtful experience, the deaf need someone to guide their thinking toward the Christian view of the problem. Deaf youth have need of counsel in friendships, the same as hearing youth.

4. *Shopping.* A deaf person may need assistance in making large purchases. He cannot make himself understood to the sales clerk, nor can the clerk explain style, colors, materials or costs to him.

5. *Spiritual.* While a deaf person may "hear" the preacher's message via an interpreter, and respond to the invitation, very often winning the deaf is done on a one-to-one basis. Knowing, trusting, loving the teacher, the deaf has confidence in the teacher's concern for his soul. When he understands his spiritual need, he seeks the help of the one who cares. It is imperative for the teacher of the deaf to know how to lead a soul to Christ.

MINISTRY TO THE HANDICAPPED

Definition

A handicapped child is one who, by reason of physical or psychological or emotional problems, is unable to benefit from the regular instruction provided to "normal" children.

1. *Mentally retarded.* (See the previous chapter on the Sunday School's ministry to the retarded.)

2. *Slow learner.* This child's IQ is just above that of the educable retarded. In most Sunday Schools, he is placed in the regular class of normal children.

3. *Super-intelligent.* Some children with an above-average IQ find instruction in a normal routine to be lacking in interest and challenge for them.

4. *Hard of hearing.* (See the previous chapter on ministering to the deaf.)

5. *Physically handicapped.* In this category are children who cannot walk or talk normally due to cerebral palsy, birth injury or polio or some other disabling disease, and those with an inherent heart weakness or other limiting condition.

6. *Blind.* While the blind student usually is in a state school for the blind much of the year, he will spend vacation times at home and accompany his family to their regular church. Older blind persons also may attend.

Special Education

The public school has for many years provided classes in special education, to meet the needs of children with some type of variation from normality. Such classes may require an environment, equipment and teaching methods exceeding those for the normal pupils.

1. *Classroom.* The room size and location should be adapted to the need. If a wheelchair patient is to be a regular pupil in a classroom, the room should be large enough so that the wheelchair will not have to be the center of attention. A ramp will be needed for any area of stairs.

2. *Seating arrangement.* A pupil with an impairment of vision or hearing (but neither blind or deaf) may need a seat near the teacher in

329

At Bellevue Baptist a medical doctor teaches the class for handicapped youngsters. She is highly skilled in ministering to the needs of these children. (Bellevue Baptist Church, Memphis, TN)

order to share in the sights and sounds of the lesson.

3. *Room decoration.* Subdued, neutral colors—such as soft green, blue or buff walls and a charcoal or green floor covering—will serve as calming factors to children who tend to be hyperactive or easily excitable. Cheerfulness without gaudiness is the rule.

4. *Methods.* In the methods section of this volume are many suggestions for visual aids which will help make lessons clear to slow learners. During picture studies, activity games, puppet presentations, role play or other group-involvement procedures, the teacher will need to be sure the handicapped child is able to participate in accordance with his ability. He, too, learns most by *doing.* In fact, he may learn more than some of his less-afflicted peers. His eagerness may exceed theirs, as may his future use of the knowledge gained.

While most Sunday School teachers are unable to have the special training required for teaching all pupils with a disability, they have God's promise to supply the wisdom needed if they will ask for it (James 1:5).

5. *Counseling.* Handicapped persons—even children—often are well aware that they are different from others. This causes grief to some

An interesting new technique uses the disabled to teach the disabled. Here special educator Joan Mallery watches a Bible study in progress. (Melodyland Christian Center)

330

whose body has not kept pace with their mental growth. The Sunday School teacher may be the one who must counsel with parents as well as child, in an effort to impart courage and determination to both. Illustrations abound of handicapped persons who have excelled in life. One need only remember perhaps the most extreme case of all—Helen Keller—to know that God can use any life truly dedicated to Him. He asks no more than an individual is able to give.

Some challenging books have been written by specialists in the field of special education. A teacher of the handicapped would profit by reading: *Why Can't I Learn?* by Robert Carpenter (Regal); *P.S. You're Not Listening,* by Eleanor Craig (R.W. Baron); *None of These Diseases,* by S.I. McMillen (Revell).

THE HOME DEPARTMENT

Sometimes called the extension department, the home department ministers to persons who, through disability, age or employment, are unable to attend Sunday School. The Sunday School goes to them instead. In the last few years this department has expanded with the increase of senior citizens' homes and nursing homes.

Purpose
1. *Provide fellowship.* Any department's outreach results in fellowship with other Christians. So the home department provides fellowship for persons whose only contact with other believers may be the department visitor's call. Elderly saints who can do little but sit in a wheelchair and pray may feel useless and unwanted by the church. The brief weekly fellowship is a link with the church.
2. *Provide instruction.* The extension department reaches pupils of many levels of understanding, education and mental standing, education and mental capacity. They need personalized, individual instruction. Such instruction may not be formal or structured as a lesson in the classroom, but it will impart fresh insight into the Word of God.
3. *Provide opportunity to participate.* Shut-ins may feel left out of the work of a church they may have served long and faithfully during their prime years. The home visitor may give the shut-in a chance to contribute the tithe of his small pension. Shut-ins should have the joy of giving as God commanded—and receiving the blessings He promised.
4. *Provide assistance in getting medical or material aid.* Elderly persons with no nearby relatives may need assistance getting to doctor's appointments, shopping for groceries or running other errands. A regular visitor will discover the needs and render or secure help.
5. *Provide a tie with the church.* In the case of a doctor, nurse, shift worker or other employed person whose hours prevent Sunday School attendance, the extension department is a tie to the church. Such people sometimes feel isolated from the church. The brief lesson presentation gives the worker a feeling of belonging.
6. *Win the unsaved.* The home visitor learns the spiritual status of the shut-in during the conversations and study. The quiet talks together about the Word of God are natural openings to make sure the shut-in is right with God.

Procedure
1. *Find the pupils.* Several avenues of search are open:
   a. The pastor and the house-to-house visitors for the church will know the names and addresses of persons unable to come to services. The roll of the home department need not include only those on the church roll. The church worker may win unchurched shut-ins to the Lord.
   b. Check the yellow pages of the telephone book for nursing homes and other community institutions where a weekly or monthly meeting or study could be held.
   c. Make a house-to-house canvass. In cities where the church serves a large residential area, volunteers should go from house to house to discover if there are persons who should be ministered to in the homes.
2. *Set up a record system.* The secretary will make an alphabetical card file and note information regarding the needs or spiritual status of home department pupils. Visits and ministry will be recorded.
3. *Assign visits to regular teachers.* Pupils in the homes expect to see the same teacher each week, just as do pupils in the church. Only when they know and trust a teacher can that teacher be of real spiritual aid.
4. *Set the visitation time.* The time cannot be arbitrarily arranged by the church. Each teacher must consider the convenience of the shut-in and those who take care of that one. The nursing home and institution schedules must be considered.
5. *Choose the curriculum.* Unless an extension department program is published by the denomination, the superintendent and teachers must plan with the shut-ins for the course of study. An elderly Christian, for instance, may have a preference that should be considered.
6. *Secure an adult class sponsor.* While the actual visits and teaching will be done by the home department, the responsibility for preparing small gifts, planning for large occasions, preparing food (where needed) should be shared by the members of an adult class. This relieves some of the load from the extension workers and at the same time gives service opportunities for adults who may not otherwise be serving the church.

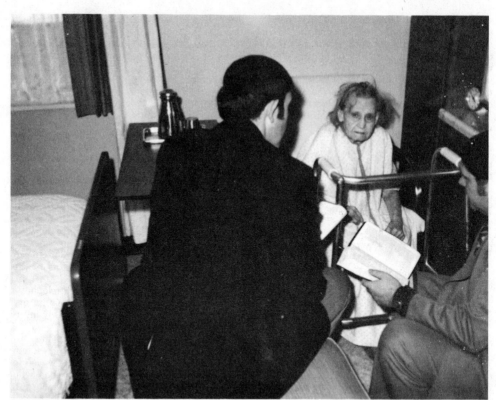

When people cannot go to Sunday School, the Sunday School can go to them. (Indianapolis Baptist Temple, Indianapolis, IN)

Personnel

1. *The superintendent.* Each department of the Sunday School must have a director. The home department superintendent will guide the work, evaluate the progress, enlist and train teachers, help with the visitation.

2. *A secretary.* The secretary will keep careful card records on each member on the extension roll. The name of the visitor in charge of each enrollee will be stated on the card, for quick reference in time of need.

3. *Teachers.* The number of teachers depends on the number of persons enrolled. Since weekly contacts are best for greatest spiritual help, one teacher should not be expected to visit more than three homes every week—although many extension workers can and do.

Program

1. *The curriculum.* A denomination's curriculum usually includes study materials in the form of quarterly magazines for both pupils and teachers. If no such literature is provided by the church, the superintendents and teachers should select the Bible book to be studied. (See number 5 under Procedure.)

2. *The teaching unit.* As with any house call, actual teaching is preceded by friendly exchange of conversation. If a shut-in is the subject of ministry, often he or she will want to sing a familiar hymn and may join with wavering voice and faulty memory. The actual teaching period usually should not exceed fifteen minutes, especially in cases of elderly persons. Give pupils opportunity for response. Allow time at the close for exchange of library books.

3. *Variations.* From time to time arrange for a group of juniors or young people from the church to go along and sing for the extension enrollee. Take a small gift, or even a large gift, as at Christmas and birthdays.

4. *Provide the pupil a chance to serve.* Plan not only to receive any money offering the pupil may present, but give opportunity for shut-in or employed enrollee to perform tasks within his strength and ability, at home, to help the church. Even wheelchair patients may be able to prepare handwork materials for Sunday School or Vacation Bible School, stuff envelopes for church mail-outs, make clothing for missionary projects, make telephone calls for revivals or conferences, and other tasks.

More than any able-bodied church member, the home department shut-in pupil needs to feel useful and wanted. The teacher will render greatest service who succeeds in creating that feeling by giving the opportunity to share.

section VIII

Origin of the
Sunday School

49

The founder of the first Sunday School did not wait for his pupils to come to the meeting place. He went to their homes and brought them. If they did not have suitable clothing to wear, he bought it for them.

The History of Sunday School[1]

Robert Raikes, the founder of the Sunday School, became a newspaper editor at age 22. He took over *The Gloucester Journal* from his father in 1757. People called him "Buck Raikes, the dandy," because of his immaculate attire. His children grew up in the clean comfort of a good home. They went to church every Sunday. In an effort to improve the beauty of that good home, the publisher went one afternoon to the rough slum district in search of a gardener. He was jostled by a gang of ragged boys. He expressed his shock and pity to the gardener's wife.

"You ought to see them on Sunday, when the factory is closed and they have nothing to do but get in trouble," she responded. Apparently, they did everything in the book.

Raikes was a churchman who carried his religion into his business. He had been concerned about the plight of poor men and women who frequently crowded the city jail for the most trivial offenses. He wrote editorials against conditions in the jail. He went to the jail, handing Bibles to the few who could read. Raikes stayed to read the Word to some who could not.

After his rough reception in the slums, Robert Raikes extended his concern to the children left at home alone while parents served their undeserved sentences. With hate, fear and ignorance filling their lives, they had no chance to be other than the half-wild creatures he had seen. Raikes took the problem to the Reverend Thomas Stock.

The pastor collected names and addresses of 90 children in his own parish, and together the two men put on a strenuous visitation campaign. If they expected a warm reception everywhere, they were disappointed. Some of the parents cursed them. But in time they gathered a class into the kitchen of a Christian woman, Mrs. Meredith. The minister became the first Sunday School superintendent and Mrs. Meredith at first did the teaching.

Robert Raikes did not start his Sunday School merely by announcing time and place. He went to the homes and brought the pupils. If some did not have sufficient clothing to come, he bought it for them. What was the price of a pair of shoes or a pair of trousers, when the investment netted a life in return? Many of his biographers claimed that Raikes marched unwilling pupils to the class with their feet hobbled like animals. One of those pupils later gave an explanation. It was the parents of some of the wild urchins who put on the hobbles to make sure they got to school. Raikes' pupils learned to read, and they read Bible lessons directly from the Bible. Raikes also wrote four textbooks used in Sunday School.

[1]Printed by permission of Regal Publishing Company, Nashville, Tennessee, from *The Bicentennial Sunday School Bible*.

Many early Sunday Schools were located in the country. This old picture shows pupils after the class session. (Museum of Sunday School Heritage, Savannah, GA)

Robert Raikes thus began "planting the seed." His pupils would grow up to become godly parents and, in turn, raise godly children. Thus began the work of lifting the city from the mire of godlessness into which it had sunk. Taught to read and encouraged to read the Word of God, the boys and girls in those first classes began to respond. The Sunday School areas became the most orderly in the city of Gloucester.

Not until three years later did Raikes use his newspaper as a platform to promote the Sunday School. When the evidence was indisputable, he informed his readers that his thesis had been correct. Starting with the children, the lives of the slum-dwellers were being transformed. His enthusiastic report caught the eyes of Christian leaders in other vice-ridden areas; they responded to the plea of Robert Raikes and started Sunday Schools throughout the nation. John Wesley urged, "There must be a Sunday School wherever there is a Methodist Society."

The first Sunday School began at 10:00 in the morning. At 12:00 they had a break, then returned for another lesson. Then it was time for the whole group to be taken to church. This at first was as disagreeable to the parishioners as to the urchins.

At first only boys were enrolled, but almost immediately both boys and girls were accepted. Discipline problems were many and severe among the lawless scholars. Indeed, the children were so unruly that the first teacher, Mrs. Meredith, resigned from her post shortly. The work moved to the kitchen of Mrs. Chritchley. The school's founder himself and a helper accompanied the offenders to their homes, watched while the punishing wallops were administered, and brought the chastened pupils back to class. No doubt the fact that the first teachers were paid for their services and for the use of the kitchen slightly eased the task.

However, Robert Raikes suggested that instructors, as well as monitors, should be volunteers. (His classes employed the system of using advanced pupils to help teach the younger children.) As Sunday School became increasingly a religious agency, Raikes's conviction grew that the workers should be voluntary.

In a letter Robert Raikes reported that in four years the Sunday School average enrollment reached 250,000 children. The 1785 "Society for the Support and Encouragement of Sunday Schools Throughout the British Dominions" (understandably shortened to "The Sunday School Society") was largely responsible for the rapid expansion of the movement. Their effort and finances founded and financed the schools.

Robert Raikes died in 1811. By the time a statue was erected in his memory in 1831, Sunday Schools in Great Britain were ministering weekly to 1,250,000 children.

THE AMERICAN
SUNDAY SCHOOL MOVEMENT

The people of Savannah, Georgia, claim that the Sunday School started 50 years before Raikes when John Wesley taught the children there on Sunday afternoons. Even though Wesley did instruct children, his classes are not technically considered a Sunday School because his efforts concerned the children of Christians, catechism instruction, and the aim of edification. A Sunday School has four unique characteristics: (a) it reaches both Christian and unsaved children; (b) its curriculum is the Word of God, rather than the catechism; (c) the purpose is to reach children for Christ through the ministry of teaching, rather than strictly edifying the children of the faithful; and (d) Sunday School is operated by laymen, whereas Wesley was a clergyman. This unique nature of the Sunday School cancels out Wesley's claim and reinforces Raikes' position as founder.

The first recorded American Sunday School was held in 1785 at Oak Grove, Virginia, by William Elliot. Both whites and blacks were instructed but at separate hours.

The Methodists were among the first to start Sunday Schools, hence their phenomenal growth as a denomination in the United States. Francis Asbury established a Sunday School in Virginia in 1786. In rapid succession Sunday Schools sprang up in South Carolina, Maryland, Rhode Island, New York and Pennsylvania. Within 11 years after Robert Raikes began the first Sunday School in England, a new Sunday School Society organized in Philadelphia in 1791. Within three months they raised $3,968 for the establishment of Sunday Schools. Sunday School societies appeared in other cities.

Sunday Schools mushroomed over the United States, tied heavily to evangelism, whereas the movement in England was tied heavily to general education. Denominations began organizing their own Sunday Schools as they saw their children going to interdenominational agencies. The movement grew at first in the established eastern seaboard cities.

From the early days Sunday School had contests. Robert Raikes gave away books, shoes, and pants for faithful attendance. Once he offered a $20 gold piece to any boy who could memorize the book of Proverbs. Toward the end of the 1700s the Christ Congregational Church, New York, gave a silver medal to the scholar bringing the most visitors during the year.

Lowell Mason, the song writer, and superintendent of the Savannah (Ga.) Sabbath School, wrote out this regulation in 1818, "Tickets are given for good behavior in school and in church, for diligently attending to lessons and memorizing Scripture. Extra tickets shall be given for extra lessons, discretionally by the teacher." Mason also wrote, "Anyone

One of the early books published by the American Sunday School Union. A Sunday School could not be certified unless it had a library. In 1859 over 30,000 of the 50,000 libraries in the U.S. were in Sunday Schools. (Museum of Sunday School Heritage, Savannah, GA)

who procures a new scholar shall receive a monthly ticket." A ticket was worth 1/16 of a dollar and could be exchanged for books.

Around 1825 the Mississippi Valley enterprise captured the imagination of Sunday School leaders on the eastern seaboard. The area west of the Alleghenies to the Rocky Mountains had a population of four million people in 1,300,000 square miles. The area was almost void of religious influence. The American Sunday School Union spearheaded a massive evangelistic thrust. In May 1830 they made a resolution to start a Sunday School in every town in the Mississippi Valley. They wanted to complete the project in two years. Two thousand people unanimously voted and subscribed over $17,000 to the project. Large gatherings in Boston, Washington and Charleston kicked off the project, including United States senators, representatives, and notables such as Daniel Webster and Francis Scott Key. Over 80 missionaries were employed and sent out. They planted libraries throughout the Midwest, each costing approximately $10 for over 50 books. It has been estimated that over one million volumes were thus placed in circulation, giving further momentum to the growth of literacy in the United States.

One of the most renowned of those missionaries was a man in the pioneer territory of Illinois, himself reached for Christ through the American Sunday School Union. "Stuttering Stephen" Paxson had overcome the double handicap of a limp and a stammer to become a successful hatter—and the favorite fiddler for the Saturday night square dance in Winchester, Illinois.

"I'll get a star if I bring a new scholar to Sunday School," said his little daughter, Mary one Sunday. She had decided that her father would be her scholar. The tired dance fiddler went,

and he found himself sitting in a class of boys who helped explain to him the hard words of the lesson. In a short time he learned that God had a place for music in His program, and Paxson's fiddle added to the enjoyment of the services. It soon became apparent that God had other plans for him in His program.

Through an American Sunday School Union missionary, Paxson caught the vision of the great task the Union had laid out. Moving his little family to the Mississippi Valley nearer the action, he set out on his horse to establish Sunday Schools. Over the next 25 years horse and

Circuit riders started some of the early Sunday Schools on the frontier. (Religious News Service Photo)

rider traveled 100,000 miles. The animal habitually stopped to wait for Stephen Paxson to speak to any child they passed. Eighty-three thousand children were reached for God in the 1,314 Sunday Schools established by this zealous missionary.

During the next 50 years 80 percent of all the churches in the Mississippi Valley came out of Sunday Schools. In one year alone 17,000 people made professions of faith. From 1824 to 1874 there were 61,299 Sunday Schools organized, with 407,244 teachers and 2,650,784 pupils. The total amount spent on this endeavor was $2,133,364. As one observer noted, never has so much been accomplished for God with such a small down payment. Another stated, "We could not do it today—that is, start a Sunday School for $1 per person." But there were a lot of people who were willing to sacrifice in those days.

Clarence Benson, writer on the Sunday School, called that era "the Babel period" because there was no Sunday School literature. Each teacher taught the Word of God as best he could. Many Sunday Schools during this period followed the successful technique later used by the Ten Largest Sunday Schools, where the pastor instructs his people at the teachers' meeting. On Sunday the teachers give the identical lesson to their pupils.

Sunday School took a decided upturn immediately after the war between the states. Mr. Vincent, a Methodist minister, published *The Sunday School Teacher* in 1866, in which he called for a curriculum that would comprehensively and consistently cover the Scripture. Out of this grew a curriculum that most denominations followed. The International Uniform Lesson came into existence. The *Sunday School Times,* first published in 1866, became the vehicle to spread Sunday School lessons throughout America. At one time it had the largest circulation of any magazine in the United States.

Massive Sunday School conventions also grew after the war between the states, although the conventions had been officially organized earlier. The first International Convention was held in Baltimore in 1875. That year 71,272 Sunday Schools existed in America. Each year the size of the Sunday School conventions grew. These conventions were unlike modern-day conventions. Today individuals from publishing houses and colleges instruct the layman. Conventions are characterized by small workshops and a few general assemblies. The older conventions were massive rallies, where laymen motivated other laymen to do the work of Sunday School. Small committees worked on resolutions, strategy and plans. These conventions paid little attention to practical techniques. They were, in fact, great Sunday School

The cover and an inside page of one of the first Sunday School quarterlies published in the United States. (Museum of Sunday School Heritage, Savannah, GA)

revival meetings. They organized large parades and made a great impact on the cities.

In 1884 the conventions reported 8,712,551 Sunday School scholars in the United States. Their accomplishments were so staggering that many thought the millennium could be ushered in. Instead of looking to spiritual horizons, the Sunday School movement began to turn academic. In 1903 the Religious Education Association was formed. The Sunday School Convention changed its name to the International Sunday School Council of Religious Education, and in 1924 the name became the International Council of Religious Education. From this organization grew the National Council of Churches.

In the early 1900s, liberalism crept into theological seminaries and sifted down to the churches. Great debates were held regarding the virgin birth of Chirst, evolution, the higher criticism of Scripture, and the resurrection. Since liberalism always kills, Sunday School zeal and expansion waned. A cold, professional spirit developed in Sunday School work. The Sunday School, which had been the most important single agency for the work of God in the preceding century, declined after 1916.

During these years most denominations developed their own Sunday School literature. Sunday School lessons lacked excitement because liberalism was closing in on many denominations. In reaction to the growing unrest, an interdenominational movement back to the Word of God developed. The Moody Bible Institute was founded in the late 1800s. In the next 50 years God raised up numerous other Bible institutes to answer the problem of growing Biblical illiteracy.

God also raised up interdenominational publishing houses such as Scripture Press, Gospel Light Press, Union Gospel Press, and David C. Cook Publishing Company. These publishers were innovative in their dedication to Biblical content, evangelistic fervor, and doctrinal orthodoxy. They laid the foundation for a Sunday School revival in the 1950s.

After World War II a new spirit spread across the Sunday School scene. Attendance took a new upturn in most denominations. Since America has experienced revival after every major war, many liberal-oriented denominations were growing along with smaller evangelical denominations and independent churches. But the growth among liberal denominations was a sociological phenomenon. A new interdenominationalism grew up around organizations such as Youth for Christ, World Vision, and other organizations committed to conservative Christianity. Large Sunday School conventions were planned by the National Sunday School Association. The Sunday School contests of *Christian Life* magazine, 1948-57, gave impetus to Sunday School growth.

The postwar Sunday School explosion occurred around 1965. Mainline denominations began registering declines in attendance and offerings. They stopped building new educational buildings. The Gallup Poll reflected a deterioration of public confidence in

Approximately 200 exhibitors maintain booths at the annual Mid-America Sunday School Convention. The exhibitors show the latest in Sunday School materials and helps. (Michigan Sunday School Assn.)

the church. Articles began to appear in the popular media questioning the effectiveness of Sunday School. *Life* magazine asked, "What is the Most Wasted Hour of the Week?" The *New York Times* accused Sunday School of being irrelevant and inefficient.

However, the evangelical denominations continued to grow. In 1968 NSSA published a press release claiming a 3.5 percent growth in Sunday School attendance among its cooperating denominations. *Christian Life* magazine introduced the listing of the 100 Largest Sunday Schools in 1968, which rocked the Sunday School world like a bombshell. Its message got through to the religious world that Sunday Schools true to the Word of God were growing in number and vitality. During the early 70s a mild Sunday School upsurge came to segments of the evangelical world. The causes of growth were Sunday School busing, renewed interest in soulwinning, revival of Sunday School contests, saturation advertisement, and a return to Biblical education.

The decade of the 70s has been characterized as the age of the big Sunday Schools. When *Christian Life* began its 100 Largest listing, only 20 Sunday Schools in America averaged over 2,000 in attendance. Within the next seven years, over 60 Sunday Schools became that large. But what are 100 out of the 350,000 Sunday Schools in America. Some people ask, "Why be concerned about the large ones?" But these successful schools prove that it is possible to grow, effectively teach the Word of God, produce godly living, and saturate communities with the Gospel.

50

Jesus, the Master Teacher, built His lessons upon everyday things—wheat, a pearl, fish, lilies.

Jesus, Master Teacher

"Go ye therefore, and teach all nations, baptizing them in the name of the Father, and of the Son, and of the Holy Ghost: Teaching them to observe all things whatsoever I have commanded you: and, lo, I am with you alway, even unto the end of the world" (Matthew 28:19,20).

Our Lord commanded Christians to teach. He knew the importance of teaching, and left us His example in the Scriptures. Often we read that He taught the people. In Matthew's threefold description of Jesus' work on earth (9:35), he places teaching first. Both Luke and John speak of His teaching before they tell of His preaching. Nicodemus called him "a teacher come from God." He is the greatest Teacher of all. He has stated our goal, "Teaching them to observe all things whatsoever I have commanded you."

He Taught with Authority

There was unmistakable authority in His very bearing and in His absolute assurance of the importance and verity of His message. He had confidence that stemmed from knowing thoroughly both *what* He would teach and *whom* He would teach. The scribes might quote at length from rabbis. But the Master Teacher could declare, "I say unto you." Jesus knew what He was teaching and spoke with conviction. Jesus was familiar with the Scriptures in His day; He quoted them freely and interpreted them well (Matthew 21:13,16; Luke 4:8).

He Understood the People He Taught

The love and sympathy of Jesus indicate His complete understanding of human nature. A master psychologist, the Master Teacher built His lessons upon everyday things. He revealed the secrets of His future kingdom in terms of the familiar—the wheat and the tares, the pearl of great price, and the good and bad fish. He promised to change fishermen into fishers of men.

1. *Curiosity.* Jesus knew that we are naturally curious. He made use of the curiosity of the woman at the well in Samaria. A Jew asked a Samaritan for water. Her curiosity grew to interest as Jesus continued. Eventually she brought others to hear Him. More deeply rooted within us is a fear of the supernatural. No doubt this element, too, was in the mind of the Samaritan woman, when a stranger suddenly began to tell her all about her past life. Through His miracles, Jesus appeals to this part of our nature. We are drawn to explore and examine incidents which we cannot explain.

2. *Emotion.* Jesus knew that emotions are an important part of life, for they color and influence all our thought and action. He used human emotion in His teaching. What greater example could we have than that of His sorrow over the city of Jerusalem (Luke 13:34)? He often spoke to people in sorrow, as He healed them or raised their loved ones from the dead. His use of marriage and feasts as examples shows His awareness of the importance of joy

342

Jesus is the greatest teacher of all. (Jesus Preaching the Gospel *by Rembrandt*)

as a component of people's lives.

3. *Thought and imagination*. People like appeals to both thought and imagination. An appeal to our ability to think flatters us; it can even stimulate us, if we let it! Jesus knew, too, that our minds require a certain logic. Luke 6:9,10 is an interesting account of Jesus' logic. He also asked pointed questions. His listeners could not evade the question in Matthew 22:42, "What do you think of the Christ?"

Imagination is quite the opposite of logic, yet very real. Some of Jesus' parables could send

"Follow me, and I will make you fishers of men." Jesus had something for His hearers to do. (Cathedral Films, Inc./Church Fotos)

imaginations soaring (Matthew 25:14-30). Imagination makes vivid any story and imprints that lesson more clearly on minds.

4. *He built on the experience of His hearers.* Jesus was familiar with the needs and experiences of all the people He taught, old and young. He did not use highly technical terms in His teaching. That would have confused people. He taught about simple, everyday things—weddings, nature, sickness and health, brotherhood and love, home and family, and vocations. These were things the people knew.

He Used Different Methods of Teaching

Jesus was aware that there are many methods to use in teaching, and He employed several of them. He used them well and got the desired results.

1. *Lecture.* Perhaps the best known of His lectures is the Sermon on the Mount in Matthew 5 to 7. In it Jesus set forth the greatest principles for living ever known. Moreover, He made his lecture colorful by use of examples, touching on things closest to hearts and vital to life.

2. *Question-and-Answer.* Jesus didn't use the question-and-answer method merely to test the knowledge of His listeners, as is often done today. He used it to stimulate their thinking. The question in Matthew 16:26, "For what is a man profited, if he shall gain the whole world, and lose his own soul?" is used to teach the value of the human soul. Luke 20:1-8 is an excellent example of Jesus' use of a question to answer a question. His questions were inescapable. They pricked the hearts of His hearers into response. They prepared the way for a story. They called for a decision.

3. *Experience.* Jesus knew that we learn best by doing. Life's most important lessons are usually learned "the hard way." When Jesus called Peter and Andrew, He didn't say, "Come, listen to what I will tell you." Rather, He said, "Follow me, and I will make you fishers of men." He called them to action; He had something for them to do. In Matthew 14:24ff., in order to teach faith to Peter, Jesus actually had Peter walk on the water. Jesus didn't tell Peter to watch Him walk on the water, but He commanded Peter to do it himself. Experience is the best way to learn.

4. *Object lessons.* Jesus often used object lessons. He knew that people remember what they see longer than what they hear. When He taught of God's provision, He pointed to birds in the sky and flowers in the field. He illustrated the characteristics of a kingdom citizen by setting in the midst of His auditors a little child. In Mark 12:13-17, Jesus used an ordinary coin to teach a lesson when the scholars of the Temple tried to trick Him. In John 13:5ff. Jesus washed the disciples' feet, a lesson in humility they never forgot. John 20:24ff. gives the story of Thomas, who believed after he saw and heard the resurrected Christ. Many of Jesus' miracles, in addition to being miracles, were, in a sense,

Jesus illustrated the characteristics of a kingdom citizen by setting a little child in the midst of His hearers. (Museum of Sunday School Heritage, Savannah, GA)

object lessons.

5. *Storytelling*. Jesus was indeed a master storyteller. Word pictures made His stories so graphic that they were told and retold by His friends after His departure. He used stories about familiar things and people to illustrate concepts previously unknown. A man repeatedly bothered his neighbor for three loaves of bread. He finally got the bread because the neighbor grew weary of his returning. "Keep on praying until your prayers are answered," Jesus was saying. An injured Jew was refused help by two of his own countrymen, but was rescued by a member of a hated race, the Samaritans. Thus Jesus answered for His hearers the question, Who is my neighbor? (Luke 10:29).

His Life Exemplified What He Taught

Jesus led an exemplary life. It is useless to teach one thing, and do another. The actions completely negate the teaching. Note how Jesus lived what He taught.

1. *Love*. In Matthew 5:44, "But I say to you, love your enemies and pray for those who persecute you." He permitted Judas to be one of His chosen twelve, knowing that he would eventually betray Him. Remember, also, His prayer for those who nailed Him to the cross.

2. *Mercy*. He taught mercy in His Sermon on the Mount in Matthew 5:7, "Blessed are the merciful, for they shall obtain mercy." Any one of the many miracles Jesus performed was an act of mercy.

3. *Brotherhood*. He taught in Matthew 12:49ff. the meaning of brotherhood. He mingled with all people, and was accused of sitting down with publicans and sinners (Luke 7:36ff.).

4. *Obedience*. He taught obedience in Matthew 19:17 when he admonished a young man to "keep the commandments." He lived a life of obedience. The Pharisees tried to find some fault with Him, but failed.

5. *Humility*. He taught humility in Matthew 6:3 and 4, warning, "But when you give alms, do not let your left hand know what your right hand is doing, so that your alms may be in secret; and your Father who sees in secret will reward you." Jesus often warned those He healed not to tell anyone else about it. And when He prayed, He liked to go off by Himself.

6. *Forgiveness*. He told Peter to forgive seventy times seven, and He forgave Peter, who denied Him.

Jesus' Teaching Got Results!

When Jesus taught, He saw definite results. When He healed a man, that man was really healed. When a man made a decision to follow Him, Jesus gained a new disciple.

Look at teaching in its totality. Don't expect everything to change at once. Jesus spoke to thousands, but the Bible doesn't say they all believed at once. True, many came to faith on occasions, but that must have been the exception rather than the rule. The very fact that the writers noted it indicates that it must have been rare. Results often come slowly, and are not always visible. A seed has been growing for quite a while before it pushes through the soil. Teachers must sow the seed, water it, and watch it grow. Teaching is a hallowed task, given by God.

section IX

Your Sunday School Tomorrow

51

Sunday School Standards

Policies

The Sunday School shall have definite governing principles so that it may function efficiently and effectively.

1. A Sunday School organized to teach Bible content.

2. A Sunday School organized to change the life according to the New Testament concept.

3. A Sunday School constituted to promote fellowship of believers one with another.

4. A Sunday School administered to work in harmony with the Christian home.

5. A place where people can administer their spiritual gifts.

6. A Sunday School composed of teachers grounded in the Word of God and trained to meet the needs of individual pupils.

7. A Sunday School designed to have an evangelistic thrust into the community.

8. A Sunday School founded to nurture the spiritual growth of teachers and staff.

9. A Sunday School departmentalized to meet each pupil on his own age level.

10. A Sunday School planned for expansion.

11. A Sunday School informed concerning the denomination and ready to cooperate with it.

12. A Sunday School established with a definite financial budget.

Personnel

The Sunday School shall have definite policy concerning the spiritual and academic standards of the personnel responsible for its ministry. The Sunday School teacher should have the following qualifications:

1. He should be saved.

2. He should have the gift of teaching (Ephesians 4:11).

3. He should have a thorough knowledge of the Word of God (II Timothy 3:15-17).

4. Daily devotions consisting of prayer and Bible study.

5. Regular church attendance (Hebrews 10:25).

6. He should have planning and administrative ability.

7. He should have leadership qualities; the ability to inspire confidence.

8. Vision—ability to view the job objectively and not become discouraged in it (Philippians 3:13-14).

9. Ability to express himself and communicate.

10. A cheerful, radiant personality.

11. A manifested love for children.

12. Patience.

13. The ability and desire to counsel.

14. Originality; ability to create an interesting and diversified class session.

Duties of teachers would include:

1. Regularity in teaching the class.

2. Visitation of the pupils' homes.

3. Be in class 15 minutes ahead of time.

4. Attendance at Sunday School teachers' meetings.

5. Acquaintance with pupils through socials, etc.

The Sunday School should have a regular progress evaluation for the teachers. The above qualifications are desirable for substitute teachers where possible.

Pupils

The Sunday School shall have definite plans for conversion and spiritual growth of the pupil. These plans are as follows:

1. Salvation of every constituent Sunday School pupil.
   a. Need of Salvation.
   b. Provision of Salvation.
   c. Acceptance of Salvation.
   d. Consequence of Salvation.
      1. Dedication.
      2. Consecration.
2. A systematic program to develop a full growth into Christian maturity.
   a. Teach pupil to grow to maturity in Christ.
      1. Bible study.
      2. Prayer.
      3. Witnessing.
      4. Memory work.
   b. Church membership.
      1. Instruction in church membership.
      2. Baptism.
      3. Reception of members.
   c. Church education.
      1. Sunday School administration.
      2. Teacher training.
      3. Personal evangelism.
3. Development of a social life that is honoring to the Lord.
   a. Teacher-pupil relationship.
   b. Participation in wholesome social activities.
4. Develop a friendly relationship between the home and the Sunday School.

Progress

The Sunday School shall make definite plans for progress. Increased attendance, improvement of organization, and the addition of equipment shall all contribute to the salvation and spiritual progress of the student. To insure progress in the Sunday School, we must have the following:

1. Teacher training for the new teacher and in-service training.
2. Promotions each year for greater interest and incentive at all age levels.
3. Evangelistic outreach within the Sunday School.
4. Mission program to broaden the vision of the home church.
5. Prayer.
6. A home department.
7. Division of departments as Sunday School grows.
8. A Board of Christian Education made up of department heads and Christian Education

Director.
9. Training in the use of audiovisual aids.
10. Extension work, ministry to prisons or hospitals, mission work, youth groups, mission Sunday School, visitation.

Public Relations

The Sunday School shall use varying methods of serving its students and reaching its community by means of visitation, advertisements, and transportation.

1. Well-organized visitation program.
2. Follow-up program for absentees.
3. Provide transportation for those who desire to come but have no means.
4. A well-organized publicity campaign to make the church and community aware of the events of the Sunday School.
5. Attention should be given to the total image of Sunday School in the minds of the public.
6. Well-planned church calendar to coordinate special events and meetings in the church.

Property

The Sunday School shall maintain adequate facilities and equipment for effectively housing and teaching its pupils.

1. 25 square feet per pupil per building or 10 square feet of prime educational space per pupil.
2. Strategic location in the center of its locale.
3. Separate classrooms for each class and separate rooms for departmental activities.
4. Windows in each room if possible.
5. Adequate heating (72° F.), lighting (natural if possible), ventilation (air conditioning).
6. Decorations—inner decor should create a cheerful, pleasant atmosphere.
7. Adequate washroom facilities, including facilities for younger children as well as adults. Drinking fountains should be found in washrooms. Maintain cleanliness.
8. Nursery department equipped with cribs, washable toys, baby bottle warmer, separate washroom.
9. Have equipment suited to each level, with chairs, tables, shelves, pictures, bulletin boards adapted to height of the children.
10. Projectors, screens, flannel boards, chalkboards, record player and other visual aids available. A visual aid file would be good.
11. Sunday School needs a library with a good selection of books for all ages.
12. Cloakroom space should be available for each department.
13. A piano should be available in each departmental area.
14. Storage space should be provided for all equipment. This should be organized and labeled.
15. Proper fire exits and equipment must be available and attention drawn to them frequently.
16. The church needs kitchen facilities to

provide for socials, programs or other needs.

17. The Sunday School office should have sufficient space for workers, records, filing system, Sunday School materials. Good office facilities aid administration.

18. First aid kit should be available in Sunday School office.

19. Waste paper baskets in each room. Proper method of disposal must be arranged for.

52

Evaluation

The following questionnaires can be of great help in evaluating your Sunday School. A good administrator solves problems. He keeps the Sunday School growing in numbers and doing a better job of teaching the Bible. Most administrators can solve the problems of which they are aware. But many times administrators know their Sunday School is in trouble, but do not know where the problems are. Hence, they can't improve the condition. These questionnaires can help you find problems in the Sunday School.

Questionnaire 1. Begin by filling out this questionnaire. It emphasizes facts, places, people and numbers. Try to fill out as many of the questions as possible. By forcing yourself to fill out each question, you force yourself to think through every aspect of your Sunday School. This is the questionnaire used in the *Ten Largest Sunday Schools* and other books that the author has written on outstanding churches. Questionnaire 1 helped him gain an immediate perspective of the total Sunday School.

Questionnaire 2. This questionnaire forces you to make a judgment on the effectiveness of your Sunday School. It is a subjective questionnaire, but it is not arbitrary. The questions parallel those in Questionnaire 1. Study the questionnaires together. In Step 1 you gather the facts, and in Step 2 you determine the effectiveness of the Sunday School in the same area.

Locating needs. After both questionnaires

are finished, a committee (usually the Board of Christian Education) should study the questionnaires and make a list of the items that scored low. Here they have a list of needs or problems that should receive their attention.

Research the need. Go to the table of contents in this volume and then study the topic to determine what should be done to solve the immediate problem. Be sure to consult the "Sunday School Standards" to determine what is acceptable.

Determine your strengths. The questionnaires will also tell you where your Sunday School is strongest. A leader always operates from his strengths. Begin here and work in areas where you can achieve the most.

Questionnaires 3-8. After you have studied the total Sunday School, next take it department by department. The following questionnaires are designed to be used by the superintendent as he visits each department on Sunday morning to determine its effectiveness. Some administrators might observe a class or department, but without training their observations may be meaningless. When an administrator observes a class in session, he should have criteria that will force him to take a total view of the class. Otherwise, he may see only those things that irritate him or those things that meet his fancy. Some administrators observe a class and come away frustrated. These questionnaires can help you be professional in your evaluations, rather than subjective.

Questionnaire 1

EDUCATIONAL PRACTICES
AND
PROCEDURES OF THE CHURCH

Name of church _____ Phone _____

Address _____ Denomination _____

Your   Name: Mr.
                 Mrs. _____
                 Miss

Your position in the church _____

Please be as exact as possible in giving your answers. Be conservative where you may have to approximate. The information you give can help your church accomplish the task Christ intended. This questionnaire will be one of the sources to help formulate a three to five year plan of growth. Your help is greatly appreciated.

****

I
THE CHURCH AND ITS COMMUNITY

A. The church

1. When was the church begun? _____

2. List all of the pastors of the church since its inception.

   Pastor   Years in Office
   _____ From _____ 19____ To _____ 19_____
   _____ From _____ 19____ To _____ 19_____
   _____ From _____ 19____ To _____ 19_____
   _____ From _____ 19____ To _____ 19_____

3. During the term of which pastor did the church see the most numerical growth?
   _____

4. What is the reputation of the church in the community? (You may check more than one item)

   _____ Bible preaching   _____ stodgy
   _____ fundamental   _____ cliquish
   _____ separatist   _____ other (specify)
   _____ friendly   _____
   _____ evangelistic   _____

5. What number of the church members who are family heads or single adults are in the following occupation?

   _____ (1) professional and proprietors of large businesses
   _____ (2) semi-professional and smaller officials of large businesses
   _____ (3) clerks and kindred workers
   _____ (4) skilled workers
   _____ (5) proprietors of small businesses
   _____ (6) semi-skilled workers
   _____ (7) unskilled workers

6. What number of the church members who are family heads or single adults have the following sources of income?

   _____ (1) inherited wealth
   _____ (2) earned wealth
   _____ (3) profits and/or fees
   _____ (4) salary
   _____ (5) wages
   _____ (6) private relief
   _____ (7) public relief
   _____ (8) other

7. What number of the church members who are family heads or single adults live in the following house types?
_____ (1) excellent houses
_____ (2) very good houses
_____ (3) good houses
_____ (4) average houses
_____ (5) fair houses
_____ (6) poor houses
_____ (7) very poor houses
8. What number of the church members who are family heads or single adults live in the following types of dwelling areas?
_____ (1) very high: north shore, etc.
_____ (2) high: the better suburbs and apartment areas, houses with spacious yards, etc.
_____ (3) above average: areas all residential, larger than average space around the houses, apartment areas in good condition, etc.
_____ (4) average: residential neighborhoods, no deterioration in the area.
_____ (5) below average: area not quite holding its own, beginning to deteriorate, business entering, etc.
_____ (6) low: considerably deteriorated, run down and semi-slum
_____ (7) very low: slum
9. Name or give other identifying phrase (beyond the tracks, etc.) for each neighborhood area in the community. List the number of church members from each neighborhood area.

Neighborhood   Number of members

_____
_____
_____
_____
_____

10. Which of the above neighborhoods have special needs or social problems? Describe the specific need or problem.

Neighborhood   Problem

_____
_____
_____
_____
_____

11. How many members of the church participate in the following civic activities?
_____ (1) high elected office (mayor, councilman, etc.)
_____ (2) elected office (school board, etc.)
_____ (3) P.T.A., neighborhood association, etc.
_____ (4) civil defense, rescue squad, volunteer fireman, etc.
_____ (5) service or fraternal organizations (Rotary, Lions, etc.)
_____ (6) other (specify)

_____
_____
_____

12. In what community activities is the pastor involved (ministerium, Rotary, etc.)?
_____
_____

B. The community
Information for this section may be obtained from:
_____ Chamber of Commerce
_____ School Board
_____ welfare and social agencies
_____ public library
_____ city planning commission
_____ urban renewal agency
_____ Census Bureau
1. When was the community first settled? _____
2. Is the community conscious of its history and heritage?

_____ very traditional
_____ traditional
_____ average
_____ progressive
_____ very progressive

3. Rate the occupation of the average family head (single individual in each of the neighborhood areas mentioned under "The church" question 8. Using the following rating system list the neighborhood name or designation, and the rating number.
   (1) Professional and proprietors of large businesses
   (2) Semi-professional and smaller officials of large businesses
   (3) Clerks and kindred workers
   (4) Skilled workers
   (5) Proprietors of small businesses
   (6) Semi-skilled workers
   (7) Unskilled workers

   _____
   _____
   _____
   _____
   _____
   _____
   _____

4. In the same manner as the above question, rate the sources of income of the average family head or single person in the neighborhood areas.
   (1) Inherited wealth
   (2) earned wealth
   (3) profits and fees
   (4) salary
   (5) wages
   (6) private relief
   (7) public relief
   (8) other

   _____
   _____
   _____
   _____

5. In the same manner rate the type of housing.
   (1) Excellent houses
   (2) Very good houses
   (3) Good houses
   (4) Average houses
   (5) Fair houses
   (6) Poor houses
   (7) Very poor houses

   _____
   _____
   _____
   _____
   _____

6. In the same manner rate the neighborhood as a dwelling area.
   (1) very high: north shore, etc.
   (2) high: the better suburbs and apartment house areas, houses with spacious yards, etc.
   (3) above average: areas all residential, larger than average
   (4) average: residential neighborhoods, no deterioration in the area
   (5) below average: area not quite holding its own, beginning to deteriorate, business entering, etc.
   (6) low: considerable deterioration, run down and semi-slum

(7) very low: slum

_____
_____
_____
_____
_____
_____

7. What zoning classifications exist in the immediate vicinity of the church? Please give an explanation of the local zoning code's symbols.

_____
_____

8. Indicate by a check the nature of any current land development in the community. In the blanks to the right record the distance in miles of the development(s) from the church.
_____ (1) very high residential _____
_____ (2) high residential including better apartments _____
_____ (3) above average residential and apartments _____
_____ (4) average residential _____
_____ (5) low income housing _____
_____ (6) clean industrial _____
_____ (7) industrial _____
_____ (8) business _____
_____ (9) shopping center _____

9. Is there undeveloped land with potential for a residential area within a one mile radius of the church? _____ yes _____ no

10. Has the church delineated a particular geographical area for its specific responsibility? _____ yes _____ no. If so give the boundaries of that area. _____

11. Is a map of the public transportation system of the community attached to this questionnaire? _____ yes _____ no

12. What is the population of the community?
Census of 1960 _____
Census of 1970 _____
Now _____

13. What population is projected for 1980? _____ 1985? _____

14. What is the population of the particular geographical area of the church's specific responsibility? _____

15. What is the population of the county?
Census of 1950 _____
Census of 1960 _____
Census of 1965 _____
Now _____

16. List the racial and/or ethnic groups living in the community, giving the population of each.

17. What is the population of the following age groups in the community?
(1) children 0-12 _____
(2) youth 13-20 _____
(3) young adult 21-40 _____
(4) middle adult 41-60 _____
(5) older adult 60- _____

18. What is the percentage of annual population turnover in the community?

19. What are the percentages of annual population turnover in the neighborhoods in the geographical area of the church's specific concern? _____

20. In what neighborhood is the population the most stable? _____

21. Are young adults remaining in the community in any sizable amount?
_____ yes _____ no. Of what occupational class(es) are most of those who are remaining?

22. What is the current form of taxation at the local level?
   _____ personal
   _____ property
   _____ real estate
   _____ sales
   _____ income
   _____ other (specify)

23. State in percentages the current dispersion of the tax dollar.
   _____
   _____

24. What are the principal industries of the community?
   Industry   Approximate number of employees

   _____
   _____
   _____
   _____

25. What percentages of the working citizens are employed within the community?
   _____

26. How many people work in the community but do not live there? _____
27. What is the current rate, in percentage, of unemployment? _____
28. How many families are there on welfare rolls? _____
29. How many of the industries are union shops?
   _____ very few
   _____ some
   _____ about half
   _____ most
   _____ all

30. Are the unionized industries open _____ or closed _____ shops?
31. What vocational training is offered the youth in terms of trades and other skills?
   _____

32. List the denominations represented in the city. _____
   _____

33. List the churches within the geographical area of the church's specific concern and their approximate membership.
   Name   Denomination   Membership

   _____
   _____
   _____

34. Name any other religious agencies in the geographical area of the church's specific concern.
   _____

35. Name the governmental social agencies in the community.
   Agency   Level of government (county, etc.)

   _____
   _____
   _____

36. Name the private social agencies in the community.
   _____
   _____

37. Are there psychological services for low income families? _____ yes _____ no. Is family counseling available for low income families? _____ yes _____ no. Check the other professional services available for low income families.
   _____ medical
   _____ dental
   _____ recreational
   _____ legal
   _____ other (specify)

38. What is the form of government in the community?
_____ mayor
_____ council
_____ city manager
_____ county board
_____ other (specify)

39. Is an annual report from the local police department attached to this questionnaire?
_____ yes _____ no
40. What recreational facilities are readily available?
_____ swimming pools
_____ gymnasiums
_____ parks
_____ youth centers
_____ tennis courts
_____ garden clubs
_____ senior citizens clubs
_____ other (specify)

41. How many of the following amusements are there in the community?
_____ bowling alleys
_____ spectator sports
_____ bars
_____ pool halls
_____ museums
_____ theatres
_____ golf courses
_____ casinos
_____ zoos
_____ parks
_____ road houses
42. Is an annual report from the Board(s) of Education attached to this questionnaire?
_____ yes _____ no

II
ENROLLMENT, ATTENDANCE AND RECORDS

1. What is the present enrollment of your Sunday School? _____
2. What was the enrollment one year ago? _____
3. What was the enrollment five years ago? _____
4. What was the average attendance one year ago? _____
5. What was the average attendance five years ago? _____
6. At what age do most children enroll in Sunday School? _____
7. At what age do most students drop out of Sunday School? _____
8. Are drop-outs increasing _____ or decreasing _____?
9. If there has been an increase or decrease in attendance, how do you account for it?
_____
10. What is the local church membership? _____
11. Who is responsible for the attendance records and other related records of the Sunday School? _____
Who is responsible for other agencies such as clubs, young people's, etc.?
_____
12. Is there a master file in the Christian Education office, or another centrally located place, that covers all church activities of each person? _____

13. Check what information is recorded about each attender.
_____ attendance
_____ Bible
_____ offering
_____ on time
_____ church
_____ study lesson

_____ visitor
_____ other (specify)

14. Check what use is made of the records.
    _____ follow up
    _____ building project
    _____ attendance
    _____ evaluation of growth
    _____ personal evaluation of individuals
    _____ other (specify)

15. Are the records used regularly? _____ yes _____ no
16. Check what recognition is made for perfect attendance.
    _____ cross and crown
    _____ yearly pins
    _____ cups
    _____ Bibles
    _____ other (specify)

17. Are student records kept up-to-date? _____ yes _____ no
18. Are the figures compiled and distributed weekly _____ monthly _____ quarterly _____ or yearly _____
19. Who has access to these records? _____
20. Is there any kind of confidential file that would describe in depth the activities of each individual student? _____ yes _____ no
    If so, check what is included.
    _____ conversion
    _____ full time service decision
    _____ emotional background
    _____ family background
    _____ date of baptism
    _____ date of membership
    _____ offices held
    _____ personal achievement
    _____ other (specify)

21. Check other sets of records that are kept.
    _____ financial
    _____ audio-visual
    _____ library
    _____ other (specify)

22. Is there a church historian? _____ yes _____ no
23. How are records preserved?
    _____ record books (bound)
    _____ card files
    _____ loose leaf forms
    _____ other (specify)

24. When is a student's name added to the Sunday School roll? _____

25. When is a student's name removed from the Sunday School roll? _____

III
ADMINISTRATION

1. Do you have a general Sunday School superintendent? _____ yes _____ no
2. Do you have departmental superintendents? _____ yes _____ no
   Check the departments for which you do have superintendents.
   _____ Cradle Roll
   _____ Nursery
   _____ Kindergarten

_____ Primary
_____ Junior
_____ Junior High
_____ Senior High
_____ College and Business Youth
_____ Young Adults
_____ Adults

3. Does the entire Sunday School staff meet together? _____ yes _____ no
   How often? _____
4. Does the Sunday School Executive Committee meet? _____ yes _____ no
   How often? _____
5. List in order of priority the matters handled when the Sunday School teachers meet. (Use 1 for most important to 8 the least important.)
   _____ Sunday School business
   _____ instruction on how to teach
   _____ inspiration
   _____ devotional approach
   _____ evaluation of past effectiveness
   _____ discussion of Sunday School lesson
   _____ information on local church educational resources, materials, etc.
   _____ planning for the future
6. Do you have the following appointed officers (please check)?
   _____ librarian
   _____ registrar
   _____ visitation chairman
   _____ assistant Sunday School superintendent
7. At what time of year do you have promotion? _____
8. Do you have a printed handbook telling the aims, duties, qualifications, etc., for Sunday School teachers? _____ yes _____ no
9. How often is this printed copy given to Sunday School teachers?
   _____
10. What do you consider to be the best new idea practiced in the administration of the Sunday School in the past two years? _____
11. What do you consider to be the main administrative problem in your local Sunday School?
    _____

IV
ORGANIZATION

Sunday School
1. Indicate the departmental attendance in your S.S. and how many classes are in each department.
   _____ _____ Cradle Roll
   _____ _____ Primary
   _____ _____ Senior High
   _____ _____ Adult
   _____ _____ Nursery
   _____ _____ Junior
   _____ _____ College
   _____ _____ Kindergarten
   _____ _____ Junior High
   _____ _____ Young Adult
2. Are all the departments closely graded? _____ yes _____ no
3. What is the average size of a single S.S. class? _____
4. Do S.S. departments meet together as departments for the opening activities?
   _____ yes _____ no
5. Does the whole church meet together for opening activities? _____ yes _____ no
6. What is the primary aim of the S.S.? (rate from 1 to 3)
   _____ evangelism   _____ Bible knowledge   _____ Christian living
7. How many are there on the total volunteer S.S. staff?
   _____ teachers   _____ staff workers
8. How are teachers elected to their position?
   _____ S.S. board

360

_____ church board
_____ Christian Education Board
_____ pastor
_____ other (specify)
9. How are substitutes elected? _____
10. Are the substitutes required to work closely with the regular S.S. teachers?
   _____ yes _____ no Sit in the class? _____
11. What are the specific aims for the S.S. classes?

12. Are the regular teachers given at least one Sunday per quarter off? _____ yes _____ no
13. What percentage of the teachers usually attend teachers' meetings?
   _____% of the substitutes _____%
14. Are teachers required to be present and sit with their class for opening activities?
   _____ yes _____ no
15. Are the teachers appointed for a regular length of time?
   _____ yes _____ no How long? _____
16. Who decides which teachers should be reappointed? _____
17. Can teachers be reappointed to the same class? _____ yes _____ no
18. To whom are teachers directly responsible?
   _____ S.S. superintendent
   _____ Christian Education Director
   _____ pastor
   _____ other (specify)

19. Are parent-teacher meetings used? _____ yes _____ no If so, how often?

20. Do teachers actively contact absentees? _____
21. Are regular reports made in writing?
   from teacher to the S.S. superintendent _____
   from the S.S. superintendent to the C.E. Board _____

Church Organization
1. Is the job of S.S. Superintendent separate from the job of chairman of the C.E. Board?
   _____ yes _____ no
2. Is there a church calendar? _____ yes _____ no If so, when is it constructed?

3. Are all church organizations required to clear their activities on this calendar?
   _____ yes _____ no
4. What persons are represented on the Executive Board of the church?
   _____ pastor
   _____ treasurer
   _____ financial secretary
   _____ Christian Education Director
   _____ Chairman of Trustees
   _____ Chairman of Deacons
   _____ moderator
   _____ church clerk
   _____ S.S. superintendent
   _____ other (specify)

5. Is the pastor also the moderator? _____ yes _____ no
6. What is the primary aim of the church? _____
7. Are new members of the church required to enter a membership class? _____ yes _____ no
8. Do new members sign a covenant? _____ yes _____ no
9. Is any member allowed to hold more than three positions of responsibility in the church?
   _____ yes _____ no
10. Who decides matters of policy in the church?

Training Courses
1. Does your church require training courses for all teachers? _____ yes _____ no
   For all substitutes? _____ yes _____ no

2. Is it required for leaders in church organizations? ＿＿＿ yes ＿＿＿ no
3. Is training made available to all interested members? ＿＿＿ yes ＿＿＿ no
4. Has the opportunity of the present training program been presented to the entire congregation? ＿＿＿ yes ＿＿＿ no
5. Are any requirements prescribed for teachers? ＿＿＿ personal ＿＿＿ spiritual
   For officers? ＿＿＿ personal ＿＿＿ spiritual
6. Does your church provide inservice training for teachers?
   ＿＿＿ yes ＿＿＿ no
7. Is there organized presentation of methods of leading people to Christ? ＿＿＿ yes ＿＿＿ no
8. Does your S.S. cooperate with local or regional S.S. conferences or workshops?
   ＿＿＿ yes ＿＿＿ no
9. What percentage of your teachers attend at least one conference or workshop a year?
   _____

10. In your training course:
    a. Are there regularly scheduled classes   ＿＿＿ yes ＿＿＿ no
    b. Is the teacher well prepared   ＿＿＿ yes ＿＿＿ no
    c. Are achievement awards given upon completion of the course   ＿＿＿ yes ＿＿＿ no
    d. Is attendance required   ＿＿＿ yes ＿＿＿ no
    e. Are tests given for successful completion of the course   ＿＿＿ yes ＿＿＿ no
    f. Is there specialized training for each age group of the S.S.   ＿＿＿ yes ＿＿＿ no
    g. Is observation of good teachers a part of the training program   ＿＿＿ yes ＿＿＿ no
    h. Does the church library have sufficient reference material for this training
                                                                              ＿＿＿ yes ＿＿＿ no
    i. Is a visual-aid program outlined   ＿＿＿ yes ＿＿＿ no
    j. Is Bible content knowledge tested   ＿＿＿ yes ＿＿＿ no
    k. Is Scripture memorization required   ＿＿＿ yes ＿＿＿ no

V
SUPERVISION

1. Are Sunday School departmental superintendents and heads of other agencies appointed by the Board of Christian Education? ＿＿＿ yes ＿＿＿ no
2. Does the Board of C.E. replace these people? ＿＿＿ yes ＿＿＿ no
3. Is there a systematic method of evaluation for these people done by the Board of C.E.? ＿＿＿ yes ＿＿＿ no Explain _____
   _____
4. Are Sunday School departmental superintendents responsible only to the Sunday School superintendent? ＿＿＿ yes ＿＿＿ no
5. Do the heads of other agencies know who they are specifically responsible to?
   ＿＿＿ yes ＿＿＿ no
6. Is there confusion in some agencies over who is really in charge? ＿＿＿ yes ＿＿＿ no (If yes, explain) _____
   _____
7. What is the title of the person that represents the Sunday School on the Board of C.E.? _____ Is he a voting member? ＿＿＿ yes ＿＿＿ no
8. Is there a board member assigned to oversee the youth activities? ＿＿＿ yes ＿＿＿ no
9. Does each member of the Board of C.E. have a specific agency to oversee and report to the Board on? ＿＿＿ yes ＿＿＿ no Explain _____
   _____
10. Do some agencies have little voice or representation on the Board of C.E.? ＿＿＿ yes ＿＿＿ no
    Explain _____
    _____
11. All Sunday School departmental superintendents have attended some form of leadership training in supervision. ＿＿＿ yes ＿＿＿ no (If no, what percentage have not?) _____%
12. Have the heads of other agencies been trained in leadership directly related to their agency? ＿＿＿ yes ＿＿＿ no Explain _____
13. Do your supervisory personnel attend additional leadership training sessions?
    ＿＿＿ yes ＿＿＿ no
14. Do the departmental superintendents meet regularly to evaluate and plan? ＿＿＿ yes ＿＿＿ no
    How regularly? _____

15. Do the supervisors within other agencies meet regularly to evaluate and plan? _____ yes _____ no How regularly? _____
16. How far ahead do most agencies plan their program? _____
17. Do most agencies evaluate past activities to build a better program for the future? _____ yes _____ no In what way? _____
18. Does the Sunday School maintain a 12 month calendar of activities? _____ yes _____ no
19. Do other agencies maintain 12 month calendars of activities? _____ yes _____ no Which do not? _____
20. Must agencies clear their dates for activities through a proper channel? _____ yes _____ no What channel? _____
21. Are there times during the year when there is competition among agencies due to too closely scheduled activities? _____ yes _____ no Examples _____
22. Is there a "fair" method of sharing important dates or services (i.e. Sunday night before Christmas) among agencies, or does one group always "get what they want"? Explain _
23. Does the Board of C.E. or the D.C.E. know what curriculum each agency is using? _____ yes _____ no
24. Is there an attempt made among agencies who serve the same age group to work together in planning the curriculum? _____ yes _____ no
25. Do Sunday School departmental superintendents ever meet together to evaluate the total curriculum of the Sunday School to point out strengths and weaknesses at various age levels? _____ yes _____ no
26. Does the curriculum of each agency require the approval of the Board of C.E.? _____ yes _____ no
27. Are there any specific weaknesses in the curriculum of any agency at the present time? Explain _____
28. Does the Sunday School superintendent confer with the departmental superintendents with regard to budget allocations? _____ yes _____ no
29. Does the head of each agency submit a budget to the C.E. Board only after he has conferred with his staff? _____ yes _____ no
30. Do the Sunday School superintendent and departmental superintendents frequently offer help and advise in problem areas? _____ yes _____ no Explain _____
31. Are there any noticeable problems in the working relationship between supervisory personnel and general workers? _____ yes _____ no Explain _____
32. Does the pastor cooperate readily with the C.E. Board? _____ yes _____ no
33. Does the pastor cooperate with and advise the S.S. superintendent? _____ yes _____ no
34. Does the pastor's relationship with general workers emphasize a spirit of helpfulness and cooperativeness? _____ yes _____ no Explain _____
35. Describe the relationship between the D.C.E. and the C.E. Board. _____
36. Describe the relationship between the D.C.E. and the S.S. superintendent. _____
37. Describe the relationship between the D.C.E. and the heads of the various agencies.
38. Does the D.C.E. have a written job description? _____ yes _____ no (If so, attach a copy)
39. Does the S.S. superintendent have a written job description? _____ yes _____ no
40. Does each agency head have a written job description? _____ yes _____ no
41. List the supervisory personnel who do not have job descriptions written out for them.
42. Do those who have written job descriptions follow their responsibilities stated therein? Explain _____

VI
BUILDINGS AND EQUIPMENT

1. How many teaching centers do you have that are used for Sunday School rooms? _____

NOTE: A teaching center is an area where a teacher meets with his class during the lesson time.

2. How many rooms do you have that could be used for Sunday School teaching centers? _____

3. What is the total educational floor space in your building? (Do not count halls, offices, and stair wells in computing floor space footage) _____

4. Please diagram the floor plan of your present building(s), specific purpose(s) for each room.

5. Have you increased floor space in your educational unit in the past two years? _____ yes _____ no How many square feet? _____

6. What is the size of your plot of ground? _____ Draw a rough scale of the plot.

7. What are your plans for future expansion? _____

   Where will you put the new building? _____

   What will be the purpose or function of the new building? _____

   How many square feet will be in the new building? _____ How many additional persons will the new building accommodate? _____

8. What building material was used for construction of your present plant? _____

9. How many toilets do you have in your present system? _____

10. Approximately how much square floor footage do you have for storage? _____

11. In the columns below, please indicate the number and size of tables and chairs in the various departments. NOTE: The number indicated under the line is that recommended by the National Sunday School Association (NSSA).

Department	No. Chairs	Height (avg.) Chairs	No. Tables	Height (avg.) Tables
Cradle Roll	____ (cribs)	____	____	____
Nursery	____	____ (8″)	____	____ (18″)
Beginner	____	____ (10″)	____	____ (20″)
Primary	____	____ (12-14″)	____	____ (24″)
Junior	____	____ (16″)	____	____ (26″)
Junior High	____	____ (18″)	____	____ (28″)
Senior High	____	____	____	____
Adult	____	____	____	____

12. Do you have at least one chair per pupil? _____ yes _____ no

13. Please list the number of items that are now used or accessible in the department indicated.

Cradle Roll
_____ cribs
_____ refrigerators
_____ bottle warmers
_____ rocking chairs
_____ change tables
_____ storage areas

Toddlers (birth-2)
_____ coat racks
_____ storage areas
_____ rugs
_____ toy boxes
_____ toys
_____ blocks
_____ pictures
_____ Bible picture books
_____ Bibles
_____ cuddle toys

NSSA indicates that there should be between 25-30 square feet per person. How many square feet do you have? _____

Nursery (2-3)

_____ low clothes hooks
_____ storage areas
_____ display tables or
    interest centers
_____ books
_____ blocks

_____ dolls
_____ puzzles
_____ picture display areas
_____ rugs
_____ bulletin boards on eye level
    of pupils

NSSA indicates that there should be between 25-30 square feet per person on the first floor near a bathroom. How many square feet do you have per person? _____
Where is it located? _____

Beginner (4-5)

_____ low clothes hooks
_____ storage areas
_____ pianos
_____ interest center
    tables
_____ crayons
_____ blunt tipped scissors
_____ Bibles

_____ books
_____ rhythm band instruments
_____ bulletin boards
_____ rugs
_____ papers
_____ flannel boards
_____ chalkboards

NSSA indicates that there should be between 25-30 square feet per person on the first floor near a bathroom. How many square feet do you have per person? _____
Where is it located? _____

Primary (6-8) (Grades 1-3)

_____ clothes racks
_____ storage areas
_____ piano for department
_____ teaching pictures
_____ display tables
_____ flannel boards

_____ Bibles
_____ crayons
_____ pencils
_____ scissors
_____ teaching aids suggested in
    curriculum
_____ chalkboards

NSSA indicates that there should be between 20-25 square feet per person. How many do you have? _____

Junior (9-11) (Grades 4-6)

_____ coat racks
_____ storage areas
_____ piano for department
_____ pencils
_____ paper
_____ hymnals
_____ display tables
_____ bookcase with Bible
    dictionary
_____ concordance

_____ pictures
_____ flannel boards
_____ bulletin boards
_____ chalkboards
_____ maps
_____ charts
_____ teaching pictures
_____ Bibles
_____ other teaching aids suggested
    in curriculum

NSSA indicates that there should be between 15-20 square feet per person. How many do you have? _____

Junior High (12-14) (Grades 7-9)

_____ coat racks
_____ storage areas
_____ piano for department
_____ hymnals
_____ bulletin boards

_____ chalkboards
_____ reference books
_____ teaching aids suggested
    in curriculum

NSSA indicates that there should be 10-15 square feet per person. How many do you have? _____

High School (15-17) (Grades 10-12)

_____ coat racks
_____ storage areas
_____ piano for department
_____ hymnals

_____ chalkboards
_____ teaching aids suggested in
    curriculum
_____ bulletin boards

NSSA indicates that there should be between 10-15 square feet per person. How many do you have? _____

Young People (18-24) (College, etc.)

_____ coat racks
_____ storage areas
_____ piano for department

_____ hymnals
_____ chalkboards
_____ teaching aids suggested
in curriculum

NSSA indicates that there should be 10-12 square feet per person. How many do you have? _____

Adults (25 and up)

_____ coat racks
_____ storage areas
_____ piano for department

_____ hymnals
_____ chalkboards
_____ teaching aids suggested in
curriculum

NSSA indicates that there should be 10-12 square feet per person. How many do you have? _____

14. How often is equipment examined for need of repair or replacement?

_____ 6 months   _____ 12 months   _____ 2 years

VII
TEACHING AIDS

1. Please list the number of teaching aids below that are available for use in the church.

_____ 16 MM projector
_____ 8 MM projector
_____ flannelgraph file
_____ flat picture file
_____ slide projector
_____ slide file
_____ filmstrip projector
_____ filmstrip file

_____ tape recorder
_____ tape file
_____ record players
_____ records
_____ other
_____
_____
_____

2. Name the audio-visual aids (other than those listed above) which you have used this past year (rent or borrow). _____
3. Where are the audio-visuals kept? _____
_____
4. Is one person designated to be in charge of all "teaching aids"? _____ yes _____ no
5. How is this person designated into office? _____
_____
6. Is he/she instructed as to the use, care and maintenance of the various pieces of equipment?
_____ yes _____ no
7. What check-out process is followed for use of an aid? _____
_____
8. What procedure do you follow to add to the present audio-visual aids? _____
_____
9. What percentage of teachers would use an aid each Sunday? _____
10. What visual aid is most generally used in classroom teaching? _____
_____
11. Do you have files on the following available to teachers? (Indicate by a check)
_____ flat pictures
_____ object lessons
_____ maps
_____ film strips
_____ flannelgraph lessons
12. How many volumes are contained in your library? _____
13. What system of classification is used? _____
14. What are the major division headings of your books? _____
_____
15. Do you have written guide lines or procedures for your library? _____ yes _____ no (If so, please enclose a copy with this report)
16. Who is in charge of the library? _____
17. To what board or committee is the library accountable? _____
_____
18. What is the annual budget of the library? _____
19. What other method do you use to acquire books? _____
_____
20. How many books are checked out each month? _____
21. Is the library considered an educational arm of the church? _____ yes _____ no

CURRICULUM

1. List those experiences which are available to students in your Christian education ministry in order of frequency. (Mark most frequent 1, next frequent 2, etc.)

   _____ service opportunities   _____ leadership opportunities
   _____ worship   _____ programs for the family together
   _____ doctrinal teaching   _____ Bible content teaching
   _____ memorization   _____ denominational doctrine
   _____ social work   _____ witnessing
   _____ missions   _____ prayer
   _____ use of talents (music, etc.)   _____ other

2. Who designs or chooses the curriculum in the Christian education ministry of the church? _____

3. Who designs or chooses the curriculum of the Sunday School? _____

4. How often is the curriculum of the Christian education ministry reviewed?
   _____ yearly   _____ other (specify)
   _____ semi-annually   _____
   _____ every five years   _____

5. Are the curricula of the other church's agencies besides the Sunday School reviewed at the same time as above? _____ yes _____ no

6. Has the curriculum material been changed in the last five years? _____ yes _____ no If so what was used before? _____
   Why was the change made? _____

7. What publishers does your denomination suggest? _____

8. Why are you or why are you not using that material? _____

   Does the Sunday School use printed materials? _____ yes _____ no List the publishers used by departments:
   Cradle Roll _____
   Nursery _____
   Kindergarten _____
   Primary _____
   Junior _____
   Junior High _____
   Senior High _____
   Young Adult _____
   Adult _____

9. How is the quarterly used in the Sunday School? (You may check more than one item)
   _____ printed scripture portion read from it
   _____ teacher teaches from quarterly
   _____ students do homework
   _____ used for lesson preparation
   _____ not used in the classroom
   _____ other (specify)
   _____
   _____

10. Are materials purchased to assist the leaders of worship time in the Sunday School?
    _____ yes _____ no Do the materials purchased suggest activities for pre-session?
    _____ yes _____ no _____ sometimes

11. What material do you purchase for each student?
    _____ pupil quarterly (workbook)   _____ other (specify)
    _____ activity packet (handwork)   _____
    _____ take home papers   _____
    _____ none

12. What additional materials will the Sunday School purchase at the request of a teacher?
_____ handwork   _____ other (specify)
_____ visual packet
_____ films
_____ filmstrips
_____ records
_____ tapes

13. Is there an official version of the Bible in the Sunday School? _____ yes _____ no
If so, what is it?
_____ King James   _____ American Standard
_____ Revised Standard   _____ New English
_____ Other (specify)
_____

14. What is the view of the Bible in your Sunday School? (You may check more than one item)
_____ good literature   _____ Word of God
_____ myth   _____ normative for faith and practice
_____ not to be taken literally

15. Who is Jesus as taught in the Sunday School? (You may check more than one item)
_____ a good man   _____ a great teacher
_____ The Messiah   _____ the Son of God
_____ truly human   _____ a dead person
_____ a living Savior   _____ other (specify)

16. Is there a Bible memory program for _____ children, _____ for youth, _____ adults.

17 In your experience how often is application to the pupils' lives made of the daily lesson in your Sunday School?
_____ very seldom   _____ not very often
_____ rather often   _____ very often
_____ always

IX
OUTREACH

1. Is there a coordinating committee of some kind that has the overall responsibility for visitation? _____ yes _____ no What positions in the church are on the committee? _____
_____

2. Do the visitation efforts of the church come under the direction of the Board of C.E.?
_____ yes _____ no

3. Do agencies which serve the same age group cooperate together in visitation efforts?
_____ yes _____ no

4. Has there been a duplication of visitation efforts in the past? _____ yes _____ no
Explain _____

5. Are visitation records kept and promptly turned in after each visit?
_____ yes _____ no

6. Are the visitation records made available to the various agencies? _____ yes _____ no

7. Is there a systematic procedure within each agency, or with the visitation committee, whereby visitation assignments are made available and/or recommended?
_____ yes _____ no Explain _____

8. Does each agency have a systematic plan of informing workers when an absentee student should be visited? _____ yes _____ no Explain _____

9. Is there a standard policy in the school as to how many times a student may miss before he should be visited? _____ yes _____ no

10. What other methods are used to contact absentees besides personal visits?
_____

11. Does each agency have a systematic plan of visiting prospects (people who have indicated an interest in attending)? _____ yes _____ no Explain _____

12. Are visitation assignments made available to laymen who are not directly involved within an agency? _____ yes _____ no
13. What other methods are used to visit prospects? _____
_____
14. Does every person who visits attempt to introduce the person to Christ? _____ yes _____ no Explain _____
15. Are visitation workers trained in personal evangelism? _____ yes _____ no
16. How many people have received Christ through the specific efforts of visitation (within the last year)? _____
17. Does the church hold any special visitation for evangelism emphases during the year? Explain _____
18. Is there a simple, but effective way for church members to turn in the names and information about possible prospects? Explain _____
_____
19. Do church members turn in the names of people they are witnessing to? _____ yes _____ no
20. Is any use made of community programs that serve new arrivals in the community (i.e. Welcome Wagon, Junior Chamber of Commerce, etc.)? _____ yes _____ no Explain _____
21. Is there a periodic canvassing of the community made to determine new prospects and make the community aware of the church? _____ yes _____ no How often? _____ Explain _____
22. When was the last canvass done? _____
What were the results? _____
_____
23. Do the church and the various agencies of the church feel responsible for locating prospects? Explain _____
24. Is there a good core of witnessing Christians in the church? _____ yes _____ no
25. Are the results of individual witnessing seen by an increase in church attendance? Explain
_____
26. Is there an emphasis by each agency of the church to encourage, train and challenge Christains to witness? _____ yes _____ no Give the strong and weak areas of this:
_____
_____
_____
27. Does each agency receive C.E. Board approval (or its properly appointed committee) before publicizing an activity in the community? _____ yes _____ no Explain the procedure
_____
_____
28. Does the public relations committee seek to develop a year-round program of consistent and regularly spaced promotion to the community? _____ yes _____ no
29. Who is included in the public relations committee? _____
_____

30. Place a check by the image (or images) that you think best represents the church as you see it.

_____ Bible-believing
_____ fundamental
_____ evangelical
_____ liberal
_____ social
_____ lower class
_____ middle class
_____ upper class
_____ conservative
_____ strict
_____ friendly
_____ youthful
_____ Republican
_____ socially concerned
_____ bigoted
_____ biased
_____ prejudiced

_____ warm
_____ community conscious
_____ politically involved
_____ growing
_____ dying
_____ religious
_____ old-fashioned

Place a zero (o) by the image (or images) that best represents the church as the community sees it.

31. What is being done to improve the image of the church? _____

32. Is there general agreement among the various agencies what the image of the church should be? Explain _____

33. Please indicate, in order of importance (1, 2, etc.) the methods and media used to promote the various programs and activities of the church to the community.
    _____ visitation
    _____ newspaper stories
    _____ newspaper advertisements
    _____ radio
    _____ posters
    _____ direct mail
    _____ telephone contacts
    _____ church newsletter
    _____ weekly bulletin
    _____ pulpit announcements
    _____ door to door flyers
    _____ television
    _____ parades (floats)
    _____ yellow pages listing
    _____ school publications
    _____ city directory listing
    _____ door to door
    _____ booths at fairs, etc.
    _____ airline terminals
    _____ bus terminals
    _____ train terminals
    _____ hotel and motel lobbies

34. What kinds of contests or special events have you used to attract outside attention? _____
    _____
    _____

35. Please list a typical plan of the outreach thrusts of the various agencies of the church. (Visitation, Promotion, Special Meetings, Contests, etc.)
    September _____
    October _____
    November _____
    December _____
    January _____
    February _____
    March _____
    April _____
    May _____
    June _____
    July _____
    August _____

36. Do all of the agencies of the church cooperate successfully in the total outreach thrust of the church? _____ yes _____ no Explain _____

37. Is there a 12 month calendar that is actually used to plan for public relations, etc.? Explain _____

38. Is there a general budget for outreach? _____ yes _____ no Explain _____
    _____

39. Must all outreach expenditures be approved by the public relations committee?

Explain _____

40. How much money is spent annually for outreach? _____
    By the Sunday School? _____ By the general church promotion? _____
    What percentage of the budget is the total outreach spending? _____
41. Has the Board of C.E. determined any goals for the outreach program of the church?
    ____ yes ____ no Explain _____
42. Have numerical goals been established for the Sunday School or other agencies? Explain
    _____
43. How many people received Christ as Savior last year as a result of the outreach program
    of the church? _____
44. Is there a transportation committee in the church or within any agency? Explain _____
    _____
45. What kind of transportation is available, and for what agencies? _____
    _____
46. Is the community aware of the available transportation? ____ yes ____ no
47. Are there agencies which suffer because of the lack of transportation for prospects?
    Explain _____
48. Do church members know who to contact to arrange transportation for people?
    ____ yes ____ no Who? _____
49. Is any remuneration given to those who provide transportation? Explain _____
    _____
50. Does the burden of providing transportation fall on the shoulders of just a few (i.e. pastor,
    D.C.E., youth sponsors, etc.)? ____ yes ____ no
    Has anything been done to rectify the situation, if no? _____
51. Are buses used to transport students to and from the church? ____ yes ____ no
52. How many buses are used? _____
53. How many are brought to Sunday School each week on these buses? _____

PARALLEL INFORMATION

To do a thorough job of evaluating your church and constructing a 3-5 year plan of growth, as much
information is needed as is available. Please attach to this questionnaire the following:
1. Church Constitution
2. Annual Budget
3. Sunday School Teachers' Handbook or Constitution
4. Copy of the Annual Report
5. Sample copies of Church Brochures or Publicity Items
6. Other printed matter that reveals the educational nature of your church

Questionnaire 2

EVALUATION

Educational Practices and Procedures of the Church

Name of Church _____ Denomination _____

Address _____ Phone _____

Mr.
Your Name: Mrs. _____

Miss
Your position in the church: _____

This evaluation should be filled out *after* you have completed the Questionnaire (Q-1). Please rate your church's level of efficiency on each item from 1 to 5. Try to be as objective as possible. This information will be used to construct a 3-5 year plan of growth for your church. Use the following scale to rate your church:

1. This item is *never* found in our church.
2. This item is *occasionally* found in our church.
3. This item is *average* in our church.
4. This item is *above average* in our church.
5. This item is one of our *strong* qualities.

Do not leave any item blank. If you leave an item blank, the scorer will assign a #1.

****

I
THE CHURCH AND COMMUNITY EVALUATION QUES-
TIONNAIRE

	1	2	3	4	5

1. Our church is concerned for the needs of our community.
2. Our church is actively involved in the affairs of our community.
3. Members of our church are active in the civic affairs of our community.
4. Our church is involved in ministering to the people in needy neighborhoods.
5. The pastor's activity in the community satisfies the members.
6. The reputation of our church in the community is what it should be.
7. Our church fulfills its role of calling attention to sin in the community.
8. The racial attitudes of our church are Biblical.
9. Our church has properly defined the specific neighborhoods for which it is concerned.
10. Our church has had a consistently Christian testimony in business and financial affairs.
11. Leadership in our church is open to anyone who is qualified.
12. Our community has opportunity for further growth.
13. Our community is a stable community.
14. Our community has been faithful to the vision of its founders.
15. The industries in our community are adequate for assuring the stability of the community.
16. Our community has an equitable tax system.
17. Our community's religious attitudes are healthy.
18. The religious nature of our community is such that our church has opportunity for growth.
19. There are enough social agencies in our community.

20. Our community is attempting to help the minority groups (racial, ethnic, and needy) who live there.
21. The racial attitudes of our community are in line with the view of Scripture.
22. The teenagers in our community are clean cut and well mannered.
23. Our community is involved in planning the future.
24. The government in our community does a good job.
25. The government of our community is honest and lawful.
26. The police department in our community does a good job.
27. The rate of crime in our community is fairly low.
28. There are adequate recreational facilities in our community.
29. Amusements in our community are constructive.
30. The schools in our community are giving our children a fine education.
31. Our community spends money on schools at a rate that is on a par with neighboring communities.
32. Our schools offer a constructive program of extra-curricular activities.
33. An adequate percentage of our high school graduates go on to college.

II
ENROLLMENT, ATTENDANCE AND RECORDS

1. Our attendance is stable and consistent.
2. Our past attendance growth has been steady.
3. We have a healthy outlook on expansion and attendance growth.
4. Our teachers have a desire to win the lost to Christ.
5. Sunday School contests are important to attendance growth.
6. Our Sunday School enrolls students at the right time of their growth. (Score less if you think the Sunday School enrolls too young or waits too late.)
7. Our church has a drop-out problem.
8. The Sunday School staff has a healthy attitude in dealing with the drop-out problem.
9. Our church enlists Sunday School pupils at the right age for church membership.
10. Our church has adequate plans to prepare people for church membership.
11. Membership in our church has meaning to our members.
12. The church has the right (general) attitudes toward the Sunday School.
13. The records and files are all centered in the responsibility of one person.
14. There is a master file that covers all church activities of each person.
15. Records are used to pin-point weak areas and realize growth.
16. Consistent attendance is important to pupils.
17. Each agency has their own set of records.
18. The records from each agency are transferred to the master file once a month.
19. The pupils are aware of the record kept on their progress.
20. All records are current and accurate.
21. The Sunday School and other agencies maintain a definite visitor and absentee record and follow-up system.
22. The congregation is satisfied in supervision of financial records.
23. There is a confidential file on each active attender kept locked in the pastor's office.
24. Records are important to all key personnel.

III
ADMINISTRATION

1. The Sunday School superintendent is given enough direction and guidance to do his job efficiently.

373

	1	2	3	4	5

2. The Sunday School teachers know what is required to perform their task properly.

3. The qualifications for teaching in our Sunday School are strictly kept.

4. The aims, duties and qualifications of Sunday School teachers are revised often enough to be up-to-date.

5. We have enough departmental superintendents to guide our Sunday School.

6. The department superintendent is given enough direction to do his job efficiently.

7. The regular Sunday School staff meeting is meaningful to teachers and necessary in the growth of the Sunday School.

8. The administration of our Sunday School welcomes and easily implements new ideas.

9. The administration of our Sunday School deals with problems in a satisfactory manner.

10. Promotion of pupils is given adequate attention by the administration.

11. When teachers are absent from class, the matter of obtaining a substitute is adequately handled.

IV
ORGANIZATION

1. Opening exercises (departmental worship) is meaningful on the whole to the students in our Sunday School. Rate each department:
    Nursery
    Kindergarten
    Primary
    Junior
    Junior High
    Senior High
    College and Business Youth
    Young Adults
    Adults

2. The individual Sunday School classes are the right size for effective teaching (rate low if classes are too large or too small).

3. The organization of the Sunday School instills a spirit of cooperation and comradeship among teachers.

4. The substitute teacher system is adequate for our Sunday School.

5. The staff personnel for running the Sunday School is adequate in keeping with the number of teachers we have.

6. The system by which new teachers are appointed is efficient.

7. The system by which former teachers are re-appointed is adequate.

8. The instruction given to prepare teachers for their positions is sufficient.

9. The instruction of *inservice training* given to those already teaching is adequate.

10. Our Sunday School benefits from denominational or interdenominational workshops and/or conferences.

11. We receive inspiration from such workshops.

12. We receive practical and helpful instruction from workshops.

V
SUPERVISION

1. The Board of C.E. usually makes wise choices in its appointment of individuals to various agencies.

2. The Board of C.E. has an adequate method of replacing vacancies within agencies.

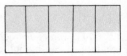

374

	1	2	3	4	5
3. The Board of C.E. has a systematic and effective method of evaluating personnel.					
4. The S.S. departmental superintendents know who they are directly responsible to.					
5. The heads of the various agencies know who they are directly responsible to.					
6. The S.S. is adequately represented on the C.E. Board.					
7. The Board of C.E. delegates one of its members to oversee the youth activities and consequently stays alert to its program.					
8. Other members of the Board of C.E. have similar responsibility with other agencies and also stay alert to their programs.					
9. Some agencies are seldom represented fairly on the Board of C.E.					
10. Departmental superintendents have received adequate training through leadership sessions they have attended.					
11. The supervisory personnel of other agencies are also well trained through the leadership sessions they have attended.					
12. All supervisory personnel attend additional leadership training sessions of great value to them.					
13. The regular meetings of the departmental superintendents usually prove to be quite valuable to the total program of the S.S.					
14. The supervisory personnel of the various agencies find that their regular meetings together help them to do their own work more effectively.					
15. Advance planning for future activities for most agencies is done quite successfully.					
16. The systematic evaluation of past activities helps the various agencies to plan more effectively for future activities.					
17. The planning of a 12 month calendar by the S.S. enables personnel to avoid unnecessary conflicts with dates.					
18. The various agencies also make successful use of a total church 12 month planning calendar.					
19. There is a simple, yet effective method for the clearing of dates for the general calendar.					
20. There is careful planning done to avoid the scheduling of activities too close together.					
21. The most important dates and services of the year are successfully shared with the various agencies over a period of several years.					
22. The Board of C.E. or the D.C.E. maintains a careful watch over the curricula of the various agencies.					
23. The cooperation among agencies who serve the same age group enables the supervisory personnel to plan the curriculum jointly.					
24. The S.S. departmental superintendents find it helpful to meet together at times to discuss the strengths and weaknesses of the curriculum.					
25. The curriculum of each agency is always approved by the Board of C.E.					
26. The overall curricula of the total church program generally meets the needs of the people.					
27. S.S. departmental superintendents are able to have a strong voice with regards to their yearly budget allocations.					
28. All supervisory personnel confer with their staff members before submitting a budget to the C.E. Board.					
29. The S.S. superintendent and the departmental superintendents are quite helpful to their staff members.					
30. There is a good spirit of cooperativeness among supervisory personnel and general workers.					
31. The pastor and the C.E. Board have a good working relationship.					
32. The pastor is very cooperative with the S. S. superintendent.					
33. The general workers in the various agencies enjoy the help and advice of the pastor.					
34. The D.C.E. and the C.E. Board enjoy a good working relationship.					
35. The S.S. superintendent and the D.C.E. are able to work closely together.					

	1	2	3	4	5

36. The D.C.E. and the heads of the various agencies work well together and the D.C.E. serves them primarily as a resource person.
37. There is an adequate job description for the D.C.E.
38. The S.S. superintendent has an adequately written job description.
39. The heads of the various agencies have adequate job descriptions.
40. There are some supervisors who do not have written job descriptions.
41. Most supervisory personnel know their job requirements and successfully fulfill their responsibilities.

VI
BUILDINGS AND EQUIPMENT

1. The church building is located geographically in the center of where the church members live.
2. The church is easily accessible from public transportation or private cars.
3. There is no traffic hazard in reaching the church.
4. The church is in a suitable environment. (It is away from noise, offensive odors, and undesirable influence of taverns, industry, etc.)
5. The landscape is neat, attractive, and adds to the purpose of the church.
6. There is enough parking for the congregation (one lot for each four in attendance).
7. The building's height is in keeping with the surrounding neighborhood. (Score low if height is out of proportion to situation and type of construction.)
8. There are at least two means of exit from every Sunday School room to the outside.
9. There are fire extinguishers available.
10. The building is considered safe from fire hazards.
11. The building is kept clean.
12. The building is properly designed for the control of sound.
13. The maintenance is adequate (score low for broken windows, unreplaced light bulbs, etc.).
14. There is adequate heating for good education.
15. There is a good amount of storage space (apart from educational materials) in the building.
16. The classroom provides natural light.
17. The classrooms are open and clean as opposed to cramped, dark, damp quarters.
18. Most of the educational rooms are flexible so that they may be adapted for use by other agencies.
19. The classrooms are so arranged that class will not be interrupted by late comers.
20. The artificial lighting is adequate.
21. The color scheme is bright, pleasing to the eyes and lends itself to creating the atmosphere of study.
22. Each teacher or at least department has its own storage unit for supplies.
23. There is adequate space for wraps and overcoats of the pupils and these are at the correct height according to student needs.
24. There are enough chairs for all students.
25. The chairs are of the correct size for the students.
26. There are enough adjustable tables for the teachers.
27. The equipment of our church is up-to-date and adequate.
28. There are plans for increasing the audio-visuals in the church.

VII
TEACHING AIDS

1. Our Sunday School has an adequate number of audio-visual teaching aids.

1	2	3	4	5

2. The teaching aids are stored where they are easily accessible to all the teachers.

3. We have an adequate method of securing up-to-date audio-visual aids.

4. The Sunday School teachers make good use of audio-visual aids.

5. The church library is adequate for our needs.

6. The library has good procedures for securing additional books.

7. The average person can find a book easily in the library.

8. The teachers make good use of the library.

9. The average pupil makes good use of the library.

10. The library has efficient administration.

11. The library is considered an educational arm of the church.

12. The library has a well-rounded service (biographies, commentaries, encyclopedias, teaching aids, fiction, youth, children's material, soul winning helps, etc.).

VIII
CURRICULUM

1. The Bible is the central text in the Sunday School.

2. The teachers stick to the assigned lessons in the quarterly.

3. The pupils do the assigned homework in the quarterly.

4. The teachers write out lesson plans at home to be used in the classroom.

5. The teachers know how to use their quarterlies and other materials.

6. Our Sunday School is satisfied with our present curriculum materials (publishing house).

7. Our Sunday School uses the present material out of choice and conviction.

8. The take home material is meaningful and used by the students.

9. Take home papers are considered part of the total teaching material.

10. Our Sunday School teachers consider practical application as important as Bible knowledge. (If one is overemphasized score low).

11. The pupils' understanding of the passage is emphasized in memory work.

12. Play activities are used to teach the younger children Christian living. Rate each department:
    Crib Room
    Nursery
    Kindergarten
    Primary

13. Handwork among the children is considered educational and helpful to cause children to grow in Christ.

14. Memory work is considered important with children.
    Memory work is considered important with youth.
    Memory work is considered important with adults.

IX
OUTREACH

1. The visitation program is effectively coordinated by a committee.

2. The Board of C.E. has careful supervision of the total visitation program.

3. There is a good cooperative effort among agencies serving the same groups toward an effective visitation program.

4. Careful planning has avoided the problem of duplication in visitation assignments among the various agencies.

5. There is an adequate system of record keeping for the visitation program.

6. The various agencies make good use of the visitation records.

7. Visitation assignments are effectively given out to the various agencies and/or staff workers.

	1	2	3	4	5

8. Each agency has a good plan whereby workers are informed of absentees who should be visited.

9. There is a general policy regarding how many times a student may miss before he should be visited.

10. There are a variety of methods used to contact absentees.

11. Each agency employs a systematic and effective plan of contacting prospects.

12. Laymen not directly involved with any agency have ample opportunities to be involved in visitation.

13. A variety of methods are used to visit prospects.

14. An attempt is made to introduce Christ to every person visited.

15. All visitation workers are effectively trained in personal evangelism.

16. There have been a good number of people who have received Christ through the visitation efforts within the last year.

17. Special emphasis on visitation for evangelism proves to be effective each year.

18. Most church members know who they should see about turning in the name of a prospect.

19. Most church members inform the pastor or someone else about specific individuals they are witnessing to.

20. The church takes advantage of community programs geared to welcome new arrivals in the community.

21. The periodic canvassing of the community provides the church with an effective way of finding prospects.

22. The latest canvass was done within the last year.

23. Church members are generally looking for opportunities of finding prospects for the church.

24. The church has many members who are regularly sharing their faith.

25. Church attendance is climbing due primarily to the effective witnessing of its members.

26. The church's programs emphasize the need for its members to be witnessing Christians.

27. The public relations committee must approve all promotion of any agency which desires to promote activities in the community.

28. The public relations committee has set up an effective year-round program of consistent promotion to the community.

29. The public relations committee is made up of a good representation of the various agencies of the church.

30. The church has a very favorable image in the community.

31. The church is constantly seeking to improve its image.

32. The agencies of the church are in agreement as to the image they would like to present to the community.

33. The public relations committee effectively uses the best methods and media (to publicize activities) which are best suited for the community.

34. Generally, the contests and special events in the church have helped to increase attendance and promote community awareness of the church.

35. The special emphasis of the various agencies are planned with a total 12 month impact in mind.

36. All of the agencies of the church play an effective role in the total outreach program.

37. The outreach activities of the church are coordinated by the use of a 12 month planning calendar.

38. There is an adequate budget for the outreach program.

39. The public relations committee has general control over the spending of money for outreach purposes.

40. The Sunday School has a sufficient portion of the outreach budget for its specialized outreach efforts.

41. The C.E. Board has written aims and objectives for the total church outreach program.

42. Numerical goals have been set as a future achievement to strive for.

43. A good number of people received Christ as Savior last year due to the effectiveness of the outreach program.

	1	2	3	4	5
44. A transportation committee functions cooperatively with the outreach program of the church.					
45. There is a sufficient amount of transportation available to those who need it.					
46. The community is aware of the available transportation.					
47. Every agency within the church is able to acquire the necessary transportation when needed.					
48. Church members know whom they should contact when some transportation is needed.					
49. Those who provide transportation are reimbursed for any personal expenses incurred in providing transportation.					
50. The providing of transportation is shared by a large number of people preventing the work from falling only to a few.					

Questionnaire 3

NURSERY

Administration
1. Crib Room superintendent: name? length of present service? appointed or elected? length of appointment or elected term?
2. Cradle Roll superintendent: name? length of present service? appointed or elected? length of appointment or elected term?
3. Coordinator of Crib Room & Cradle Roll: name? length of present service? appointed or elected? length of appointment or elected term?
4. Authority: Who is administrator directly responsible to? Are expenses included in annual church or C.E. budget? How much are you allowed to spend or charge?

Personnel in Crib Room
1. Is there at least one permanent attendant for each service? SS ____, AM ____, Training Hour ____, Evening ____, Prayer Meeting ____ Are they R.N.s? Salaried? (amount per week or month)
2. What system is used to enlist volunteers? to schedule workers? length of rotation? more than one service? (e.g. SS, AM, Training-PM)
3. What qualifications do you look for in Crib Room attendants?
4. What training (if any) is given to new attendants/volunteers?
5. What specific instructions (written or verbal) do you give to Crib Room attendants?
6. Are there a few persons that can be called upon in emergency or large services?
7. Are clean uniform smocks provided?
8. Are badges or distinguishing tags provided?
9. Are attendants listed on bulletin board or in Sunday bulletin?
10. Is there a system of "retirement" or "vacation" used to reward or refresh long term attendants, or are they given "life sentences"?

Ministry to Mothers
1. Is there an active mother's club for Crib Room & Cradle Roll mothers? How often does it meet?
Where? Main attraction for attending?
2. What is the functional purpose of the mother's club?
3. Is an effort made to include or enlist "outside" mothers into mother's club or other Cradle Roll & Crib Room sponsored events? How? By whom?
4. Have any mothers been saved through the direct or indirect ministry of mother's club in the last year? (give details)

Personnel in Cradle Roll Department
1. Is there someone who is personally responsible for outreach?
2. Does the Cradle Roll Department have a secretary? How many hours per week/month?
3. How are workers selected?
4. How many workers presently do you have and use?
5. How many infants presently listed on cradle roll?
6. Function in relation to member families of church and Sunday School rolls?
7. Function in relationship to marginal families (clubs, V.B.S., camps)?
8. Function in relationship to families in community? by newspaper scanning? Radio announcements? Membership referrals?
9. Procedure of follow-up used for those listed on Cradle Roll: mail only? mail & telephone? combo. mail, phone, visits? mail & visits? visits with materials only?
10. Procedure of follow-up for those families listed on Cradle Roll but who have stopped leaving child in Crib Room or not attending services altogether?
11. What publisher do you purchase Crade Roll materials from?
12. Copies of any form letters worked up by individuals or staff?

Procedure of check-in and check-out
1. Are new parents given any token used to claim their infant?
2. Is space provided (or form) to leave directions for feeding, sleeping, changing, etc.?
3. Are parents allowed into the room for delivery and pick-up?
4. Are new parents given a cordial and complete tour of facilities, or at least is an offer made?

5. Are multiple (sticky or pin-on) tags available to identify child, outer wear, diaper bag?
6. Is an opportunity (informally or other) given for parents and others to suggest improvements in care *or* legitimate criticism? Suggestion box?

Housekeeping
1. Are regular supplies purchased for Crib Room? By whom?
2. How often are crib sheets and other linen changed? After each child? weekly? when soiled? other time?
3. How often are toys, cribs, floor disinfected? weekly? monthly? other?
4. How often is the Crib Room completely housecleaned? weekly? monthly? other?
5. By whose standard is it housecleaned?

Records, trends, promotion
1. Is Crib Room attendance regularly posted in a conspicuous place? Where?
2. Are there usually enough cribs?
3. What is the capacity in no. of infants?
4. What is average percentage of capacity?
5. What is record attendance?
6. What is the average attendance on special occasions (Easter, Christmas program)?
7. Is there an effort through attendance graphs, explanation of services rendered, or other ways to encourage leaving of child for more services than now used?
8. Are there take-home papers (weekly)? or novelties (for infant)? or literature (for parents) given out periodically to encourage or reward attendance and greater understanding?

Supplies and Equipment
Are the following supplies and equipment available?
1. Atmosphere: light and pleasant?
2. Baby's schedule: list or card?
3. Books: cloth and washable for baby? child care for mothers? inspirational for mothers?
4. Book shelves: for child's books? for adult giveaways?
5. Bulletin board: promotional for parents?
6. Cabinets: Cradle Roll supplies? Crib Room supplies? attendants' coats and purses?
7. Ceiling: light and reflective? high or low?
8. Cribs: separate, in line, or stacked? no. _____ and washable? mattress, mattress covers and rubber sheets?
9. Diaper bag bins or racks? no.?
10. Door(s): solid, dutch, with window, or with ventilator?
11. First aid kit and materials?
12. Floor: varnished wood, tile, rug, color?
13. Garbage pail with plastic bag liner?
14. Interest center: location? impact?
15. Listing of emergency and authorized personnel? medical doctor? hospital?
16. Pictures or wall mottos: adult content and height? infant content and location? the Savior?
17. Playpen(s): washable pads? Number?
18. Record or tape player?
19. Record or tapes?
20. Refrigerator?
21. Registry: attendance?
22. Regulations posted (for parent's knowledge): Neat? Conspicuous?
23. Rocker(s) for adults?
24. Rug (in rocking chair area)?
25. Supplies: baggies (for soiled diapers)? hand tissue? diapers - service? disposable? clean linen - crib sheets? receiving blankets? wash cloths? talcum powder? bottle warmer? smocks (for attendants? name tags? sterilization solution? other _____? _____? _____?
26. Sink with hot water?
27. Toilet?
28. Thermostat/thermometer?
29. Waste basket(s)?
30. Walls: color? washability?
31. Windows: height from floor _____? proximity to cribs _____? shades or drapes to shield from direct sunlight _____? storm windows (drafty)? can they be opened?
32. Washable rubber toys?
33. Diagram in scale the layout showing all facilities, heating, windows, doors.

Questionnaire 4

PRESCHOOL DEPARTMENT

Personnel
1. Is there a department superintendent?
2. How many workers are in the department?
3. There should be one teacher or helper for every six to ten pupils. What is your ratio?
4. How many classes are in the department?
5. How is the department divided?
6. How are the teachers and workers selected?
7. Are they trained for the job? How?
8. How often are departmental meetings held?
9. Are there any male workers in the department? If not, has anything been done to recruit workers?
10. Do the teachers conduct a visitation program?
11. Is there a consistent follow-up on absentees?
12. Has anything been done to involve parents?

Pupils
1. What is the department's average attendance?
2. How many of the pupils are boys? How many are girls?
3. How many of the children are from homes in which at least one parent is a church member?
4. How many are from homes in which the parents attend church but are not members?
5. How many of the pupils are from non-churched homes?
6. Do any of the children have physical defects? For example, hearing, sight, etc. What provisions are made for these students?
7. What divisions are made in the department?
8. How many children are in each group?
9. How many of the Sunday School students remain for the morning worship service?
10. Are there children in the worship service who are not in attendance in Sunday school?

Environment
1. How often are bulletin boards and other displays changed?
2. What is the height of
   a. The windows
   b. The bulletin boards
   c. The coat racks
   d. The chairs
   e. The tables
3. What is the size in square feet of the department?
4. What is the average square feet per child?
5. Is there enough storage space?
6. Where are the restroom facilities in relation to the classrooms? Are the sinks and toilets low enough for the children?
7. What provision is made for early arrivers?

Teaching Time
1. Approximately how much time is spent on listening activities and how much time is spent on participation activities?
2. Is the study of missions included in your program?
3. Which of the following methods are used at least once a month?
   activity time
   group singing
   play time
   prayer time
   Bible memorization
   review of past learned Bible verses
   review of past learned lessons
   giving
   sharing
   rest time
   role play

Questionnaire 5

PRIMARY DEPARTMENT

Personnel
1. Is there a department superintendent?
2. How many workers are in the department?
3. How many classes are in the department?
4. How is the department divided?
5. How are the teachers and workers selected?
6. Are they trained for the job? How?
7. How often are departmental meetings held?
8. Are there any male workers in the department? If not, has anything been done to recruit them?
9. Do the teachers conduct a visitation program?
10. Has anything been done to involve parents?

Pupils
1. What is the department's average attendance?
2. How many of the pupils are boys?
3. How many are girls?
4. How many of the children are from homes in which at least one parent is a church member?
5. How many are from homes in which the parents attend church but are not members?
6. How many of the pupils are from non-churched homes?
7. Do any of the children have physical defects? For example, hearing, sight, etc.? What provisions are made for these students?
8. What divisions are made in the department?
9. How many children are in each group?
10. How many of the Sunday School students remain for the morning worship service?
11. Are there children in the worship service who are not in attendance in Sunday School?

Environment
1. How often are the bulletin boards changed?
2. What is the height of
   a. The windows
   b. The bulletin boards
   c. The tables and chairs
3. What is the size in square feet of the department?
4. What is your average square feet per child?
5. Is there adequate storage space?
6. What provision is made for early arrivers?
7. Do you have necessary equipment available?

Teaching Time
1. Approximately how much time is spent on listening activities and how much time is spent on participation activities?
2. Is the study of missions included in your program?
3. Are the children taught stewardship?
4. Do you use a variety of teaching methods?
5. Are the children encouraged to memorize Scripture?
6. Is any opportunity given for the children to respond to Christ's offer of salvation?

Primary Department
Observation

Personnel
1. Do the teachers arrive early?
2. Are they neat in appearance?
3. Do the staff members visit among themselves or tend to the pupils?
4. Do the teachers appear to be well prepared in advance?
5. Do they employ creative teaching methods?

Environment

1. Does the room have plenty of light?
2. Is the room located above or below the ground level?
3. Where is the entrance into the room located?
4. Are there attractive bulletin boards and visuals?
5. Are the pictures arranged at the child's eye level?
6. What type of floor covering has been used?
7. Is the room sound proof?
8. What color has the room been painted?
9. Is the room neat and clean?
10. Are all unnecessary articles of equipment, etc., removed?

Teaching Time

1. Is there a variety of activities planned providing the child with opportunity to worship, study, serve, etc.
2. Are visuals used and handled well?
3. Is the story told or read? Is it applied to the child's life?
4. Are the activities pupil-centered or lesson-centered?
5. Is the Bible or the teacher's manual used as textbook?
6. Is the class teacher-dominated or is there pupil-teacher and pupil-pupil interaction?
7. Are the children encouraged to participate?
8. Are there any situations which lead to discipline problems which would be avoided?

Questionnaire 6

JUNIOR DEPARTMENT

Personnel
1. Is there a department superintendent?
2. What is the department enrollment?
3. What is the average attendance?
4. What is the record attendance?
5. How is the department divided?
6. How many workers are there in the department? Describe the function of each.
7. NSSA advises 1 teacher to 6-8 pupils. What is your ratio?
   Do men teach the boys' classes?
8. How do you recruit your teachers? What training do they receive?

Pupils
1. Do your curriculum materials require student work before, during, or after the lesson session?
2. Do you think the materials should be changed?
3. Do you have presession activities for early comers?

Equipment
1. Check the equipment you use in your department
   pencils _____
   hymnals _____
   bookcase _____
   Bible atlas _____
   pictures _____
   bulletin boards _____
   maps _____
   Bibles _____
   other _____
   paper _____
   display table _____
   Bible dictionary _____
   concordance _____
   flannelboards _____
   chalkboards _____
   charts _____
   teaching aids _____

Teaching time
1. Do you have opening exercises? _____ How long do they last _____
   How long is class time? _____ minutes.
2. What teaching methods are used most frequently by the teachers in your department? (In order of frequency, 1, most frequent, etc.)
   chalkboard _____
   charts _____
   buzz groups _____
   conversation _____
   maps _____
   object lessons _____
   quiz _____
   storytelling _____
   discussion _____
   field trips _____
   filmstrips _____
   flannelgraph _____
   projects _____
   question-and-answer _____
   role-play _____
   other _____
3. How often do you hold departmental meetings?

Miscellaneous
 1. What is your procedure for follow-up of newcomers (visitors)? Absentees?
 2. How often do your teachers visit their pupils?
 3. Do your teachers have socials for their classes? Date of last _____
 4. What is your potential for growth?
 5. What are the aims and goals of the teachers?
    Content-centered?   Need-centered?
 6. How do you evaluate your education results?
 7. When was the last child won to Christ in your Sunday School class?
 8. What measures are taken to handle discipline problems in your class?
 9. Do you emphasize memory work for your pupils?
10. How close are the washroom facilities? Are they adequate?

Equipment and Facilities
 1. Are there coat racks?
 2. Is there storage area?
 3. Is there a piano?
 4. Are pencils available?
 5. Are hymnals available?
 6. Is there a display table?
 7. Is there a bookcase? Bible atlas _____
 8. Are chairs suitable in height? 15" to 17"
 9. Is lighting adequate?
10. Is there a desk for the secretary?
11. What is the shape of tables in classes?
12. Are movable partitions adequately soundproof?
13. Are windows low enough to see out?
14. What type floor-covering is used? Resiliant? Noise-resistant?
15. Is ceiling of acoustical tile?
16. Are audiovisuals adequate? handy? used?
17. Attitude of students toward superintendent and teachers _____
18. How many come early?

Questionnaire 7

JUNIOR AND SENIOR HIGH
COLLEGE AND CAREER

There are three basic breakdowns or groups to be considered here: (a) junior high students, (b) senior high students, (c) college and career.

General Questions
1. What is the general status of these three groupings at the present time? i.e.:
2. Are separate classes being conducted for each group? Or:
3. Is there a mixing within the three groups? Or:
4. Are any of these groups mixed with others outside the young adult category?
5. Where would a visitor(s) in any of these three groups be placed for Sunday School?
6. How many people are there (or how many couples in group "C") in each of the three groups?

Questions regarding individual classes in the Young Adult Division
1. What is the size of the class?
2. What type of format does the class follow: or, how is the class conducted?
3. Is there a good deal of interaction and discussion?
4. What subject material is presently being studied in the class?
5. Who determines what subject material will be studied in the class, and on what basis is the choice made?
6. If the class has a teacher, as such, how much time does he spend in weekly preparation?
7. What has been the attendance pattern in this class during the past three years?
8. What is the attendance carry over from the high school department to the college age section of the young adult department of the church?
9. Are there any people in these three groups who attend church services but not Sunday School?
10. What do you consider to be the potential of the church locale with regard to the addition of new people to each of these three groups?
11. What are the teacher's aims and goals for each of the classes in the young adult category?
12. Have the teachers in the young adult category classes had any teacher training?
13. Do teachers (especially in the college class) have contact with the members of their class outside Sunday School?

Questions regarding the social area
1. What social activities are presently being carried on in each of these groups?
2. What do you feel are the social needs of each of these three groups?
3. Do you feel that the people in each of the three groups are satisfied with present social activities?
4. Are any social activities being used to reach people of these three groups who might not normally come to church?
5. What has been the response of the three groups to past social activities?
6. Who is responsible for planning social activities in each of the three groups?
7. How are the social activities of each of the three groups related to the Sunday School program (and other areas of the church program)?

Questions regarding service opportunities
1. What positions of service in the church are presently open to people in these three groups?
2. What positions of service in the church are presently filled by people in these three groups?
3. Are there presently any programs within the various young adult groups designed to stimulate, develop, and train leadership?

Questions regarding classrooms (for observation not interview)
1. Is the room of adequate size for the number of people present? (there should be at least 10-12 square feet of space per person)
2. Is the room sufficiently sight and sound proof to prevent constant distraction?
3. Does the room contain enough proper furnishings, and are these furnishings in good condition?
4. Are there chalk boards and bulletin boards?
5. If the answer to question four is "yes," are there erasers and chalk for the chalk board and tacks for the bulletin board?

6. Is the room properly cleaned and maintained?
7. Is the lighting proper and adequate?
8. Does the color and atmosphere of the room promote the best state of mind for the purpose of the room?
9. Is the furniture and equipment arranged in the best manner?

Questionnaire 8

ADULT DEPARTMENT

Questions
1. What is the philosophy behind the teaching in the class?
2. What type of curriculum is used in the class?
3. How is the curriculum used in teaching the class?
4. How does the teacher follow up absentees?
5. What do the students need: indoctrination or specific needs fulfilled?
6. How much teacher-training has the teacher had?
7. How much preparation does the teacher need per week?
8. What kind of teaching methods have been used in the past?
9. What kind of organization is there in the class?
10. What kind of outside class activities are there, parties, prayer meetings, etc.?
11. What kind of growth has been seen in the adult class within the two past years?
12. Is the class made up of new or mature Christians?

Observations
1. Where does the class meet?
2. How is the class arranged?
3. What form of opening is used?
4. What type of teaching is being done, buzz groups, lecture, discussion, etc.?
5. What kind of teaching tools does the teacher use, visual aids, etc.?
6. How are the Scriptures used in presenting the lesson?
7. How many people of your class stay for church?
8. How many people come to church who don't come to Sunday School?
9. What kind of class participation is there?
10. How does the room environment lend itself to effective teaching?
11. What is the number of people in relationship to the size of the classroom (is there enough room)?
12. How are the adult department classes grouped?
13. How are new people welcomed?
14. What kind of class organization is there?
15. What percentage of the class's enrollment attends regularly?
16. How do students react to teaching methods being used?
17. What kind of new member enrollment methods are used?

SUNDAY SCHOOL ENROLLMENT AMONG AMERICAN CHURCHES[1]

The Sunday School statistics in the following charts represent the number of pupils on the rolls. This is the potential "outreach" not actual attendance. Earlier in this guidebook the 100 largest Sunday Schools and the 50 fastest growing Sunday Schools were listed. Figures for these churches represent actual attendance.

The material in the following charts has been taken from *The Yearbook of American and Canadian Churches*. This is compiled by the Office of Research, National Council of Churches, New York City, and is the most reliable available. The statistics were compiled from questionnaires submitted by officials from the designated religious bodies. The information was not verified or "adjusted" but is reported as submitted.

---

[1]From *The Yearbook of American and Canadian Churches*, 1974 edited by Constance Jacquet. Copyright © 1974 by The National Council of the Churches of Christ in the U.S.A. Used by permission of Abingdon Press.

Caution should be exercised in comparing the following figures. Some organizations practice "pure member" roles. They list only those who are considered a member of the "in group," i.e., people who have met all of the criteria for membership. Many smaller holiness denominations count only members who do not smoke, drink, and indulge in other worldly practices. As a result, their attendance may be much larger than the figures represent. Other groups practice "open membership" whereby all those who make a profession are counted as members. These groups usually have much larger figures but in reality have a smaller attendance than the figures represent.

Many organizations are not included, such as the Baptist Bible Fellowship with approximately 2,700 churches and an estimated 1,156,600 members in the Sunday School. The Southwide Baptist Fellowship and other sectarian organizations also are not included. The reader may not be interested in all these religious bodies, but each is included to give an overall picture of the Sunday School.

TABLE 1-A: UNITED STATES CURRENT AND NON-CURRENT STATISTICS

The following table provides current and non-current statistics for United States religious bodies alphabetically. Current statistics are defined as those gathered and reported for 1973 and 1972. Non-current statistics are those for 1971, or earlier. No statistics for "Full, Communicant, or Confirmed Members," "Number of Sunday or Sabbath Schools," and "Total Enrollment" are reported for bodies having non-current statistics.

	Year Reported	No. of Churches	Inclusive Membership	Full, Communicant, or Confirmed Members	No. of Pastors Serving Parishes	Total No. of Clergy	No. of Sunday or Sabbath Schools	Total Enrollment
Albanian Orthodox Diocese of America	1973	10	5,150	410	2	4	2	130
American Baptist Association	1973	3,336	955,900	955,900	3,300	3,338	3,369	470,000
American Baptist Churches in the U.S.A.	1972	6,029	1,484,393	1,484,393	4,648	7,599	N.R.	N.R.
The American Carpatho-Russian Orthodox Greek Catholic Church	1972	70	108,400	108,400	61	68	56	5,104
The American Catholic Church (Syro-Antiochian)	1973	5	495	495	8	8	2	33
The American Lutheran Church	1972	4,825	2,492,355	1,773,416	4,071	6,264	4,549	670,571
American Rescue Workers	1972	25	2,500	2,500	N.R.	45	25	3,000
The Anglican Orthodox Church	1972	37	2,630	2,050	12	14	35	N.R.
Apostolic Christian Church (Nazarean)	1972	54	3,771	2,400	132	134	52	1,650
Apostolic Christian Churches of America	1973	78	9,500	9,500	N.R.	273	77	9,160
The Apostolic Faith	1972	45	4,100	4,100	75	75	44	6,600
Armenian Apostolic Church of America	1972	29	125,000	125,000	23	34	29	2,550
Armenian Church of America, Diocese of the (including Diocese of California)	1972	58	372,000	372,000	N.R.	67	120	10,000
Assemblies of God	1973	8,871	1,099,606	700,071	8,237	12,087	9,200	1,078,332
Associate Reformed Presbyterian Church (General Synod)	1972	148	28,711	28,711	102	154	146	16,883
Baptist General Conference	1972	686	111,364	111,364	773	1,032	686	120,453
Baptist Missionary Association of America	1972	1,437	199,640	199,640	2,500	2,500	1,437	102,479
Beachy Amish Mennonite Church	1972	62	4,069	4,069	160	163	55	N.R.
Berean Fundamental Church	1972	50	2,530	2,530	53	57	50	4,210
Bethel Ministerial Association	1971	25	4,000		48	49	50	4,466

	Year Reported	No. of Churches	Inclusive Membership	Full, Communicant or Confirmed Members	No. of Pastors Serving Parishes	Total No. of Clergy	No. of Sunday or Sabbath Schools	Total Enrollment
Brethren Churches, National Fellowship of	1972	243	33,514	33,514	290	443	243	41,000
Brethren in Christ Church	1972	151	9,730	9,730	127	197	155	17,729
Christ Catholic Church (Diocese of Boston)	1972	4	429	391	4	5	2	77
The Christian and Missionary Alliance	1972	1,154	136,154	77,991	953	1,259	1,266	180,745
Christian Church (Disciples of Christ)	1972	4,569	1,352,211	881,467	4,105	6,749	4,569	580,503
Christian Church of North America, General Council	1972	110	8,500	8,500	135	137	N.R.	7,000
Christian Churches and Churches of Christ	1973	5,479	1,036,460	1,036,460	4,665	6,934	5,479	N.R.
The Christian Congregation, Inc.	1972	297	52,585	52,585	295	305	294	33,960
Christian Reformed Church	1972	750	287,114	157,667	581	1,027	750	92,715
Church of Christ	1972	32	2,400	2,400	169	188	N.R.	N.R.
The Church of God	1973	2,035	75,890	75,890	1,910	2,737	2,025	96,500
Church of God (Anderson, Ind.)	1972	2,261	155,920	155,920	1,783	2,906	2,233	244,921
Church of God (Cleveland, Tenn.)	1972	4,152	297,103	297,103	7,240	8,000	5,497	483,565
Church of God General Conference (Oregon, Ill.)	1972	132	7,400	7,400	104	115	N.R.	8,850
The Church of God of Prophecy	1973	1,711	59,535	59,535	3,557	5,195	2,149	86,276
The Church of God of the Mountain Assembly	1973	90	3,500	3,500	100	206	90	5,600
The Church of Jesus Christ (Bickertonites)	1972	50	2,439	2,439	80	220	50	4,430
The Church of Jesus Christ of Latter-day Saints	1972	5,112	2,185,810	1,797,584	17,133	17,133	4,663	2,023,287
Church of the Brethren	1972	1,037	179,686	179,686	686	2,026	1,045	80,077
Church of the Lutheran Brethren of America	1972	97	9,010	5,310	98	119	97	8,760
Church of the Lutheran Confession	1972	69	9,490	6,818	54	70	61	1,667
Church of the Nazarene	1972	4,861	404,732	404,732	3,846	7,195	4,882	992,668
Churches of Christ	1968	18,000	2,400,000		N.R.	6,200	N.R.	N.R.
Churches of Christ in Christian Union	1973	256	8,771	8,771	N.R.	310	254	16,182
Churches of God in North America (General Eldership)	1972	364	35,833	29,640	225	357	364	36,715
Congregational Christian Churches, National Association of	1972	344	85,000	85,000	319	459	205	16,500
Conservative Congregational Christian Conference	1972	121	20,400	20,400	170	247	116	13,467
Cumberland Presbyterian Church	1972	879	88,738	56,212	539	710	853	64,966
Duck River (and Kindred) Association of Baptists	1972	86	8,909	8,909	129	N.R.	N.R.	N.R.
Eastern Orthodox Catholic Church in America	1972	2	265	265	6	7	1	100

Church	Year							
Elim Fellowship	1973	70	5,000	5,000	70	128	N.R.	N.R.
The Episcopal Church	1972	6,891	3,062,734	2,099,896	7,352	11,566	N.R.	606,156
Ethical Culture Movement	1972	25	5,000	4,000	30	37	20	1,325
The Evangelical Church of North America	1972	118	9,843	9,843	113	168	118	13,406
Evangelical Congregational Church	1973	160	29,434	29,434	126	187	159	27,580
The Evangelical Covenant Church of America*	1972	523	68,771	68,771	428	671	531	66,173
Evangelical Lutheran Synod	1972	89	16,179	11,532	50	63	84	3,680
Evangelical Mennonite Brethren Conference	1972	32	3,784	3,784	32	36	32	4,338
Evangelical Mennonite Church, Inc.	1972	20	3,136	3,136	25	37	N.R.	4,350
Free Methodist Church of North America	1972	1,091	65,167	48,455	N.R.	1,744	1,023	116,976
Free Will Baptists	1973	2,275	203,000	203,000	2,300	3,600	2,300	165,000
Friends United Meeting	1972	515	68,717	54,927	299	566	416	33,345
General Association of Regular Baptist Churches	1973	1,473	214,000	214,000	N.R.	N.R.	N.R.	N.R.
General Baptists (General Association of)	1973	834	70,000	70,000	850	1,200	834	80,800
Greek Orthodox Archdiocese of North and South America	1972	502	1,950,000	1,950,000	545	675	639	75,191
Independent Fundamental Churches of America	1972	598	77,794	77,794	686	1,264	N.R.	111,384
Jehovah's Witnesses	1972	5,794	431,179	431,179	N.R.	N.R.	N.R.	N.R.
Jewish Congregations	1972	5,000	6,115,000	N.R.	5,100	6,400	N.R.	N.R.
Lutheran Church in America	1972	5,788	3,034,366	2,165,591	4,797	7,450	5,568	844,195
The Lutheran Church—Missouri Synod	1972	5,741	2,781,297	1,963,262	4,748	7,174	5,563	783,952
Mennonite Church	1972	1,036	89,505	89,505	1,840	2,207	888	111,747
Mennonite Church, The General Conference	1972	189	36,129	36,129	173	329	192	29,939
The Missionary Church	1972	273	20,078	20,078	327	470	273	44,161
Moravian Church in America, Northern Province	1972	99	34,041	25,763	82	153	96	9,311
Moravian Church in America, Southern Province	1972	49	22,784	16,963	48	60	49	9,938
New Apostolic Church of North America	1972	276	21,023	21,023	356	428	276	7,810
North American Baptist General Conference	1973	246	41,516	41,516	257	354	224	35,052
North American Old Roman Catholic Church	1973	121	60,098	58,774	79	111	33	8,186
Old Order Amish Church	1972	368	14,720	14,720	1,472	1,479	N.R.	N.R.
Old Order (Wisler) Mennonite Church	1972	38	8,000	8,000	60	101	None	None

	Year Reported	No. of Churches	Inclusive Membership	Full, Communicant, or Confirmed Members	No. of Pastors Serving Parishes	Total No. of Clergy	No. of Sunday or Sabbath Schools	Total Enrollment
The Old Roman Catholic Church (English Rite)	1972	186	65,128	65,128	186	201	N.R.	N.R.
Open Bible Standard Churches, Inc.	1972	275	25,000	25,000	425	730	275	25,000
Orthodox Church in America	1972	370	1,000,000	1,000,000	390	455	N.R.	N.R.
The Orthodox Presbyterian Church	1972	123	14,871	9,946	N.R.	205	125	N.R.
Pentecostal Church of Christ	1973	45	1,365	1,365	50	52	44	3,103
Pentecostal Holiness Church, Inc.	1972	1,340	74,108	74,108	N.R.	1,878	1,300	143,724
Presbyterian Church in the U.S.	1972	4,284	946,536	946,536	2,984	5,139	N.R.	489,050
Primitive Advent Christian Church	1972	10	551	551	14	14	7	518
The Protestant Conference (Lutheran)	1972	7	2,660	1,650	10	13	7	600
Reformed Church in America	1972	911	372,681	218,415	854	1,470	908	119,822
Reformed Church in the United States	1973	24	4,008	3,045	18	21	24	805
Reformed Presbyterian Church of North America	1972	68	5,560	4,383	50	97	N.R.	3,039
Reorganized Church of Jesus Christ of Latter Day Saints	1972	1,031	179,763	179,763	15,872	15,872	N.R.	N.R.
The Roman Catholic Church	1972	23,880	48,460,427	N.R.	N.R.	57,332	11,376	9,778,361
The Romanian Orthodox Episcopate of America	1972	45	50,000	N.R.	42	49	38	1,636
Russian Orthodox Church in the U.S.A., Patriarchal Parishes of the	1972	41	50,000	50,000	48	53	N.R.	N.R.
The Salvation Army	1972	1,101	358,626	79,439	2,337	5,181	1,131	106,754
Seventh-day Adventists	1972	3,278	449,188	449,188	1,539	3,422	3,312	383,239
Seventh Day Baptist General Conference	1972	68	5,284	5,284	42	63	55	2,986
Southern Baptist Convention	1972	34,512	12,065,333	12,065,333	30,500	54,150	33,549	7,175,186
Syrian Orthodox Church of Antioch (Archdiocese of the U.S.A. and Canada)	1972	10	50,000	25,000	14	14	10	530
Triumph the Church and Kingdom of God in Christ (International)	1972	495	54,307	44,460	860	1,375	495	51,777
Ukrainian Orthodox Church in America (Ecumenical Patriarchate)	1973	23	30,000	30,000	22	26	23	3,500
United Brethren in Christ	1972	284	26,409	26,409	153	255	286	32,009
United Christian Church	1973	12	422	422	8	12	10	960

Church	Year							
United Church of Christ	1972	6,635	1,895,016	1,895,016	4,990	9,480	N.R.	659,122
The United Methodist Church	1972	39,626	10,334,521	10,334,521	20,518	34,974	37,607	5,380,147
United Pentecostal Church, International	1972	2,650	250,000	200,000	4,000	5,250	2,550	325,500
The United Presbyterian Church in the United States of America	1972	8,732	2,908,958	2,908,958	7,412	13,624	N.R.	1,109,570
United Zion Church	1973	16	877	877	23	28	13	1,336
Volunteers of America	1973	546	30,730	30,730	392	473	102	9,574
The Wesleyan Church	1970	1,898	84,499		1,918	2,925		N.R.
Wesleyan Holiness Association of Churches	1972	67	2,000	2,000	67	112	67	
Wisconsin Evangelical Lutheran Synod	1972	991	385,077	278,442	791	995	918	56,527

TABLE 1-B: SUMMARY OF UNITED STATES CURRENT AND NON-CURRENT STATISTICS

"Current" statistics are those reported for the years 1973 and 1972. "Non-Current" statistics are for the years 1971 and earlier. Only current data are provided in the following categories: Full, Communicant, or Confirmed Members; Number of Sunday or Sabbath Schools; Total Enrollment.

1974 Yearbook - Current	117	234,296	112,235,890	52,057,877	200,379	360,978	170,837	36,697,785
1973 Yearbook - Current	128	237,870	114,369,013	55,020,752	194,704	295,154	185,149	38,487,453

List of Charts

Index

improving leadership ability, 184-5
Lesson planning, 181, 305-7

M

Master teacher plan, 136, 247-9
Memory work, 318-22
Misconceptions regarding Sunday
    School, 62-4
Missions education, 308-10
Multi-media project, 301-4
Music, 311-14

O

Organization
    future trends, 57
    grading the Sunday School, 92-5
        (chart), 94
    natural factors in, 206-8
    principles for, 87-92
    spiritual factors in, 205-6

P

Pastor and Christian Education, 67-71
Pastoral care, 27

R

Record-keeping, 124-6
Retarded, ministry to, 325-7
Review games, 322-4
Role-play, 297-9

S

Shut-ins, ministry to, 331-2
Size
    advantages of small Sunday
        Schools, 26-8
    largest Sunday Schools in U.S.,
        29-49
Special days
    ideas for, 236
    value of, 234-6
Special ministries
    to the deaf, 327-9
    to the handicapped, 329-31
    to the retarded, 325-7
    to shut-ins, 331-2

Standards
    equipment
        general equipment standards
            (chart), 141
        Nursery, 143-4
        Beginner, 145-6
        Primary, 147
        Junior, 148
        Junior High, 149
        Senior High, 150
        Adult, 151
    for Sunday School, 349-51
Superintendents
    departmental
        Cradle Roll, 84
        Toddler, 84
        Beginner, 84
        Primary, 85
        Junior, 85
        Intermediate, 86
        Senior High, 86
        Adult, 86
    general, 83-4

T

Teachers
    covenant for, 181-2
    duties of, 178
    enlisting, 191-2
    qualifications of, 179-80
    retaining, 193-4
    training, 192-3
Teachers' meeting
    organizing, 187
    program for, 188-9,
    value of, 186
Teaching methods
    discussion
        brainstorm, 261
        buzz groups, 256
        case study, 266-7
        circular response, 261
        colloquy, 265-6
        debate, 263-5
        dyads or neighbor nudge, 259
        listening teams, 259
        panel discussion, 260
        symposium, 263
    future trends, 58-9
    Jesus' teaching techniques, 342-6
    lecture, 250-5
    question and answer, 268

return to traditional, 22-5
story telling, 269-72
Team teaching, 134, 243-7

U

Unified service, 137

V

VBS, 95
Visitation
lack of, 214
misconception regarding, 63
outreach
factor in growth, 200-5
test of educational ministry, 69
procedures for, 225-8

Visual aids
nonprojected
bulletin boards, 278
chalkboard, 274-5
charts, 279
exhibits, 281
flannelgraph, 279-81
flashcards, 278-9
flat pictures, 277
graphs, 278
maps, 275-7
models, 281
object lessons, 281-2
posters, 278
puppets, 282-5
sandtable, 281
principles for use, 273-4
projected
overhead projector, 287-9
slides, films, motion pictures
principles for use, 286-7